The European Tour
Yearbook 2008

OFFICIAL

PUBLICATION

Introduction from The European Tour

The 20th Anniversary edition of The European Tour Yearbook provides an ideal opportunity to reflect on the past and look into the future. First and foremost, however, I must pay tribute to the stars of the show – the players. To the record breaking achievements of Angel Cabrera and Padraig Harrington. To the arrival of Justin Rose as Europe's Number One. To every player who performs on The European Tour International Schedule. Without their dedication and skills we would not be where we are today; showcasing our game to the world.

In fewer than 40 days in the summer of 2007 Angel and Padraig earned global recognition. They also completed a double not achieved by European Tour Members since The European Tour was born in 1971. Angel won the United States Open at Oakmont Country Club; Padraig captured The 136th Open Championship at Carnoustie. Their stories are told in two fascinating chapters in this Yearbook in which all victories by Tour Members are vividly

recorded in words and pictures including Henrik Stenson's outstanding triumph in the WGC – Accenture Match Play and Ernie Els's record seventh win in the HSBC World Match Play Championship at Wentworth Club.

Justin reached for the stars, swathed in smiles, as one contributor wrote, and won the Volvo Masters to secure Number One honours in The European Tour Order of Merit. Fifty weeks

earlier he had won the MasterCard Masters – the third of 52 events on The European Tour International Schedule which in 2007 visited 25 countries. Now here was Justin earning the Harry Vardon Trophy with the penultimate putt of a seriously engrossing season.

There have been many milestones in the short life of The European Tour. We expect many more as our vision becomes reality. During four

The Headquarters of The European Tour at Wentworth

decades of development we have received magnificent support from a multitude of sponsors and promoters. Volvo becoming the Tour's first corporate sponsor, commencing in 1988, was a proud announcement. In early November we celebrated the 20th anniversary of the Volvo Masters. The longevity of this relationship owes much to many people. The Volvo Board, Don Jaime Ortiz-Patiño, the past President of Valderrama, and The European Tour. Most of all it owes much to the hugely popular Mel Pyatt, the President and CEO of Volvo Event Management. Mel retired at Valderrama after 21 years at the helm. His distinctive blend of excellence and style will be missed but never forgotten.

Now to the future. On November 19, 2007, in Dubai, The European Tour and Leisurecorp, the company developing Dubai's leading residential golf community at Jumeirah Golf Estates, announced a wide-ranging partnership which will create The US $ 10,000,000 Dubai World Championship, the world's richest golf tournament, and provide a thrilling crescendo for spectators as it brings together the leading 60 players on "The Race to Dubai" – formerly the Order of Merit – with an initial annual bonus pool of US $10,000,000 on offer. The inaugural Dubai World Championship will take place on November 19-22, 2009, on either the Fire or Earth course at Jumeirah Golf Estates in Dubai, UAE.

A unique agreement will also see the construction of a new International Headquarters for The European Tour at Jumeirah Golf Estates in addition to significant support for selected European Tour events; funding of The European Tour's Physio Truck; and the creation of a global property company, in a joint initiative with Leisurecorp, to develop new tournament venues.

This announcement unquestionably endorsed our desire to partner with excellence through endeavour and cultivate perfection. Across the globe interest in golf is intensifying. We have our ideals and our aspirations. We are dedicated to using the global experience to provide the very best for our players and their fans. What matters is that we use our skills, our insight and our creativity to develop the game and grow our brand through strong marketing and shrewd operations designed to generate luxury golf course developments in expanding territories for the golfers of tomorrow.

The future now beckons for the 20 graduates who earned their places on The 2008 European Tour International Schedule from the European Challenge Tour and I congratulate Michael Lorenzo-Vera, of France, on leading the way as I do Carl Mason on finishing Number One on the European Seniors Tour Order of Merit for the third time in five years. Both Michael and Carl reached the top with record earnings and Michael, no doubt, will have high hopes of following in the footsteps of Germany's Martin Kaymer, the Sir Henry Cotton Rookie of the Year in 2007.

These are exciting times. In looking forward to The 2008 Ryder Cup at Valhalla on the outskirts of Louisville in Kentucky, and wishing Nick Faldo, The European Team Captain, all the best, I also hope you enjoy recalling the theatrically spellbinding achievements of all our players in 2007 through this the 20th Anniversary edition of The European Tour Yearbook.

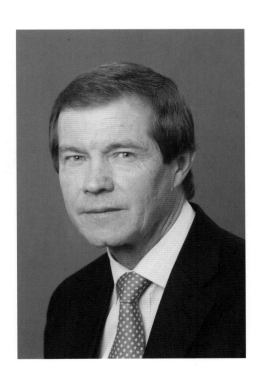

George O'Grady
Chief Executive
The European Tour

Acknowledgements

Executive Editor
Mitchell Platts

Production Editor
Frances Jennings

Editorial Consultants
Scott Crockett
Chris Plumridge

Picture Editors
Andrew Redington
Rob Harborne

Art Direction
Tim Leney
Andrew Wright
TC Communications Plc

Print Managed by
Peter Dane
Mark Baldwin
LPD Ltd.

The European Tour Yearbook 2008 is published by The PGA European Tour, Wentworth Drive, Virginia Water, Surrey GU25 4LX.
Distributed through Aurum Press Ltd.
7 Greenland Street
London NW1 0ND

© PGA European Tour.

GET MORE CONTROL
BY CONTROLLING LESS.
UNLEARN OUTSOURCING.

Gaining control and flexibility through outsourcing isn't a contradiction. At least not for those who've unlearned outsourcing misconceptions and know the true benefits of outsourcing. Unisys Outsourcing Solutions are tailored to provide the best fit for your organization and change as your needs change. Our solution design models enable us to collaboratively define your initial service requirements and fine-tune service management over time. Whether you're expanding into new markets or integrating for growth in existing ones, Unisys Solutions for Secure Business Operations provides better control of your business performance and your customer experience. Perfect for unleashing your full business potential. Unlearning is just the beginning.

Security unleashed. **UNISYS**
Secure Business Operations. imagine it. done.

www.securityunleashed.com

Contents

Mirror
Image

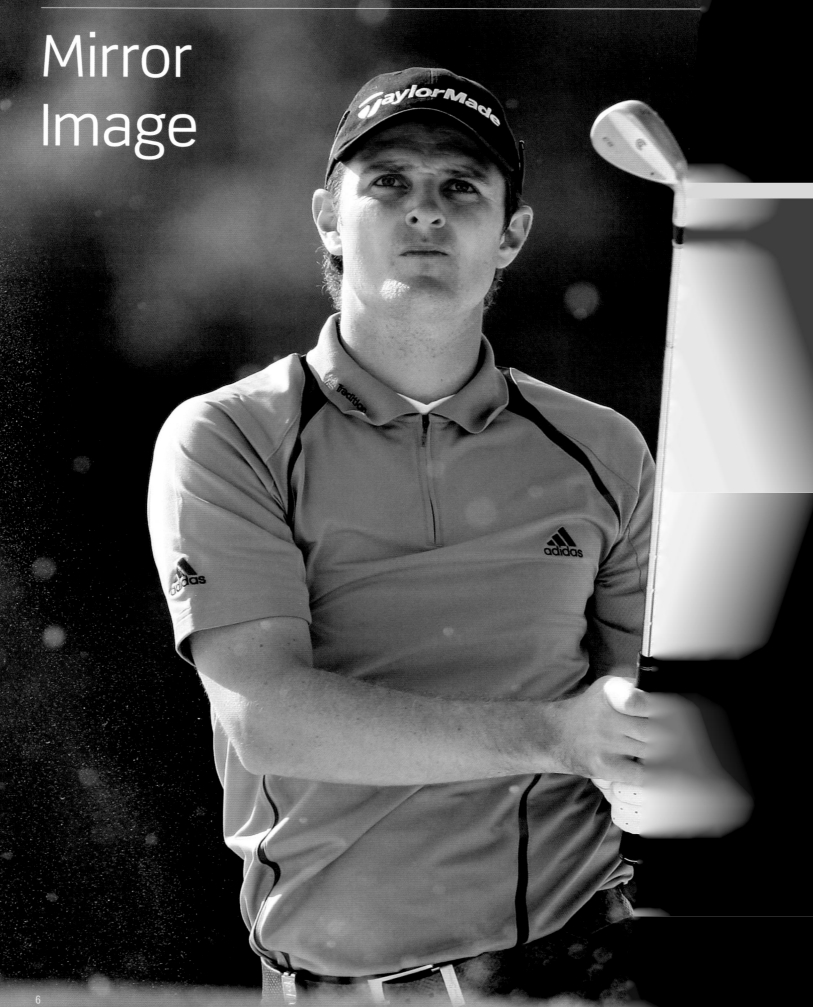

In the end the biggest victory of Justin Rose's professional life was a mirror image of everything that had gone before. Inordinately talented as a golfer and blessed with a temperament that embraces tranquillity when all around him are in danger of losing focus, Rose has had much to endure as well as to enjoy since turning professional on his 18th birthday in the high summer of 1998.

Justin with his late father Ken at Muirfield in 2002

Justin with his wife, Kate, the Volvo Masters trophy and the Harry Vardon Trophy

Since then it has been a long and winding road to his present position as the winner of The 2007 European Tour Order of Merit. His victory at Club de Golf Valderrama in the season-climaxing Volvo Masters was a high-flying yet stumbling affair. His final nine holes over Don Jaime Ortiz-Patiño's Spanish masterpiece suggested at times a young man losing his nerve just when he needed it most.

There was little time for regrets, however, as the game which had taken him into a four stroke lead with victory apparently his, began to slide away alarmingly. That he regrouped, recovered and ultimately won a play-off against compatriot Simon Dyson and Søren Kjeldsen of Denmark clearly marked him out as a player of sublime promise. But then, his working life has been a potpourri of achievement and setback.

To uncork the centre of this golfer we must return to that summer of 1998. He entered The Open Championship at Royal Birkdale as an amateur and surfed into town on the wrong end of a bitterly

disappointing month for he had failed to win The Amateur Championship he coveted so much.

Beside him, as he confirmed his name on the registration list for the greatest tournament of them all, was his father Ken. It was he who had nurtured and encouraged his son as a golfer. Not cajoled, mind you, for here was a father determined that his son would grow his talent only if he really wanted to. Ken Rose saw himself as a facilitator. He protected his boy as much as he exposed him to the high risk that is playing a game for a living.

Born in Johannesburg before his family returned to England, Justin grew up in the middle of a golf obsession. By the time he was 12 years old he knew he was good. By the time he was 17 he knew he wanted to play professionally. But by the time he arrived at Royal Birkdale in 1998, however, he had no clue what was about to happen.

What happened, of course, was that he finished a tempestuous week in a share of fourth place, a

final, holed pitch shot echoing around the sporting world like a trumpet call announcing the arrival of someone special. Of course, just when it seems as good as it can be, it tends to turn an awful lot worse.

Ushered onto the European circuit with every media gun blazing, Rose fell spectacularly from grace, missing 21 cuts in succession. Only in his case this difficult period was made much harder to bear because, while other rookies were floundering anonymously, his low points were magnified by high publicity. Eighteen months after he had strode so hopefully into the limelight, he was just another jittery kid on the Challenge Tour.

It was at one of these events in 1999 that your correspondent bumped into him. After chatting for a spell he departed with the phrase which now resonates hugely: "Don't worry about me. I believe in my ability to play this game. I'll be okay. I'll make it one day."

Now he has. Sadly his father is not around to witness his coronation as Number One in Europe for Ken died from cancer in 2002, leaving a void in the Rose family life that can never be filled. It was

touching to hear Justin say, as he cradled the Harry Vardon Trophy in Spain, that he thought his dad would be proud of him.

There is no doubt, however, that the hard times have helped this golfer develop. The amateur who wowed us in 1998 is now a seasoned player, the optimism of youth has been replaced by a steelier determination and a veneer of ambition that is as closely and realistically focused as it once was dreamy. The boy is now a proper man.

"It's been a long trip since 1998," he said. "It's had its moments when it's been tough. Missing all those cuts, losing my dad, just growing up really. It has toughened me up and made me appreciative of the good times. It's taught me also that you've got to work hard, got to dedicate yourself. Dad's passing put a lot of things into perspective for me as did getting married last year. Golf is what I do, means a lot to me. It's what I am, but it is not who I am."

His confidence, meanwhile, soared on the back of a simplified swing technique. Few things in sport are more boring than the concept of a swing technique but, in layman's terms, the simpler it is, the better it

Justin secures a share of fourth place as an amateur at The Open Championship at Royal Birkdale in 1998

Groovy washing up!

Justin with the 2002 Alfred Dunhill Championship trophy

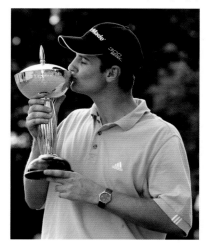

is and it is better because, when the big moments arrive and every nerve end jangles, a player has to know he can trust his body to do the right things. Often in sport, a blank mind is a good mind and it is this thoughtless state that Rose is now embracing more often.

He switched coaches last summer from David Leadbetter to the lesser-known Nick Bradley who, interestingly, learned his coaching skills from, yes, Leadbetter. "Before Nick, I was expending my energy on things that weren't bearing fruit," he said. "Nick simplifies things and when things are simple they're easier to trust and to replicate. Maybe before I'd been trying to get too perfect."

Well, maybe, but if it works for him then fine and the detail since tends to show it has indeed been a good move. Leadbetter had been coaching him for several years and sometimes, merely a change of emphasis is what works for men who are forever tinkering here and fine-tuning there. In professional golf the illusion of movement is often as important as the reality of any perceived progress.

Ken Rose (far right), who was in the gallery to see Justin win the British Masters in June 2002, died three months later following a long and courageous fight against leukaemia. The family pictured shows: Margie Rose, Annie Rose, Justin and Ken

Justin was joint top points scorer for the Great Britain and Ireland team that won the Seve Trophy against Continental Europe at Campo de Golf Parador El Saler, Valencia, Spain in 2003

He now believes his strength is that he does not really have a weakness, his chipping and putting are as sound as his tee shots and his approach shots are considered. He also enjoys a champion's ability to exist in the moment, to shut out all that is going on and to concentrate instead on the job in hand. This sounds easy but it is the hardest bit of all to achieve. His coach's interest in meditation and a relevant spirituality undoubtedly has helped. It does not matter how you cope, it just matters that you do.

Before he won the Volvo Masters, Rose already had secured the Order of Merit by virtue of a guaranteed top three place in Spain but it then became even more significant that he should succeed in the three man play-off. By doing so he not only capped a stellar year with winnings of €2,944,945, he also held off the circling vultures of doubt that suggested he was a top ten golfer any week, but not enough of a winner.

That may seem harsh but it is the reality of this perverse game. No-one doubted Rose's ability but too often, when push came to back nine, he stuttered slightly. As Jack Nicklaus pointed out all those years ago: "Playing terrific golf is one thing, winning titles is another."

He had begun his 2007 European season 50 weeks earlier when he won the MasterCard Masters in Australia but to end it the way he did removed any doubt and he may now properly savour a year that also saw him finish second only to Tiger Woods in the four Major Championships in terms of scoring aggregates – he was tied fifth in the Masters Tournament, tied tenth in the US Open Championship, tied 12th in The Open Championship and tied 12th in the US PGA Championship – as well as so nearly lifting Europe's own BMW PGA Championship at Wentworth Club in May.

On the "Road Hole"

Justin with the first cup he won, the Monthly Mug at Tylney Park, and the under 14 title at Worplesdon Junior Open in 1990

Left Justin with his good friend Ian Poulter

Justin the student

One summer's trophies!

Justin and Kate Rose

For Justin Rose, his golfing career will no doubt be a continuing rollercoaster but the likelihood now is that it will be much more roller than coaster. Ahead, there are more Major Championships to contend, most likely Ryder Cups to embroider and much else to anticipate. Beside him will be his family and his wife Kate who has done so much to barricade him against the bad moments. Together they form a seriously class act.

Would Ken Rose be inordinately proud of his lad? You bet your bottom euro he would.

Bill Elliott
The Observer

Dissecting the Majors

The Year In Retrospect

I t was, in retrospect, the year of living a bit dangerously, a season that witnessed the emergence of not one, but two European Tour Major Champions, and a summer that continued to confirm the breathtaking dominance of one Eldrick Tiger Woods.

But first, a question: What connects ladybirds and cigarettes? The answer: The Open Championship at Carnoustie, Scotland, and the US Open Championship at Oakmont Country Club, Pennsylvania. More specifically, it concerns Padraig Harrington's young son Patrick and Argentina's answer to Superman – Angel Cabrera.

It was young Paddy's innocence that charmed millions watching on television when his dad showed him the Claret Jug he had just won and the child asked : "Can we put ladybirds in it dad?" Harrington's grin at this childish quip split an already sunlit scene with its radiance. "Yes we can. We definitely can," said the new Open Champion before wheeling away to enjoy his moment.

It was a wonderful postscript to an afternoon embroidered with drama. The Irishman's wet-dry-wet-dry-perfect chip-putt routine at that pulsating final hole in Scotland is not the way to try to win an Open. It is, however, the way to set everyone's pulses racing. Spain's Sergio Garcia, meanwhile, will forever wonder why his putt on this final green failed to turn a smidgeon right, but he will know that when it came to the play-off the man who had so nearly thrown away his own chance simply dominated.

Garcia's downbeat postscript interview was criticised by some of the media but they should know better. The young Spaniard was in pain at this point as

well as in denial. Somehow sensitivity seems a rare commodity in this modern, hard-nosed world. There is no criticism from this quarter, however, for Garcia richly entertained us that week, as did Harrington.

Cabrera, too, lived dangerously. Indeed those who believe sucking on a cigarette represents too much flirtation with the sharp side of life will contest that, in mid-summer, he was living perilously already. Interestingly, the Argentine took their fears to heart later in the year when he quit the weed but in June, its calming influence helped him cope with the cloying US Open rough that forced the majority of players, including Woods, to opt for safety off the tee.

Not Cabrera. His game plan was as simple as a JCB's on entering a china shop...just crush it. It may be politically incorrect – amongst other things – to light up, take a puff, throw your cigarette down on the tee and whack a drive a million miles down a fairway so tight it encourages claustrophobia, but he did it anyway. Cabrera has always been a class act in the making but few of us really believed he could break through at a US Open Championship. The fact that he did so, lit up the season in the most thrilling fashion.

Of course, the only danger American Zach Johnson faced at Augusta National during the Masters Tournament in April was the possibility

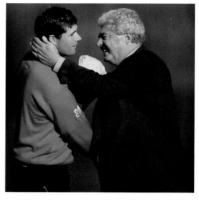

Padraig Harrington became the first Irishman to win The Irish Open since John O'Leary (right) in 1982

The European Tour's Chief Referee, John Paramor (right) confers with Tournament Administrator Tony Gray

Below Left *Genworth Financial celebrated its inaugural year as Official Sponsor of The European Tour Statistics, with the end of year Awards ceremony at Valderrama. Left to right with their awards: Peter O'Malley (Driving Accuracy), Richard Sterne (Sand Saves), Andres Romero, who received a special award for an outstanding performance backed by statistical success, and Alvaro Quiros (Driving Distance)*

Martin Kaymer - The 2007 Sir Henry Cotton Rookie of the Year

Bertie Ahern, Ireland's Taoiseach, welcomed Padraig Harrington and his wife Caroline to a reception at the Government Buildings in Dublin where he paid tribute to the "skill, courage and nerve, of The 2007 Open Champion."

Martin Kaymer

of hypothermia. This was the coldest Masters on record, so chilly that even the Georgia peach crop was hit hard. For those of us who rejoice in a Peach Cobbler in the grand old clubhouse, this was very bad news indeed. Out on the course, however, Johnson was sewing his own seeds of greatness.

Quiet and serious, the American plodded along serenely while all around him men were finding excuses not to win the tournament. Among those who chased him to the finishing line, it was pleasing to see the figure of England's Justin Rose. In 2007 Rose came of age, conceding only to Woods when it came to working out aggregate performances in the four Majors, and winning the MasterCard Masters at Huntingdale Golf Club in Melbourne, Australia, his third European Tour title and then the season ending Volvo Masters with which he secured the Number One spot in The European Tour Order of Merit.

Ah yes, Mr Woods. For a nano-second in 2007 it seemed the World Number One had taken his eye off the ball to concentrate instead on becoming a father. Rivals clutched hold of this thought with

the eagerness of a child reaching out for a comfort blanket. Before there was time to savour any respite from the American's eternal success, however, he was back. This time, if anything, he seemed more serious than ever in his attempt to crush the opposition.

Woods, of course, is not a Member of The European Tour but he does play on it, winning, in order of importance, the US PGA Championship at Southern Hills Country Club in Oklahoma, the World Golf Championships - CA Championship at Doral Golf Resort and Spa in Florida, and the WGC –Bridgestone Invitational at Firestone Country Club in Ohio.

He leads the way in the Multiple Winners Category compiled so assiduously by Steve Doughty, The European Tour's Statistician, followed by six who each won twice including that man Harrington and, of course, Rose. Harrington warmed up for his Open victory by winning The Irish Open. His victory at the Adare Manor Hotel and Golf Resort in County Limerick was the first home win since John O'Leary highlighted his own career in 1982.

The other double champions were: Ernie Els, who followed victory in the South African Airways Open at Humewood Golf Club, Port Elizabeth, with an historic seventh success in the HSBC World Match Play Championship at Wentworth Club, Surrey, England; Henrik Stenson, the tall, elegant Swede who prevailed in the Dubai Desert Classic at the Emirates Golf Club, Dubai and the WGC – Accenture Match Play at the Gallery Golf Club, Tucson, Arizona; Finland's Mikko Ilonen, who scored the most geographically split double of the year with victories in the Enjoy Jakarta Astro Indonesia Open – his debut win – at Damai Indah Golf and Country Club, Indonesia and then confirmed his emergence from the pack, a little further north, in the Scandinavian Masters at Arlandastad Golf in Stockholm, Sweden; and, Lee Westwood, that most resolute of Englishmen, who took the titles at Valle Romano Open de Andalucia at Aloha Golf Club, Spain, and The Quinn Direct British Masters at The Belfry, England.

While winning more than once in a season represents sensational achievement, winning for the first time on Tour is, arguably, the more significant move. Clearly, Ilonen takes the honours here with his brace of titles but 17 other players also took the most relevant step of their careers – a European Tour record for a single season – when they broke through the toughest barrier of all.

So, step forward please...Korea's YE Yang (HSBC Champions, Sheshan International Golf Club, Shanghai, China), Spain's José Manuel Lara (UBS Hong Kong Open, Hong Kong Golf Club, Fanling), Australia's Nathan Green (Blue Chip New Zealand Open, Gulf Harbour Country Club, Auckland), Spain's Alvaro Quiros (Alfred Dunhill Championship, Leopard Creek, Mpumalanga, South Africa), Argentina's Ariel Canete (Joburg Open, Royal Johannesburg and Kensington Golf Club, South Africa), South Africa's Anton Haig (Johnnie Walker Classic, Blue Canyon Country Club, Phuket, Thailand), China's Liang Wen-chong (Clariden Leu Singapore Masters, Laguna National Golf Club, Singapore), Thailand's Chapchai Nirat (TCL Classic, Yalong Bay Golf Club, Sanya, Hainan Island, China), Argentina's Daniel Vancsik (Madeira Islands Open BPI, Santo da Serra, Madeira, Portugal), Spanish amateur Pablo Martin (Estoril Open de Portugal, Quinta da Marinha Oitavos Golfe, Estoril, Portugal), Spain's Carl Suneson (OPEN DE SAINT OMER, presented by NEUFLIZE OBC, Aa Saint Omer Golf Club, Lumbres, France), England's Graeme Storm (Open de France ALSTOM, Le Golf National, Paris, France), Argentina's Andres Romero, (The Deutsche Bank Players' Championship of Europe, Gut Kaden,

Hamburg, Germany), England's Ross Fisher (The KLM Open, Kennemer Golf and Country Club, Zandvoort, The Netherlands), Denmark's Mads Vibe-Hastrup (Open de Madrid Valle Romano, Real Sociedad Hípica Española Club de Campo, Madrid, Spain) and France's Grégory Bourdy (Mallorca Classic, Pula Golf Club, Majorca, Spain). Congratulations to you all. The task now, of course, is to do it again in 2008.

While the year's lowest rounds were compiled by Germany's Martin Kaymer (Oceânico Victoria Golf Club), The 2007 Sir Henry Cotton Rookie of the Year, Nirat (Yalong Bay Golf Club) and Westwood (Golf Club Gut Lärchenhof), all three returning 11 under par 61s, it is how a man finishes rather than how he starts that counts in this contrarily challenging game. Therefore, step forward England's Steve Webster and take a bow for the eight under par 64, which swept him to an emotional win in the Portugal Masters at the Oceânico Victoria Golf Club at Vilamoura, and which took the honours ahead of the respective seven under par 65s of Paul Casey (Abu Dhabi Golf Championship, Abu Dhabi Golf Club), Gonzalo Fernandez-Castaño (Telecom Italia Open, Castello di Tolcinasco Golf and Country Club, Milan), Els (Humewood Golf Club), and that man Westwood again (this time at The Belfry).

Colin Montgomerie of Scotland and South Africa's Richard Sterne also sealed victories thanks to closing 65s but at courses where the par was lower. Montgomerie took the Smurfit Kappa European Open at The K Club, Straffan, Co. Kildare, Ireland, while Sterne prevailed at The Celtic Manor Wales Open, The Celtic Manor Resort, Newport, South Wales.

Michael Lorenzo-Vera, of France, finished first with a record €128,927 on the 2007 European Challenge Tour Rankings from which the leading 20 players qualify to play on The 2008 European Tour International Schedule

Don Jaime Ortiz-Patiño, the Past President of Valderrama, holds The Ryder Cup during the playing of the 20th Volvo Masters in the company of (from left to right) Sergio Garcia, Luke Donald, Robert Karlsson, Mel Pyatt, President & CEO of Volvo Event Management, George O'Grady, Chief Executive of The European Tour, David Howell and Henrik Stenson

Open at Golfclub München Eichenried, Germany, while Frenchman Grégory Havret was victorious in The Barclays Scottish Open at Loch Lomond, Glasgow, Scotland. Clearly, the Auld Alliance between Scotland and France lives on.

A decade after he last won, Per-Ulrik Johansson of Sweden returned to the limelight when the 40 year old won The Russian Open Golf Championship at Le Meridien Moscow Country Club, and The 2006 Sir Henry Cotton Rookie of the Year, Marc Warren of Scotland, confirmed the wisdom of that accolade when he won the Johnnie Walker Championship at The Gleneagles Hotel, Perthshire, Scotland, to the delight of the home country fans.

Australian Brett Rumford took his third title in four years via the eternally spectacular Omega European Masters at Crans-sur-Sierre, Crans Montana, Switzerland, and the Danish Hansens were at it again, this time when Søren won his second Tour title in the Mercedes-Benz Championship at Golf Club Gut Lärchenhof, Cologne, Germany. Furthermore, England's Nick Dougherty, who had thrilled everyone with a spirited display in the US Open Championship in June, followed up with an outstanding victory in Scotland in the Alfred Dunhill Links Championship at the Old Course, St Andrews, Carnoustie and Kingsbarns.

Back in Ireland, Nick Faldo began to hone his Ryder Cup captaincy skills when he cunningly led Great Britain and Ireland to victory over Seve Ballesteros' Continental Europe in the Seve Trophy. The Heritage Golf and Spa Resort, Killenard, Co. Laois, Ireland, proved a brilliant setting for a match that is now very much GB&I property no matter how hard Seve tries to stir his troops.

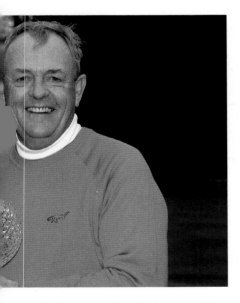

Carl Mason receives from John Jacobs, appointed Tournament Director-General of the PGA in 1971 which marked the official birth of The European Tour, The John Jacobs Trophy for finishing Number One with a record €412,376 on the 2007 European Seniors Tour

Left *Henrik Stenson (right) and Niclas Fasth, both of Sweden, finished fourth and fifth respectively in The 2007 European Tour Order of Merit*

While winning might be everything in the professional game, the biggest bouquets are reserved for those with the nerve, focus and energy to lead over all four days. South Africa's Retief Goosen did this when winning The Commercialbank Qatar Masters at Doha Golf Club, as did France's Raphaël Jacquelin for his victory in the BMW Asian Open at Tomson Shanghai Pudong Golf Club, Shanghai, China. Goosen now holds the record for most consecutive winning years on Tour, nine.

Anders Hansen of Denmark is definitely a player to watch. Well, every five years he is. He won the hugely coveted PGA Championship in 2002 and until this season it was his only European Tour victory. Now he has two, winning the 2007 BMW PGA Championship at Wentworth Club, Surrey, England. Extraordinary, but also very impressive.

Elsewhere South African golf continued to offer up champions when Charl Schwartzel won the Open de España at Centro Nacional de Golf, Madrid, Spain, while Austrian fans rejoiced when Markus Brier won the Volvo China Open at Shanghai Silport Golf Club, China.

Left-handers everywhere raised a glass when Australia's Richard Green took the title in the BA-CA Golf Open, presented by Telekom Austria, at Fontana Golf Club in Vienna. Sweden's Peter Hedblom won the Maybank Malaysian Open at Saujana Golf and Country Club, Kuala Lumpur, and compatriot Niclas Fasth won the BMW International

While the hole in one remains the most glamorous target in the game, the albatross remains the rarest bird of all, for while The 2007 European Tour International Schedule produced 17 holes in one, there were just four albatrosses. These were achieved by Gavin Flint (Maybank Malaysian Open), Frankie Minoza (TCL Classic), Tadd Fujikawa (Omega European Masters) and Graeme McDowell (Volvo Masters).

Ladybirds? Who needs them? Give me albatrosses every time. Mind you, you would not fit many of those into the Claret Jug!

Bill Elliott
The Observer

Bigger and Better

1	**Y E YANG**		274	-14
2	Tiger WOODS		276	-12
3	Michael CAMPBELL		277	-11
	Retief GOOSEN		277	-11
5	Marc WARREN		278	-10
6	Paul CASEY		280	-8
	Padraig HARRINGTON		280	-8
	Robert KARLSSON		280	-8
9	K J CHOI		281	-7
	Johan EDFORS		281	-7
	Jim FURYK		281	-7
	Francesco MOLINARI		281	-7
	Jyoti RANDHAWA		281	-7

With Paul Casey and Tiger Woods sitting alongside him at the pre-tournament press conference, it was easy to understand what defending champion David Howell meant when he referred to the HSBC Champions as Asia's Major. The event was about to be contested for only the second time and yet boasted an elite field of 74 players that included ten of the top 20 from the Official World Golf Ranking.

Marc Warren

Robert Karlsson

Also competing in the first event of The 2007 European Tour International Schedule was India's Jeev Milkha Singh, winner of the final event of the 2006 season, the Volvo Masters at Club de Golf Valderrama, and Korean Y E Yang, who began the week largely unheralded, but who ensured he did not end it that way.

It was difficult, however, to look beyond Woods, who had arrived on the back of an extraordinary run of success. The World Number One had taken five weeks off since winning the World Golf Championships - American Express Championship at The Grove in England and was looking to win his seventh stroke play title in succession, a run which began at The Open Championship at Royal Liverpool Golf Club.

A year earlier, Woods had also been the star attraction for the inaugural event at the Sheshan International Golf Club in Shanghai where, in typical fashion, he fought to the end before accepting second best to Howell, for whom victory proved the springboard to the Englishman's most successful season on Tour.

Once again, thousands turned out in force to witness the game's greatest golfer going about his business. Among them, on the opening day, was Roger Federer – the equivalent of the American in the world of tennis – who was also competing in Shanghai that week. The last time they met, Woods had watched the Swiss maestro waltz towards the US Open title in New York, and so he confessed to being slightly embarrassed to have compiled a lacklustre level par round of 72 in front of his friend and fellow great.

"For him to come out here and watch me was pretty special," said Woods. "The only thing was that he played well when I watched him at the US Open, whereas I thrashed it around the place out here!"

Ironically, Federer would have seen the real Woods had he turned up the following day when the American – who had trailed Jyoti Randhawa of India by seven shots overnight – moved back into contention after an exceptional course record equalling round of 64 that included seven birdies and an eagle. It was exactly what those who turned up to watch had been hoping to see, and Woods, who coped admirably with the inevitable crowd distractions, did not disappoint them. Suddenly, he was a mere two shots off the lead and prowling dangerously.

Local Rules

PROTECTIVE FENCES AROUND GREENS
a) A protective fence around a green is an Immovable
Obstruction(Rule 24-2 applies)
b) If a ball strikes any part of a protective fence around
a green the player MAY disregard that stroke, abandon
the ball and play another ball as nearly as possible at
the spot from which the original ball was played in
accordance with Rule 20-5 (playing next stroke from
where previous ball played).

BRORA GOLF CLUB SCOTLAND

Different golf courses have different rules. How wonderful.

However, in the end it was to prove a rollercoaster week for the American, who stumbled to a 73 in the third round to go into the final day trailing South African Retief Goosen by five shots. First round leader Randhawa was third but, more importantly, the man in second was Yang.

Although Woods gave it his all in the final round to finish second, as did European Tour Members Michael Campbell, Padraig Harrington, Robert Karlsson, Marc Warren, Casey and Goosen who, between them filled the next six places, they were all kept at arm's length by Yang, who, at 34, went on to claim the biggest win of his career with a round of 69, for a 14 under par total of 274.

So, Woods' run of stroke play victories was brought to an end by a player he confessed he had never seen, or heard of, before. As ever, though, he was generous and gracious in defeat, pointing out that the Korean's victory simply illustrated the strength of the game worldwide. "Golf has changed, it's evolved," he said. "It has become more international and it has more depth. In each and every field now there are different guys who can win. That wasn't the case 15 or 20 years ago."

Yang, who previously played mainly in Japan, went quietly about his business with rounds of 66-72-67-69, and was, charmingly, a little bemused by his achievement. He was also amazed to find Woods waiting for him in the clubhouse to congratulate him and the Korean admitted he became a little tongue-tied. "I didn't know what to say," he said. "Because he's a player that always seems to win, I didn't know whether I should congratulate him on finishing second." Better not, one suspects.

As his victory was sinking in, Yang was told that he could now join The European Tour and had 14 days to make up his mind. Needless to say, within half an hour he had already signed up. After all, bigger and better things were beckoning.

Peter Dixon
The Times

Francesco Molinari

A golf coach corrects a young player's posture during a golf clinic at the driving range

Y E Yang (left) receives the trophy from Vincent Cheng, Chairman, Hongkong and Shanghai Banking Corporation Limited

> This is such a big thing, such a big moment in my life. I want to play a lot of tournaments overseas, in Europe, the United States and Japan. I just want to be able to compete with the best players in the world, and I think this win has given me that chance.
> **Y E Yang**

The Course

Located 32 kilometres from Shanghai's central business district, the Nelson and Haworth designed course sits in tranquil surroundings at the base of the city's tallest mountain. The tree-lined American-style course has been built up to 20 metres in some places giving exciting shot variations from the undulating fairways.

Paul Casey

Sheshan International Golf Club

Par 72   Yards **7165**   Metres **6551**

Final Results

Pos	Name		Rd1	Rd2	Rd3	Rd4	Total		€	£
1	Y E YANG	KOR	66	72	67	69	274	-14	655,883.50	438,325.18
2	Tiger WOODS	USA	72	64	73	67	276	-12	437,268.79	292,225.56
3	Retief GOOSEN	RSA	68	67	69	73	277	-11	221,566.31	148,072.17
	Michael CAMPBELL	NZL	66	70	77	64	277	-11	221,566.31	148,072.17
5	Marc WARREN	SCO	66	71	70	71	278	-10	167,650.53	112,040.40
6	Paul CASEY	ENG	73	68	68	71	280	-8	118,063.75	78,901.69
	Padraig HARRINGTON	IRL	67	70	73	70	280	-8	118,063.75	78,901.69
	Robert KARLSSON	SWE	73	68	69	70	280	-8	118,063.75	78,901.69
9	Francesco MOLINARI	ITA	72	68	69	72	281	-7	74,222.75	49,602.86
	Johan EDFORS	SWE	68	74	69	70	281	-7	74,222.75	49,602.86
	Jyoti RANDHAWA	IND	65	69	72	75	281	-7	74,222.75	49,602.86
	Jim FURYK	USA	73	66	74	68	281	-7	74,222.75	49,602.86
	K J CHOI	KOR	68	72	71	70	281	-7	74,222.75	49,602.86
14	Colin MONTGOMERIE	SCO	69	70	76	67	282	-6	58,323.49	38,977.43
	John BICKERTON	ENG	68	71	71	72	282	-6	58,323.49	38,977.43
	Luke DONALD	ENG	70	69	71	72	282	-6	58,323.49	38,977.43
17	Jeev Milkha SINGH	IND	70	69	71	73	283	-5	53,837.07	35,979.17
18	Henrik STENSON	SWE	76	64	70	74	284	-4	51,121.61	34,164.43
	Shiv KAPUR	IND	71	67	74	72	284	-4	51,121.61	34,164.43
20	Charl SCHWARTZEL	RSA	72	72	71	70	285	-3	46,674.54	31,192.47
	Nick O'HERN	AUS	72	69	71	73	285	-3	46,674.54	31,192.47
	Bradley DREDGE	WAL	71	70	70	74	285	-3	46,674.54	31,192.47
23	Kevin STADLER	USA	74	70	71	71	286	-2	42,581.66	28,457.21
	Camilo VILLEGAS	COL	71	71	75	69	286	-2	42,581.66	28,457.21
	Anton HAIG	RSA	71	71	72	72	286	-2	42,581.66	28,457.21
26	Chris DIMARCO	USA	70	74	73	70	287	-1	39,630.07	26,484.67
	Gaurav GHEI	IND	72	70	71	74	287	-1	39,630.07	26,484.67
28	Anthony WALL	ENG	73	67	78	70	288	0	37,859.11	25,301.14
29	Alan MCLEAN	SCO	71	68	78	72	289	1	36,088.15	24,117.61
	Chinarat PHADUNGSIL	THA	72	69	74	74	289	1	36,088.15	24,117.61
31	Mark PILKINGTON	WAL	74	70	75	71	290	2	33,726.88	22,539.58
	Ian POULTER	ENG	72	74	72	72	290	2	33,726.88	22,539.58
33	Markus BRIER	AUT	71	75	72	73	291	3	31,365.60	20,961.55
	Thaworn WIRATCHANT	THA	75	67	71	78	291	3	31,365.60	20,961.55
35	Craig PARRY	AUS	77	69	75	71	292	4	29,004.33	19,383.52
	Chawalit PLAPHOL	THA	67	70	82	73	292	4	29,004.33	19,383.52
37	Scott STRANGE	AUS	70	76	74	73	293	5	27,548.21	18,410.39
38	Cesar MONASTERIO	ARG	74	68	80	72	294	6	26,761.12	17,884.38
39	Peter O'MALLEY	AUS	69	79	73	74	295	7	24,793.39	16,569.36
	Jean VAN DE VELDE	FRA	74	71	77	73	295	7	24,793.39	16,569.36
	Simon DYSON	ENG	78	71	74	72	295	7	24,793.39	16,569.36
	Grégory BOURDY	FRA	73	68	76	78	295	7	24,793.39	16,569.36
43	Chris RODGERS	ENG	74	76	73	73	296	8	21,645.02	14,465.31
	Alejandro CANIZARES	ESP	68	75	78	75	296	8	21,645.02	14,465.31
	Warren ABERY	RSA	74	66	76	80	296	8	21,645.02	14,465.31
	Niclas FASTH	SWE	76	70	74	76	296	8	21,645.02	14,465.31
47	Darren FICHARDT	RSA	71	69	80	77	297	9	18,496.65	12,361.26
	David HOWELL	ENG	73	72	76	76	297	9	18,496.65	12,361.26
	Tadahiro TAKAYAMA	JPN	72	67	81	77	297	9	18,496.65	12,361.26
	Gonzalo FDEZ-CASTAÑO	ESP	78	71	77	71	297	9	18,496.65	12,361.26
51	Lian-Wei ZHANG	CHN	72	76	73	77	298	10	15,741.83	10,520.22
	Ter-Chang WANG	TPE	71	75	76	76	298	10	15,741.83	10,520.22
	Stephen DODD	WAL	72	73	79	74	298	10	15,741.83	10,520.22
54	Wen-Chong LIANG	CHN	78	75	74	72	299	11	12,987.01	8,679.18
	Wen-Tang LIN	TPE	76	75	77	71	299	11	12,987.01	8,679.18
	Paul SHEEHAN	AUS	77	72	77	73	299	11	12,987.01	8,679.18
	Kane WEBBER	AUS	77	73	79	70	299	11	12,987.01	8,679.18
58	Thomas BJÖRN	DEN	75	76	74	75	300	12	11,019.28	7,364.16
59	Hendrik BUHRMANN	RSA	75	73	77	76	301	13	9,838.65	6,575.14
	Adam BLAND	AUS	74	77	78	72	301	13	9,838.65	6,575.14
61	Jong Yul SUK	KOR	76	75	76	75	302	14	8,658.01	5,786.12
62	Gui Ming LIAO	CHN	75	74	76	78	303	15	7,870.92	5,260.11
	Louis OOSTHUIZEN	RSA	71	75	83	74	303	15	7,870.92	5,260.11
	Paul BROADHURST	ENG	76	77	78	72	303	15	7,870.92	5,260.11
65	Prom MEESAWAT	THA	75	75	80	74	304	16	7,083.83	4,734.10
66	Chao LI	CHN	75	78	75	79	307	19	6,493.51	4,339.59
	Mardan MAMAT	SIN	74	80	78	75	307	19	6,493.51	4,339.59
68	Zeng Fa QI	CHN	77	77	74	81	309	21	6,099.96	4,076.59
69	Steven BOWDITCH	AUS	72	71	79	89	311	23	5,903.19	3,945.08
70	Ming Jie HUANG	CHN	78	78	80	76	312	24	5,706.41	3,813.58
71	Hao YUAN	CHN	80	74	84	75	313	25	5,509.64	3,682.08
	Mu HU (Am)	CHN	83	73	77	80	313	25		
73	Wei-Huang WU	CHN	76	78	83	79	316	28	5,312.87	3,550.58
74	Bradford VAUGHAN	RSA	85	73	82	77	317	29	5,116.10	3,419.07

Total Prize Fund

€3,935,458 £2,630,056

Coming of Age

1	**José Manuel LARA**		**265**	**-15**
2	Juvic PAGUNSAN		266	-14
3	Thongchai JAIDEE		268	-12
	Jyoti RANDHAWA		268	-12
	Jeev Milkha SINGH		268	-12
6	Miguel Angel JIMÉNEZ		269	-11
	Søren KJELDSEN		269	-11
8	Alejandro CAÑIZARES		270	-10
	Francesco MOLINARI		270	-10
	Jean VAN DE VELDE		270	-10

UBS

For years Hong Kong was known as 'The Pearl of the Orient', a romantic sobriquet full of old world charm. Then, tourism chiefs threw millions of dollars at advertising agencies to reinvent the special administrative region which on July 1, 2007, celebrated the tenth anniversary of its return to China. From 'Love it, Live it', to the 'City of Life' and the 'Events Capital of Asia', Hong Kong has always proved a magnet for tourists, business people and the sporting world.

Now it is branded 'Asia's World City', a slogan which might be disputed in Tokyo, Singapore and a few other destinations around the region, but whatever the spin doctors decide to call it, golfers need little encouragement to come to Hong Kong. In fact, most of them cannot wait to travel there.

Tradition, atmosphere, prestige – the UBS Hong Kong Open has it all – and more. "It is a unique event and because it is always at the same venue, it is like the Masters of Asia," said Kyi Hla Han, Executive Chairman of the Asian Tour. "The European players enjoy coming here, too, because of all those things...and of course the city itself."

The latest golfer to fall in love with Hong Kong was Spaniard José Manuel Lara, who finally buried his bridesmaid's tag to claim his first title in the co-sanctioned tournament between The European Tour and the Asian Tour.

The Tourism Board needs little investment in promoting Hong Kong in Spain, however. The talented Alejandro Cañizares, who finished in a share of eighth place, the experienced Miguel Angel Jiménez, winner in Hong Kong in the 2005 season, and Lara will do that for them.

"You wouldn't believe the number of people before who asked me when I was going to win. Now I can say I have," said the 29 year old Lara, who had four ties for second place over the past three years preying on his mind as he came down the final hole.

But that was precisely where he came of age as a tournament winner. "Every day I had split that fairway in two," he said. "But I was tense on the final afternoon and I hooked my drive left. However, from a downhill lie in the rough, I hit my best shot of the week." His approach stopped on the edge of the green and from there he routinely two putted for par and a one stroke victory over rookie Juvic Pagunsan of the Philippines.

Cañizares and Jiménez were amongst the thousands of spectators greenside, and eagerly embraced Lara after the winning putt had dropped. "I was trying to concentrate and imagine that I was alone out there, but there were so many people following us it was difficult," he said.

"It is a great victory and a new thing for me. But this was my time."

The three Spaniards spent the week together – on the golf course and off it – their camaraderie never compromised even though they were in direct competition.

"We had dinner together and Miguel talked about Spanish politics – he loves getting into that. Or football," said Lara. "We practised together too and he was good to play with. He has lots of experience and knows Fanling as he has won here. He gave me some tips on the greens and that helped a lot."

Jiménez admitted that a good meal and some wine with friends was an important part of his life. "To play well you need some good spirits," he laughed, acknowledging his unintentional reference to the previous night's bottle of red. "The most important thing to know is that you are human and not a machine."

In second place, that was exactly what Pagunsan proved too, much to the delight of the record crowds. The Filipino with the positive attitude made a rookie mistake when he fluffed a three wood from a bunker on the 13th in the final round to hand the initiative to Lara, but the 28 year old never stopped smiling. "I always smile when I play," he said. "I smile for the crowd, I smile for my fans. I don't want to be sad. There is no point."

Jyoti Randhawa

José Manuel Lara is presented with the trophy by Kathryn Shih, Chief Executive, UBS Hong Kong Branch

Thongchai Jaidee

Søren Kjeldsen

Simon Khan

Although the €259,178 (£174,335) first prize was in Lara's safekeeping, Pagunsan had €172,785 (£116,223) reasons to keep smiling himself. It will be enough for him to build a dream mansion for his wife and child. "This is the biggest result in my career. This performance will help a lot. My confidence is big now," he said.

There was also cause for celebration for European Tour Member Jeev Milkha Singh after his tie for third place alongside Thongchai Jaidee and Jyoti Randhawa sealed the UBS Order of Merit title.

It capped a dream year for the Indian which saw him win the 2006 Volvo China Open in Beijing in April before becoming at that time only the third Asian golfer to win a European Tour event on European soil since 1972 when he captured the 2006 Volvo Masters at Club de Golf Valderrama in October.

Noel Prentice
South China Morning Post

The first step to understanding is listening.

A thoughtful, meticulous approach. Success at golf depends on it. At UBS Wealth Management we take a similar view to success in investments. By devoting time to understanding your financial needs and maintaining an ongoing dialog, we continually assess your situation and respond to opportunities in line with your goals. Come meet with us and see the difference.

Wealth
Management

You & Us

 UBS

The Course

Not one of the longest courses on The European Tour, but the tree-lined fairways and the firm fast greens on the Peter Thomson and Michael Wolveridge layout place a premium on accuracy. The numerous dog-legs and narrowness from many of the tees neutralises the long hitters and present an intriguing test.

DANGER
GOLF BALLS
PROCEED WITH CAUTION
危險
前行時小心
留意擊球

Miguel Angel Jiménez

i European Tour history was created in the 2003 event when Lo Shih-Kai became the youngest player to compete in a European Tour event, aged 13 and 280 days. He beat the then previous record of Sergio Garcia, who was 15 and 45 days when he competed in the 1995 Turespaña Open Mediterrania The Land of Valencia.

Hong Kong Golf Club
Par **70**   Yards **6703**   Metres **6129**

Final Results

Pos	Name		Rd1	Rd2	Rd3	Rd4	Total		€	£
1	José Manuel LARA	ESP	64	66	66	69	265	-15	259,178.03	174,335.78
2	Juvic PAGUNSAN	PHI	67	65	66	68	266	-14	172,785.35	116,223.85
3	Thongchai JAIDEE	THA	68	66	67	67	268	-12	80,345.99	54,044.63
	Jeev Milkha SINGH	IND	66	67	69	66	268	-12	80,345.99	54,044.63
	Jyoti RANDHAWA	IND	64	69	69	66	268	-12	80,345.99	54,044.63
6	Miguel Angel JIMÉNEZ	ESP	68	67	66	68	269	-11	50,540.22	33,995.82
	Søren KJELDSEN	DEN	69	68	65	67	269	-11	50,540.22	33,995.82
8	Jean VAN DE VELDE	FRA	68	67	67	68	270	-10	34,937.55	23,500.70
	Francesco MOLINARI	ITA	68	69	67	66	270	-10	34,937.55	23,500.70
	Alejandro CAÑIZARES	ESP	71	69	63	67	270	-10	34,937.55	23,500.70
11	Grégory BOURDY	FRA	65	66	69	71	271	-9	28,613.54	19,246.86
12	Andrew BUCKLE	AUS	67	65	72	68	272	-8	26,747.44	17,991.63
13	Angelo QUE	PHI	69	66	69	70	274	-6	22,445.04	15,097.63
	Wen-Chong LIANG	CHN	65	72	70	67	274	-6	22,445.04	15,097.63
	Gary SIMPSON	AUS	69	68	69	68	274	-6	22,445.04	15,097.63
	Anthony KANG	USA	70	70	68	66	274	-6	22,445.04	15,097.63
	Simon KHAN	ENG	66	68	68	72	274	-6	22,445.04	15,097.63
	Raphaël JACQUELIN	FRA	69	67	71	67	274	-6	22,445.04	15,097.63
19	Cesar MONASTERIO	ARG	68	70	67	70	275	-5	17,883.46	12,029.29
	James KINGSTON	RSA	70	68	70	67	275	-5	17,883.46	12,029.29
	Colin MONTGOMERIE	SCO	69	66	70	70	275	-5	17,883.46	12,029.29
	Graeme STORM	ENG	65	73	71	66	275	-5	17,883.46	12,029.29
	Scott STRANGE	AUS	68	68	69	70	275	-5	17,883.46	12,029.29
	Bryan SALTUS	USA	68	70	69	68	275	-5	17,883.46	12,029.29
25	Matthew MILLAR	AUS	69	71	64	72	276	-4	15,006.56	10,094.14
	Daniel CHOPRA	SWE	72	67	67	70	276	-4	15,006.56	10,094.14
	Thaworn WIRATCHANT	THA	68	70	69	69	276	-4	15,006.56	10,094.14
	Christian CÉVAËR	FRA	68	68	68	72	276	-4	15,006.56	10,094.14
	Thammanoon SRIROT	THA	68	66	74	68	276	-4	15,006.56	10,094.14
	Peter LAWRIE	IRL	71	64	71	70	276	-4	15,006.56	10,094.14
31	Gary EMERSON	ENG	70	69	67	71	277	-3	12,471.77	8,389.12
	Lian-Wei ZHANG	CHN	69	63	70	75	277	-3	12,471.77	8,389.12
	Mark PILKINGTON	WAL	69	67	67	74	277	-3	12,471.77	8,389.12
	Wen-Tang LIN	TPE	70	68	68	71	277	-3	12,471.77	8,389.12
	José-Filipe LIMA	POR	69	68	75	65	277	-3	12,471.77	8,389.12
36	Tom WHITEHOUSE	ENG	70	70	70	68	278	-2	10,574.57	7,112.97
	Prom MEESAWAT	THA	69	69	73	67	278	-2	10,574.57	7,112.97
	Ron WON	USA	68	68	70	72	278	-2	10,574.57	7,112.97
	Jarmo SANDELIN	SWE	66	71	73	68	278	-2	10,574.57	7,112.97
	Rick GIBSON	CAN	68	71	68	71	278	-2	10,574.57	7,112.97
	Damien MCGRANE	IRL	68	66	73	71	278	-2	10,574.57	7,112.97
42	Joakim BÄCKSTRÖM	SWE	70	69	73	67	279	-1	8,708.47	5,857.74
	Gaurav GHEI	IND	70	70	69	70	279	-1	8,708.47	5,857.74
	K J CHOI	KOR	71	69	70	69	279	-1	8,708.47	5,857.74
	Jun-Won PARK	KOR	67	69	72	71	279	-1	8,708.47	5,857.74
	Lee SUNG	KOR	67	72	68	72	279	-1	8,708.47	5,857.74
	Gary RUSNAK	USA	68	71	71	69	279	-1	8,708.47	5,857.74
48	James STEWART	HKG	67	73	75	65	280	0	6,842.37	4,602.51
	Kane WEBBER	AUS	70	70	73	67	280	0	6,842.37	4,602.51
	Jong Yul SUK	KOR	66	70	72	72	280	0	6,842.37	4,602.51
	Adam BLYTH	AUS	66	68	73	73	280	0	6,842.37	4,602.51
	Adam LE VESCONTE	AUS	70	69	70	71	280	0	6,842.37	4,602.51
	Johan AXGREN	SWE	67	73	73	67	280	0	6,842.37	4,602.51
54	Robert-Jan DERKSEN	NED	68	68	70	75	281	1	5,598.30	3,765.69
	Anton HAIG	RSA	69	65	71	76	281	1	5,598.30	3,765.69
56	Terry PILKADARIS	AUS	70	70	71	71	282	2	4,613.42	3,103.21
	Darren FICHARDT	RSA	71	68	68	75	282	2	4,613.42	3,103.21
	Hendrik BUHRMANN	RSA	67	71	74	70	282	2	4,613.42	3,103.21
	Simon YATES	SCO	67	70	69	76	282	2	4,613.42	3,103.21
	David CARTER	ENG	70	69	71	72	282	2	4,613.42	3,103.21
	Phillip PRICE	WAL	68	68	73	73	282	2	4,613.42	3,103.21
62	Michael CAMPBELL	NZL	68	71	69	75	283	3	3,965.46	2,667.36
	Rahil GANGJEE	IND	70	70	71	72	283	3	3,965.46	2,667.36
64	Clay DEVERS	USA	68	72	71	74	285	5	3,732.20	2,510.46
65	Martin ROMINGER	SUI	68	72	72	75	287	7	3,576.69	2,405.86
66	Scott BARR	AUS	69	71	80	69	289	9	3,421.18	2,301.26
67	David BRANSDON	AUS	67	73	77	75	292	12	3,265.68	2,196.65
68	Wen Teh LU	TPE	70	70	DISQ		140	-2	3,110.17	2,092.05

Total Prize Fund

€1,549,291   £1,042,128

Striking
A Chord

1	Justin ROSE		276	-12
2	Greg CHALMERS		278	-10
	Richard GREEN		278	-10
4	Aaron PIKE (Am)		279	-9
5	Aaron BADDELEY		280	-8
6	Kurt BARNES		281	-7
7	Mathew GOGGIN		282	-6
	Simon KHAN		282	-6
	Jarrod LYLE		282	-6
10	Adam BLAND		283	-5
	Raphaël JACQUELIN		283	-5
	Peter LONARD		283	-5
	Matthew MILLAR		283	-5

B eing English in the week of the MasterCard Masters at Huntingdale Golf Club was always going to be tricky because of the poor showing of the nation's cricketers in the first Ashes Test. Therefore, the victory of Justin Rose was welcome, not only for those draped in the flag of St George, but also for those followers of European golf who welcomed one of the game's brightest talents back to the winners' circle.

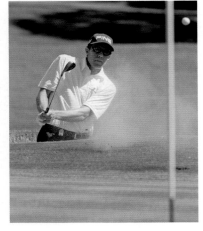

Nick O'Hern

Richard Green

Rose became the first Englishman to earn a Gold Jacket – an idea, if not colour, pinched unashamedly from the Masters Tournament at Augusta National – and was an appropriate winner in the tournament's debut on The European Tour International Schedule as a co-sanctioned event with the PGA Tour of Australasia.

While the English cricketers – photographed on one newspaper's front page under the heading 'Eleven of the Worst' – had to handle sneers and jeers in Brisbane, Rose had nothing to worry about on that score further south in Melbourne. The 26 year old was cheered and applauded all the way by the knowledgeable fans, appreciative of his golf and ambivalent to his nationality.

From the first day they admired the coolness of his temperament, the accuracy of his driving, the excellence of his iron play and most of all, perhaps, according to five time Open Champion Peter Thomson, the quality of his putting. Rose holed out beautifully throughout to win by two shots and bring the calendar year to a perfect close, just days after rejoining The European Tour with a view, he readily admitted, to making The Ryder Cup Team in 2008.

It had been over four years since his last victory following a play-off in the British Masters at Woburn, but he arrived in Australia fresh from a confidence-boosting end of season run on the US PGA Tour. However, he needed a win to make a significant move up the Official World Golf Ranking and he got it, success lifting him from 69th to 51st.

Curiously, what steeled him for the test was a comment made a week earlier by Australian golfer Nathan Green during the MFS Australian Open. Watching the event, while playing in the Dunlop Phoenix tournament in Japan where he finished fourth, Rose heard Green's comment that : "There is no better way to learn about winning than winning." It struck a chord.

Despite dropping shots over the demanding last three holes on the first day, Rose carded a 69 and declared himself pleased nevertheless as he trailed surprise leader, unheralded Australian amateur Aaron Pike, by five. The burly 21 year old from Queensland equalled Nick O'Hern's course record and, unfazed by the publicity, continued to lead on day two when Rose added a superbly competent 66 to close to within two shots.

When the Englishman fired a third round 68 – helped by a glorious eagle at the 14th where he described his two iron 275 yard second to two feet as his shot of the year – he moved smoothly into a two shot lead. He was enjoying the chance to play links-style golf albeit on a course on the famous Melbourne sandbelt that is a few miles from the sea.

Changes made to Huntingdale in recent years, mainly to solve drainage problems, had made the course easier to play according to many of the established Australian stars. They claimed the fear factor had disappeared but it was back with a vengeance on the final day. The wind blew strongly from the south east, the greens were faster than they had been all week and the pins were tight. Rose, the only man to have had three rounds in the 60's, knew he needed to dig deep to win. He did, but not without a scare or two.

At the long seventh he found the left hand trap from the tee and, while many thought he had been too ambitious when the ball hit the lip and spun into the trees, he confirmed later that was not the case. He had played conservatively from the sand with an eight iron, he said, but had simply thinned the shot. He ended up with a triple-bogey eight, yet kept the lead before showing immense character by making a birdie immediately at the eighth.

Ahead, the 2004 champion Richard Green was compiling one of only two rounds in the 60's on the final day to set the pace on ten under par 278. Further back, fellow Australian Greg Chalmers was recovering bravely after five putting the ninth and amateur Pike, enjoying every minute in the spotlight, was maintaining his challenge admirably. When he holed from a bunker for an eagle three at the 14th, he drew level with Rose. There, however, the dream ended. He dropped two shots in the run in to finish fourth.

Rose kept cool and after Chalmers holed a devilish putt on the last to tie Green in the clubhouse, the Englishman stepped onto the last tee with a two shot cushion. He made four and victory was assured.

For him it was the perfect way to start his holidays. It had been his week and he had also played his part in restoring some battered English sporting pride down under.

Renton Laidlaw
The Golf Channel

Jarmo Sandelin

Raphaël Jacquelin

The Course

Originally designed by C H Allison in 1941, the redesign by Newton-Grant-Spencer in 2001 sees course management now at the forefront of any successful round. Strategically positioned bunkers place the emphasis on accuracy as do testing pin positions. Wind direction also plays a large part in club selection on every hole.

Nick Dougherty

Justin Rose (left) is presented with the trophy by Leigh Clapham, Executive Vice President Australasia MasterCard Worldwide

i Playing on a sponsors invitation, England's Justin Rose claimed his third European Tour International Schedule victory. He was the first winner on the 2007 European Tour to win whilst playing via an invite.

Huntingdale Golf Club
Par **72**   Yards **6980**   Metres **6383**

Final Results

Pos	Name		Rd1	Rd2	Rd3	Rd4	Total		€	£
1	Justin ROSE	ENG	69	66	68	73	276	-12	170,353.28	115,359.23
2	Greg CHALMERS	AUS	70	67	68	73	278	-10	80,208.00	54,314.97
	Richard GREEN	AUS	70	71	68	69	278	-10	80,208.00	54,314.97
4	Aaron PIKE (Am)	AUS	64	69	72	74	279	-9		
5	Aaron BADDELEY	AUS	68	71	70	71	280	-8	45,427.54	30,762.46
6	Kurt BARNES	AUS	70	66	75	70	281	-7	37,856.29	25,635.39
7	Jarrod LYLE	AUS	72	69	69	72	282	-6	30,600.50	20,721.94
	Mathew GOGGIN	AUS	74	70	71	67	282	-6	30,600.50	20,721.94
	Simon KHAN	ENG	71	66	72	73	282	-6	30,600.50	20,721.94
10	Peter LONARD	AUS	68	71	69	75	283	-5	22,240.57	15,060.79
	Raphaël JACQUELIN	FRA	66	72	67	78	283	-5	22,240.57	15,060.79
	Adam BLAND	AUS	72	70	67	74	283	-5	22,240.57	15,060.79
	Matthew MILLAR	AUS	76	69	68	70	283	-5	22,240.57	15,060.79
14	John SENDEN	AUS	69	68	74	73	284	-4	16,088.92	10,895.04
	Nick O'HERN	AUS	73	68	69	74	284	-4	16,088.92	10,895.04
	Peter O'MALLEY	AUS	74	68	68	74	284	-4	16,088.92	10,895.04
17	Jarrod MOSELEY	AUS	73	70	71	71	285	-3	11,983.88	8,115.20
	Craig PARRY	AUS	68	72	69	76	285	-3	11,983.88	8,115.20
	Paul CASEY	ENG	71	70	67	77	285	-3	11,983.88	8,115.20
	Nathan GREEN	AUS	73	67	71	74	285	-3	11,983.88	8,115.20
21	Andrew TSCHUDIN	AUS	71	73	70	72	286	-2	9,653.35	6,537.02
	Daniel CHOPRA	SWE	75	69	72	70	286	-2	9,653.35	6,537.02
	Peter WILSON	ENG	65	74	72	75	286	-2	9,653.35	6,537.02
	Peter SENIOR	AUS	72	70	67	77	286	-2	9,653.35	6,537.02
25	Damien MCGRANE	IRL	76	67	69	75	287	-1	7,571.26	5,127.08
	Jarmo SANDELIN	SWE	71	73	68	75	287	-1	7,571.26	5,127.08
	Gary SIMPSON	AUS	75	65	71	76	287	-1	7,571.26	5,127.08
	Andrew BUTTERFIELD	ENG	70	70	70	77	287	-1	7,571.26	5,127.08
	Brad KENNEDY	AUS	74	70	70	73	287	-1	7,571.26	5,127.08
	Rafael CABRERA BELLO	ESP	74	71	70	72	287	-1	7,571.26	5,127.08
	Brendan CHANT	AUS	75	68	71	73	287	-1	7,571.26	5,127.08
32	Wade ORMSBY	AUS	74	71	70	73	288	0	5,489.16	3,717.13
	Marcus FRASER	AUS	74	69	66	79	288	0	5,489.16	3,717.13
	Steven BOWDITCH	AUS	68	69	75	76	288	0	5,489.16	3,717.13
	Robert ALLENBY	AUS	69	71	72	76	288	0	5,489.16	3,717.13
	Gavin COLES	AUS	71	73	70	74	288	0	5,489.16	3,717.13
	Tony CAROLAN	AUS	68	69	72	79	288	0	5,489.16	3,717.13
	Jason NORRIS	AUS	74	71	73	70	288	0	5,489.16	3,717.13
39	Nick DOUGHERTY	ENG	65	77	73	74	289	1	4,448.11	3,012.16
	Graeme STORM	ENG	71	73	68	77	289	1	4,448.11	3,012.16
	Aron PRICE	AUS	71	71	70	77	289	1	4,448.11	3,012.16
	James NITTIES	AUS	71	68	76	74	289	1	4,448.11	3,012.16
43	Peter NOLAN	AUS	71	71	72	76	290	2	3,312.42	2,243.10
	Terry PILKADARIS	AUS	72	72	75	71	290	2	3,312.42	2,243.10
	Simon DYSON	ENG	77	68	69	76	290	2	3,312.42	2,243.10
	Lee S JAMES	ENG	74	69	71	76	290	2	3,312.42	2,243.10
	Peter FOWLER	AUS	71	70	74	75	290	2	3,312.42	2,243.10
	Steve COLLINS	AUS	75	70	70	75	290	2	3,312.42	2,243.10
	Steve ALKER	NZL	73	72	73	72	290	2	3,312.42	2,243.10
	Aaron BLACK	AUS	70	74	71	75	290	2	3,312.42	2,243.10
51	Stephen DARTNALL (Am)	AUS	70	72	74	75	291	3		
52	Luke HICKMOTT	AUS	72	72	73	75	292	4	2,082.09	1,409.95
	James HEATH	ENG	75	70	73	74	292	4	2,082.09	1,409.95
	Brett RUMFORD	AUS	75	70	68	79	292	4	2,082.09	1,409.95
	Stuart APPLEBY	AUS	75	67	74	76	292	4	2,082.09	1,409.95
	Carl SUNESON	ESP	68	71	69	84	292	4	2,082.09	1,409.95
57	Gary MURPHY	IRL	74	70	71	78	293	5	1,656.21	1,121.55
58	Marcus CAIN	AUS	72	73	76	73	294	6	1,585.23	1,073.48
	Danny VERA	AUS	72	72	77	73	294	6	1,585.23	1,073.48
60	Adam PORKER	AUS	76	69	72	78	295	7	1,523.72	1,031.82
	Andrew TAMPION	AUS	75	69	75	76	295	7	1,523.72	1,031.82
	Mahal PEARCE	NZL	71	74	74	76	295	7	1,523.72	1,031.82
63	Dean KINNEY	AUS	74	70	76	76	296	8	1,485.86	1,006.19
64	Michael WRIGHT	AUS	74	71	75	77	297	9	1,457.47	986.96
	Henry EPSTEIN	AUS	72	70	78	77	297	9	1,457.47	986.96
66	Adam CRAWFORD	AUS	71	73	73	81	298	10	1,429.07	967.74
67	Denny LUCAS	ENG	71	73	75	85	304	16	1,410.15	954.92

Total Prize Fund
€892,396   £608,840

Cloaked in Success

1	Nathan GREEN		279	-5
2	Michael CAMPBELL		281	-3
	Nick DOUGHERTY		281	-3
	Marcus FRASER		281	-3
	Jarrod MOSELEY		281	-3
	Wade ORMSBY		281	-3
	Brett RUMFORD		281	-3
8	Greg CHALMERS		282	-2
	Peter O'MALLEY		282	-2
	Scott STRANGE		282	-2
	Simon WAKEFIELD		282	-2

Every golf tournament has its own character and style. One might depend on its location for its popularity, another for the test it provides, while the remainder might simply be memorable for the friendly welcome always on offer to visitors.

Peter O'Malley

Michael Campbell

The Blue Chip New Zealand Open ticked all the boxes. Only the punitive cross winds on Saturday and Sunday were not on the wish list of most of the visitors to the Gulf Harbour Country Club, but eventual winner Nathan Green did not agree. He had no complaints.

The Robert Trent Jones Jnr designed golf course, a fiercely undulating test on a cliff-top site near Auckland, boasts some of the most dramatic views across the bay where competitors in the America's Cup have long battled the strong and often gusting winds.

Conditions which suit yachtsmen, surfers and kite-fliers are, however, not always welcomed by golfers and for the late starters on Sunday, the wind was a title wrecker. Indeed the strong south-westerlies turned the tournament into a

test of survival in the latter stages of both the third and fourth rounds.

Winner Green was a prime example of how your tee-time on the weekend affected your finishing position. The Australian's 76 on Saturday, when he was a late starter, saw him slip down the leaderboard from tied fifth to tied 39th, while on Sunday, out in the 23rd last group of the day and a full three and a half hours before the final pairing, he moved from tied 39th to first thanks to a sensational closing 65.

Green, who alongside José Maria Olazábal had lost a play-off to Tiger Woods in the Buick Invitational on the US PGA Tour in January, was understandably elated at his first professional victory of note, although he had to spend an anxious time waiting and wondering if he had done enough.

He watched the second Ashes Test from Adelaide on television, had a tasty steak and egg pie for lunch, indulged in a spot of commentary for The Golf Channel and even cancelled his planned afternoon flight back to Australia....just in case!

What he opted not to do was watch what was happening on the golf course as challenger after challenger faltered coming down the stretch. Seldom can any eventual winner have sat longer and more nervously in the locker room than he did. He paced the floor for almost four hours before he knew he had won.

Going into the final day an incredible 29 players were within four shots of the leaders, Australians Kim Felton and Marcus Fraser and England's Graeme Storm. With conditions leading to such fluctuation in the scoring, it seemed anyone who made the cut could have won.

Into the closing stages, the challenge to Green was reduced to six golfers but, one by one, they fell away, including pre-tournament favourite and local hero Michael Campbell who tried hard – maybe too hard he admitted later – to win his national Open for a second time.

Campbell finished on three under par 281, two shots adrift of Green, as did Australians Jarrod Moseley, Wade Ormsby, Brett Rumford and Fraser, and Englishman Nick Dougherty, who partnered Green and whose 67 was the second best score of the final afternoon.

In addition to the first prize cheque of €145,831 (£98,763) and subsequent Membership of The European Tour which he took up two days later, Green was also draped, as tradition demands in the event, in a multi-coloured cloak, the Maori equivalent of the Masters Tournament Green Jacket, proud Maori Michael Campbell doing the honours.

"That was the longest afternoon I have ever endured," admitted Green. "But I've always enjoyed playing in New Zealand and I'll definitely be back to defend next year in the centenary year of the event."

Renton Laidlaw
The Golf Channel

Nathan Green (right) is presented with the trophy by Mark Bryers, Managing Director of Blue Chip

Above *Marcus Fraser*

Left *Simon Wakefield*

View across the 16th tee and beyond

Damian McGrane

The Course

Designed by Robert Trent Jones Jnr and first opened in 1997, the course is on undulating land which offers spectacular views over the city of Auckland. With wide fairways and a moderate length, the key to scoring is good iron play and putting the ball in the right part of the green.

Michael Campbell

> It was freezing out there at the presentation, so the jacket served a double purpose. I'm just so thrilled to receive it off someone like Michael Campbell who has done so much for New Zealand golf and his fellow Maoris.
> *Nathan Green*

Gulf Harbour Country Club

Par **71**   Yards **6953**   Metres **6358**

Final Results

Pos	Name		Rd1	Rd2	Rd3	Rd4	Total		€	£
1	Nathan GREEN	AUS	71	67	76	65	279	-5	145,831.11	98,763.42
2	Brett RUMFORD	AUS	71	70	69	71	281	-3	43,951.88	29,766.20
	Nick DOUGHERTY	ENG	69	66	79	67	281	-3	43,951.88	29,766.20
	Michael CAMPBELL	NZL	71	65	73	72	281	-3	43,951.88	29,766.20
	Jarrod MOSELEY	AUS	68	70	73	70	281	-3	43,951.88	29,766.20
	Marcus FRASER	AUS	69	69	70	73	281	-3	43,951.88	29,766.20
	Wade ORMSBY	AUS	72	63	76	70	281	-3	43,951.88	29,766.20
8	Scott STRANGE	AUS	67	70	74	71	282	-2	20,861.95	14,128.66
	Peter O'MALLEY	AUS	72	71	66	73	282	-2	20,861.95	14,128.66
	Greg CHALMERS	AUS	68	70	72	72	282	-2	20,861.95	14,128.66
	Simon WAKEFIELD	ENG	69	73	71	69	282	-2	20,861.95	14,128.66
12	Daniel CHOPRA	SWE	74	68	71	70	283	-1	13,286.84	8,998.45
	Kim FELTON	AUS	68	72	68	75	283	-1	13,286.84	8,998.45
	Damien MCGRANE	IRL	70	70	70	73	283	-1	13,286.84	8,998.45
	Michael LONG	NZL	69	70	73	71	283	-1	13,286.84	8,998.45
	Peter LAWRIE	IRL	72	66	73	72	283	-1	13,286.84	8,998.45
	Tim WILKINSON	NZL	72	70	72	69	283	-1	13,286.84	8,998.45
18	Rafael CABRERA BELLO	ESP	73	71	69	71	284	0	8,822.78	5,975.19
	Kurt BARNES	AUS	71	70	69	74	284	0	8,822.78	5,975.19
	Shaun P WEBSTER	ENG	70	68	74	72	284	0	8,822.78	5,975.19
	Peter SENIOR	AUS	69	69	71	75	284	0	8,822.78	5,975.19
	Graeme STORM	ENG	74	69	65	76	284	0	8,822.78	5,975.19
23	David GRIFFITHS	ENG	70	70	72	73	285	1	7,291.56	4,938.17
	Jarmo SANDELIN	SWE	71	71	73	70	285	1	7,291.56	4,938.17
	Mahal PEARCE	NZL	72	72	70	71	285	1	7,291.56	4,938.17
	Gareth PADDISON	NZL	73	69	69	74	285	1	7,291.56	4,938.17
27	Brad KENNEDY	AUS	73	68	70	75	286	2	5,468.67	3,703.63
	Ben BUNNY	AUS	70	72	71	73	286	2	5,468.67	3,703.63
	David LUTTERUS	AUS	71	70	71	74	286	2	5,468.67	3,703.63
	Terry PRICE	AUS	70	70	76	70	286	2	5,468.67	3,703.63
	Andrew TSCHUDIN	AUS	72	72	69	73	286	2	5,468.67	3,703.63
	Richard GREEN	AUS	72	70	70	74	286	2	5,468.67	3,703.63
	David BRANSDON	AUS	70	68	74	74	286	2	5,468.67	3,703.63
	Doug HOLLOWAY	NZL	72	70	71	73	286	2	5,468.67	3,703.63
35	Doug BATTY	NZL	70	74	68	75	287	3	3,726.80	2,523.95
	Daniel VANCSIK	ARG	71	68	71	77	287	3	3,726.80	2,523.95
	Scott HEND	AUS	76	65	73	73	287	3	3,726.80	2,523.95
	Lee S JAMES	ENG	69	72	72	74	287	3	3,726.80	2,523.95
	Aron PRICE	AUS	72	71	72	72	287	3	3,726.80	2,523.95
	Andrew W JOHNSON	RSA	73	67	73	74	287	3	3,726.80	2,523.95
	Jason NORRIS	AUS	71	71	70	75	287	3	3,726.80	2,523.95
	Eric EGLOFF	USA	70	73	72	72	287	3	3,726.80	2,523.95
	Terry PILKADARIS	AUS	73	69	74	71	287	3	3,726.80	2,523.95
	James HEATH	ENG	70	69	75	73	287	3	3,726.80	2,523.95
	Matthew MILLAR	AUS	70	72	72	73	287	3	3,726.80	2,523.95
46	Marc LEISHMAN	AUS	71	70	75	72	288	4	2,592.55	1,755.79
	Henry EPSTEIN	AUS	75	69	72	72	288	4	2,592.55	1,755.79
	Craig PARRY	AUS	69	71	71	77	288	4	2,592.55	1,755.79
49	Denny LUCAS	ENG	70	69	79	71	289	5	2,106.45	1,426.58
	Stephen SCAHILL	NZL	69	71	75	74	289	5	2,106.45	1,426.58
	Andrew RAITT	ENG	71	67	74	77	289	5	2,106.45	1,426.58
52	Carl SUNESON	ESP	70	70	69	81	290	6	1,701.37	1,152.24
	Chris DOWNES	AUS	76	68	72	74	290	6	1,701.37	1,152.24
54	James NITTIES	AUS	71	69	74	77	291	7	1,397.55	946.48
	Gavin COLES	AUS	75	65	72	79	291	7	1,397.55	946.48
	Tim MILFORD	ENG	71	71	74	75	291	7	1,397.55	946.48
	Philip TATAURANGI	NZL	78	66	72	75	291	7	1,397.55	946.48
58	Christian L NILSSON	SWE	77	67	75	73	292	8	1,296.28	877.90
	Mark PURSER	NZL	69	72	77	74	292	8	1,296.28	877.90
	Aaron TOWNSEND	AUS	74	68	71	79	292	8	1,296.28	877.90
	Steven JEFFRESS	AUS	73	71	73	75	292	8	1,296.28	877.90
62	Hamish ROBERTSON	NZL	76	68	71	78	293	9	1,247.67	844.98
	David MCKENZIE	AUS	71	72	72	78	293	9	1,247.67	844.98
64	Marcus HIGLEY	ENG	74	66	75	79	294	10	1,215.26	823.03
	Tony CHRISTIE	NZL	70	73	76	75	294	10	1,215.26	823.03
66	James HEPWORTH	ENG	74	70	74	77	295	11	1,190.95	806.57
67	Brendan CHANT	AUS	71	73	71	82	297	13	1,174.75	795.59

Total Prize Fund

€766,302   £518,974

Worth the Wait

ALFRED DUNHILL CHAMPIONSHIP						
PLAYER	SCORE	HOLE	**PLAYER**	SCORE	HOLE	
QUIROS A	-13	18	PILKINGTON	-7	18	
SCHWARTZEL	-12	18	MCLEAN	-6	18	
WESTWOOD	-9	18	TADINI	-6	18	
FICHARDT	-8	18	ELS	-6	18	
FISHER R	-8	18				
OTTO	-7	18				

1	**Alvaro QUIROS**	275	-13
2	Charl SCHWARTZEL	276	-12
3	Lee WESTWOOD	279	-9
4	Darren FICHARDT	280	-8
	Ross FISHER	280	-8
6	Hennie OTTO	281	-7
	Mark PILKINGTON	281	-7
8	Ernie ELS	282	-6
	Alan McLEAN	282	-6
	Alessandro TADINI	282	-6

M any a true word, it is said, is spoken in jest – just ask Alvaro Quiros. A mere four weeks before his stunning maiden victory in the Alfred Dunhill Championship in South Africa, the 23 year old found himself deep in the heart of battle in The European Tour Qualifying School – Final Stage at San Roque in Spain.

Scott Drummond

Charl Schwartzel

As if keeping his nerve to progress through the six round examination was not demanding enough, at the end of his second round, the Spaniard was asked to spare 15 minutes to fill in a biography form to ensure all his details, both personal and professional, would be correct in the 2007 Media Guide.

Name, date of birth and residence passed by unremarkably but, when he arrived at the section entitled 'European Tour Wins', he paused, smiled, and said, in disarming fashion: "None yet, but soon... maybe? You never know!"

You never know indeed! Less than a month later, after securing the 34th and penultimate card on offer at San Roque, the player coached by former Ryder Cup golfer José Rivero became the first golfer in history to win on his first start as a full European Tour Member.

It continued the current trend of young Spanish golfers achieving rapid success on The European Tour, started by Gonzalo Fernandez-Castaño in 2005 when victory in only his 16th professional start in The KLM Open helped him win The Sir Henry Cotton Rookie of the Year title that year, and continued by Alejandro Cañizares in 2006 who became the quickest Affiliate Member of The European Tour to win when, in only his third event, he claimed The Imperial Collection Russian Open.

There is also every reason to believe that Quiros can build on this success. Standing well over six feet tall, he has the power to be one of the longest hitters on Tour, but he also possesses a deft short game which, when allied to the former ability, can produce a winning combination, as he proved at the beautiful Leopard Creek in Mpumalanga.

However, deep within his fun-loving temperament, burns a never-say-die attitude which will stand him

in good stead in professional golf where, due to the very nature of the sport, things will not always go your way even if you are playing well.

He proved it in the Qualifying School - Final Stage where matching 73s in the third and fourth rounds left him languishing in a share of 40th place before battling back over the final two days to ensure his card, and he showed similar resilience in South Africa.

At the end of round one, Quiros stood in a share of 75th place after a disappointing two over par 74. Alongside him were 13 other players who posted similar scores on the opening day. Come Friday night, eight of those players were packing their bags for home and by the end of play on Sunday, four others had not even made their way into the top 30. Thanks to subsequent rounds of 66-68-67 for a 13 under par total of 275, Quiros did and, what is more, made his way right to number one.

At the start of the week, much had been made of another shining young star in the golfing firmament, England's Oliver Fisher, who was making his professional debut in Mpumalanga.

Like Quiros, the 18 year old – who in 2005 at the age of 16 had been the youngest player to represent Great Britain and Ireland in the Walker Cup – had come through the Qualifying School – Final Stage, finishing 29 places above the Spaniard in fifth place.

He started well and his opening two rounds in the paid ranks returned respective under par scores of 71 and 70. But, as he will quickly learn, the crux of any professional golf tournament is the weekend action and, although he slipped back on Saturday and Sunday to eventually finish in a tie for 58th, the English teenager is undoubtedly a name to ponder for the future.

A name on everybody's lips in the run-up to the event was defending champion Ernie Els who began, understandably, as favourite. But, in a mirror image of Fisher's week, the three time Major winner started conservatively and indeed flirted with the cut for a spell before consecutive 69s on the weekend saw him elevate to his final resting place of tied eighth; thrilling for the spectators to watch but never really a danger for those at the head of affairs.

The year before Els' triumph, the winner had been his fellow countryman Charl Schwartzel and, having taken a two shot lead into the final round of this year's event and a four shot advantage over Quiros, a double success looked on the cards for the 22 year old.

However three bogeys between the fourth and tenth handed the impetus to the Spaniard who took full advantage with four birdies in the closing six holes. It meant Quiros, playing two groups in front of Schwartzel, had to stand and watch and hope his opponent did not birdie the last to force a play-off. When the South African's second shot to the par

five ended in the water surrounding the green, that eventuality disappeared along with the ball.

Many a true word might, indeed, be spoken in jest but it also appears that good things come to those who wait – ask Alvaro Quiros.

Scott Crockett

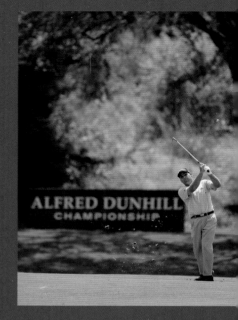

Above *Hennie Otto*

Left *Mark Pilkington*

Below *(left to right) Tom Whitehouse, Benn Barham, Richard McEvoy, Edward Rush and James Heath don springbok skins for their game drive through the Kruger National Park*

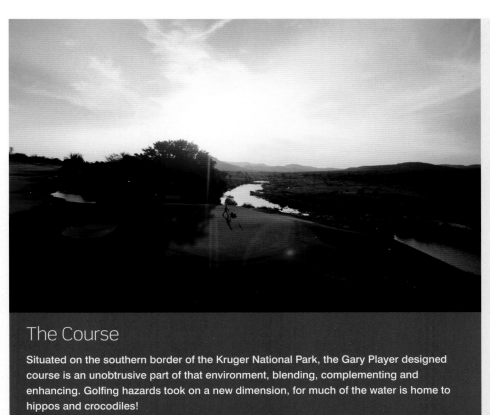

The Course

Situated on the southern border of the Kruger National Park, the Gary Player designed course is an unobtrusive part of that environment, blending, complementing and enhancing. Golfing hazards took on a new dimension, for much of the water is home to hippos and crocodiles!

Phillip Archer

Alvaro Quiros is presented with the trophy by Gaynor Rupert, wife of Johann Rupert, Chairman of Richemont International

European Tour history was made by Spain's Alvaro Quiros in claiming the Alfred Dunhill Championship. After graduating from the 2006 European Tour Qualifying School, he became the first player to win his first event as a full European Tour Member.

Leopard Creek
Par **72**   Yards **7249**   Metres **6631**

Final Results

Pos	Name		Rd1	Rd2	Rd3	Rd4	Total		€	£
1	Alvaro QUIROS	ESP	74	66	68	67	275	-13	158,500.00	106,627.74
2	Charl SCHWARTZEL	RSA	68	68	68	72	276	-12	115,000.00	77,363.97
3	Lee WESTWOOD	ENG	73	66	67	73	279	-9	69,100.00	46,485.66
4	Ross FISHER	ENG	73	69	68	70	280	-8	45,100.00	30,340.13
	Darren FICHARDT	RSA	72	70	69	69	280	-8	45,100.00	30,340.13
6	Hennie OTTO	RSA	71	69	69	72	281	-7	32,100.00	21,594.64
	Mark PILKINGTON	WAL	70	71	65	75	281	-7	32,100.00	21,594.64
8	Alan MCLEAN	SCO	77	69	69	67	282	-6	21,433.33	14,418.85
	Ernie ELS	RSA	72	72	69	69	282	-6	21,433.33	14,418.85
	Alessandro TADINI	ITA	68	74	71	69	282	-6	21,433.33	14,418.85
11	Phillip ARCHER	ENG	68	72	74	69	283	-5	15,350.00	10,326.41
	Scott DRUMMOND	SCO	71	70	73	69	283	-5	15,350.00	10,326.41
	Titch MOORE	RSA	76	64	73	70	283	-5	15,350.00	10,326.41
	Des TERBLANCHE	RSA	70	72	65	76	283	-5	15,350.00	10,326.41
	Edward RUSH	ENG	73	72	71	67	283	-5	15,350.00	10,326.41
	Alexandre ROCHA	BRA	74	67	70	72	283	-5	15,350.00	10,326.41
17	Jaco VAN ZYL	RSA	73	69	72	70	284	-4	12,600.00	8,476.40
	Robert ROCK	ENG	70	74	71	69	284	-4	12,600.00	8,476.40
	Johan AXGREN	SWE	70	74	68	72	284	-4	12,600.00	8,476.40
20	Sven STRÜVER	GER	76	70	70	69	285	-3	11,020.00	7,413.49
	Liam BOND	WAL	71	71	70	73	285	-3	11,020.00	7,413.49
	Henrik NYSTROM	SWE	75	70	69	71	285	-3	11,020.00	7,413.49
	Steve VAN VUUREN	RSA	69	74	73	69	285	-3	11,020.00	7,413.49
	Simon NASH	AUS	69	75	70	71	285	-3	11,020.00	7,413.49
25	Rafael CABRERA BELLO	ESP	69	69	77	71	286	-2	9,214.29	6,198.73
	Lee SLATTERY	ENG	72	73	69	72	286	-2	9,214.29	6,198.73
	André CRUSE	RSA	71	73	72	70	286	-2	9,214.29	6,198.73
	David DRYSDALE	SCO	73	73	68	72	286	-2	9,214.29	6,198.73
	Ian HUTCHINGS	RSA	70	70	75	71	286	-2	9,214.29	6,198.73
	Jesus Maria ARRUTI	ESP	73	72	71	70	286	-2	9,214.29	6,198.73
	Euan LITTLE	SCO	72	70	70	74	286	-2	9,214.29	6,198.73
32	Pelle EDBERG	SWE	70	76	68	73	287	-1	7,600.00	5,112.75
	Grégory HAVRET	FRA	73	68	71	75	287	-1	7,600.00	5,112.75
	Fredrik ANDERSSON HED	SWE	74	72	74	67	287	-1	7,600.00	5,112.75
	Michiel BOTHMA	RSA	73	73	71	70	287	-1	7,600.00	5,112.75
	Alan MICHELL	RSA	69	73	73	72	287	-1	7,600.00	5,112.75
	Anton HAIG	RSA	78	68	70	71	287	-1	7,600.00	5,112.75
	Oliver WILSON	ENG	68	70	72	77	287	-1	7,600.00	5,112.75
39	Joakim BÄCKSTRÖM	SWE	73	72	70	73	288	0	6,700.00	4,507.29
	Grant MULLER	RSA	71	73	69	75	288	0	6,700.00	4,507.29
41	Andrew COLTART	SCO	69	76	71	73	289	1	6,100.00	4,103.65
	Benn BARHAM	ENG	70	72	72	75	289	1	6,100.00	4,103.65
	Vaughn GROENEWALD	RSA	71	73	75	70	289	1	6,100.00	4,103.65
	Rafael ECHENIQUE	ARG	72	74	70	73	289	1	6,100.00	4,103.65
45	Werner GEYER	RSA	71	74	73	72	290	2	5,400.00	3,632.74
	Jean-Baptiste GONNET	FRA	75	69	76	70	290	2	5,400.00	3,632.74
	Marc CAYEUX	ZIM	74	69	74	73	290	2	5,400.00	3,632.74
48	Sam LITTLE	ENG	74	70	74	73	291	3	4,700.00	3,161.83
	Keith HORNE	RSA	72	71	75	73	291	3	4,700.00	3,161.83
	Patrik SJÖLAND	SWE	72	72	72	75	291	3	4,700.00	3,161.83
	Brandon PIETERS	RSA	70	71	74	76	291	3	4,700.00	3,161.83
52	Tom WHITEHOUSE	ENG	71	73	76	72	292	4	3,700.00	2,489.10
	Adilson DA SILVA	BRA	72	72	74	74	292	4	3,700.00	2,489.10
	Neil CHEETHAM	ENG	73	72	70	77	292	4	3,700.00	2,489.10
	Mattias ELIASSON	SWE	73	69	68	82	292	4	3,700.00	2,489.10
	Andrew MCLARDY	RSA	70	75	69	78	292	4	3,700.00	2,489.10
	Tyrone VAN ASWEGEN	RSA	73	70	72	77	292	4	3,700.00	2,489.10
58	Oliver FISHER	ENG	71	70	77	75	293	5	2,750.00	1,850.01
	Trevor FISHER JNR	RSA	71	72	78	72	293	5	2,750.00	1,850.01
	Wayne DE HAAS	RSA	68	72	75	78	293	5	2,750.00	1,850.01
	Richard FINCH	ENG	78	66	74	75	293	5	2,750.00	1,850.01
	Ross WELLINGTON	RSA	75	71	76	71	293	5	2,750.00	1,850.01
	Sam WALKER	ENG	69	74	71	79	293	5	2,750.00	1,850.01
	Juan PARRON	ESP	75	70	70	78	293	5	2,750.00	1,850.01
	James KAMTE	RSA	71	74	71	77	293	5	2,750.00	1,850.01
66	Jean HUGO	RSA	73	73	74	74	294	6	2,300.00	1,547.28
67	Jonathan LOMAS	ENG	73	73	74	75	295	7	2,150.00	1,446.37
	Gareth DAVIES	ENG	73	68	77	77	295	7	2,150.00	1,446.37
69	Lee S JAMES	ENG	72	73	73	78	296	8	2,000.00	1,345.46
70	Mark MURLESS	RSA	74	71	77	75	297	9	1,900.00	1,278.19
71	Hendrik BUHRMANN	RSA	71	75	75	77	298	10	1,750.00	1,177.28
	Jean-François LUCQUIN	FRA	76	70	77	75	298	10	1,750.00	1,177.28

Total Prize Fund

€995,000   £669,366

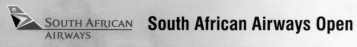

The Perfect Remedy

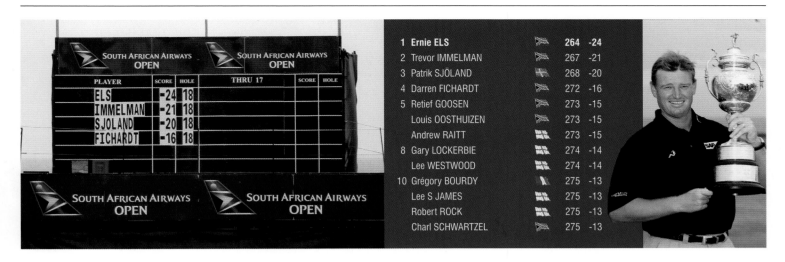

	PLAYER		SCORE	HOLE			
1	Ernie ELS		264	-24			
2	Trevor IMMELMAN		267	-21			
3	Patrik SJÖLAND		268	-20			
4	Darren FICHARDT		272	-16			
5	Retief GOOSEN		273	-15			
	Louis OOSTHUIZEN		273	-15			
	Andrew RAITT		273	-15			
8	Gary LOCKERBIE		274	-14			
	Lee WESTWOOD		274	-14			
10	Grégory BOURDY		275	-13			
	Lee S JAMES		275	-13			
	Robert ROCK		275	-13			
	Charl SCHWARTZEL		275	-13			

The legendary South African Bobby Locke, who knew a thing or two about how to play a links course, once declared that Humewood Golf Club was worthy of hosting The Open Championship should it ever be played outside the United Kingdom.

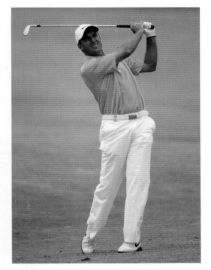

Darren Fichardt

Grégory Bourdy

Retief Goosen

Aside from Locke, who won The Open at four of Britain's most celebrated links, only two other South African golfers have claimed the Claret Jug and it was appropriate that one of them, Ernie Els, returned to the winner's circle as Humewood Golf Club played host to the South African Airways Open for the first time since 1957.

As he sprayed photographers with champagne at the conclusion of the prize giving ceremony, Els said: "I love this course and anyone who knows me knows how much I love links golf. What is more, Humewood is the step I needed to get me going again. The knee injury in 2005 set me back, I was going backwards and was frustrated, like a bear with a sore head. Quite frankly, my wife Liezl deserves a medal for putting up with me!"

As he basked in the glory of his 58th win worldwide, so the officials and members of Humewood were delighted to learn that their club would again host the South African Airways Open in 2010 when the Championship celebrates its Centenary. Khaya Ngqula, President and CEO of South African Airways, said: "Through the Open we showcase the best international talent as well as our world-class golfing facilities. Humewood has been a superb venue and we're delighted that we'll be returning."

Humewood was designed by a Briton, Colonel Stafford Vere Hotchkin, who teamed up with Major Horace Hutchinson and Sir Guy Campbell to form one of the great triumvirates of golf course architecture in the 1920's, the best known of which is probably Woodhall Spa, home of the English Golf Union. At Humewood, Hotchkin took into consideration the prevailing winds so that the majority of holes are usually played into the wind or downwind and the defined entrances to the greens encourage bump and run shots to be played.

The winds in Port Elizabeth, where Humewood is located on a stretch of exposed links land close to where the Indian Ocean meets Algoa Bay, have been known to reach gale force proportions. "Calm days at Humewood are pretty rare," said Els. He knew well enough since one of his six wins in his native South Africa just happened to be in the 1992 Goodyear Classic played at...Humewood. "I beat Retief Goosen by a shot, shooting 67 in the last round so let's hope history repeats itself," he added, at the start of the week.

Ironically Goosen, the defending champion, looked like sweeping clear of the field on the opening day until an 11 at the 17th dropped him back, two behind joint leaders Trevor Immelman, Andrew Raitt, Carl Suneson and...Els.

Trevor Immelman

Ironically, there was little wind to talk of in the second round when Patrik Sjöland's 64 enabled him to take a one shot lead ahead of Els and Immelman, who both shot 66s. Sjöland, who lost his Tour card following the 2005 season, admitted: "I was tired of travelling, and in a way it was nice to lose my card. It allowed me to spend some time at home and think things over." Goosen, two shots further back in a share of fourth with Raitt, took revenge on the 17th – a two iron, a 275 yard three wood and a 20 foot putt bringing an eagle three and the comment: "The 11 is history; there's nothing more to say."

Huge crowds basked in the sun and watched fabulous golf in the third round when Immelman celebrated his 27th birthday by hitting all 18 greens in regulation for nine birdies and nine pars in a course record 63.

Els stayed in touch, albeit three shots behind his young compatriot, courtesy of a round which included two master strokes which once again emphasised his ability to conjure such shots on the links. At the 15th he used a rescue club off an upslope to set up an eagle three, then at the next

hit a pitch off a hard lie and over a bunker on his way to a birdie three, a shot one observer described as almost incomprehensible.

Immelman was the man to beat as the fourth round began but Els ensured he maintained his record of a tournament win every year since 1991. He carded an excellent closing 65 in the breeze and his 24 under par total of 264 set a new scoring record for the Championship. "That's as good as I can play," said Els, who won by three from Immelman and four from Sjöland. "There were a lot of different emotions out there. I view the South African Open like I do a Major Championship."

Els, winner of two US Opens and The 2002 Open Championship, had played like a Major Champion again and found the perfect remedy to cure that sore head.

Mitchell Platts

Richard Sterne

The Course

Humewood Golf Club, redesigned by Donald Steel in the 1980s, is one of the world's most challenging links courses and consistently ranked in the top ten in South Africa. Bobby Locke considered it the best in the country and felt it compared favourably with the top links courses in the British Isles.

Richard Finch

Above Fans of Ernie Els show their support during the final round

(left to right) Neale Kunhardt, President of South African Golf Association, Ernie Els and Khaya Ngqula, President & CEO of South African Airways

> After injuring my knee following The 2005 Open I basically spent a year playing patch-up golf. I did not want my winning run of at least one victory every year to end. Humewood was my last chance to set the record straight. Now I have done so and the relief is immense.
>
> **Ernie Els**

Humewood Golf Club

Par 72 **Yards 6963** **Metres 6366**

Final Results

Pos	Name		Rd1	Rd2	Rd3	Rd4	Total		€	£
1	Ernie ELS	RSA	67	66	66	65	264	-24	158,500.00	107,062.77
2	Trevor IMMELMAN	RSA	67	66	63	71	267	-21	115,000.00	77,679.61
3	Patrik SJÖLAND	SWE	68	64	69	67	268	-20	69,100.00	46,675.31
4	Darren FICHARDT	RSA	72	67	65	68	272	-16	49,100.00	33,165.82
5	Retief GOOSEN	RSA	69	66	68	70	273	-15	35,100.00	23,709.17
	Andrew RAITT	ENG	67	68	68	70	273	-15	35,100.00	23,709.17
	Louis OOSTHUIZEN	RSA	71	65	70	67	273	-15	35,100.00	23,709.17
8	Gary LOCKERBIE	ENG	73	66	70	65	274	-14	22,600.00	15,265.73
	Lee WESTWOOD	ENG	68	68	68	70	274	-14	22,600.00	15,265.73
10	Lee S JAMES	ENG	71	69	67	68	275	-13	17,225.00	11,635.05
	Robert ROCK	ENG	70	68	69	68	275	-13	17,225.00	11,635.05
	Charl SCHWARTZEL	RSA	71	69	65	70	275	-13	17,225.00	11,635.05
	Grégory BOURDY	FRA	71	68	68	68	275	-13	17,225.00	11,635.05
14	Jaco VAN ZYL	RSA	71	65	72	68	276	-12	14,600.00	9,861.93
15	Ross FISHER	ENG	70	69	66	72	277	-11	14,100.00	9,524.20
16	Justin WALTERS	ENG	73	67	71	67	278	-10	12,012.50	8,114.14
	Richard FINCH	ENG	71	71	70	66	278	-10	12,012.50	8,114.14
	James KAMTE	RSA	73	68	69	72	278	-10	12,012.50	8,114.14
	Lee SLATTERY	ENG	71	70	69	68	278	-10	12,012.50	8,114.14
	Richard STERNE	RSA	73	69	66	70	278	-10	12,012.50	8,114.14
	Angel CABRERA	ARG	75	65	69	69	278	-10	12,012.50	8,114.14
	Bradford VAUGHAN	RSA	70	68	71	69	278	-10	12,012.50	8,114.14
	Pelle EDBERG	SWE	69	68	73	68	278	-10	12,012.50	8,114.14
24	Alan MCLEAN	SCO	69	68	71	71	279	-9	10,100.00	6,822.30
	Benn BARHAM	ENG	71	71	68	69	279	-9	10,100.00	6,822.30
	Sam WALKER	ENG	72	69	72	66	279	-9	10,100.00	6,822.30
27	Nic HENNING	RSA	71	68	70	71	280	-8	9,050.00	6,113.05
	Carl SUNESON	ESP	67	76	65	72	280	-8	9,050.00	6,113.05
	Keith HORNE	RSA	73	68	68	71	280	-8	9,050.00	6,113.05
	Edward RUSH	ENG	70	67	70	73	280	-8	9,050.00	6,113.05
31	Juan PARRON	ESP	71	72	70	68	281	-7	7,600.00	5,133.61
	Eirik Tage JOHANSEN	NOR	75	66	71	69	281	-7	7,600.00	5,133.61
	Tongoona CHARAMBA	ZIM	75	69	67	70	281	-7	7,600.00	5,133.61
	James HEATH	ENG	70	70	74	67	281	-7	7,600.00	5,133.61
	Steve BASSON	RSA	71	69	69	72	281	-7	7,600.00	5,133.61
	Chris Jnr SWANEPOEL	RSA	73	70	70	68	281	-7	7,600.00	5,133.61
	Mattias ELIASSON	SWE	75	69	70	67	281	-7	7,600.00	5,133.61
	David FROST	RSA	72	69	68	72	281	-7	7,600.00	5,133.61
	Des TERBLANCHE	RSA	68	70	71	72	281	-7	7,600.00	5,133.61
40	Chris WILLIAMS	RSA	72	70	70	70	282	-6	5,900.00	3,985.30
	Fredrik ANDERSSON HED	SWE	69	67	73	73	282	-6	5,900.00	3,985.30
	Warren BENNETT	ENG	73	69	68	72	282	-6	5,900.00	3,985.30
	Oliver FISHER	ENG	77	67	65	73	282	-6	5,900.00	3,985.30
	Branden GRACE (AM)	RSA	73	71	67	71	282	-6		
	Rafael CABRERA BELLO	ESP	72	69	66	75	282	-6	5,900.00	3,985.30
	Mark MURLESS	RSA	72	71	70	69	282	-6	5,900.00	3,985.30
	Ulrich VAN DEN BERG	RSA	72	70	69	71	282	-6	5,900.00	3,985.30
	Andrew MCLARDY	RSA	71	71	70	70	282	-6	5,900.00	3,985.30
49	Hennie OTTO	RSA	70	73	68	72	283	-5	4,400.00	2,972.09
	Desvonde BOTES	RSA	73	68	72	70	283	-5	4,400.00	2,972.09
	Adilson DA SILVA	BRA	71	71	73	68	283	-5	4,400.00	2,972.09
	André CRUSE	RSA	72	70	73	68	283	-5	4,400.00	2,972.09
	Edoardo MOLINARI	ITA	70	69	66	78	283	-5	4,400.00	2,972.09
	Michiel BOTHMA	RSA	75	69	72	67	283	-5	4,400.00	2,972.09
	Ian HUTCHINGS	RSA	73	70	70	70	283	-5	4,400.00	2,972.09
56	Mathias GRÖNBERG	SWE	72	70	70	72	284	-4	3,142.86	2,122.92
	Sam LITTLE	ENG	73	71	68	72	284	-4	3,142.86	2,122.92
	Ross WELLINGTON	RSA	76	67	67	74	284	-4	3,142.86	2,122.92
	Oliver WILSON	ENG	74	69	71	70	284	-4	3,142.86	2,122.92
	Johan AXGREN	SWE	72	70	72	70	284	-4	3,142.86	2,122.92
	Phillip ARCHER	ENG	75	68	69	72	284	-4	3,142.86	2,122.92
	Andrew TAMPION	AUS	72	67	72	73	284	-4	3,142.86	2,122.92
63	Alessandro TADINI	ITA	74	70	71	70	285	-3	2,350.00	1,587.37
	Divan VAN DEN HEEVER	RSA	71	73	70	71	285	-3	2,350.00	1,587.37
	Gareth DAVIES	ENG	69	75	69	72	285	-3	2,350.00	1,587.37
	Nigel EDWARDS (AM)	WAL	73	68	71	73	285	-3		
	Michael LAMB	ZIM	76	68	66	75	285	-3	2,350.00	1,587.37
	Alexandre ROCHA	BRA	74	70	67	74	285	-3	2,350.00	1,587.37
	Nico VAN RENSBURG	RSA	70	70	70	75	285	-3	2,350.00	1,587.37
	Sean FARRELL	ZIM	75	69	69	72	285	-3	2,350.00	1,587.37
	Titch MOORE	RSA	71	69	73	72	285	-3	2,350.00	1,587.37
72	Dion FOURIE	RSA	72	70	73	71	286	-2	1,700.00	1,148.31
	Grégory HAVRET	FRA	73	68	71	74	286	-2	1,700.00	1,148.31
	Steve VAN VUUREN	RSA	71	65	77	73	286	-2	1,700.00	1,148.31
	David CARTER	ENG	74	69	69	74	286	-2	1,700.00	1,148.31
	Wade ORMSBY	AUS	71	69	73	73	286	-2	1,700.00	1,148.31
77	Thomas AIKEN	RSA	76	68	71	72	287	-1	1,394.00	941.61
	Julien FORET	FRA	75	69	74	69	287	-1	1,394.00	941.61
	Garry HOUSTON	WAL	71	72	76	68	287	-1	1,394.00	941.61
	Grant MULLER	RSA	73	71	72	71	287	-1	1,394.00	941.61
	Joakim BÄCKSTRÖM	SWE	72	72	73	70	287	-1	1,394.00	941.61
82	Birgir HAFTHORSSON	ISL	74	69	70	75	288	0	1,385.00	935.53
	Christiaan BASSON (AM)	RSA	73	70	73	72	288	0		
84	Daniel VANCSIK	ARG	71	71	75	72	289	1	1,380.50	932.49
	Tony JOHNSTONE	ZIM	72	72	74	71	289	1	1,380.50	932.49
86	Anton HAIG	RSA	75	68	71	76	290	2	1,376.00	929.45
87	Werner GEYER	RSA	73	71	74	73	291	3	1,371.50	926.41
	Trevor FISHER	RSA	79	65	75	72	291	3	1,371.50	926.41
89	Scott DRUMMOND	SCO	73	67	70	85	295	7	1,367.00	923.37
90	Matthew RICHARDSON	ENG	74	68	78	76	296	8	1,364.00	921.35

Total Prize Fund

€1,016,066 £686,326

Happy Holidays

Joburg Open 2007					
PLAYER	SCORE	HOLE	PLAYER	SCORE	HOLE
CANETE	-19	18	DA SILVA	-12	18
MCLARDY	-17	18	RUSH	-12	18
OTTO	-16	18			
HAINDL	-13	18			
MURLESS	-13	18			

1	Ariel CANETE		266	-19
2	Andrew MCLARDY		268	-17
3	Hennie OTTO		269	-16
4	Alex HAINDL		272	-13
	Mark MURLESS		272	-13
6	Adilson DA SILVA		273	-12
	Edward RUSH		273	-12
8	James KINGSTON		274	-11
	Doug McGUIGAN		274	-11
	Edoardo MOLINARI		274	-11
	Terry PILKADARIS		274	-11

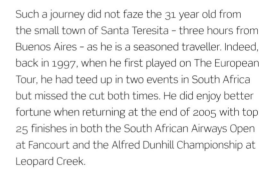

I t was inevitable that, with a name like Ariel Canete, headline writers would offer such gems as 'Ariel Cleans Up' following the Argentine's victory in the Joburg Open at the Royal Johannesburg and Kensington Golf Club. Yet the manner in which Canete not only kept his card tidy but also his rivals at bay in the final round, gave real substance to those newspaper captions.

James Kingston

Edoardo Molinari

For this was truly a remarkable turnaround in the fortunes of a player who had endured a lacklustre twelve months during which time he lost his European Tour card and which, after finishing 53rd at the Qualifying School, left him contemplating a full-time return to the Challenge Tour.

The European Tour had resumed in the same country where the last event on the 2007 schedule had been staged prior to the Christmas festivities. However, Canete's original plan did not have South Africa on the radar as he considered extending his own break further into the New Year.

As he explained: "I was in Argentina and it was the holidays. I was sitting there doing nothing. I was not even practising. Then a friend of mine 'phoned me and said I must go to South Africa because it offered me a real chance to get my career back on track."

Such a journey did not faze the 31 year old from the small town of Santa Teresita - three hours from Buenos Aires - as he is a seasoned traveller. Indeed, back in 1997, when he first played on The European Tour, he had teed up in two events in South Africa but missed the cut both times. He did enjoy better fortune when returning at the end of 2005 with top 25 finishes in both the South African Airways Open at Fancourt and the Alfred Dunhill Championship at Leopard Creek.

Yet this time there was much more at stake because, after eight Qualifying School visits, he knew in his heart of hearts it was time he used his considerable talent to emulate his Argentine compatriots Jorge Berendt, Angel Cabrera, José Coceres, Vicente Fernandez, Ricardo Gonzalez, Cesar Monasterio and Eduardo Romero by winning on The European Tour International Schedule.

That he should become the first Argentine to win a Tour event in South Africa came courtesy of a new event announced only a few weeks earlier and organised as a celebration of the City of Johannesburg. Counsellor Amos Masondo, the Executive Mayor of Johannesburg, said: "We want everyone in the city to feel that the Joburg Open belongs to them and for the tournament to showcase the city and its people to sports lovers throughout the world."

What is more an additional objective of the Joburg Open, co-sanctioned by The European Tour and the Sunshine Tour, was to raise funds for the establishment of a driving range near Diepsloot, north of Sandton on the outskirts of the city. The range will offer schoolchildren, and other members of the community, regular coaching sessions and those who show talent and persistence will receive free second-hand equipment and, eventually, club membership.

Canete and his fellow Argentines know all about coming through the ranks – Angel Cabrera was originally a caddie who received financial assistance from Eduardo Romero – and so 12 years after turning professional it was Canete's turn to take a giant stride forward.

Initially one of South Africa's own took the lead with Andrew McLardy notching two eagles in the last four holes of an inward 29 for a 63 on the West Course while Italy's Edoardo Molinari scored 64 on the tougher East Course. With a field of 200, two courses were used to reach the halfway stage by which time South Africans James Kingston, Hennie Otto and Jakobus Roos had moved to 11 under par 132, one ahead of Australian Terry Pilkadaris.

Canete finished the third day on top of the leaderboard, but business was not concluded. Play had been suspended because of lightning leaving Canete and his rivals to complete their third rounds on Sunday morning before setting out for the final time on the East Course in the afternoon. By then Canete was one ahead, and when he conjured up a brilliant up and down from a greenside bunker for birdie at the 18th, he had increased that margin to two shots to realise his dream, claim victory, and earn exempt European Tour status for virtually three years.

Charl Schwartzel

Naturally enough his first call was to his travel agent. Canete, who had intended to compete in Colombia, Costa Rica and Guatemala on the Challenge Tour in the following weeks, was instead heading for the abundant riches of The European Tour's Abu Dhabi Golf Championship.

And, of course, another chance to clean up.

Mitchell Platts

Storm clouds gather

Andrew McLardy

The Course

The West Course and East Course are a fine example of how two courses in close proximity can create a different golfing experience. The West, the original course on site, has sweeping fairways and generous greens albeit alongside trees and water. The East, at 7590 yards, is 505 yards longer than its neighbour and a true championship layout which has hosted seven South African Open Championships. The 518 yard tenth and the 500 yard 11th are reputed to be the longest back-to-back par fours in the world.

Tom Whitehouse

Sven Strüver

Ariel Canete receives the trophy from Johan Immelman (left) Commissioner of the Sunshine Tour, Moss Ngoasheng (second left) Chairman of easyGolf Worldwide and Councillor Amos Masondo (right) the Executive Mayor of Johannesburg

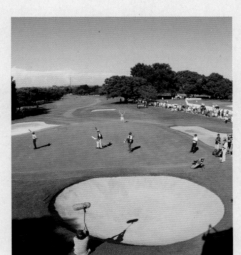

i The inaugural Joburg Open was played over two courses at the Royal Johannesburg and Kensington Golf Club layout – the East and West Courses. The East measured 7,590 yards, making it the longest course ever played on The European Tour.

Royal Johannesburg and Kensington Golf Club
(East and West Courses)

| Par **71** | Yards **7590** | Metres **6940** (East) |
| Par **72** | Yards **7085** | Metres **6478** (West) |

Final Results

Pos	Name		Rd1	Rd2	Rd3	Rd4	Total		€	£
1	Ariel CANETE	ARG	66	68	65	67	266	-19	158,500.00	106,774.99
2	Andrew MCLARDY	RSA	63	72	65	68	268	-17	115,000.00	77,470.81
3	Hennie OTTO	RSA	65	67	70	67	269	-16	69,100.00	46,549.85
4	Mark MURLESS	RSA	64	71	69	68	272	-13	45,100.00	30,382.03
	Alex HAINDL	RSA	68	68	66	70	272	-13	45,100.00	30,382.03
6	Adilson DA SILVA	BRA	71	65	69	68	273	-12	32,100.00	21,624.46
	Edward RUSH	ENG	70	67	67	69	273	-12	32,100.00	21,624.46
8	Doug McGUIGAN	RSA	68	67	71	68	274	-11	20,475.00	13,793.17
	James KINGSTON	RSA	66	66	72	70	274	-11	20,475.00	13,793.17
	Edoardo MOLINARI	ITA	64	71	69	70	274	-11	20,475.00	13,793.17
	Terry PILKADARIS	AUS	67	66	74	67	274	-11	20,475.00	13,793.17
12	Alastair FORSYTH	SCO	67	68	69	71	275	-10	14,900.00	10,037.52
	Jean-Baptiste GONNET	FRA	69	67	69	70	275	-10	14,900.00	10,037.52
	Sven STRÜVER	GER	65	71	68	71	275	-10	14,900.00	10,037.52
	Ulrich VAN DEN BERG	RSA	68	69	70	68	275	-10	14,900.00	10,037.52
	Keith HORNE	RSA	67	71	69	68	275	-10	14,900.00	10,037.52
17	Ricardo GONZALEZ	ARG	68	72	71	65	276	-9	12,850.00	8,656.52
	Richard STERNE	RSA	69	66	71	70	276	-9	12,850.00	8,656.52
19	Tom WHITEHOUSE	ENG	67	73	69	68	277	-8	11,360.00	7,652.77
	Charl SCHWARTZEL	RSA	69	68	69	71	277	-8	11,360.00	7,652.77
	Louis OOSTHUIZEN	RSA	65	69	74	69	277	-8	11,360.00	7,652.77
	Euan LITTLE	SCO	69	71	68	69	277	-8	11,360.00	7,652.77
	Dion FOURIE	RSA	71	68	70	68	277	-8	11,360.00	7,652.77
24	David PARK	WAL	65	71	69	73	278	-7	10,250.00	6,905.01
	Matthew ZIONS	AUS	67	68	71	72	278	-7	10,250.00	6,905.01
26	Lee S JAMES	ENG	69	71	67	72	279	-6	9,500.00	6,399.76
	Maarten LAFEBER	NED	72	66	68	73	279	-6	9,500.00	6,399.76
	Kalle BRINK	SWE	69	68	72	70	279	-6	9,500.00	6,399.76
29	Jan-Are LARSEN	NOR	70	66	74	70	280	-5	8,420.00	5,672.21
	Magnus A CARLSSON	SWE	69	66	72	73	280	-5	8,420.00	5,672.21
	Benn BARHAM	ENG	68	70	69	73	280	-5	8,420.00	5,672.21
	Justin WALTERS	ENG	68	69	74	69	280	-5	8,420.00	5,672.21
	Oliver WILSON	ENG	69	68	73	70	280	-5	8,420.00	5,672.21
34	Ryan TIPPING	RSA	70	69	69	73	281	-4	7,100.00	4,782.98
	Garth MULROY	RSA	69	69	71	72	281	-4	7,100.00	4,782.98
	Shaun NORRIS	RSA	69	69	72	71	281	-4	7,100.00	4,782.98
	Antti AHOKAS	FIN	73	66	71	71	281	-4	7,100.00	4,782.98
	Brett LIDDLE	RSA	69	68	70	74	281	-4	7,100.00	4,782.98
	Jaco VAN ZYL	RSA	67	68	71	75	281	-4	7,100.00	4,782.98
	Michiel BOTHMA	RSA	71	68	71	71	281	-4	7,100.00	4,782.98
	Richard BLAND	ENG	68	72	72	69	281	-4	7,100.00	4,782.98
42	Raphaël EYRAUD	FRA	70	67	72	73	282	-3	5,800.00	3,907.22
	Brandon PIETERS	RSA	65	71	73	73	282	-3	5,800.00	3,907.22
	Des TERBLANCHE	RSA	73	67	70	72	282	-3	5,800.00	3,907.22
	Trevor FISHER JNR	RSA	67	72	73	70	282	-3	5,800.00	3,907.22
	Andrew CURLEWIS	RSA	70	70	71	71	282	-3	5,800.00	3,907.22
47	Robert WIEDERKEHR	SUI	69	70	74	70	283	-2	4,500.00	3,031.47
	Jakobus ROOS	RSA	67	65	75	76	283	-2	4,500.00	3,031.47
	David DIXON	ENG	66	71	73	73	283	-2	4,500.00	3,031.47
	Darren FICHARDT	RSA	68	72	69	74	283	-2	4,500.00	3,031.47
	Stuart LITTLE	ENG	74	65	72	72	283	-2	4,500.00	3,031.47
	Marc CAYEUX	ZIM	65	73	75	70	283	-2	4,500.00	3,031.47
	Stuart CAGE	ENG	67	72	74	70	283	-2	4,500.00	3,031.47
	Bobby LINCOLN	RSA	67	71	70	75	283	-2	4,500.00	3,031.47
55	Peter KAENSCHE	NOR	69	71	73	71	284	-1	2,875.00	1,936.77
	Warren ABERY	RSA	64	73	73	74	284	-1	2,875.00	1,936.77
	Jamie LITTLE	ENG	66	74	72	72	284	-1	2,875.00	1,936.77
	Andrew MARSHALL	ENG	69	69	69	77	284	-1	2,875.00	1,936.77
	Marcus HIGLEY	ENG	71	69	72	72	284	-1	2,875.00	1,936.77
	Paul NILBRINK	NOR	71	68	73	72	284	-1	2,875.00	1,936.77
	Julio ZAPATA	ARG	70	69	71	74	284	-1	2,875.00	1,936.77
	Gareth DAVIES	ENG	66	71	70	77	284	-1	2,875.00	1,936.77
	Ross WELLINGTON	RSA	69	71	71	73	284	-1	2,875.00	1,936.77
	Henrik NYSTROM	SWE	66	69	75	74	284	-1	2,875.00	1,936.77
	Patrik SJÖLAND	SWE	66	72	71	75	284	-1	2,875.00	1,936.77
	Christiaan BASSON	RSA	74	66	73	71	284	-1	2,875.00	1,936.77
67	Jaco AHLERS	RSA	72	68	72	73	285	0	2,100.00	1,414.68
	David HIGGINS	IRL	69	69	72	75	285	0	2,100.00	1,414.68
	Michael LAMB	ZIM	68	71	71	75	285	0	2,100.00	1,414.68
70	Vaughn GROENEWALD	RSA	65	74	74	74	287	2	1,800.00	1,212.59
	Paul DWYER	ENG	68	71	72	76	287	2	1,800.00	1,212.59
	Gustavo ROJAS	ARG	70	70	73	74	287	2	1,800.00	1,212.59
73	Chris DAVISON	RSA	68	71	74	75	288	3	1,447.00	974.78
	Dean LAMBERT	RSA	68	66	76	78	288	3	1,447.00	974.78
	Hendrik BUHRMANN	RSA	72	68	73	75	288	3	1,447.00	974.78
	Grant MULLER	RSA	68	72	75	73	288	3	1,447.00	974.78
	Sion E BEBB	WAL	69	71	76	72	288	3	1,447.00	974.78
	Robert DINWIDDIE	ENG	69	69	76	74	288	3	1,447.00	974.78
79	Tyrone VAN ASWEGEN	RSA	68	72	77	72	289	4	1,388.00	935.04
80	Simon NASH	AUS	72	68	72	78	290	5	1,382.00	931.00
	Magnus PERSSON	SWE	68	67	79	76	290	5	1,382.00	931.00
	Chris GANE	ENG	65	72	75	78	290	5	1,382.00	931.00
83	Omar SANDYS	RSA	70	69	75	77	291	6	1,376.00	926.96

Total Prize Fund

€1,010,592 £680,794

Walking on Air

1	**Paul CASEY**		271	-17
2	Peter HANSON		272	-16
	Miguel Angel JIMÉNEZ		272	-16
4	Chris DiMARCO		273	-15
5	Retief GOOSEN		274	-14
	Padraig HARRINGTON		274	-14
	Jean-François LUCQUIN		274	-14
8	Henrik STENSON		275	-13
9	Robert-Jan DERKSEN		276	-12
	Phillip PRICE		276	-12

O ne of George O'Grady's Christmas presents might have taken until January to arrive but it was no less welcome for that. It came when the Chief Executive of The European Tour arrived in The Gulf and noted how well the Abu Dhabi Golf Championship had bedded down.

Though only in its second season, it had acquired status which some tournaments take years to achieve and, what is more, it offered more points towards the Official World Golf Ranking than the Bob Hope Chrysler Classic on the US PGA Tour in the same week. To cap it all, the event also produced a world class winner in Paul Casey, a true son of Europe, who had grown in stature in front of our eyes during 2006 and at the end of which had been named The European Tour Golfer of the Year.

In mid September, Casey had won the HSBC World Match Play Championship at Wentworth Club; a week later he was the cornerstone of Europe's victory in The Ryder Cup; and a month after that, he only failed to become Number One on The European Tour Order of Merit when the redoubtable Padraig Harrington played a remarkable last few holes of the Volvo Masters, taking one putt on each of the last eight greens to finish second behind Jeev Milkha Singh and claim the Harry Vardon Trophy for himself.

In Abu Dhabi, however, an exceptional last round of 65 gave Casey victory over a field that contained five of his Ryder Cup team-mates in Sergio Garcia, Robert Karlsson, Colin Montgomerie, Henrik Stenson and Harrington,

and in all eight of the world's top 21, including American Chris DiMarco, who had won in 2006, and South African Retief Goosen, the US Open Champion in 2001 and 2004.

Casey is beginning to dominate in Europe. His eighth victory worldwide was also the fourth from his past 27 events on The European Tour International Schedule. How had he improved so quickly? Part of the answer lies in his relationship with Peter Kostis, his coach.

"He has been pushing me," Casey said. "Without him doing that, things like this would not have happened." Casey revealed, for example, that he and Kostis have on-going bets. When Casey does not win a tournament, he has to buy dinner and Kostis, a wine enthusiast, chooses the wine. When Casey does triumph, he is allowed to choose a couple of bottles from Kostis' vast cellar.

As well as being in excellent condition, the National Course that Casey won on had matured and been toughened up since DiMarco won with a 20 under par total of 268. It had been lengthened by 150 yards and the fairways slightly narrowed. The rough was longer and rye grass had been planted in it. New bunkers and tees had also been added on several holes.

Miguel Angel Jiménez

Robert-Jan Derksen

Peter Hanson

Left *Paul Casey with a group of volunteer marshalls after he won the 2007 Abu Dhabi Golf Championship*

Below *Padraig Harrington receives a special players' badge as winner of The 2006 Order of Merit from George O'Grady, Chief Executive of The European Tour*

Thomas Björn

Paul Casey (centre) displays the trophy flanked by Sheikh Hamed Bin Zayed Al Nahyan, Head of the Crown Prince Court in Abu Dhabi, (left) and Sheikh Sultan Bin Tahnoon Al Nahyan, Chairman of The Abu Dhabi Tourism Authority (right)

Phillip Price

However, once you see the size of Casey's forearms you know he has the strength to hit the ball a long way and one shot in his last round confirmed that.

It came on the eighth, a 572 yard par five that dog legs to the left. It was into a 12 mph wind, which may have explained why his drive only travelled 310 yards, but his second, a three wood that carried 280 yards, even impressed the man himself. It was a perfect demonstration of the Englishman's brute strength, whereas a shot from a bunker with a five iron on the 71st hole was as notable for its deftness. A teaspoonful too much sand and his ball would not have cleared the lip.

After everyone had jostled for position over the first three days, the fourth turned out to be a humdinger with many of The European Tour's leading golfers approaching their best in the hot sun. For 17 holes, Casey gave a masterclass of straight and powerful hitting, moving from ten under par and a share of sixth place overnight to 18 under par and in the lead coming down the 72nd hole. No-one could stay with him, though several players were tied with him for the lead at various times, and Peter Hanson and Miguel Angel Jiménez would end one stroke behind him, with DiMarco one shot further back.

The only moment of slight concern came on the 18th green when he misjudged a three foot putt for par on the grainy surface and had to accept the bitter pill of a bogey six, eliciting an anxious 20 minute wait before it became clear that his total of 17 under par 271 was good enough.

The only question then remaining was, who was happier on Sunday evening, Casey or Hanson? "I am flying at the moment," said Hanson, referring to his happiness at the birth of his baby girl one week earlier. Hanson had a doughty 68 in the fourth round, after which he said: "I have been walking on clouds since then,"

In all probability, Casey was walking alongside him.

John Hopkins
The Times

The official sponsor of the European Tour Statistics

think it possible.com℠

Genworth®
Financial

The Course

New tees, additional bunkering and reshaping of rough on several holes led to the National Course being a tougher test in this, its second year of European Tour competition. The variety of holes, some which required length while others demanded shot-making, kept the professionals on their toes throughout.

Sergio Garcia

Last year's event was fantastic, but this year was just so much better. This is a world-class event and I think everyone involved should be very, very proud with what they put on this week.
Paul Casey

Abu Dhabi Golf Club
Par **72** Yards **7433**   Metres **6795**

Final Results

Pos	Name		Rd1	Rd2	Rd3	Rd4	Total		€	£
1	Paul CASEY	ENG	71	68	67	65	271	-17	257,876.56	170,266.13
2	Peter HANSON	SWE	70	68	66	68	272	-16	134,388.55	88,731.67
	Miguel Angel JIMÉNEZ	ESP	71	65	68	68	272	-16	134,388.55	88,731.67
4	Chris DIMARCO	USA	69	70	68	66	273	-15	77,363.74	51,080.35
5	Retief GOOSEN	RSA	66	72	68	68	274	-14	55,392.44	36,573.53
	Jean-François LUCQUIN	FRA	70	69	67	68	274	-14	55,392.44	36,573.53
	Padraig HARRINGTON	IRL	68	67	68	71	274	-14	55,392.44	36,573.53
8	Henrik STENSON	SWE	66	72	70	67	275	-13	38,681.87	25,540.17
9	Robert-Jan DERKSEN	NED	70	69	69	68	276	-12	32,802.23	21,658.07
	Phillip PRICE	WAL	69	65	71	71	276	-12	32,802.23	21,658.07
11	Gary ORR	SCO	70	68	70	69	277	-11	26,664.70	17,605.69
	Phillip ARCHER	ENG	63	75	71	68	277	-11	26,664.70	17,605.69
	Nick DOUGHERTY	ENG	66	72	70	69	277	-11	26,664.70	17,605.69
14	Thongchai JAIDEE	THA	68	71	67	72	278	-10	21,378.18	14,115.20
	Alastair FORSYTH	SCO	71	66	69	72	278	-10	21,378.18	14,115.20
	Sergio GARCIA	ESP	68	72	69	69	278	-10	21,378.18	14,115.20
	Stephen DODD	WAL	69	70	72	67	278	-10	21,378.18	14,115.20
	Robert KARLSSON	SWE	73	67	69	69	278	-10	21,378.18	14,115.20
	Colin MONTGOMERIE	SCO	69	71	69	69	278	-10	21,378.18	14,115.20
20	Marcel SIEM	GER	71	72	67	69	279	-9	16,573.03	10,942.55
	Paul LAWRIE	SCO	67	72	69	71	279	-9	16,573.03	10,942.55
	James HEPWORTH	ENG	68	71	68	72	279	-9	16,573.03	10,942.55
	Steve WEBSTER	ENG	70	73	69	67	279	-9	16,573.03	10,942.55
	Andrew MCLARDY	RSA	70	72	70	67	279	-9	16,573.03	10,942.55
	Graeme STORM	ENG	68	70	69	72	279	-9	16,573.03	10,942.55
	Richard STERNE	RSA	70	67	71	71	279	-9	16,573.03	10,942.55
	Kyron SULLIVAN	WAL	72	71	70	66	279	-9	16,573.03	10,942.55
	Shiv KAPUR	IND	70	66	68	75	279	-9	16,573.03	10,942.55
29	Niclas FASTH	SWE	71	69	73	67	280	-8	12,864.49	8,493.93
	Richard GREEN	AUS	67	72	69	72	280	-8	12,864.49	8,493.93
	Anthony WALL	ENG	68	75	66	71	280	-8	12,864.49	8,493.93
	Raphaël JACQUELIN	FRA	70	71	68	71	280	-8	12,864.49	8,493.93
	Christian CÉVAËR	FRA	73	68	71	68	280	-8	12,864.49	8,493.93
	Emanuele CANONICA	ITA	70	73	68	69	280	-8	12,864.49	8,493.93
	Ian GARBUTT	ENG	69	74	69	68	280	-8	12,864.49	8,493.93
36	Gary MURPHY	IRL	72	68	68	73	281	-7	10,830.92	7,151.25
	Garry HOUSTON	WAL	70	67	71	73	281	-7	10,830.92	7,151.25
	David CARTER	ENG	71	68	71	71	281	-7	10,830.92	7,151.25
	Julien GUERRIER (AM)	FRA	68	72	69	72	281	-7		
	Alejandro CAÑIZARES	ESP	75	68	70	68	281	-7	10,830.92	7,151.25
41	Oliver WILSON	ENG	70	72	73	67	282	-6	9,283.65	6,129.64
	Graeme MCDOWELL	NIR	71	72	69	70	282	-6	9,283.65	6,129.64
	Nick O'HERN	AUS	68	68	75	71	282	-6	9,283.65	6,129.64
	Alessandro TADINI	ITA	70	66	71	75	282	-6	9,283.65	6,129.64
	Maarten LAFEBER	NED	71	70	71	70	282	-6	9,283.65	6,129.64
	Peter HEDBLOM	SWE	71	69	72	70	282	-6	9,283.65	6,129.64
47	Thomas BJÖRN	DEN	71	71	71	70	283	-5	7,891.10	5,210.20
	Damien MCGRANE	IRL	72	68	71	72	283	-5	7,891.10	5,210.20
	Grégory BOURDY	FRA	70	73	72	68	283	-5	7,891.10	5,210.20
50	Alvaro QUIROS	ESP	70	70	75	69	284	-4	6,962.74	4,597.23
	James KINGSTON	RSA	71	68	70	75	284	-4	6,962.74	4,597.23
	Søren HANSEN	DEN	73	69	69	73	284	-4	6,962.74	4,597.23
53	Andrew MARSHALL	ENG	73	70	73	69	285	-3	5,570.19	3,677.79
	Miles TUNNICLIFF	ENG	72	71	73	69	285	-3	5,570.19	3,677.79
	Juan PARRON	ESP	71	71	70	73	285	-3	5,570.19	3,677.79
	Oliver FISHER	ENG	68	71	73	73	285	-3	5,570.19	3,677.79
	Brett RUMFORD	AUS	70	70	72	73	285	-3	5,570.19	3,677.79
	Stephen GALLACHER	SCO	70	73	71	71	285	-3	5,570.19	3,677.79
59	Mark PILKINGTON	WAL	73	70	69	74	286	-2	4,177.64	2,758.34
	Robert ROCK	ENG	69	72	71	74	286	-2	4,177.64	2,758.34
	Matthew MILLAR	AUS	73	69	75	69	286	-2	4,177.64	2,758.34
	Chinarat PHADUNGSIL	THA	71	71	73	71	286	-2	4,177.64	2,758.34
	Gary EMERSON	ENG	67	70	74	75	286	-2	4,177.64	2,758.34
	David PARK	WAL	73	70	71	72	286	-2	4,177.64	2,758.34
	Kenneth FERRIE	ENG	74	68	75	69	286	-2	4,177.64	2,758.34
66	Søren KJELDSEN	DEN	75	68	71	73	287	-1	3,404.00	2,247.54
	Benn BARHAM	ENG	75	67	72	73	287	-1	3,404.00	2,247.54
	Francesco MOLINARI	ITA	69	71	74	73	287	-1	3,404.00	2,247.54
69	Yasin ALI	ENG	71	70	71	76	288	0	2,699.43	1,782.33
	Ariel CANETE	ARG	68	74	74	72	288	0	2,699.43	1,782.33
	Notah BEGAY III	USA	72	71	74	71	288	0	2,699.43	1,782.33
	John BICKERTON	ENG	74	68	72	74	288	0	2,699.43	1,782.33
	Terry PRICE	AUS	74	69	71	74	288	0	2,699.43	1,782.33
74	Markus BRIER	AUT	73	69	73	74	289	1	2,315.00	1,528.51
75	Lee SLATTERY	ENG	71	70	76	74	291	3	2,312.00	1,526.53

Total Prize Fund
€**1,556,541** £**1,027,724**

Bang on Target

1	**Retief GOOSEN**		**273**	**-15**
2	Nick O'HERN		274	-14
3	Ernie ELS		275	-13
4	Stuart APPLEBY		276	-12
	Richard GREEN		276	-12
	Graeme McDOWELL		276	-12
7	Andres ROMERO		277	-11
	Henrik STENSON		277	-11
9	Thongchai JAIDEE		278	-10
	Wen-Chong LIANG		278	-10

Few tournaments could claim to have begun in such explosive fashion as the 2007 Commercialbank Qatar Masters, nor to have ended four days later with such a spectacular finale served up by the eventual winner, Retief Goosen, as the country celebrated a decade of golf with The European Tour.

For the unwary with a nervous disposition there was some consternation when, on two occasions during the morning's play in the first round, the magnificent Doha Golf Club clubhouse and the many temporary buildings erected for the event were rocked to their foundations by the sound of two huge explosions.

The club members in the know, however, just shrugged their shoulders. For several weeks they had endured the dynamiting of rocks on a nearby building site outside the course boundary and, even if a few backswings were disturbed, the big bangs eventually became the subject of good natured humour amongst the tournament professionals.

As the affable Englishman John Bickerton remarked: "I was out on the course for the first one and just thought it was Paul Casey hitting another one of his drives!" Possibly, and not just by coincidence, two of the most unflappable heads in European golf ended up amongst the names on the first day leaderboard.

Goosen produced a seven under par 65 and said his golf had been good enough to threaten the course record of 63, a feat which would have seen him claim the prize of a sporty BMW on offer to anyone who achieved it.

Miguel Angel Jiménez showed no ill effects after swapping the ice and snow of a recent skiing holiday for the desert heat to card a 66 and the multi-cultural nature of a tournament co-sanctioned with the Asian Tour was reflected in the matching 66 posted by Australia's Nick O'Hern and the 67 returned by India's Shiv Kapur.

Day two, January 26, was the Republic Day of India but sadly Kapur could not celebrate it by challenging the lead. It left the Asian standard to be flown by the highly promising Thai teenager Chinarat Phadungsil who moved into the top ten and within sight of two Antipodean left handers who were determined not to let what was also, by coincidence, Australia Day, pass quietly.

Andres Romero

Left *Henrik Stenson*

Below *Graeme McDowell and Ernie Els*

HOLE	PLAYER	PAR
18	GOOSEN	-15
18	OHERN	-14
18	ELS	-13
18	APPLEBY	-12
18	MCDOWELL	-12
18	GREEN	-12
18	ROMERO	-11

Richard Green spent his early morning in an unsuccessful hunt for vegemite to spread on his breakfast toast, but later he and O'Hern had good reason to visit the temporary beer garden situated close to the tenth tee where their favourite amber nectar was readily available.

Despite tighter pin placements and a tricky breeze Green and O'Hern had moved to 11 and nine under par respectively to form part of a triumvirate, alongside Goosen, at the top of the leaderboard, a trio that remained pretty much in place through to the tournament's gripping climax.

There were late assaults on their domination from another Australian, Stuart Appleby, and Northern Ireland's Graeme McDowell and so when on the Sunday afternoon Ernie Els birdied three of his last four holes the murmurs in the stands around the 18th green were all about the possibility of a play-off involving several players.

Ironically, and struggling to join them was Goosen, somewhat treading water after his heroics of the opening day. With two holes to play he was two shots behind O'Hern, who appeared to be closing in on his first European Tour success.

Goosen halved the deficit with a birdie at the 17th before playing the par five final hole in imperious style to take the title. His drive split the fairway and his three wood from 280 yards out nestled in the first cut of rough at the back of the green.

After missing the fairway with his drive, O'Hern could only hold his breath and hope that his subsequent par five would lead to a play-off, as most observers were convinced Goosen would get up and down in two to tie him so that both finished one ahead of Els and two in front of Appleby, Green and McDowell.

Instead Goosen went one better. The South African sized up his putt from 30 feet, worked out how to negotiate two different slopes as well as the five foot right to left borrow and coolly produced the decisive eagle three that settled the destination of the €282,743 (£185,566) first prize.

After enduring more than 12 months without a victory on The European Tour International Schedule, Goosen was a relieved man. "It's a great feeling to have a European Tour win under the belt again," he said. "It's been a while since the last one."

O'Hern digested his disappointment and declared: "I wasn't expecting Retief to make it, but that's golf. You have to expect the unexpected."

Goosen, who had been labelled the "hakeem", or wise man, among the visiting professionals, gave his thoughts on that putt. "You are shaking on the inside like every other player does – even Tiger. When you're under pressure, it's a sort of 'must' thing. You must focus and you must make the putt." He did, and a 14th European Tour title was his for the keeping.

Graham Otway

Johan Edfors

Achieving in Qatar since 1975

Commercialbank lifestyle banking services

Richard Green

Retief Goosen (left) with the trophy alongside Hassan Al-Naimi (centre), President of The Qatar Golf Association, and Andrew Stevens (right), Group CEO, Commercialbank

Miguel Angel Jiménez

> The course has changed quite a bit since I was last here in 1999. It is a lot tougher than it was in those days. The rough has grown up and it is consistent and thick. Then there's the wind. I have always enjoyed the wind and playing a range of different shots.
> **Sergio Garcia**

The Course

Designed by Peter Harradine in 1996, the uniquely challenging course has been host to all ten editions of the tournament. With eight artificial lakes weaving their way alongside the majority of the holes, utmost accuracy was required as was the ability to hit the ball a long way as length was a factor.

Doha Golf Club

Par **72**   Yards **7355**   Metres **6725**

Final Results

Pos	Name		Rd1	Rd2	Rd3	Rd4	Total		€	£
1	Retief GOOSEN	RSA	65	68	71	69	273	-15	282,743.30	185,566.06
2	Nick O'HERN	AUS	66	69	69	70	274	-14	188,495.53	123,710.71
3	Ernie ELS	RSA	69	71	68	67	275	-13	106,200.31	69,699.88
4	Stuart APPLEBY	AUS	70	69	71	66	276	-12	72,044.30	47,283.09
	Richard GREEN	AUS	68	65	71	72	276	-12	72,044.30	47,283.09
	Graeme MCDOWELL	NIR	73	68	68	67	276	-12	72,044.30	47,283.09
7	Andres ROMERO	ARG	70	71	67	69	277	-11	46,653.49	30,618.96
	Henrik STENSON	SWE	68	68	70	71	277	-11	46,653.49	30,618.96
9	Wen-Chong LIANG	CHN	69	67	72	70	278	-10	35,965.60	23,604.43
	Thongchai JAIDEE	THA	71	67	72	68	278	-10	35,965.60	23,604.43
11	Oliver FISHER	ENG	73	68	70	68	279	-9	27,720.66	18,193.23
	Søren KJELDSEN	DEN	72	69	66	72	279	-9	27,720.66	18,193.23
	Paul LAWRIE	SCO	69	67	71	72	279	-9	27,720.66	18,193.23
	Chris DIMARCO	USA	69	71	70	69	279	-9	27,720.66	18,193.23
	David LYNN	ENG	73	69	71	66	279	-9	27,720.66	18,193.23
16	Paul MCGINLEY	IRL	71	68	72	69	280	-8	22,902.62	15,031.12
	Peter O'MALLEY	AUS	73	67	67	73	280	-8	22,902.62	15,031.12
	Nick DOUGHERTY	ENG	68	71	71	70	280	-8	22,902.62	15,031.12
19	Ariel CANETE	ARG	69	70	72	70	281	-7	20,357.89	13,361.00
	Sergio GARCIA	ESP	70	71	73	67	281	-7	20,357.89	13,361.00
	Miguel Angel JIMÉNEZ	ESP	66	70	73	72	281	-7	20,357.89	13,361.00
22	Jeev Milkha SINGH	IND	69	68	75	70	282	-6	18,152.45	11,913.56
	Emanuele CANONICA	ITA	70	68	72	72	282	-6	18,152.45	11,913.56
	Robert KARLSSON	SWE	70	71	70	71	282	-6	18,152.45	11,913.56
	Alejandro CAÑIZARES	ESP	70	69	70	73	282	-6	18,152.45	11,913.56
	Edward MICHAELS	USA	68	69	69	76	282	-6	18,152.45	11,913.56
27	Shiv KAPUR	IND	67	73	72	71	283	-5	15,098.77	9,909.41
	Stephen DODD	WAL	72	68	73	70	283	-5	15,098.77	9,909.41
	Michael CAMPBELL	NZL	70	70	70	73	283	-5	15,098.77	9,909.41
	Robert-Jan DERKSEN	NED	71	71	70	71	283	-5	15,098.77	9,909.41
	Chawalit PLAPHOL	THA	73	69	70	71	283	-5	15,098.77	9,909.41
	Søren HANSEN	DEN	72	72	68	71	283	-5	15,098.77	9,909.41
	Johan EDFORS	SWE	73	67	74	69	283	-5	15,098.77	9,909.41
34	Lee WESTWOOD	ENG	71	70	72	71	284	-4	12,723.68	8,350.62
	Thaworn WIRATCHANT	THA	73	70	73	68	284	-4	12,723.68	8,350.62
	Alvaro QUIROS	ESP	70	70	71	73	284	-4	12,723.68	8,350.62
37	Jason KNUTZON	USA	73	71	70	71	285	-3	11,027.19	7,237.21
	Scott STRANGE	AUS	70	71	74	70	285	-3	11,027.19	7,237.21
	Jong Yul SUK	KOR	69	73	72	71	285	-3	11,027.19	7,237.21
	Andrew COLTART	SCO	69	73	72	71	285	-3	11,027.19	7,237.21
	Simon HURD	ENG	71	70	71	73	285	-3	11,027.19	7,237.21
	Jean VAN DE VELDE	FRA	75	69	70	71	285	-3	11,027.19	7,237.21
	Peter HANSON	SWE	70	73	71	71	285	-3	11,027.19	7,237.21
44	José Manuel LARA	ESP	73	71	71	71	286	-2	8,652.10	5,678.42
	Raphaël JACQUELIN	FRA	73	70	71	72	286	-2	8,652.10	5,678.42
	Phillip ARCHER	ENG	72	70	72	72	286	-2	8,652.10	5,678.42
	Mardan MAMAT	SIN	69	70	76	71	286	-2	8,652.10	5,678.42
	Anton HAIG	RSA	71	70	72	73	286	-2	8,652.10	5,678.42
	Chinarat PHADUNGSIL	THA	69	68	75	74	286	-2	8,652.10	5,678.42
	Terry PILKADARIS	AUS	71	70	72	73	286	-2	8,652.10	5,678.42
51	Phillip PRICE	WAL	70	72	73	72	287	-1	7,125.26	4,676.35
	Anthony KANG	USA	72	70	71	74	287	-1	7,125.26	4,676.35
53	Frankie MINOZA	PHI	75	69	73	71	288	0	5,937.72	3,896.96
	Simon KHAN	ENG	72	71	74	71	288	0	5,937.72	3,896.96
	Chris RODGERS	ENG	70	70	72	76	288	0	5,937.72	3,896.96
	Cesar MONASTERIO	ARG	73	70	74	71	288	0	5,937.72	3,896.96
	Marcus BOTH	AUS	71	73	74	70	288	0	5,937.72	3,896.96
58	Seve BENSON (AM)	ENG	72	72	74	71	289	1		
	Gary RUSNAK	USA	72	71	76	70	289	1	5,004.65	3,284.58
	Paul BROADHURST	ENG	71	69	74	75	289	1	5,004.65	3,284.58
61	Steve WEBSTER	ENG	71	72	73	74	290	2	4,750.17	3,117.57
62	David BRANSDON	AUS	70	73	74	74	291	3	4,410.88	2,894.88
	Bradley DREDGE	WAL	71	72	74	74	291	3	4,410.88	2,894.88
	Prom MEESAWAT	THA	71	70	75	75	291	3	4,410.88	2,894.88
65	S.S.P CHOWRASIA	IND	72	71	75	74	292	4	3,986.75	2,616.53
	Prayad MARKSAENG	THA	71	73	72	76	292	4	3,986.75	2,616.53
67	Thammanoon SRIROT	THA	71	72	74	76	293	5	3,562.63	2,338.17
	Juvic PAGUNSAN	PHI	70	71	77	75	293	5	3,562.63	2,338.17
	Mahal PEARCE	NZL	70	73	75	75	293	5	3,562.63	2,338.17
70	Gary SIMPSON	AUS	72	69	74	79	294	6	3,161.64	2,075.00
	Gonzalo FDEZ-CASTAÑO	ESP	70	73	74	77	294	6	3,161.64	2,075.00
72	Jarmo SANDELIN	SWE	74	70	76	75	295	7	2,545.00	1,670.30
73	Kenneth FERRIE	ENG	70	74	75	77	296	8	2,542.00	1,668.33
74	Yasin ALI	ENG	69	75	78	75	297	9	2,539.00	1,666.36
75	Clay DEVERS	USA	74	70	80	80	304	16	2,536.00	1,664.39

Total Prize Fund

€1,706,653   £1,120,086

Home Comforts

1	Henrik STENSON	269	-19
2	Ernie ELS	270	-18
3	Niclas FASTH	271	-17
	Tiger WOODS	271	-17
5	Ross FISHER	272	-16
6	Peter HANSON	274	-14
7	Simon DYSON	275	-13
	Prom MEESAWAT	275	-13
	Jyoti RANDHAWA	275	-13
10	Thomas BJÖRN	276	-12
	Miguel Angel JIMÉNEZ	276	-12
	Robert KARLSSON	276	-12
	Maarten LAFEBER	276	-12
	Colin MONTGOMERIE	276	-12

F ew sponsorship opportunities that have come Henrik Stenson's way have surely carried the same appeal as the day he was invited to become one of the ambassadors for Golf in Dubai. Here is a man who fell for the place long before anyone offered him a financial inducement. When looking for reasons why he recovered from a troubled spell to rise from 176th on the Official World Golf Ranking to inside the top ten, Dubai looms every bit as large as the world's tallest building which will, by 2008, grace an already imposing skyline.

Robert Karlsson

Maarten Lafeber

This golfing pleasuredome is not only the place he goes to hone his game when the snow is thick on the ground in his native Sweden. It was here that he and coach, Pete Cowen, who has an academy in Dubai, rebuilt his game so successfully that he can now compete with anyone.

When not plying his considerable trade around the globe, Stenson can often be found playing social golf on the Majlis Course at the Emirates Golf Club where he is a member. Imagine, therefore, the pleasure that came following a thrilling tussle for the 18th edition of the Dubai Desert Classic. In 2005 Stenson had lost a sudden-death play-off

in Stockholm for the Scandinavian Masters by Carlsberg - an event in which he was also runner-up in 2004. Now he went one better in his adopted home. "Everyone wants to win their home town event," he said.

Everything else was in place as well. Watching from the packed grandstands around the 18th green as the newlywed nervelessly wrapped up a one shot victory, was his bride, Emma, and many of their friends.

Then there was the quality of the opposition. On Saturday night, Stenson had dinner with Cowen, who reminded him of the fate of Thomas Björn at this event in 2001. "Thomas won after playing all four days with Tiger Woods, and now you have the chance to do the same after playing all four rounds with Ernie Els," Cowen said.

The South African, a three-time winner of the event, would eventually finish runner-up. Then there were the two men a further stroke adrift; Niclas Fasth, who is rightly proud of his excellent record of winning when in contention; and Woods, who is no slouch in that department either.

If you had to pick one hole to define this pleasing triumph it would be the 18th. This fabulous risk and reward par five has, of course, played a major part in deciding previous editions, and did so again.

Stenson began it with a one shot lead, and could have gone for the green in two with a three wood.

By his side was his caddy Fanny Sunesson, who played her part in so many of Nick Faldo's triumphs. Between them, they devised a more cunning strategy, playing short of the water. The worst score a player of Stenson's calibre could now make was five, the worst case scenario a play-off.

This moved into view, however, when Els birdied the hole. Now Stenson had to get down in two from 80 yards to win. It is not revealing any state secrets to say this was the Swede's weak shot until months of intense work on the range under the steely gaze of Cowen put matters right. Would it come back to haunt him now when the pressure was at its most intense?

Not a bit. As ever on the final day the flag was cut close to the water but Stenson gutsily took it on, and left himself a six foot uphill putt. When he rolled it in, Sunesson's mind must have flashed back to all those times at Faldo's side, when he won so many titles in the same manner.

As for Woods, for once he could not hole the putts that mattered, despite being watched on the final day by his sporting brethren from Mount Olympus, the Formula One giant Michael Schumacher and the tennis great Roger Federer.

By the American's side was a young Englishman by the name of Ross Fisher, whose week of weeks hinted at a future laden with many such exciting times to come. Two 65s to open the tournament showcased all his playing ability. But while 12 shots worse in terms of scoring, his two 71s to finish and earn fifth place were equally impressive. For here he had swapped a quiet place where he could concentrate on his own game, for the full glare of the limelight.

Playing with Els and Woods for the first time has awed many, but not this engaging young man who was taken on by Wentworth Club on a golf scholarship at the age of 13. He broke par playing with the South African in the third round and then completed a notable double by emulating the feat alongside Woods on the final day.

At the finish, Woods told him: "You are young and strong and you're only going to get better if you keep going." Fisher may care to reflect on another player on whom Woods bestowed similar words in 2004. His name? Henrik Stenson.

Derek Lawrenson
Daily Mail

Above Colin Montgomerie

David Griffiths

Roger Federer and Tiger Woods

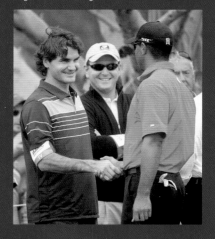

The Course

Named by Golf Digest as one of the top 100 courses outside the United States, the Majlis Course was the first all grass course in the Gulf and has played host to 16 of the 18 Dubai Desert Classics. Once again presented in immaculate condition with the perfect putting surfaces drawing glowing praise from all competitors.

Above *Ross Fisher*

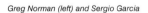

> It's always nice to beat Tiger obviously, but to play four rounds with Ernie and to beat him by a shot coming down the stretch gives me pretty much the same satisfaction.
> *Henrik Stenson*

Above *Henrik Stenson (left) is presented with the trophy by Mohamed Ali Alabbar, Chairman of Golf in Dubai*

Greg Norman (left) and Sergio Garcia

Emirates Golf Club

Par 72   **Yards 7301**   **Metres 6677**

Final Results

Pos	Name		Rd1	Rd2	Rd3	Rd4	Total		€	£
1	Henrik STENSON	SWE	68	64	69	68	269	-19	309,862.23	204,102.46
2	Ernie ELS	RSA	66	65	68	71	270	-18	206,569.66	136,064.91
3	Tiger WOODS	USA	68	67	67	69	271	-17	104,671.46	68,945.81
	Niclas FASTH	SWE	69	69	65	68	271	-17	104,671.46	68,945.81
5	Ross FISHER	ENG	65	65	71	71	272	-16	78,828.95	51,923.66
6	Peter HANSON	SWE	69	65	69	71	274	-14	65,071.07	42,861.52
7	Jyoti RANDHAWA	IND	66	68	67	74	275	-13	47,966.67	31,595.06
	Simon DYSON	ENG	67	69	69	70	275	-13	47,966.67	31,595.06
	Prom MEESAWAT	THA	68	68	68	71	275	-13	47,966.67	31,595.06
10	Maarten LAFEBER	NED	70	71	69	66	276	-12	32,349.62	21,308.30
	Thomas BJÖRN	DEN	70	69	66	71	276	-12	32,349.62	21,308.30
	Robert KARLSSON	SWE	70	67	68	71	276	-12	32,349.62	21,308.30
	Colin MONTGOMERIE	SCO	73	66	68	69	276	-12	32,349.62	21,308.30
	Miguel Angel JIMÉNEZ	ESP	67	68	71	70	276	-12	32,349.62	21,308.30
15	Stuart APPLEBY	AUS	69	69	71	68	277	-11	26,214.34	17,267.07
	Johan EDFORS	SWE	72	68	69	68	277	-11	26,214.34	17,267.07
	Andrew COLTART	SCO	69	71	67	70	277	-11	26,214.34	17,267.07
18	Thongchai JAIDEE	THA	67	70	72	69	278	-10	23,518.54	15,491.38
	Ignacio GARRIDO	ESP	71	67	68	72	278	-10	23,518.54	15,491.38
20	Darren CLARKE	NIR	68	70	68	73	279	-9	21,045.84	13,862.64
	Phillip PRICE	WAL	67	71	69	72	279	-9	21,045.84	13,862.64
	Paul CASEY	ENG	70	68	68	73	279	-9	21,045.84	13,862.64
	David PARK	WAL	70	70	70	69	279	-9	21,045.84	13,862.64
	Robert-Jan DERKSEN	NED	70	66	71	72	279	-9	21,045.84	13,862.64
25	Lee WESTWOOD	ENG	68	69	75	68	280	-8	17,941.02	11,817.53
	David GRIFFITHS	ENG	71	67	69	73	280	-8	17,941.02	11,817.53
	Paul MCGINLEY	IRL	69	69	71	71	280	-8	17,941.02	11,817.53
	Taichi TESHIMA	JPN	69	69	68	74	280	-8	17,941.02	11,817.53
	Andrew MARSHALL	ENG	69	70	68	73	280	-8	17,941.02	11,817.53
	Paul BROADHURST	ENG	73	66	71	70	280	-8	17,941.02	11,817.53
31	Marcel SIEM	GER	68	71	69	73	281	-7	15,431.14	10,164.30
	Jean-François LUCQUIN	FRA	70	67	70	74	281	-7	15,431.14	10,164.30
	Oliver WILSON	ENG	73	67	71	70	281	-7	15,431.14	10,164.30
34	Jeev Milkha SINGH	IND	70	69	67	76	282	-6	12,642.38	8,327.38
	Damien MCGRANE	IRL	72	69	70	71	282	-6	12,642.38	8,327.38
	Raphaël JACQUELIN	FRA	68	71	75	68	282	-6	12,642.38	8,327.38
	Richard GREEN	AUS	72	67	71	72	282	-6	12,642.38	8,327.38
	Joakim HAEGGMAN	SWE	69	67	69	77	282	-6	12,642.38	8,327.38
	Andrew MCLARDY	RSA	75	66	70	71	282	-6	12,642.38	8,327.38
	Richard STERNE	RSA	69	70	70	73	282	-6	12,642.38	8,327.38
	Nick DOUGHERTY	ENG	72	68	69	73	282	-6	12,642.38	8,327.38
	Christopher HANELL	SWE	72	69	70	71	282	-6	12,642.38	8,327.38
	David LYNN	ENG	70	69	72	71	282	-6	12,642.38	8,327.38
44	Stephen GALLACHER	SCO	71	69	68	75	283	-5	10,039.54	6,612.92
	Graeme MCDOWELL	NIR	65	69	73	76	283	-5	10,039.54	6,612.92
	Mark FOSTER	ENG	71	68	68	76	283	-5	10,039.54	6,612.92
	José Manuel LARA	ESP	66	71	70	76	283	-5	10,039.54	6,612.92
48	Charl SCHWARTZEL	RSA	69	72	69	74	284	-4	8,552.20	5,633.23
	Grégory HAVRET	FRA	71	70	73	70	284	-4	8,552.20	5,633.23
	Emanuele CANONICA	ITA	74	66	69	75	284	-4	8,552.20	5,633.23
	Francesco MOLINARI	ITA	70	70	70	74	284	-4	8,552.20	5,633.23
52	Alastair FORSYTH	SCO	70	70	70	75	285	-3	7,622.61	5,020.92
	Rory MCILROY (AM)	NIR	69	69	71	76	285	-3		
54	Gonzalo FDEZ-CASTAÑO	ESP	73	68	71	74	286	-2	6,507.11	4,286.15
	Phillip ARCHER	ENG	69	71	75	71	286	-2	6,507.11	4,286.15
	Garry HOUSTON	WAL	71	67	71	77	286	-2	6,507.11	4,286.15
	Notah BEGAY III	USA	71	69	73	73	286	-2	6,507.11	4,286.15
	Peter HEDBLOM	SWE	71	69	69	77	286	-2	6,507.11	4,286.15
59	Hennie OTTO	RSA	71	69	71	76	287	-1	5,391.60	3,551.38
	Cesar MONASTERIO	ARG	68	70	74	75	287	-1	5,391.60	3,551.38
	Alvaro QUIROS	ESP	69	68	72	78	287	-1	5,391.60	3,551.38
62	Stephen DODD	WAL	72	68	73	75	288	0	5,019.77	3,306.46
63	Grégory BOURDY	FRA	71	70	73	75	289	1	4,833.85	3,184.00
64	Greg NORMAN	AUS	70	71	71	78	290	2	4,647.93	3,061.54
65	Bradley DREDGE	WAL	69	72	79	71	291	3	4,462.02	2,939.08
66	Lee SLATTERY	ENG	70	71	76	83	300	12	4,276.10	2,816.61

Total Prize Fund

€1,840,535 £1,212,338

Celebration of Independence

1	Peter HEDBLOM		280	-8
2	Jean-François LUCQUIN		281	-7
3	Simon DYSON		282	-6
	Ignacio GARRIDO		282	-6
5	Marcus HIGLEY		283	-5
	Gary LOCKERBIE		283	-5
7	Mikko ILONEN		284	-4
	Prom MEESAWAT		284	-4
	Chinarat PHADUNGSIL		284	-4
	Simon YATES		284	-4

At first glance it might not appear obvious, but delve a little deeper under the surface and, perhaps, there was no more fitting winner of the Maybank Malaysian Open than Peter Hedblom.

In the towns and cities across Malaysia there was a palpable sense of joy that a lengthy journey had finally given way to an extended period of festivity, namely a yearlong series of events throughout 2007 to mark the Golden Jubilee of the country itself.

It was a celebration that Hedblom – who became the eighth winner of the Maybank Malaysian Open in its co-sanctioned format between The European Tour and the Asian Tour – could identify with, for his own journey in search of a second European Tour victory had also reached a successful conclusion, 11 years after it had begun.

Back in 1996 the then 26 year old Swede, one of the hottest properties to come out of European junior golf, strode confidently to victory in the Moroccan Open at the Royal Golf Resort Dar es Salam and a bright future in the game seemed guaranteed.

However loss of form and confidence, allied to injury, saw his progress stall until the memorable Sunday afternoon in the steamy heat of the Saujana Golf and Country Club in the nation's capital of Kuala Lumpur where all the delightful feelings associated with being a winner blossomed once again.

It was an appropriate setting for Hedblom to triumph, for in the 50 years since Malaysia gained independence from Great Britain, the country, too, had blossomed to become a leading sports nation in Asia, hosting the 1998 Commonwealth Games as well as the annual Formula One Grand Prix and the MotoGP.

The foundation for such growth was laid in 1956 when Tunku Abdul Rahman, the country's first Prime Minister, led a delegation comprising four members of the Alliance coalition and four Rulers' representatives to London to negotiate Malaysia's independence.

Three weeks into the negotiations, the London Independence Agreement was signed with the British Government agreeing to give Malaysia her independence on August 31, 1957. Fifty years later, the Golden Anniversary Celebrations honoured the nation's past, present and future. Malaysia is an exotic country with a diverse culture which draws significant influence from other Asian countries and boasts a heritage derived from its racial mix of Malay, Chinese and Indian.

Such diversity was exhibited in the field for the Maybank Malaysian Open which featured players

Ignacio Garrido

Ricardo Gonzalez

from no less than 27 countries amongst the 150 men who teed off on Thursday morning on Saujana's famous Cobra Course.

All were battling for a prestigious title, first contested in 1962, and which became the first tournament to be co-sanctioned between The European Tour and the Asian Tour in February 1999 when Gerry Norquist – now Senior Vice President for Commercial Development on the Asian Tour – held off Germany's Alex Cejka and American compatriot Bob May to win by three shots at Saujana.

Without doubt golf has become one of the success stories for Malaysia over the years and therefore it seemed only fitting that the Maybank Malaysian Open was chosen as one of a series of marquee events staged throughout the country in 2007 to mark the Golden Jubilee.

In honour of the occasion, the tournament was given the royal seal of approval when the King of Malaysia teed-up in the Pro-Am alongside the 2005 US Open Champion Michael Campbell. The 45 year old monarch, Sultan Seri Paduka Baginda Yang di-Pertuan Agon, played off a handicap of 14 and when Campbell asked to which club His Highness belonged, the response from a burly minder was: "He's the King of Malaysia. He can play anywhere he likes." Given his wayward nature with the driver, he apparently did.

Ironically, Hedblom knew exactly how he felt after an erratic beginning to the tournament. One over par after the first round, a triple bogey seven at the first and a bogey six at the third at the start of round two moved him to five over par for the tournament and in severe danger of missing the cut. Eagle threes at the seventh and 13th rescued the day, however, allowing the Swede to begin his forward momentum.

Three shots off the pace going into the last round, Hedblom – cheered on by wife Anna, his three children and his parents – clawed back the deficit with a fine final round 68, a round which even allowed him the luxury of a bogey six at the final hole to triumph by a shot from Frenchman Jean-François Lucquin, the Swede finishing with an eight under par total of 280.

"This is unbelievable," he said. "When you have not won for that long, you question whether you can win again – now I know I can."

The Golden Jubilee celebrations raged on into the night in Kuala Lumpur. One can only imagine that Peter Hedblom needed no second invitation to join in.

Bernie McGuire

Simon Dyson

Jean-François Lucquin

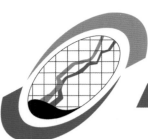

BURSA MALAYSIA
SWING 06/07

UBS Hong Kong Open
Championship 2006

Maybank
MALAYSIAN OPEN 2007

Enjoy Jakarta
astro
Indonesia Open 2007

Clariden Leu
Singapore Masters

TCL CLASSIC
高尔夫精英赛
SANYA · 三亚 · 2007

MIKKO ILONEN
SWING 06/07 Champion

The Course

The Palm Course, popularly referred to as 'The Cobra', is one of the most celebrated layouts in Asia and provides an exacting examination of every club in the bag. The course features tight, undulating fairways lined by dense clusters of palm trees, leading to super slick greens.

Robert-Jan Derksen

Above *Peter Hedblom (right) is presented with the trophy by Datuk Amirsham A. Aziz, President & CEO of Maybank*

Prom Meesawat

Thongchai Jaidee of Thailand claimed his first European Tour International Schedule victory in the 2004 Malaysian Open and went on to make a successful defence 12 months later. He became only the second player in European Tour history to win the same event in consecutive years for their first two European Tour titles. The first player to achieve the feat was Trevor Immelman (2003 and 2004 South African Airways Open).

Saujana Golf and Country Club

Par **72**   Yards **6971**   Metres **6370**

Final Results

Pos	Name		Rd1	Rd2	Rd3	Rd4	Total		€	£
1	Peter HEDBLOM	SWE	73	71	68	68	280	-8	165,895.10	109,347.98
2	Jean-François LUCQUIN	FRA	72	68	74	67	281	-7	110,594.16	72,896.96
3	Ignacio GARRIDO	ESP	76	69	68	69	282	-6	56,039.37	36,937.75
	Simon DYSON	ENG	71	68	73	70	282	-6	56,039.37	36,937.75
5	Gary LOCKERBIE	ENG	72	71	70	70	283	-5	38,520.84	25,390.60
	Marcus HIGLEY	ENG	72	67	70	74	283	-5	38,520.84	25,390.60
7	Simon YATES	SCO	73	69	70	72	284	-4	24,237.27	15,975.74
	Prom MEESAWAT	THA	72	69	70	73	284	-4	24,237.27	15,975.74
	Chinarat PHADUNGSIL	THA	70	67	77	70	284	-4	24,237.27	15,975.74
	Mikko ILONEN	FIN	69	70	74	71	284	-4	24,237.27	15,975.74
11	Amandeep JOHL	IND	73	71	71	70	285	-3	16,264.36	10,720.48
	Angelo QUE	PHI	70	73	68	74	285	-3	16,264.36	10,720.48
	Ricardo GONZALEZ	ARG	69	71	69	76	285	-3	16,264.36	10,720.48
	Graeme STORM	ENG	72	72	69	72	285	-3	16,264.36	10,720.48
	David BRANSDON	AUS	70	72	70	73	285	-3	16,264.36	10,720.48
16	Keith HORNE	RSA	73	73	71	69	286	-2	12,484.79	8,229.22
	Damien MCGRANE	IRL	70	73	70	73	286	-2	12,484.79	8,229.22
	David DRYSDALE	SCO	73	73	70	70	286	-2	12,484.79	8,229.22
	Andrew COLTART	SCO	74	69	70	73	286	-2	12,484.79	8,229.22
	Gavin FLINT	AUS	71	71	72	72	286	-2	12,484.79	8,229.22
	S.S.P CHOWRASIA	IND	67	77	71	71	286	-2	12,484.79	8,229.22
	Gerald ROSALES	PHI	70	75	70	71	286	-2	12,484.79	8,229.22
23	Sam WALKER	ENG	72	71	72	72	287	-1	10,501.16	6,921.73
	Frankie MINOZA	PHI	72	70	71	74	287	-1	10,501.16	6,921.73
	Alessandro TADINI	ITA	70	72	74	71	287	-1	10,501.16	6,921.73
	Robert-Jan DERKSEN	NED	70	73	70	74	287	-1	10,501.16	6,921.73
27	Andrew MARSHALL	ENG	75	69	71	73	288	0	8,858.80	5,839.18
	Garry HOUSTON	WAL	75	70	74	69	288	0	8,858.80	5,839.18
	Darren CLARKE	NIR	74	72	71	71	288	0	8,858.80	5,839.18
	Christian CÉVAËR	FRA	75	68	76	69	288	0	8,858.80	5,839.18
	Simon WAKEFIELD	ENG	71	74	75	68	288	0	8,858.80	5,839.18
	Stephen GALLACHER	SCO	71	73	72	72	288	0	8,858.80	5,839.18
	Gary SIMPSON	AUS	71	72	73	72	288	0	8,858.80	5,839.18
34	Alastair FORSYTH	SCO	69	73	73	74	289	1	6,967.59	4,592.62
	Wen-Chong LIANG	CHN	73	71	72	73	289	1	6,967.59	4,592.62
	Unho PARK	AUS	75	71	73	70	289	1	6,967.59	4,592.62
	Terry PILKADARIS	AUS	72	74	68	75	289	1	6,967.59	4,592.62
	Grégory BOURDY	FRA	73	72	74	70	289	1	6,967.59	4,592.62
	Airil RIZMAN	MAS	71	75	72	71	289	1	6,967.59	4,592.62
	Marcus BOTH	AUS	71	72	73	73	289	1	6,967.59	4,592.62
	Matthew MILLAR	AUS	74	72	71	72	289	1	6,967.59	4,592.62
42	Kyron SULLIVAN	WAL	73	70	72	75	290	2	5,673.61	3,739.70
	Lee WESTWOOD	ENG	75	70	71	74	290	2	5,673.61	3,739.70
	Shaifubari MUDA	MAS	73	73	73	71	290	2	5,673.61	3,739.70
	Jeev Milkha SINGH	IND	71	71	76	72	290	2	5,673.61	3,739.70
	Søren KJELDSEN	DEN	70	70	81	69	290	2	5,673.61	3,739.70
47	Thomas BJÖRN	DEN	73	72	74	72	291	3	4,976.85	3,280.44
	Robert ROCK	ENG	66	78	76	71	291	3	4,976.85	3,280.44
49	Anton HAIG	RSA	74	69	72	77	292	4	4,379.63	2,886.79
	Adam GROOM	AUS	73	71	75	73	292	4	4,379.63	2,886.79
	Kane WEBBER	AUS	68	73	77	74	292	4	4,379.63	2,886.79
	Jong Yul SUK	KOR	71	72	74	75	292	4	4,379.63	2,886.79
53	Steven JEPPESEN	SWE	74	72	76	71	293	5	3,583.33	2,361.92
	Wei-Tze YEH	CHN	69	75	77	72	293	5	3,583.33	2,361.92
	Mark FOSTER	ENG	69	75	75	74	293	5	3,583.33	2,361.92
	Gaurav GHEI	IND	72	72	74	75	293	5	3,583.33	2,361.92
57	Cesar MONASTERIO	ARG	71	71	76	76	294	6	2,986.11	1,968.26
	Rafael ECHENIQUE	ARG	68	71	77	78	294	6	2,986.11	1,968.26
	José-Filipe LIMA	POR	74	70	76	74	294	6	2,986.11	1,968.26
60	Gary RUSNAK	USA	74	71	75	75	295	7	2,687.50	1,771.44
	Chapchai NIRAT	THA	70	75	73	77	295	7	2,687.50	1,771.44
	Prayad MARKSAENG	THA	75	70	75	75	295	7	2,687.50	1,771.44
63	Mike CUNNING	USA	74	72	77	74	297	9	2,388.89	1,574.61
	Hendrik BUHRMANN	RSA	72	72	80	73	297	9	2,388.89	1,574.61
	Edward LOAR	USA	68	71	72	86	297	9	2,388.89	1,574.61
66	Supramaniam SIVACHANDRAN	MAS	75	71	73	79	298	10	2,189.82	1,443.39
67	Emanuele CANONICA	ITA	75	69	79	79	302	14	2,090.28	1,377.78
68	Rafael CABRERA BELLO	ESP	73	72	75	83	303	15	1,990.74	1,312.18
69	Michael CAMPBELL	NZL	75	70	74	W/D	223	7		

Total Prize Fund

€991,663   £654,890

Ring of Fire

1	Mikko ILONEN		275	-9
2	Shiv KAPUR		276	-8
	Frankie MINOZA		276	-8
	Andrew TAMPION		276	-8
5	Thammanoon SRIROT		279	-5
	Jong Yul SUK		279	-5
7	Alexandre ROCHA		280	-4
8	Tony CAROLAN		281	-3
	James HEATH		281	-3
	Chapchai NIRAT		281	-3

T he promotional flags lining the final leg of the bus journey to Damai Indah Golf and Country Club contained an unusual juxtaposition of images. There was a putter and a golf ball, fairly obvious stuff for publicising a golf event, but dominating the whole picture was a bright yellow pig bedecked with a large nose ring.

Shiv Kapur

Thaworn Wiratchant

Given Jakarta's unique place in the world – it lies near the equator and on the Ring of Fire where 75 per cent of the world's volcanoes can be found - we should have probably expected the unexpected. After all, the city's lifeblood is one of extreme diversity – a contrast between rich and poor, between Eastern tradition and Western modernity, and between golden sun-kissed mornings and grey stormy afternoons.

Yet another striking contradiction was provided by the winner of the third co-sanctioned Enjoy Jakarta Astro Indonesia Open, Mikko Ilonen of Finland. That a man from the Arctic Circle should capture his maiden European Tour title in the sweltering heat and humidity of Indonesia's capital seemed entirely appropriate following a roller-coaster week in which Ilonen kept total focus in the face of numerous weather disruptions.

Torrential rainfall had hit Jakarta during the week prior to the tournament, causing flooding to low lying areas, and the course managers at Damai Indah were taking no chances about further downpours affecting the tournament. So a call was made to draft in some expert assistance. In Europe this might have involved a team of top-level agronomists, but in Jakarta, as suggested earlier, things are very different.

Instead they hired what is locally known as a pawang hujan, a sort of mystical rain-mover rather than a rain-maker. The pawang fasted on the eve of the tournament and then walked the course each day to perform a series of chants and rituals directed at moving, or postponing, the rain clouds.

Apparently, this ancient mysticism does not work on thunder and lightning, which may explain why all four rounds suffered suspensions due to afternoon storms but, remarkably, on only one occasion did it actually rain.

The reigning champion, England's Simon Dyson, a four-time winner in Asia and joint runner-up at the previous week's event in Malaysia - started in solid fashion with a one under par 70, only to find himself overshadowed by, amongst others, Thailand's Chawalit Plaphol and Ilonen, who carded scores of 65 and 66 respectively to head the first round leaderboard.

The following day Ilonen added a 68 to move into a share of the lead alongside one of The European Tour's newest bright young things, Australian Andrew Tampion, who only turned professional in November after winning his card at the Qualifying School.

Displaying a classic swing and wonderful tempo, the 22 year old Tampion produced a best of the day 66 to tie Ilonen on eight under par 134, three strokes clear of their nearest challengers.

Plaphol, meanwhile, slipped into a share of tenth spot with a three over par 74 and found himself alongside a man who would go on to have a big part to play in the rest of the tournament, Filipino veteran Frankie Minoza.

Having previously won the Indonesia Open in 1986 and 1990, Minoza was especially keen to make it a hat-trick now the event was part of The European Tour International Schedule and he set about this task with a third round 66 to tie Ilonen, who added a level par 71, on eight under par 205.

The two leaders had moved to nine under par after ten holes of the final round when play was suspended due to lightning for the fourth consecutive afternoon. After a delay lasting one hour and 45 minutes, the players headed back out onto the course and Ilonen was soon hitting the ball even sweeter than before the cessation.

Minoza saw his victory hopes fade with a double bogey six at the 14th while India's Shiv Kapur and Tampion both mounted late challenges to Ilonen, but in the end the talented Finn could afford the luxury of bogeying the last for a winning aggregate of nine under par 275, one better than his three rivals.

By now, the yellow pig made perfect sense. Sunday was the first day of the Year of the Pig on the Chinese Lunar Calendar, but it was also the beginning of something new for Ilonen and The European Tour, as this was the first victory by a Finnish player since the Tour's inception in 1972.

Ilonen had closed out the tournament with a one under par 70 and, as he walked off the 18th green, holding his arms triumphantly in the air, it began to rain. Maybe there was something in those rituals, after all.

Steven Franklin

Andrew Tampion

__Below left__ James Heath

__Below__ Andrew Marshall

The Course

The Pantai Indah Kapuk course, one of two in the vast Damai Indah Golf and Country Club resort, was designed by Robert Trent Jones in 1992. Located adjacent to the Java Sea, the course is highlighted by several ponds and streams and features rustic fieldstone walls and bridges, reminiscent of many courses throughout Europe.

Mikko Ilonen receives the trophy from Mdm. Nelia M. Sutrisno, CEO of PT. Direct Vision (Astro Indonesia)

> How much you drink, what you drink, what you eat, what you do off the course is everything when you play in weather like this. I am experienced enough now to not do the wrong thing when I am playing tournament golf. I am not having a beer in the evening, if you were wondering.
> *Mikko Ilonen*

Damai Indah Golf and Country Club
Par **71**   Yards **7120**   Metres **6511**

Final Results

Pos	Name		Rd1	Rd2	Rd3	Rd4	Total		€	£
1	Mikko ILONEN	FIN	66	68	71	70	275	-9	134,563.99	89,688.40
2	Frankie MINOZA	PHI	71	68	66	71	276	-8	60,205.21	40,127.44
	Shiv KAPUR	IND	67	73	69	67	276	-8	60,205.21	40,127.44
	Andrew TAMPION	AUS	68	66	73	69	276	-8	60,205.21	40,127.44
5	Thammanoon SRIROT	THA	72	67	71	69	279	-5	31,245.76	20,825.65
	Jong Yul SUK	KOR	69	68	69	73	279	-5	31,245.76	20,825.65
7	Alexandre ROCHA	BRA	72	68	73	67	280	-4	24,221.52	16,143.91
8	James HEATH	ENG	70	70	70	71	281	-3	18,139.23	12,090.00
	Chapchai NIRAT	THA	68	69	72	72	281	-3	18,139.23	12,090.00
	Tony CAROLAN	AUS	71	71	67	72	281	-3	18,139.23	12,090.00
11	Chawalit PLAPHOL	THA	65	74	70	73	282	-2	12,074.88	8,048.04
	Rick GIBSON	CAN	72	70	72	68	282	-2	12,074.88	8,048.04
	Thaworn WIRATCHANT	THA	75	69	72	66	282	-2	12,074.88	8,048.04
	Christian CÉVAËR	FRA	68	72	71	71	282	-2	12,074.88	8,048.04
	Simon DYSON	ENG	70	71	71	70	282	-2	12,074.88	8,048.04
	Henrik NYSTROM	SWE	70	69	72	71	282	-2	12,074.88	8,048.04
	Scott STRANGE	AUS	69	69	72	72	282	-2	12,074.88	8,048.04
	Gareth DAVIES	ENG	71	67	72	72	282	-2	12,074.88	8,048.04
	Thongchai JAIDEE	THA	72	67	71	72	282	-2	12,074.88	8,048.04
20	Peter GUSTAFSSON	SWE	70	73	67	73	283	-1	9,392.57	6,260.25
	Mark MOULAND	WAL	70	70	71	72	283	-1	9,392.57	6,260.25
	Sam LITTLE	ENG	72	69	71	71	283	-1	9,392.57	6,260.25
23	Iain STEEL	MAS	74	70	74	66	284	0	7,791.25	5,192.96
	Gaurav GHEI	IND	68	69	79	68	284	0	7,791.25	5,192.96
	Andrew MARSHALL	ENG	70	71	72	71	284	0	7,791.25	5,192.96
	Steve ALKER	NZL	70	71	72	71	284	0	7,791.25	5,192.96
	Mike CUNNING	USA	71	72	71	70	284	0	7,791.25	5,192.96
	Mardan MAMAT	SIN	74	67	71	72	284	0	7,791.25	5,192.96
	David BRANSDON	AUS	69	72	74	69	284	0	7,791.25	5,192.96
	Airil-Rizman ZAHARI	MAS	70	69	74	71	284	0	7,791.25	5,192.96
	Adam GROOM	AUS	69	71	77	67	284	0	7,791.25	5,192.96
	Mark BROWN	NZL	75	69	68	72	284	0	7,791.25	5,192.96
33	S.S.P CHOWRASIA	IND	68	72	72	73	285	1	5,823.26	3,881.27
	Prom MEESAWAT	THA	71	68	74	72	285	1	5,823.26	3,881.27
	Bryan SALTUS	USA	68	74	74	69	285	1	5,823.26	3,881.27
	Oliver FISHER	ENG	74	67	72	72	285	1	5,823.26	3,881.27
	Adam BLYTH	AUS	73	70	69	73	285	1	5,823.26	3,881.27
	Chih-Bing LAM	SIN	72	72	72	69	285	1	5,823.26	3,881.27
	David CARTER	ENG	72	72	75	66	285	1	5,823.26	3,881.27
	Ignacio GARRIDO	ESP	71	71	74	69	285	1	5,823.26	3,881.27
41	Danny CHIA	MAS	71	71	75	69	286	2	4,763.57	3,174.97
	Simon YATES	SCO	74	69	71	72	286	2	4,763.57	3,174.97
	Anthony KANG	USA	73	69	70	74	286	2	4,763.57	3,174.97
	James HEPWORTH	ENG	71	70	74	71	286	2	4,763.57	3,174.97
	Marcus FRASER	AUS	74	70	69	73	286	2	4,763.57	3,174.97
46	Ted OH	KOR	69	74	72	72	287	3	3,794.70	2,529.21
	Chinarat PHADUNGSIL	THA	70	71	72	74	287	3	3,794.70	2,529.21
	Matthew MILLAR	AUS	71	73	69	74	287	3	3,794.70	2,529.21
	Emanuele CANONICA	ITA	72	72	70	73	287	3	3,794.70	2,529.21
	François DELAMONTAGNE	FRA	72	71	71	73	287	3	3,794.70	2,529.21
	Chris RODGERS	ENG	72	71	75	69	287	3	3,794.70	2,529.21
	Ross BAIN	SCO	73	70	67	77	287	3	3,794.70	2,529.21
53	Gary EMERSON	ENG	71	72	73	72	288	4	2,758.56	1,838.61
	Young-Woo NAM	KOR	68	69	75	76	288	4	2,758.56	1,838.61
	Keith HORNE	RSA	73	71	71	73	288	4	2,758.56	1,838.61
	Patrik SJÖLAND	SWE	69	74	73	72	288	4	2,758.56	1,838.61
	José-Filipe LIMA	POR	68	76	71	73	288	4	2,758.56	1,838.61
	Mads VIBE-HASTRUP	DEN	67	75	71	75	288	4	2,758.56	1,838.61
59	Jun-Won PARK	KOR	69	75	72	73	289	5	2,301.04	1,533.67
	Birgir HAFTHORSSON	ISL	71	72	74	72	289	5	2,301.04	1,533.67
61	Mark FOSTER	ENG	69	74	70	78	291	7	2,058.83	1,372.23
	Marcus BOTH	AUS	70	73	73	75	291	7	2,058.83	1,372.23
	Daniel VANCSIK	ARG	74	68	74	75	291	7	2,058.83	1,372.23
	Alexander NOREN	SWE	69	69	76	77	291	7	2,058.83	1,372.23
65	Taichiro KIYOTA	JPN	74	70	78	70	292	8	1,816.61	1,210.79
	Richard MCEVOY	ENG	72	70	72	78	292	8	1,816.61	1,210.79
67	Kane WEBBER	AUS	68	72	83	70	293	9	1,655.14	1,103.17
	Scott BARR	AUS	69	71	76	77	293	9	1,655.14	1,103.17

Total Prize Fund

€804,374   £536,123

Right Place, Right Time

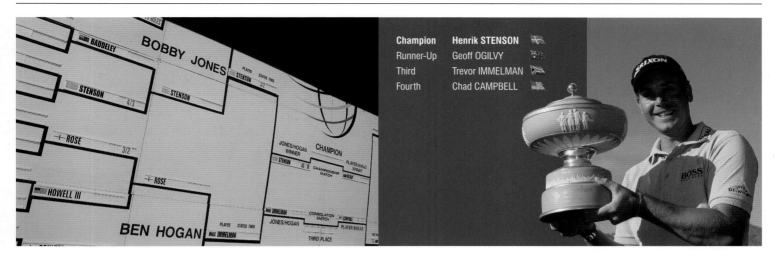

Champion	**Henrik STENSON**
Runner-Up	Geoff OGILVY
Third	Trevor IMMELMAN
Fourth	Chad CAMPBELL

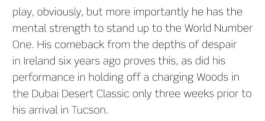

I n the summer of 2001, Henrik Stenson was playing so badly that he walked off The K Club midway through his opening round of the Smurfit European Open ready to give up the game. "You guys will get on better without me," he told his playing partners after hitting two tee shots, one heading far left and the other even further right.

Six years later it was hard to believe the talented and confident Swede, the man who returned to The K Club and holed the winning putt in The 2006 Ryder Cup, could ever say such a thing.

It was even harder to believe after Stenson walked away from the picturesque Gallery Golf Club in Arizona as the newly crowned World Golf Championships – Accenture Match Play champion, as Europe's highest ranked player on the Official World Golf Ranking, and as the man most likely to thwart Tiger Woods' hopes of dominating world golf into the distant future.

Modern professional golf is awash with players who voice defiance in the face of Woods' brilliance but few mean it, and those who do rarely deliver. Stenson stands out from this crowd. He can

Below Nick O'Hern

play, obviously, but more importantly he has the mental strength to stand up to the World Number One. His comeback from the depths of despair in Ireland six years ago proves this, as did his performance in holding off a charging Woods in the Dubai Desert Classic only three weeks prior to his arrival in Tucson.

Even when he performs fitfully - as he did for long stretches during the 36 hole final against the defending champion Geoff Ogilvy - the Swede seldom took his eye off the prize. When it came to the crux he was more than up to the task, hitting a nine iron at the par three 16th hole of the afternoon round to less than two feet for a conceded birdie. He ended the match at the next, a 601 yard par five, where he reached the green in two shots before rolling a long and winding putt to within tap-in distance to claim the €1,027,631 (£692,343) winner's cheque. The victory lifted Stenson to fifth on the Official World Golf Ranking and top of The 2007 European Tour Order of Merit.

That position, the highest of the 30 year old's career, was a superb achievement and no doubt his bank manager was delighted. But the Swede is a man with his eyes fixed on horizons far beyond his bank balance. Golfing historians demand far meatier fare than simply World Golf Championships and ranking points and Stenson knows this as well as anyone. "I want to be as good as I can be in the Majors," he admitted.

The prospect of watching him strive for such a goal is a lip-smacking one, but for the time being there was his contest against the equally impressive Ogilvy to savour. Stenson had the best of the morning's play and headed into lunch two up. But whatever was on the menu clearly did not

Paul Casey

agree with the Swede because in the opening nine holes of the afternoon round he had four bogeys and five pars. That kind of scoring might win an umbrella in the Saturday morning medal but in such exalted company it is liable to earn you nothing but trouble.

Sure enough, Ogilvy took advantage and opened up a two hole lead of his own. But just when the Australian appeared to have the match within his grasp, he faltered, bogeying the ninth and 11th holes to restore parity. The Swede regained the lead at the next hole and never lost it.

He had moved past six opponents including Zach Johnson, who was to win the Masters Tournament only six weeks later, during a week when he, and other Europeans including Paul Casey and Justin Rose, embellished their credentials and established their claims to be regarded as future winners of Major Championships.

Rose, in particular, caught the eye. He beat Michael Campbell, Phil Mickelson and Charles Howell III before eventually succumbing in the quarter-finals to Trevor Immelman. His 3 and 1

success over Mickelson suggested that at the age of 26 the Englishman was truly poised to rise to a new level.

Casey was another who shone once again in the head-to-head format, five months after his victory in the HSBC World Match Play Championship at Wentworth Club. Like his fellow countryman, he succumbed at the quarter-final stage but there is no denying his lofty status in the European game these days, as his 4 and 3 victory in the second round over Colin Montgomerie illustrated all too well, following an equally fine victory against Mike Weir.

This, then, was a week that European golf could savour and most certainly one during which Stenson knew his place was on – not off – the fairways.

Lawrence Donegan
The Guardian

Justin Rose

The Course

Designed by John Fought, the South Course at The Gallery Golf Club was nominated as one of Golf Digest's 100 Best Courses and has a links style reminiscent in many ways of Donald Ross' Pinehurst No.2. Tight pin positions place a premium on approach shot accuracy while the local Sagauros cacti ensure focus from the tee.

Gallery Golf Club

Par **72**   Yards **7466**   Metres **6829**

Total Prize Fund

€6,089,666   £4,102,774

	€	£
Champion:	1,027,631	692,343
Runner-up:	608,966	410,277
Third Place:	437,694	294,886
Fourth Place:	361,573	243,602
Quarter Finalists:	197,914	133,340
Third Round:	98,957	66,670
Second Round:	68,508	46,156
First Round:	30,448	20,513

Henrik Stenson (left) with William Green, Chairman and CEO of Accenture, and the Walter Hagen Cup

Ian Poulter

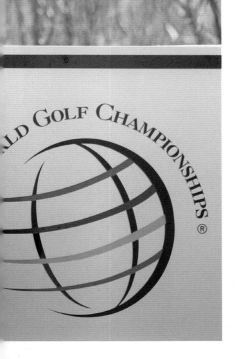

> A lot of great things happened for me this week – such as becoming the first Swede to win a World Golf Championships and achieving the highest placing for a Swede on the World Ranking - and I'm just exhausted. I mean, my feet are aching, my head is aching, and (thanks to the winner's cheque for €1,027,631) my wallet is aching!
>
> *Henrik Stenson*

Final Results

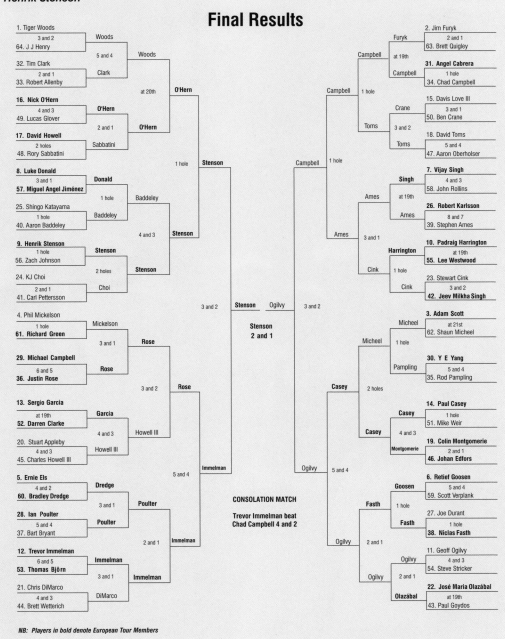

CONSOLATION MATCH

Trevor Immelman beat
Chad Campbell 4 and 2

NB: Players in bold denote European Tour Members

Perfect Blend

1	Anton HAIG		275	-13
2	Richard STERNE		275	-13
	Oliver WILSON		275	-13
4	Retief GOOSEN		278	-10
5	Mike WEIR		279	-9
6	Ernie ELS		280	-8
	David FROST		280	-8
	Gaurav GHEI		280	-8
	Colin MONTGOMERIE		280	-8
10	Richard BLAND		281	-7
	Simon HURD		281	-7
	Iain STEEL		281	-7
	Jean VAN DE VELDE		281	-7

W hat would we have done without the trustees of young John Walker in the early 19th century? After the death of the wee boy's father, the aforementioned fellows paid £417 for a shop in Kilmarnock, Scotland. It was on these premises that the teenage Johnnie began a whisky blending dynasty.

Colin Montgomerie

Ernie Els

Fortunately his Walker descendants shared a flair for combining malts and from those origins in the west of Scotland, much of the world was to acquire a taste for the Johnnie Walker blend. Nowadays worldwide sales are around 150 million bottles in 200 countries.

Such a global presence was to manifest itself in Phuket, Thailand, at the beginning of March 2007 for the 15th staging of the Johnnie Walker Classic, won by the newest golfing sensation to come out of South Africa, Anton Haig.

As well as wonderful golf, it was a week in keeping with the sponsor's key policy, responsible drinking. Naturally the players would wait until the evening for a tipple; Adam Scott – the highest ranked player on show at World Number Four – was particularly partial to a drop but only after gallons of water had been consumed during his day's work.

You could not ask for a bigger contrast between the town the Scots colloquially call 'Killie' and the paradise holiday island of Phuket. The Johnnie Walker Classic was played in searing temperatures of which they could only dream in Ayrshire. On the second day the heat index – or how hot it actually feels when humidity is taken into account – was nudging 40 degrees Celsius.

Colin Montgomerie looked as though he might expire at any time, particularly after trudging up the steps to the recorders' hut at the end of his round. "Every time I bent down to pick up my ball I felt faint. On some of the tees it felt like there was no air at all," said the famous son of Troon, coincidentally a neighbouring town to Kilmarnock.

"My Scottish skin isn't made for this lark," he added. "I drank eight bottles of water out there, that's four litres and I don't know where it's gone - it's evaporated! I've not been to the loo and if you're interested, I don't want to either!"

Oliver Wilson, the highly promising young Englishman, was taking on board even more liquid. "I basically was having a sip after every shot, water or energy drinks," he said. That made 66 gulps in a second round that gave him the halfway lead.

Wilson might have gone on to share the lead a round later had, ironically, a discarded drinks can not interfered with his swing as he tried to escape from the bank of the water that guards the treacherous par three 17th at the Blue Canyon Country Club. Instead he dropped a shot and was one behind South African Richard Sterne going into what proved to be a dramatic final round.

Johnnie Walker Classic

Despite the field boasting Major winners such as Ernie Els, Retief Goosen, Paul Lawrie, Mike Weir and Ian Woosnam it was young guns Haig, Sterne and Wilson who ultimately starred. Haig – another name linked to whisky heritage – had no lack of bottle to go with his undoubted talent.

Heading to his second shot at the last this massively long hitting South African looked to be in trouble. He had hooked his drive and tall palm trees obscured his view of the green. Undaunted, he launched his wedge with purpose and the ball, as if on a string, danced close to the pin. It was a truly majestic stroke and one later voted The European Tour Shot of the Month for March. He tapped in for birdie to secure his place in the play-off alongside Sterne and Wilson.

Sterne had checked out of his hotel on the Friday morning after an opening 75. He thought the spectacular course was impossible, but then shot 64 to make the cut with ease before adding another to top the leaderboard on Saturday. Into

the play-off he had a chance for birdie at the first extra hole but his ball lipped out.

Wilson had also missed, leaving Haig to hole a right to left ten foot curler that secured his maiden European Tour title. "I've been given a few bottles of Johnnie Walker this week, I think I'll be opening them tonight," he said.

At only 20, his game possesses a perfect blend of power and finesse – rather like his great hero Els had demonstrated at a similar age and something which led Darren Clarke to label him as a certain Major Championship winner of the future.

Els, of course, is a multiple Major winner, global superstar and, by the way, the owner of a hugely successful wine label. One is only left to ponder the dynasty that Haig might have begun in Phuket.

Iain Carter
BBC Radio Five Live

Richard Sterne

Oliver Wilson

David Frost

The Course

One of the most distinguished and prestigious championship courses in Asia, the Canyon Course is carved into lush landscape surrounded by freshwater lakes and in harmony with the earth. It features natural hazards, towering trees, rolling fairways, long carries, narrow landing areas and well guarded, slick greens.

Retief Goosen has a close encounter with 'Yum Yum'
a four year old female Thai elephant

Vorathep Rangchaikul (left), President of Diageo Moet Hennessy Thailand, presents the trophy to Anton Haig

History was made in the Johnnie Walker Classic at Lake Karrinyup Country Club in Perth, Australia, where in 2003 Ernie Els broke The European Tour record for the lowest 72 hole total in relation to par. His rounds of 64-65-64-66 gave the South African a score of 259 (-29), beating the previous best of 27 under par by Jerry Anderson, which had stood since the 1984 European Masters.

Blue Canyon Country Club
Par **72**   Yards **7203**   Metres **6548**

Final Results

Pos	Name		Rd1	Rd2	Rd3	Rd4	Total		€	£
1	Anton HAIG	RSA	71	64	70	70	275	-13	310,801.29	208,330.00
2	Oliver WILSON	ENG	68	66	70	71	275	-13	161,964.87	108,565.00
	Richard STERNE	RSA	75	64	64	72	275	-13	161,964.87	108,565.00
4	Retief GOOSEN	RSA	68	68	72	70	278	-10	93,241.88	62,500.00
5	Mike WEIR	CAN	66	78	68	67	279	-9	79,069.11	53,000.00
6	Colin MONTGOMERIE	SCO	69	70	70	71	280	-8	52,401.94	35,125.00
	Gaurav GHEI	IND	69	73	74	64	280	-8	52,401.94	35,125.00
	David FROST	RSA	69	70	72	69	280	-8	52,401.94	35,125.00
	Ernie ELS	RSA	73	70	67	70	280	-8	52,401.94	35,125.00
10	Richard BLAND	ENG	68	70	72	71	281	-7	33,427.21	22,406.25
	Simon HURD	ENG	73	71	66	71	281	-7	33,427.21	22,406.25
	Jean VAN DE VELDE	FRA	72	69	71	69	281	-7	33,427.21	22,406.25
	Iain STEEL	MAS	69	73	70	69	281	-7	33,427.21	22,406.25
14	Marc WARREN	SCO	68	72	71	71	282	-6	27,972.56	18,750.00
	Richard LEE	NZL	67	70	70	75	282	-6	27,972.56	18,750.00
16	Terry PILKADARIS	AUS	70	70	73	70	283	-5	22,688.86	15,208.33
	Graeme STORM	ENG	66	73	70	74	283	-5	22,688.86	15,208.33
	Chris RODGERS	ENG	71	70	71	71	283	-5	22,688.86	15,208.33
	Alastair FORSYTH	SCO	74	70	69	70	283	-5	22,688.86	15,208.33
	Adam BLAND	AUS	71	67	75	70	283	-5	22,688.86	15,208.33
	Garry HOUSTON	WAL	72	68	73	70	283	-5	22,688.86	15,208.33
	Robert-Jan DERKSEN	NED	71	71	73	68	283	-5	22,688.86	15,208.33
	Ter-Chang WANG	TPE	68	70	71	74	283	-5	22,688.86	15,208.33
	Aron PRICE	AUS	74	68	67	74	283	-5	22,688.86	15,208.33
25	Stephen GALLACHER	SCO	66	76	68	74	284	-4	17,715.96	11,875.00
	Mark FOSTER	ENG	72	70	72	70	284	-4	17,715.96	11,875.00
	Jeev Milkha SINGH	IND	67	72	71	74	284	-4	17,715.96	11,875.00
	James NITTIES	AUS	69	67	74	74	284	-4	17,715.96	11,875.00
	Matthew MILLAR	AUS	71	70	71	72	284	-4	17,715.96	11,875.00
	Adam SCOTT	AUS	74	69	70	71	284	-4	17,715.96	11,875.00
	Brad KENNEDY	AUS	65	77	71	71	284	-4	17,715.96	11,875.00
32	Simon DYSON	ENG	71	70	73	71	285	-3	14,471.14	9,700.00
	Damien MCGRANE	IRL	71	72	69	73	285	-3	14,471.14	9,700.00
	Phillip ARCHER	ENG	74	69	67	75	285	-3	14,471.14	9,700.00
	David LYNN	ENG	73	69	73	70	285	-3	14,471.14	9,700.00
	Jong Yul SUK	KOR	70	74	70	71	285	-3	14,471.14	9,700.00
37	Kyung-Tae KIM	KOR	71	73	72	70	286	-2	12,494.41	8,375.00
	Peter HANSON	SWE	66	72	76	72	286	-2	12,494.41	8,375.00
	Wen-Chong LIANG	CHN	72	70	67	77	286	-2	12,494.41	8,375.00
	Rahil GANGJEE	IND	72	69	71	74	286	-2	12,494.41	8,375.00
	Bryan SALTUS	USA	74	69	72	71	286	-2	12,494.41	8,375.00
42	Jun-Won PARK	KOR	71	73	71	72	287	-1	9,697.16	6,500.00
	Scott STRANGE	AUS	73	69	69	76	287	-1	9,697.16	6,500.00
	Edward MICHAELS	USA	70	74	74	69	287	-1	9,697.16	6,500.00
	Thammanoon SRIROT	THA	71	71	74	71	287	-1	9,697.16	6,500.00
	Jean-François REMESY	FRA	75	69	74	69	287	-1	9,697.16	6,500.00
	Lian-Wei ZHANG	CHN	70	71	75	71	287	-1	9,697.16	6,500.00
	Gary ORR	SCO	73	68	74	72	287	-1	9,697.16	6,500.00
	Jean-François LUCQUIN	FRA	73	69	71	74	287	-1	9,697.16	6,500.00
	Peter O'MALLEY	AUS	70	73	73	71	287	-1	9,697.16	6,500.00
	Jarrod MOSELEY	AUS	70	71	72	74	287	-1	9,697.16	6,500.00
52	Craig PARRY	AUS	69	74	77	68	288	0	6,899.90	4,625.00
	Keith HORNE	RSA	68	71	73	76	288	0	6,899.90	4,625.00
	Wen Teh LU	TPE	69	75	75	69	288	0	6,899.90	4,625.00
	Rafael CABRERA BELLO	ESP	70	72	74	72	288	0	6,899.90	4,625.00
	Thongchai JAIDEE	THA	71	68	75	74	288	0	6,899.90	4,625.00
57	Kim FELTON	AUS	70	68	74	77	289	1	5,594.51	3,750.00
	Marcus BOTH	AUS	73	70	71	75	289	1	5,594.51	3,750.00
	Nick FLANAGAN	AUS	70	69	77	73	289	1	5,594.51	3,750.00
60	Shiv KAPUR	IND	72	70	75	73	290	2	5,035.06	3,375.00
	Graeme MCDOWELL	NIR	67	76	70	77	290	2	5,035.06	3,375.00
	Peter FOWLER	AUS	68	72	77	73	290	2	5,035.06	3,375.00
63	Andrew COLTART	SCO	72	72	74	73	291	3	4,568.85	3,062.50
	Thaworn WIRATCHANT	THA	71	71	75	74	291	3	4,568.85	3,062.50
65	Simon KHAN	ENG	70	74	72	76	292	4	4,009.40	2,687.50
	Andrew MARSHALL	ENG	73	71	77	71	292	4	4,009.40	2,687.50
	Wen-Tang LIN	TPE	70	74	75	73	292	4	4,009.40	2,687.50
	Barry HUME	SCO	68	74	79	71	292	4	4,009.40	2,687.50
69	Adam BLYTH	AUS	70	72	75	76	293	5	3,252.19	2,179.94
	David DIAZ	AUS	73	74	76	73	293	5	3,252.19	2,179.94
	Ken Chi LING	TPE	70	71	80	72	293	5	3,252.19	2,179.94
72	Unho PARK	AUS	70	74	75	75	294	6	2,794.00	1,872.82
73	Markus BRIER	AUT	74	68	76	77	295	7	2,791.00	1,870.81
74	Ignacio GARRIDO	ESP	71	71	76	78	296	8	2,786.50	1,867.79
	Lee SUNG	KOR	71	72	78	75	296	8	2,786.50	1,867.79
76	Scott GARDINER	AUS	65	77	79	74	297	9	2,780.50	1,863.77
	Chris CAMPBELL	AUS	72	72	77	76	297	9	2,780.50	1,863.77
78	Hendrik BUHRMANN	RSA	71	73	76	88	308	20	2,776.00	1,860.75

Total Prize Fund

€1,887,130 £1,264,942

Memorable Gesture

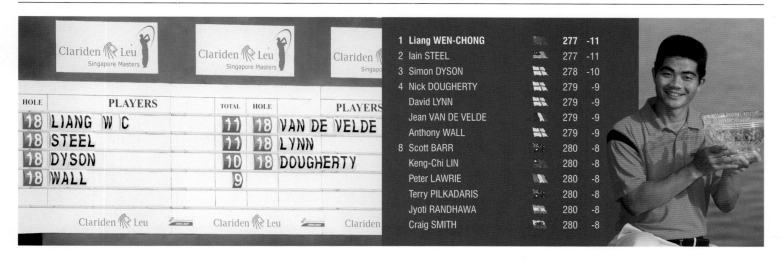

1	Liang WEN-CHONG		277	-11
2	Iain STEEL		277	-11
3	Simon DYSON		278	-10
4	Nick DOUGHERTY		279	-9
	David LYNN		279	-9
	Jean VAN DE VELDE		279	-9
	Anthony WALL		279	-9
8	Scott BARR		280	-8
	Keng-Chi LIN		280	-8
	Peter LAWRIE		280	-8
	Terry PILKADARIS		280	-8
	Jyoti RANDHAWA		280	-8
	Craig SMITH		280	-8

The first interview of what was to be an intriguing week was conducted in Mandarin, the second would preferably have been in Hindi and the third was in Japanese. If anything illustrated the explosion of top class golf throughout Asia and the Far East it was the field for the Clariden Leu Singapore Masters, coming as it did from no fewer than 32 countries, with the favourites spread evenly throughout the co-sanctioned event between The European Tour and the Asian Tour.

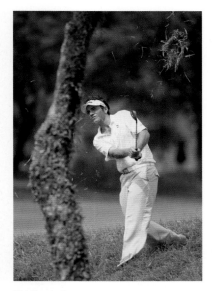

Nick Dougherty

Simon Dyson

First man in the media centre, for instance, was Liang Wen-chong from China, next came India's Jyoti Randhawa and third was Japan's Shingo Katayama, wearing his distinctive cowboy hat.

Perhaps it was fate or indeed pre-ordained then, that first should be first, that Liang should go from the interview room to the winner's podium to savour his first victory on The European Tour International Schedule.

He did not get there easily, though. An incredible last nine holes, which saw player after player throw away a winning chance, left two men standing, Iain Steel of Malaysia and Liang. They both finished on 11 under par 277 and had to go back to the 18th tee for a sudden-death play-off that was over almost before it started. Steel whipped his tee shot into the lake that runs all the way down the left of Laguna National Golf Club's attractive finishing hole before almost putting his third into the same stretch of water.

Liang played two conservative shots en route to a straightforward par four and a cheque for €139,075 (£94,218). He then made a memorable gesture, one which showed he knew how important it was to grow the game in China.

"I want to do my part as a golfer and give all my prize money to a golf foundation back home," he said. "There are only two role models in golf in China, Zhang Lian-wei and myself, and this money will help to bring more youngsters into the game." Zhang, of course, was a previous winner of this very title in 2003.

It might have been just as appropriate for Steel to claim his maiden win, for if anyone characterises the melting pot that is cosmopolitan Singapore it is this man who was born in Sabah, Malaysia, of a Scottish father and a Malaysian mother; who studied at Strathallan in Scotland, the same school as Colin Montgomerie, but who now lives in Birmingham, Alabama.

Although Steel's day would be tinged with disappointment, the fact that two Asian Tour-based golfers contested the play-off delighted local officials. As Spencer Robinson, the doyen of golf writers in Asia, explained: "It is crucial, critical if our Tour is to grow, that Asians do well in these co-sanctioned events.

"We have to create our own stars, players, who by winning at co-sanctioned level, can then be seen to go and play in Europe on the two year exemption they earn by their victory. And it is important that they are Asian. Anton Haig is a member of the Asian Tour as well as The European Tour and was a wonderful winner of the Johnnie Walker Classic in Phuket, but Asian youngsters would probably not relate to him in the same way as they would to a Liang."

It helped, too, that Liang won against what started as a strong field. However, when the 204 contestants – whose first two rounds were split between the established Masters Course and the newer Classic Course – reached the halfway mark, Darren Clarke, David Howell, Lee Westwood and Haig were among those who did not make it.

Peter Lawrie

They missed an extraordinary final afternoon over the Masters Course which played host to the entire weekend's action. The lead changed hands repeatedly with eight of the last nine players in the field playing pass the parcel with the trophy. First it looked as though the experienced Thongchai Jaidee might win, as he opened with four birdies in his first five holes, to reach 13 under par. But 32 out was followed by 42 back and an eventual share of 14th place.

The gritty Australian Terry Pilkadaris featured in the early stages but also suffered in the late afternoon malaise with halves of 32-40, while Nick Dougherty and Simon Dyson both finished furious with themselves.

Dougherty led the tournament after 15 holes at 13 under par but successive double bogeys at the 16th and 17th consigned him to 'near but yet so far' status once again in the event, adding a share of fourth to his second place last year when, realistically, he could have won three times in succession following his maiden Tour victory at Laguna National in 2005. Dyson three putted the 16th before horseshoeing out from 15 feet at the last when a birdie would have seen him join the play off.

Even Liang and Steel were not immune to mistakes, the Chinese golfer double bogeying the 15th and Steel doing the same at the 16th. But, in the end, they were the survivors –importantly both for themselves and for the whole of golf in Asia.

David Davies

Thongchai Jaidee

Jean Van de Velde

The Course

The established Masters Course played host to three of the four rounds and presented a sterner test than in previous years thanks to its increased length and demanding rough. Its sister layout, the adjacent Classic Course, although shorter, proved to be no pushover especially over the closing holes, the 200 yard par three 17th and the 470 yard par four 18th.

Roland Knecht (right), Member of the Executive Board, Clariden Leu, presents the trophy to Liang Wen-Chong

i Since the event was first played in 2001, three different countries have entered the winners circle for the first time on The European Tour. They were: India (2002 - Arjun Atwal), China (2003 - Zhang Lian-wei) and Singapore (2006 - Mardan Mamat).

Laguna National Golf Club

Par **72** Yards **7208** Metres **6589** - Masters Course
Par **72** Yards **7099** Metres **6493** - Classic Course

Final Results

Pos	Name		Rd1	Rd2	Rd3	Rd4	Total		€	£
1	Liang WEN-CHONG	CHN	64	72	68	73	277	-11	139,075.66	94,218.32
2	Iain STEEL	MAS	70	65	71	71	277	-11	92,717.11	62,812.21
3	Simon DYSON	ENG	71	69	67	71	278	-10	52,237.77	35,389.05
4	Nick DOUGHERTY	ENG	70	72	66	71	279	-9	32,836.36	22,245.35
	David LYNN	ENG	72	68	70	69	279	-9	32,836.36	22,245.35
	Anthony WALL	ENG	68	72	72	67	279	-9	32,836.36	22,245.35
	Jean VAN DE VELDE	FRA	68	71	71	69	279	-9	32,836.36	22,245.35
8	Jyoti RANDHAWA	IND	65	68	72	75	280	-8	16,564.21	11,221.60
	Peter LAWRIE	IRL	66	70	70	74	280	-8	16,564.21	11,221.60
	Keng-Chi LIN	TPE	73	68	69	70	280	-8	16,564.21	11,221.60
	Terry PILKADARIS	AUS	69	72	67	72	280	-8	16,564.21	11,221.60
	Craig SMITH	WAL	72	70	71	67	280	-8	16,564.21	11,221.60
	Scott BARR	AUS	70	69	71	70	280	-8	16,564.21	11,221.60
14	Scott STRANGE	AUS	69	73	70	69	281	-7	11,529.58	7,810.84
	Chinarat PHADUNGSIL	THA	69	71	71	70	281	-7	11,529.58	7,810.84
	Thongchai JAIDEE	THA	69	69	69	74	281	-7	11,529.58	7,810.84
	Peter SENIOR	AUS	70	70	73	68	281	-7	11,529.58	7,810.84
	Francesco MOLINARI	ITA	69	70	70	72	281	-7	11,529.58	7,810.84
	Peter O'MALLEY	AUS	71	70	69	71	281	-7	11,529.58	7,810.84
20	Joakim BÄCKSTRÖM	SWE	73	69	69	71	282	-6	9,575.53	6,487.05
	Robert ROCK	ENG	71	70	68	73	282	-6	9,575.53	6,487.05
	Oliver WILSON	ENG	69	72	70	71	282	-6	9,575.53	6,487.05
	Martin KAYMER	GER	66	73	71	72	282	-6	9,575.53	6,487.05
24	Marcus BOTH	AUS	72	69	72	70	283	-5	8,302.97	5,624.94
	Matthew ZIONS	AUS	68	71	73	71	283	-5	8,302.97	5,624.94
	Andrew COLTART	SCO	69	69	72	73	283	-5	8,302.97	5,624.94
	Hendrik BUHRMANN	RSA	71	69	71	72	283	-5	8,302.97	5,624.94
	Robert-Jan DERKSEN	NED	73	69	72	69	283	-5	8,302.97	5,624.94
	Mardan MAMAT	SIN	68	73	70	72	283	-5	8,302.97	5,624.94
30	Chawalit PLAPHOL	THA	75	67	72	70	284	-4	6,711.52	4,546.79
	Gary ORR	SCO	71	71	69	73	284	-4	6,711.52	4,546.79
	Graeme STORM	ENG	66	74	72	72	284	-4	6,711.52	4,546.79
	Shingo KATAYAMA	JPN	65	76	70	73	284	-4	6,711.52	4,546.79
	Tony LASCUNA	PHI	69	72	71	72	284	-4	6,711.52	4,546.79
	Gary LOCKERBIE	ENG	68	67	69	80	284	-4	6,711.52	4,546.79
	Prom MEESAWAT	THA	71	71	70	72	284	-4	6,711.52	4,546.79
37	Gary SIMPSON	AUS	69	72	72	72	285	-3	5,841.28	3,957.24
	Barry HUME	SCO	65	69	76	75	285	-3	5,841.28	3,957.24
39	Ariel CANETE	ARG	70	72	73	71	286	-2	5,090.26	3,448.45
	Brad KENNEDY	AUS	68	74	72	72	286	-2	5,090.26	3,448.45
	Gerald ROSALES	PHI	72	69	72	73	286	-2	5,090.26	3,448.45
	Mark FOSTER	ENG	76	65	71	74	286	-2	5,090.26	3,448.45
	Marcus FRASER	AUS	64	73	74	75	286	-2	5,090.26	3,448.45
	Rahil GANGJEE	IND	72	68	77	69	286	-2	5,090.26	3,448.45
	Lee SUNG	KOR	69	72	72	73	286	-2	5,090.26	3,448.45
46	Jong Yul SUK	KOR	69	73	69	76	287	-1	3,922.01	2,657.00
	Wei Chih LU	TPE	70	72	75	70	287	-1	3,922.01	2,657.00
	Ross FISHER	ENG	74	66	73	74	287	-1	3,922.01	2,657.00
	Jeev Milkha SINGH	IND	69	73	70	75	287	-1	3,922.01	2,657.00
	Steve WEBSTER	ENG	71	69	73	74	287	-1	3,922.01	2,657.00
	Stephen DODD	WAL	69	73	69	76	287	-1	3,922.01	2,657.00
	Mark PILKINGTON	WAL	72	67	73	75	287	-1	3,922.01	2,657.00
53	Scott HEND	AUS	71	70	74	73	288	0	3,170.98	2,148.22
	Carlos RODILES	ESP	71	70	72	75	288	0	3,170.98	2,148.22
55	Jean-François LUCQUIN	FRA	69	70	76	74	289	1	2,492.98	1,688.89
	Richard BLAND	ENG	72	67	73	77	289	1	2,492.98	1,688.89
	Frankie MINOZA	PHI	69	71	71	78	289	1	2,492.98	1,688.89
	Simon KHAN	ENG	69	70	77	73	289	1	2,492.98	1,688.89
	Gaurav GHEI	IND	68	70	77	74	289	1	2,492.98	1,688.89
	Ross BAIN	SCO	69	70	73	77	289	1	2,492.98	1,688.89
	Wen-Tang LIN	TPE	69	70	77	73	289	1	2,492.98	1,688.89
	Mark BROWN	NZL	66	73	76	74	289	1	2,492.98	1,688.89
63	Adam GROOM	AUS	70	72	72	76	290	2	2,002.73	1,356.77
	Adam BLYTH	AUS	67	73	74	76	290	2	2,002.73	1,356.77
	Brett RUMFORD	AUS	68	74	77	71	290	2	2,002.73	1,356.77
66	Angelo QUE	PHI	66	73	80	72	291	3	1,835.83	1,243.70
67	David GRIFFITHS	ENG	74	68	74	76	292	4	1,710.66	1,158.91
	Simon YATES	SCO	68	73	75	76	292	4	1,710.66	1,158.91
69	David CARTER	ENG	74	66	72	81	293	5	1,585.49	1,074.11
70	Shaun P WEBSTER	ENG	69	73	79	73	294	6	1,524.80	1,032.99
71	Phillip PRICE	WAL	69	71	70	85	295	7	1,252.00	848.18

Total Prize Fund

€835,721 £566,168

Wild Young Thing

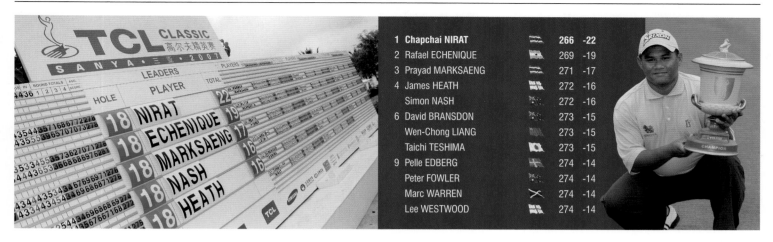

1	**Chapchai NIRAT**		266	-22
2	Rafael ECHENIQUE		269	-19
3	Prayad MARKSAENG		271	-17
4	James HEATH		272	-16
	Simon NASH		272	-16
6	David BRANSDON		273	-15
	Wen-Chong LIANG		273	-15
	Taichi TESHIMA		273	-15
9	Pelle EDBERG		274	-14
	Peter FOWLER		274	-14
	Marc WARREN		274	-14
	Lee WESTWOOD		274	-14

I n October 2003, Thai golfer Thaworn Wiratchant battled gamely down the stretch in the Kolon Korean Open before succumbing by a shot to an American by the name of John Daly, who claimed the title at the Woo Jung Hills Country Club thanks to a final round 68.

Oliver Fisher

James Heath

Four years on, and watching from behind the 18th green at the Yalong Bay Golf Club on Hainan Island as the final act of the 2007 TCL Classic played out, Wiratchant might have been forgiven for casting his mind back to that afternoon in South Korea.

For coming up the 18th fairway of the Sanya venue was a burly figure so reminiscent of a young Daly that, from a distance, it was hard to tell them apart. Throw in an identical power game, the same 'grip it and rip it' philosophy and the same over turn at the top of the backswing and the similarity was complete.

But as the TCL Classic drew to a close, one final resemblance between the pair also became apparent, namely, like Daly, the talented young Thai Chapchai Nirat knew exactly how to win.

Just as the American burst onto the scene spectacularly in 1991 when, as ninth and final alternate for the US PGA Championship he not only gained entry to the tournament at Crooked Stick but went on to win by three shots, Nirat, without any Asian Tour victories to his credit, burst forth from relative obscurity to triumph in the co-sanctioned tournament between The European Tour and the Asian Tour.

The 23 year old did not merely win: he blew the field away, starting with a stunning 11 under par course record 61 in the first round which made him the man to catch all week. Subsequent rounds of 66-68-71 ensured it was a task no-one was up to.

Nearest pursuer, as he had been since his opening 64, was Argentina's Rafael Echenique but the graduate from the 2006 European Challenge Tour knew he had to take every opportunity which presented itself in the final afternoon if he was to have a chance of making up his six shot deficit.

Three birdies in a flawless outward half of 33 gave the 26 year old from San Luis a glimmer of hope but when he missed birdie opportunities from inside six feet on both the 13th and 14th, he knew second place was his optimum return.

In the final group behind, Nirat, who had his only minor wobble of the week at the end of the third round when he bogeyed both the 17th and 18th holes to reduce a seven shot advantage to five, from Japan's Taichi Teshima and England's Miles Tunnicliff, knew he only had to play conservatively to claim the €127,046 (£86,271) first prize, and did just that.

Eight straight pars began his round and he was still level par for the day after 14 holes before a superb birdie two at the testing 240 yard par three 15th, where he holed a curling 30 foot putt from the bottom of the green, put the destiny of the trophy beyond doubt. It also enabled him to enjoy the walk up the final three holes and in particular the 18th where his proud compatriot Wiratchant looked on.

It was appropriate that the 40 year old, who along with Thongchai Jaidee had been the only Thai golfer to win on The European Tour previously, was there to watch as both he and Jaidee had been instrumental in young Nirat's progress; a point alluded to by the Executive Chairman of the Asian Tour, Kyi Hla Han.

"A lot of credit goes to the old guard like Thaworn and Thongchai who have not only paved the way for the younger Thai players to shine through, but they have also been influential in their careers by playing the role of big brother to the new and young players like Chapchai," he said.

"Along with Prom (Meesawat) and Chinarat (Phadungsil) who are 24 and 18 respectively, Chapchai represents a new breed of emerging Thai players who look set to emulate, if not better, the feats of their elders."

One way Nirat has already emulated his illustrious senior countrymen is by taking up Membership of The European Tour, which he did a mere three days after his triumph in China.

"I cannot wait to play in Europe and broaden my experience," said the young man whose booming drives and swashbuckling attitude to the game seem certain to enthral spectators wherever he plays.

Remind you of anyone?

Scott Crockett

Lee Westwood

Miles Tunnicliff

Yalong Bay Golf Club

Par **72**   Yards **7189**   Metres **6572**

Final Results

Pos	Name		Rd1	Rd2	Rd3	Rd4	Total		€	£
1	Chapchai NIRAT	THA	61	66	68	71	266	-22	127,046.55	86,271.87
2	Rafael ECHENIQUE	ARG	64	69	68	68	269	-19	84,700.24	57,516.31
3	Prayad MARKSAENG	THA	71	68	65	67	271	-17	47,720.59	32,405.01
4	James HEATH	ENG	72	63	68	69	272	-16	35,218.71	23,915.52
	Simon NASH	AUS	67	66	71	68	272	-16	35,218.71	23,915.52
6	Wen-chong LIANG	CHN	69	68	66	70	273	-15	22,869.29	15,529.56
	David BRANSDON	AUS	67	66	74	66	273	-15	22,869.29	15,529.56
	Taichi TESHIMA	JPN	69	65	66	73	273	-15	22,869.29	15,529.56
9	Pelle EDBERG	SWE	71	64	69	70	274	-14	14,865.04	10,094.21
	Peter FOWLER	AUS	69	68	68	69	274	-14	14,865.04	10,094.21
	Lee WESTWOOD	ENG	66	70	68	70	274	-14	14,865.04	10,094.21
	Marc WARREN	SCO	70	67	70	67	274	-14	14,865.04	10,094.21
13	Oliver FISHER	ENG	67	69	67	72	275	-13	11,472.76	7,790.66
	Kane WEBBER	AUS	67	71	66	71	275	-13	11,472.76	7,790.66
	Nick DOUGHERTY	ENG	66	69	69	71	275	-13	11,472.76	7,790.66
	Miles TUNNICLIFF	ENG	70	65	65	75	275	-13	11,472.76	7,790.66
17	Thaworn WIRATCHANT	THA	69	68	68	71	276	-12	9,681.33	6,574.18
	François DELAMONTAGNE	FRA	73	62	70	71	276	-12	9,681.33	6,574.18
	Adam BLYTH	AUS	67	66	70	73	276	-12	9,681.33	6,574.18
	Ashley HALL	AUS	67	69	69	71	276	-12	9,681.33	6,574.18
21	Brad KENNEDY	AUS	67	67	69	74	277	-11	8,499.75	5,771.82
	Scott STRANGE	AUS	69	69	70	69	277	-11	8,499.75	5,771.82
	Scott BARR	AUS	69	68	71	69	277	-11	8,499.75	5,771.82
	Chawalit PLAPHOL	THA	68	69	70	70	277	-11	8,499.75	5,771.82
25	Iain STEEL	MAS	71	68	67	72	278	-10	7,013.25	4,762.40
	Mardan MAMAT	SIN	68	70	72	68	278	-10	7,013.25	4,762.40
	Gaurav GHEI	IND	70	69	68	71	278	-10	7,013.25	4,762.40
	Gary RUSNAK	USA	67	70	67	74	278	-10	7,013.25	4,762.40
	Patrik SJÖLAND	SWE	69	69	69	71	278	-10	7,013.25	4,762.40
	Stephen SCAHILL	NZL	71	68	71	68	278	-10	7,013.25	4,762.40
	Carl SUNESON	ESP	66	68	72	72	278	-10	7,013.25	4,762.40
	Birgir HAFTHORSSON	ISL	68	70	72	68	278	-10	7,013.25	4,762.40
	Richard LEE	NZL	65	70	70	73	278	-10	7,013.25	4,762.40
34	Jean-Baptiste GONNET	FRA	67	66	73	73	279	-9	5,259.94	3,571.80
	Rafael CABRERA BELLO	ESP	68	70	71	70	279	-9	5,259.94	3,571.80
	Wade ORMSBY	AUS	66	71	70	72	279	-9	5,259.94	3,571.80
	Wei-chih LU	TPE	72	66	71	70	279	-9	5,259.94	3,571.80
	Wen-teh LU	TPE	65	69	68	77	279	-9	5,259.94	3,571.80
	Mark PILKINGTON	WAL	68	70	71	70	279	-9	5,259.94	3,571.80
	Fredrik ANDERSSON HED	SWE	69	69	72	69	279	-9	5,259.94	3,571.80
	James KINGSTON	RSA	66	70	74	69	279	-9	5,259.94	3,571.80
	Paul MCGINLEY	IRL	72	67	72	68	279	-9	5,259.94	3,571.80
43	Steve ALKER	NZL	67	71	70	72	280	-8	4,345.17	2,950.62
	Mads VIBE-HASTRUP	DEN	67	70	70	73	280	-8	4,345.17	2,950.62
	Gareth PADDISON	NZL	69	69	72	70	280	-8	4,345.17	2,950.62
46	Unho PARK	AUS	68	71	74	68	281	-7	3,659.09	2,484.73
	François CALMELS	FRA	69	68	74	70	281	-7	3,659.09	2,484.73
	Barry LANE	ENG	68	71	70	72	281	-7	3,659.09	2,484.73
	Keith HORNE	RSA	65	72	70	74	281	-7	3,659.09	2,484.73
	Simon GRIFFITHS	ENG	68	70	72	71	281	-7	3,659.09	2,484.73
	Juvic PAGUNSAN	PHI	68	68	69	76	281	-7	3,659.09	2,484.73
52	Sam LITTLE	ENG	68	67	74	73	282	-6	2,973.01	2,018.84
	Neven BASIC	AUS	71	67	71	73	282	-6	2,973.01	2,018.84
	Alexandre ROCHA	BRA	67	70	73	72	282	-6	2,973.01	2,018.84
55	Adam GROOM	AUS	69	70	72	72	283	-5	2,319.60	1,575.14
	Julien FORET	FRA	69	70	72	72	283	-5	2,319.60	1,575.14
	Matthew ZIONS	AUS	69	68	72	74	283	-5	2,319.60	1,575.14
	Carlos RODILES	ESP	68	66	73	76	283	-5	2,319.60	1,575.14
	Lian-wei ZHANG	CHN	73	65	72	73	283	-5	2,319.60	1,575.14
	Ter-chang WANG	TPE	73	66	72	72	283	-5	2,319.60	1,575.14
	Luis CLAVERIE	ESP	68	70	73	72	283	-5	2,319.60	1,575.14
62	Simon HURD	ENG	71	67	74	72	284	-4	1,905.77	1,294.13
	Danny CHIA	MAS	68	70	74	72	284	-4	1,905.77	1,294.13
	Scott HEND	AUS	66	73	74	71	284	-4	1,905.77	1,294.13
65	Lee SUNG	KOR	71	68	70	76	285	-3	1,753.31	1,190.60
66	Matthew RICHARDSON	ENG	71	67	74	75	287	-1	1,677.08	1,138.83

The Course

Shaped like a dragon's claw, the Yalong Bay course is bordered by adjacent green hills and the South China Sea which provided testing breezes. Although the links-styled rolling fairways remained generous, the rough had grown from previous years placing a premium on accuracy on both the drives and the approach shots into a series of fast and undulating, well bunkered greens.

Bo Lianming (left), Vice President of TCL Corporation, presents the trophy to Chapchai Nirat

Rafael Echenique

" This is my first big win and I'd like to dedicate it to my parents. I was feeling serious on the back nine because Rafael (Echenique) was getting close so I didn't want to make a mistake, but at the finish I was very happy. To win a big tournament like this means a great deal to me and I will definitely play in Europe. "
Chapchai Nirat

Total Prize Fund

€756,341   £513,598

Reverting to Type

1	Daniel VANCSIK		270	-18
2	David FROST		277	-11
	Santiago LUNA		277	-11
4	Christian CÉVAËR		279	-9
	Euan LITTLE		279	-9
	Mads VIBE-HASTRUP		279	-9
7	Grégory BOURDY		280	-8
	Simon NASH		280	-8
	Alexander NOREN		280	-8
10	Francesco MOLINARI		281	-7

D aniel Vancsik made the headlines. Vicente Fernandez, formerly a journalist in Buenos Aires, would have been delighted to write the story for his protégé had just provided one of the surprise victories of the season.

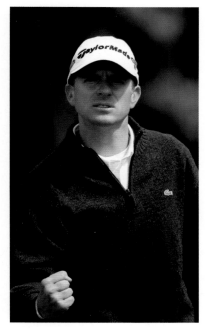

Christian Cévaër

David Frost

Fernandez, during his time on The European Tour, had been pretty adept at making headlines himself. His unerring 90 foot putt at The Belfry in 1992 to claim the English Open title is legendary. Similar to Costantino Rocca's mammoth effort from the Valley of Sin three years later to force a play-off with John Daly in The Open Championship at St Andrews, it is still one of those dramatic finales on The European Tour that lives in the memory.

Vancsik had no need of a huge putt to take the Madeira Islands Open BPI title but his triumph out of the blue was no less dramatic than his mentor's accomplishment 15 years earlier. After a 2006 rookie season that was hardly sensational - only ten cuts made out of 24 starts - the man from Posadas, who had previously fashioned a successful Challenge Tour career, lost his card.

After regaining it at the Qualifying School, his 2007 season was not exactly setting the heather on fire either. Four missed cuts out of seven events

and very few pesos in the bank account did not forecast the heady happenings that unfolded up the mountain at Santo da Serra.

One of the keys to Vancsik's amazing transformation lay with one of Fernandez's contemporaries and fellow countryman - José Cantero.

Disturbed by languishing 215th on the Order of Merit following the TCL Classic the week before, Vancsik turned to Cantero for coaching. He was impressed, he said, by the fact that his teacher had "won on every continent". He wanted some of that to brush off on him.

Vancsik went into the week in Madeira with his head buzzing with tips but, most importantly, Cantero had sharpened up his pupil's short game. It was a lesson the 30 year old used to utmost advantage, gradually distancing himself from the field and showing such authority that he stretched his victory margin to seven strokes. It was easily the biggest winning margin of the season at that juncture.

On the opening morning, however, it was a player who made his mark in 1988 by launching himself spectacularly on The European Tour, who led the way. Indeed, there were shades of Fernandez's feat about Peter Baker's claim to fame.

The Englishman will be forever remembered, not for a closing putt, but for eagling the 18th twice in succession at Fulford to snatch the Benson and Hedges International Open from a certain Nick Faldo in his pomp. Baker, boosted by the success of his Vice-Captaincy to Ian Woosnam in The 2006 Ryder Cup at The K Club, briefly turned back the clock with an excellent 67. By the end of the day, however, Ricardo Santos, the son of an Algarve florist, proved to be the pick of the bunch with a 66.

Vancsik, starting to find his touch around the greens, soon nipped everyone's challenge in the bud. With a little help from his friends, the tall Argentine with Hungarian and German roots, slowly but surely overwhelmed the field.

Armed with additional advice from compatriots Angel Cabrera and Ricardo Gonzalez, who had given him a run through of most of The European Tour courses at the start of the season, Vancsik began to come to terms with Santo da Serra and took a one shot lead over Christian Cévaër at the halfway stage.

On Saturday it got even better for the Argentine as a flawless 68 took him four shots clear of the field. Showing little sign of nerves the next day, he doubled that advantage by the turn with the help of a masterful short game which proved that Cantero's tuition was reaping dividends.

It may have only been a five footer, rather than the massive effort Fernandez had coaxed home at The Belfry all those years ago, but Vancsik's final act sparked off the same sort of celebrations that had greeted the eight previous Argentine winners before him, since the Tour's 1972 beginning. He was doused in champagne as the distinctive blue and white national flag was draped around his shoulders.

Back home, Fernandez might not have been hitting the typewriter keyboard, but plenty more were.

Norman Dabell

David Lynn

Left *Santiago Luna*

Mads Vibe-Hastrup

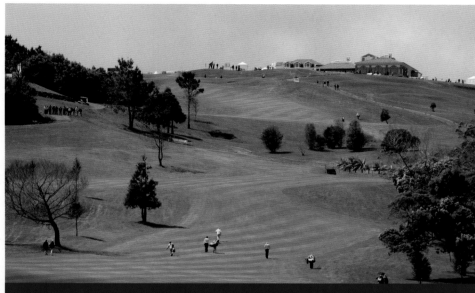

The Course

Looking over the bay of Machico where the Portuguese navigators first landed, Santo da Serra is one of the most picturesque locations on The European Tour International Schedule. Originally built in 1937, a redesign in 1991 by Robert Trent Jones Snr and subsequent work have made it one of the most improved courses on Tour while ensuring golf and nature continue to live in perfect harmony.

Daniel Vancsik (left) celebrates with the trophy with Jose Carlos Agrellos from BPI

Peter Baker

i Des Smyth created European Tour history by becoming the oldest player to win a European Tour event. He was 48 and 34 days when he claimed the 2001 Madeira Islands Open BPI, beating the old record of Neil Coles, who was 48 and 14 days when he triumphed at the 1982 Sanyo Open.

madeira Islands

Santo da Serra
Par **72**   Yards **6826**   Metres **6241**

Final Results

Pos	Name		Rd1	Rd2	Rd3	Rd4	Total		€	£
1	Daniel VANCSIK	ARG	68	66	68	68	270	-18	116,660.00	79,925.46
2	David FROST	RSA	72	65	72	68	277	-11	60,795.00	41,651.54
	Santiago LUNA	ESP	69	67	72	69	277	-11	60,795.00	41,651.54
4	Euan LITTLE	SCO	73	66	69	71	279	-9	29,726.67	20,366.17
	Christian CÉVAÉR	FRA	70	65	72	72	279	-9	29,726.67	20,366.17
	Mads VIBE-HASTRUP	DEN	68	70	68	73	279	-9	29,726.67	20,366.17
7	Alexander NOREN	SWE	72	66	72	70	280	-8	18,060.00	12,373.17
	Grégory BOURDY	FRA	74	67	68	71	280	-8	18,060.00	12,373.17
	Simon NASH	AUS	70	69	71	70	280	-8	18,060.00	12,373.17
10	Francesco MOLINARI	ITA	75	70	67	69	281	-7	14,000.00	9,591.60
11	Stuart LITTLE	ENG	71	69	72	70	282	-6	12,880.00	8,824.27
12	Grégory HAVRET	FRA	71	69	73	70	283	-5	11,340.00	7,769.20
	Jamie SPENCE	ENG	74	65	74	70	283	-5	11,340.00	7,769.20
	Iain PYMAN	ENG	77	67	70	69	283	-5	11,340.00	7,769.20
15	Tom WHITEHOUSE	ENG	74	71	70	69	284	-4	8,694.00	5,956.39
	Jamie DONALDSON	WAL	71	69	70	74	284	-4	8,694.00	5,956.39
	Martin KAYMER	GER	68	73	75	68	284	-4	8,694.00	5,956.39
	Miguel RODRIGUEZ	ARG	77	68	70	69	284	-4	8,694.00	5,956.39
	Peter BAKER	ENG	67	72	72	73	284	-4	8,694.00	5,956.39
	Johan AXGREN	SWE	75	70	68	71	284	-4	8,694.00	5,956.39
	Ian GARBUTT	ENG	71	69	73	71	284	-4	8,694.00	5,956.39
	Bradley DREDGE	WAL	73	72	70	69	284	-4	8,694.00	5,956.39
	David LYNN	ENG	71	70	74	69	284	-4	8,694.00	5,956.39
	António SOBRINHO	POR	74	70	71	69	284	-4	8,694.00	5,956.39
25	David PARK	WAL	71	68	72	74	285	-3	6,650.00	4,556.01
	Andrew MARSHALL	ENG	73	71	69	72	285	-3	6,650.00	4,556.01
	Sam LITTLE	ENG	70	69	74	72	285	-3	6,650.00	4,556.01
	Robert-Jan DERKSEN	NED	68	72	70	75	285	-3	6,650.00	4,556.01
	Wade ORMSBY	AUS	76	67	72	70	285	-3	6,650.00	4,556.01
	Oliver WILSON	ENG	70	69	75	71	285	-3	6,650.00	4,556.01
	François DELAMONTAGNE	FRA	74	68	70	73	285	-3	6,650.00	4,556.01
32	Tiago CRUZ	POR	73	71	73	69	286	-2	5,432.00	3,721.54
	Eirik Tage JOHANSEN	NOR	77	67	73	69	286	-2	5,432.00	3,721.54
	Steve ALKER	NZL	72	71	70	73	286	-2	5,432.00	3,721.54
	Jean VAN DE VELDE	FRA	75	67	74	70	286	-2	5,432.00	3,721.54
	Pelle EDBERG	SWE	74	70	72	70	286	-2	5,432.00	3,721.54
37	Jean-Baptiste GONNET	FRA	78	67	70	72	287	-1	4,620.00	3,165.23
	Simon WAKEFIELD	ENG	74	67	73	73	287	-1	4,620.00	3,165.23
	Ivó GINER	ESP	74	71	72	70	287	-1	4,620.00	3,165.23
	Peter GUSTAFSSON	SWE	74	70	70	73	287	-1	4,620.00	3,165.23
	Notah BEGAY III	USA	67	71	75	74	287	-1	4,620.00	3,165.23
	Andrew TAMPION	AUS	74	68	70	75	287	-1	4,620.00	3,165.23
43	Gary MURPHY	IRL	74	67	70	77	288	0	3,920.00	2,685.65
	Jean-François REMESY	FRA	71	74	69	74	288	0	3,920.00	2,685.65
	Fredrik ANDERSSON HED	SWE	70	69	71	78	288	0	3,920.00	2,685.65
	Birgir HAFTHORSSON	ISL	74	70	71	73	288	0	3,920.00	2,685.65
47	Benn BARHAM	ENG	74	69	73	73	289	1	3,290.00	2,254.03
	Denny LUCAS	ENG	72	73	73	71	289	1	3,290.00	2,254.03
	David GRIFFITHS	ENG	74	69	72	74	289	1	3,290.00	2,254.03
	Pedro LINHART	ESP	73	71	75	70	289	1	3,290.00	2,254.03
	Edoardo MOLINARI	ITA	71	72	74	72	289	1	3,290.00	2,254.03
52	Ricardo SANTOS	POR	66	74	77	73	290	2	2,800.00	1,918.32
	Luis CLAVERIE	ESP	71	70	76	73	290	2	2,800.00	1,918.32
54	Philip TALBOT	ENG	73	71	77	70	291	3	2,450.00	1,678.53
	David DRYSDALE	SCO	73	72	74	72	291	3	2,450.00	1,678.53
	David HIGGINS	IRL	74	70	74	73	291	3	2,450.00	1,678.53
57	Alvaro SALTO	ESP	74	71	77	70	292	4	2,135.00	1,462.72
	Sven STRÜVER	GER	70	71	73	78	292	4	2,135.00	1,462.72
59	Alessandro TADINI	ITA	73	71	73	76	293	5	1,890.00	1,294.87
	Garry HOUSTON	WAL	75	69	70	79	293	5	1,890.00	1,294.87
	Nicolas VANHOOTEGEM	BEL	75	70	73	75	293	5	1,890.00	1,294.87
	Steven O'HARA	SCO	71	70	76	76	293	5	1,890.00	1,294.87
	Manuel QUIROS	ESP	73	70	75	75	293	5	1,890.00	1,294.87
64	Phillip ARCHER	ENG	71	74	79	70	294	6	1,680.00	1,150.99
65	David BRANSDON	AUS	72	73	78	72	295	7	1,575.00	1,079.06
	Kenneth FERRIE	ENG	74	70	78	73	295	7	1,575.00	1,079.06
67	Adrien MÖRK	FRA	73	72	78	81	304	16	1,470.00	1,007.12

Total Prize Fund
€695,980   £476,826

The Joy of Six

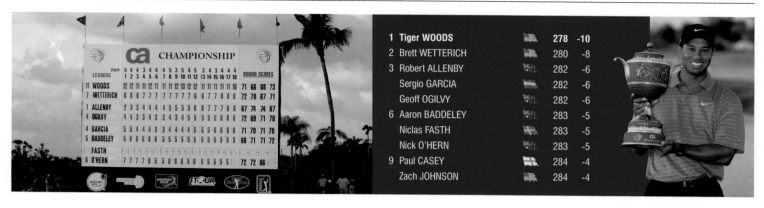

1	Tiger WOODS		278	-10
2	Brett WETTERICH		280	-8
3	Robert ALLENBY		282	-6
	Sergio GARCIA		282	-6
	Geoff OGILVY		282	-6
6	Aaron BADDELEY		283	-5
	Niclas FASTH		283	-5
	Nick O'HERN		283	-5
9	Paul CASEY		284	-4
	Zach JOHNSON		284	-4

In 2007, the annual Tiger Woods Benefit Fund, now also known as the World Golf Championships - CA Championship, moved to Florida for the first time. Only two men have prevented Woods from winning this tournament in its eight year history and there was not about to be a third. The blessed one came home in cruise control to win by two shots from Ryder Cup colleague Brett Wetterich despite a flicker of excitement on the 72nd hole.

Thomas Björn

Niclas Fasth

The 467 yard, par four 18th is the hole that put the monster into the Doral Golf Resort and Spa's Blue Monster course. It is a dog-leg round a lake with treacherous cross winds and a narrow fairway. After Sergio Garcia drew hoots of derision from the gallery for putting one in the water, he turned to the crowd and said: "If you think it's easy, try and hit it yourself." When Woods reached the tee for the final time, he had a three shot lead.

Wisely, the World Number One was not about to fool with the water and played the hole as if it were a par five, hitting a three iron from the tee and an eight iron and wedge onto the green. Meanwhile Wetterich smashed his drive up the fairway and an approach shot to eight feet. Suddenly if Wetterich holed and Woods three putted....?

Except that Woods does not three putt; at least not in these circumstances. However, he had hit a very conservative wedge to a spot some 50 feet from the hole, the same spot from where, earlier in the day, Mark Calcavecchia had putted clean off the green and into the water. But, before Wetterich could entertain any fanciful notions of a play-off or better, Woods hit the perfect lag putt and that was that.

Indeed many people thought the tournament had finished the day before. When Wetterich birdied four of his first six holes on the Saturday, eyes glanced over to Woods on the first tee to see how he would react. He reacted with an eagle three.

Paul Casey, who had just finished his own fine round of 66 on his way to eventually sharing ninth place, said: "If it was any other player you

couldn't believe that he had eagled the first. But because it's Tiger you kind of expect it. He's got such an unbelievable record leading from the front. He's gone. I don't think we'll see him again."

Indeed Woods was so far gone that most in the field resigned themselves to playing for second. After tacking a third round 68 onto his decisive second round 66 for a four shot lead, he was so relaxed that he drove himself down to the tennis that evening where he watched his good friend Roger Federer tenderise another hapless victim.

After finishing second, Wetterich said: "I never thought I was going to win. It would have been nice to see how he played when someone had pressure on him, to see if he fired at the flags more or still kind of played the same way. But I didn't get to see that part and it just looked easy to him out there today."

Certainly the new venue has done nothing to reduce Woods' chances of dominating the tournament. The 31 year old American won the Ford Championship at Doral on the US PGA Tour in both 2005 and 2006 before adding the CA Championship to his CV.

There is every chance that Woods will add a few more titles yet as the WGC - CA Championship is scheduled to return to Doral through to the 2010 season.

Nevertheless, the manicured Doral fairways and greens look great on television, and this resort course, with a fine match play-style finish, has also rewarded European Tour Members in the past - indeed Nick Faldo won there in 1995 and Ernie Els triumphed in 2002.

The clubhouse, to a British eye, takes a bit of getting used to, and when you think of other clubhouses of the world like Royal West Norfolk's snug windcheater, the grand panorama of Congressional or the more traditional virtues of Winged Foot, Doral gives more of the appearance of a vast shopping mall, a feeling enhanced by the fact it contains a Starbucks store within its walls. Cleaning contractors had even been hired to vacuum the clubhouse stairs on a 24 hour basis – a Sisyphean task if ever there were one.

For Tiger Woods, however, the ball keeps rolling upwards as his personal cash register for this event alone underlines, now standing at $7,312,500.

Ker-ching!

Mark Reason
The Sunday Telegraph

Above *Vijay Singh*
Left *Sergio Garcia*

Below *Padraig Harrington*

Paul Casey

Tiger Woods (left) with John Swainson, President and CEO of CA

After his latest World Golf Championships triumph in the WGC – CA Championship, Tiger Woods made history by becoming the first golfer to win the same official European Tour Order of Merit events six times. His other wins were in 1999, 2002, 2003, 2005 and 2006.

The Course

Originally designed by Dick Wilson and later restored by Ray Floyd, The Blue Monster course demands both length and finesse from the tee to avoid the strategically placed bunkers while the undulating greens, water hazards and deep Bermuda rough demand respect. The 18th hole, with its signature fountain, was ranked by GOLF Magazine as one of the top 100 holes in the world.

Doral Golf Resort and Spa

Par **72**   Yards **7266**   Metres **6645**

Final Results

Pos	Name		Rd1	Rd2	Rd3	Rd4	Total		€	£
1	Tiger WOODS	USA	71	66	68	73	278	-10	1,014,505.24	695,052.27
2	Brett WETTERICH	USA	72	70	67	71	280	-8	601,188.29	411,882.82
3	Robert ALLENBY	AUS	67	74	74	67	282	-6	284,311.96	194,786.25
	Sergio GARCIA	ESP	71	70	71	70	282	-6	284,311.96	194,786.25
	Geoff OGILVY	AUS	72	69	71	70	282	-6	284,311.96	194,786.25
6	Niclas FASTH	SWE	72	70	70	71	283	-5	159,690.64	109,406.38
	Nick O'HERN	AUS	72	72	66	73	283	-5	159,690.64	109,406.38
	Aaron BADDELEY	AUS	69	71	71	72	283	-5	159,690.64	109,406.38
9	Paul CASEY	ENG	76	70	66	72	284	-4	118,358.94	81,089.43
	Zach JOHNSON	USA	72	68	73	71	284	-4	118,358.94	81,089.43
11	Tom PERNICE Jnr	USA	71	70	70	74	285	-3	83,414.87	57,148.74
	Vijay SINGH	FIJ	74	68	69	74	285	-3	83,414.87	57,148.74
	Robert KARLSSON	SWE	74	74	68	69	285	-3	83,414.87	57,148.74
	Ernie ELS	RSA	70	70	71	74	285	-3	83,414.87	57,148.74
	Thomas BJÖRN	DEN	68	72	71	74	285	-3	83,414.87	57,148.74
16	Dean WILSON	USA	73	75	66	72	286	-2	65,629.72	44,963.87
	Ian POULTER	ENG	73	68	75	70	286	-2	65,629.72	44,963.87
	Charles HOWELL III	USA	69	71	71	75	286	-2	65,629.72	44,963.87
19	Angel CABRERA	ARG	72	70	75	70	287	-1	60,118.83	41,188.28
	Padraig HARRINGTON	IRL	73	70	73	71	287	-1	60,118.83	41,188.28
	K J CHOI	KOR	71	73	71	72	287	-1	60,118.83	41,188.28
	Henrik STENSON	SWE	67	73	72	75	287	-1	60,118.83	41,188.28
23	Phil MICKELSON	USA	77	72	70	69	288	0	55,609.92	38,099.16
	Thongchai JAIDEE	THA	72	74	70	72	288	0	55,609.92	38,099.16
25	Mark WILSON	USA	74	72	72	71	289	1	53,355.46	36,554.60
26	Lucas GLOVER	USA	73	73	72	72	290	2	52,228.23	35,782.32
	Luke DONALD	ENG	74	70	75	71	290	2	52,228.23	35,782.32
28	John ROLLINS	USA	73	70	70	78	291	3	49,973.78	34,237.76
	Jeev Milkha SINGH	IND	74	70	70	77	291	3	49,973.78	34,237.76
	Rodney PAMPLING	AUS	70	69	74	78	291	3	49,973.78	34,237.76
	Stephen AMES	CAN	74	70	74	73	291	3	49,973.78	34,237.76
32	Mark CALCAVECCHIA	USA	74	71	70	77	292	4	47,343.58	32,435.77
	Anton HAIG	RSA	75	69	74	74	292	4	47,343.58	32,435.77
	Chris DIMARCO	USA	76	72	69	75	292	4	47,343.58	32,435.77
35	Chad CAMPBELL	USA	75	74	72	72	293	5	42,458.92	29,089.22
	Carl PETTERSSON	SWE	72	72	74	75	293	5	42,458.92	29,089.22
	Rory SABBATINI	RSA	71	75	73	74	293	5	42,458.92	29,089.22
	Bart BRYANT	USA	71	73	75	74	293	5	42,458.92	29,089.22
	Charl SCHWARTZEL	RSA	75	74	70	74	293	5	42,458.92	29,089.22
	Jim FURYK	USA	70	73	72	78	293	5	42,458.92	29,089.22
	José Maria OLAZÁBAL	ESP	69	80	72	72	293	5	42,458.92	29,089.22
	Steve STRICKER	USA	74	69	73	77	293	5	42,458.92	29,089.22
	Trevor IMMELMAN	RSA	72	68	74	79	293	5	42,458.92	29,089.22
	Stuart APPLEBY	AUS	79	72	71	71	293	5	42,458.92	29,089.22
45	Stewart CINK	USA	74	68	73	79	294	6	36,822.78	25,227.82
	Johan EDFORS	SWE	74	73	74	73	294	6	36,822.78	25,227.82
	Paul BROADHURST	ENG	73	71	73	77	294	6	36,822.78	25,227.82
	Arron OBERHOLSER	USA	74	76	71	73	294	6	36,822.78	25,227.82
	David TOMS	USA	72	72	76	74	294	6	36,822.78	25,227.82
50	Brett QUIGLEY	USA	73	72	73	77	295	7	33,816.84	23,168.41
	Louis OOSTHUIZEN	RSA	74	75	77	69	295	7	33,816.84	23,168.41
	John BICKERTON	ENG	77	72	74	72	295	7	33,816.84	23,168.41
	Paul GOYDOS	USA	74	75	70	76	295	7	33,816.84	23,168.41
	Mike WEIR	CAN	73	75	73	74	295	7	33,816.84	23,168.41
55	David HOWELL	ENG	74	73	73	76	296	8	32,313.87	22,138.70
	Colin MONTGOMERIE	SCO	76	72	73	75	296	8	32,313.87	22,138.70
	J J HENRY	USA	73	74	78	71	296	8	32,313.87	22,138.70
58	Ben CURTIS	USA	76	75	69	77	297	9	31,186.64	21,366.42
	Nathan GREEN	AUS	72	71	76	78	297	9	31,186.64	21,366.42
	Retief GOOSEN	RSA	77	70	78	72	297	9	31,186.64	21,366.42
61	Adam SCOTT	AUS	76	71	72	80	299	11	30,247.29	20,722.85
	Charley HOFFMAN	USA	75	75	77	72	299	11	30,247.29	20,722.85
63	Tim CLARK	RSA	76	78	71	75	300	12	29,495.80	20,208.00
	Hennie OTTO	RSA	74	73	74	79	300	12	29,495.80	20,208.00
65	Anthony WALL	ENG	80	73	75	73	301	13	28,556.44	19,564.43
	Joe DURANT	USA	73	73	77	78	301	13	28,556.44	19,564.43
	Y E YANG	KOR	76	77	73	75	301	13	28,556.44	19,564.43
68	Kevin STADLER	USA	73	71	78	82	304	16	27,617.09	18,920.87
	Prom MEESAWAT	THA	74	71	82	77	304	16	27,617.09	18,920.87
70	Hideto TANIHARA	JPN	80	75	73	77	305	17	27,053.47	18,534.73
71	Michael CAMPBELL	NZL	77	76	78	75	306	18	26,865.60	18,406.01
72	Shingo KATAYAMA	JPN	81	78	74	75	308	20	26,677.73	18,277.30
73	Davis LOVE III	USA	74	73	W/D					

Total Prize Fund

€5,959,091 £4,082,660

Breasting the Tape

		277	-7
1	Pablo MARTIN (AM)	277	-7
2	Raphaël JACQUELIN	278	-6
3	David GRIFFITHS	281	-3
	Martin KAYMER	281	-3
	Charl SCHWARTZEL	281	-3
	Graeme STORM	281	-3
7	Alastair FORSYTH	282	-2
	Michael JONZON	282	-2
	Andrew OLDCORN	282	-2
	Sven STRÜVER	282	-2

R aces are all about patience, pacing yourself and putting in sprint finishes as Pablo Martin ably demonstrated when he rewrote golfing history by becoming the first amateur to win an event on The European Tour International Schedule.

Martin Kaymer

Raphaël Jacquelin

The key to the 20 year old's success in the Estoril Open de Portugal at Quinta da Marinha Oitavos Golfe was zooming home in 29 for a sizzling Saturday 66, then breasting the tape the next day with a flawless closing 68.

What made this race extra special, however, was that it boiled down to a battle royal between some of golf's most gifted newcomers to provide a thrilling glimpse of some of the shining lights of the future in Europe's golfing firmament.

Martin became the first amateur to take a Tour title since the International Schedule was launched 1145 tournaments earlier in 1972. His impressive panache in writing his name into the record books echoed the youthful derring deeds of illustrious compatriots Seve Ballesteros, Sergio Garcia and José Maria Olazábal.

But it was the manner in which the Oklahoma State University student became the 11th first time winner of the 2007 season that marked him out as a potential heir to the aforementioned Spanish legends.

The former British Boys Champion and Spanish Amateur Championship winner had hinted at great things to come by romping to a share of the 54 hole lead in the 2003 Open de España before eventually finishing tied 22nd.

He recalled: "I was 17 and I was shaking all over after my first round. I asked Miguel Angel Jiménez, who comes from Malaga like me, how to deal with the situation and he said everybody gets nervous and everyone is human – that's a good sign. He said to focus on my own game. It helped me a lot."

He learned the Jiménez lesson well, staying cool, calm and collected in Portugal after opening rounds of 73-70 left him seven strokes behind English rookie professional Ross McGowan, the

2006 English Amateur Champion who, in only his second main circuit event, had opened with a brace of 68s.

University of Tennessee graduate McGowan slipped a stroke behind fellow 24 year old Alexander Noren of Sweden at the 54 hole stage as Martin dramatically moved within two of the lead. The rest, as they say, is history and Pablo's father Gonzala, mother Elena, sister Maria and brother Gonzalo were in the gallery to witness the heroics.

Afterwards the young champion recalled: "When Scott Verplank was at Oklahoma State he won as an amateur on the US PGA Tour and my coaches have been giving me stick for three years that I couldn't do the same on The European Tour. It was a joke, obviously, but it definitely inspired me and I am proud that I managed to prove them wrong.

"It helped me to be partnered the last day with Alex, who was also at Oklahoma State and played with me in my freshman year, and Ross who is also a good friend. It might have been different if I'd been with big name players I watch on television.

"University golf helped me. It is really the same pressure when I play in college. I was in a play-off to win a team event in the Nationals last year and all my team-mates and families were watching. I was thinking if I miss this putt they are going to kill me!"

A final round 67 saw Frenchman Raphaël Jacquelin take second place, one shot adrift of Martin, and also take delivery of the €208,330 (£141,157) winner's cheque, as the young Spaniard left with the title only. There were no complaints from Martin, however, who announced he would not turn professional immediately, instead preferring to honour his commitments to his college.

"I will definitely play for the rest of the term there," he said. "They have done so much for me and I want to pay them back. I plan to turn professional in the summer."

The Estoril Open de Portugal might have ended on April 1 but Pablo Martin and his old college pals were certainly not kidding around at Quinta da Marinha Oitavos Golfe. They served up some seriously exciting golf which bodes well for the future of The European Tour.

Gordon Richardson

Graeme Storm

The Course

Designed by American Arthur Hills, the routing is a continuous loop of holes; nine out and nine in, similar to many links layouts in Scotland. Spectacular views of the nearby Sintra Mountains and the distant Atlantic Ocean augment a course described by Ireland's Paul McGinley as having the potential to be the best in Europe.

Sven Strüver

Duarte Nobre Guedes (left), President of the Estoril Tourism Board, presents the trophy to Pablo Martin

Paul Broadhurst

> This golf course has magnificent potential. I am designing a golf course at the moment so I am watching golf courses very closely now, and I think that this course has the potential to be the best course in Europe - that's how much potential I think it has.
> **Paul McGinley**

Quinta da Marinha Oitavos Golfe
Par **71**   Yards **6893**   Metres **6303**

Final Results

Pos	Name		Rd1	Rd2	Rd3	Rd4	Total		€	£
1	Pablo MARTIN (AM)	ESP	73	70	66	68	277	-7		
2	Raphaël JACQUELIN	FRA	70	69	72	67	278	-6	208,330.00	141,157.42
3	Charl SCHWARTZEL	RSA	74	71	67	69	281	-3	83,157.50	56,344.73
	Martin KAYMER	GER	72	69	73	67	281	-3	83,157.50	56,344.73
	Graeme STORM	ENG	72	67	70	72	281	-3	83,157.50	56,344.73
	David GRIFFITHS	ENG	76	69	68	68	281	-3	83,157.50	56,344.73
7	Alastair FORSYTH	SCO	73	69	69	71	282	-2	35,125.00	23,799.52
	Michael JONZON	SWE	71	71	69	71	282	-2	35,125.00	23,799.52
	Sven STRÜVER	GER	70	70	72	70	282	-2	35,125.00	23,799.52
	Andrew OLDCORN	SCO	76	69	66	71	282	-2	35,125.00	23,799.52
11	Mark FOSTER	ENG	77	67	70	69	283	-1	21,187.50	14,355.94
	Peter LAWRIE	IRL	73	70	71	69	283	-1	21,187.50	14,355.94
	Stephen GALLACHER	SCO	68	71	73	71	283	-1	21,187.50	14,355.94
	Tom WHITEHOUSE	ENG	74	71	68	70	283	-1	21,187.50	14,355.94
	Alejandro CAÑIZARES	ESP	71	72	71	69	283	-1	21,187.50	14,355.94
	Alexander NOREN	SWE	71	68	68	76	283	-1	21,187.50	14,355.94
17	Lee S JAMES	ENG	73	71	70	70	284	0	16,531.25	11,201.02
	Luis CLAVERIE	ESP	72	68	73	71	284	0	16,531.25	11,201.02
	Gary ORR	SCO	70	73	73	68	284	0	16,531.25	11,201.02
	Ross McGOWAN	ENG	68	68	72	76	284	0	16,531.25	11,201.02
21	Jamie SPENCE	ENG	72	73	66	74	285	1	14,343.75	9,718.84
	Pelle EDBERG	SWE	71	71	72	71	285	1	14,343.75	9,718.84
	Simon DYSON	ENG	67	74	73	71	285	1	14,343.75	9,718.84
	Nick DOUGHERTY	ENG	69	69	75	72	285	1	14,343.75	9,718.84
25	Fredrik ANDERSSON HED	SWE	76	68	74	68	286	2	11,875.00	8,046.10
	Benn BARHAM	ENG	72	67	77	70	286	2	11,875.00	8,046.10
	Euan LITTLE	SCO	72	69	72	73	286	2	11,875.00	8,046.10
	Søren KJELDSEN	DEN	72	73	72	69	286	2	11,875.00	8,046.10
	Paul LAWRIE	SCO	72	72	67	75	286	2	11,875.00	8,046.10
	Van PHILLIPS	ENG	75	70	72	69	286	2	11,875.00	8,046.10
	Simon KHAN	ENG	73	68	76	69	286	2	11,875.00	8,046.10
	Emanuele CANONICA	ITA	73	70	71	72	286	2	11,875.00	8,046.10
	Paul MCGINLEY	IRL	76	70	70	70	286	2	11,875.00	8,046.10
34	Grégory HAVRET	FRA	72	74	68	73	287	3	8,510.42	5,766.37
	Sam LITTLE	ENG	72	73	70	72	287	3	8,510.42	5,766.37
	Jesus Maria ARRUTI	ESP	75	71	69	72	287	3	8,510.42	5,766.37
	Carl SUNESON	ESP	74	71	73	69	287	3	8,510.42	5,766.37
	Alessandro TADINI	ITA	77	66	73	71	287	3	8,510.42	5,766.37
	Taichi TESHIMA	JPN	71	69	70	77	287	3	8,510.42	5,766.37
	Robert-Jan DERKSEN	NED	70	75	72	70	287	3	8,510.42	5,766.37
	Barry LANE	ENG	69	75	72	71	287	3	8,510.42	5,766.37
	Markus BRIER	AUT	75	71	68	73	287	3	8,510.42	5,766.37
	Henrik NYSTROM	SWE	76	69	74	68	287	3	8,510.42	5,766.37
	Daniel VANCSIK	ARG	72	72	75	68	287	3	8,510.42	5,766.37
	Oliver FISHER	ENG	73	71	73	70	287	3	8,510.42	5,766.37
46	Mads VIBE-HASTRUP	DEN	76	70	72	70	288	4	6,000.00	4,065.40
	Adrien MÖRK	FRA	73	73	72	70	288	4	6,000.00	4,065.40
	José Manuel LARA	ESP	72	71	73	72	288	4	6,000.00	4,065.40
	Santiago LUNA	ESP	73	71	70	74	288	4	6,000.00	4,065.40
	David BRANSDON	AUS	71	70	74	73	288	4	6,000.00	4,065.40
	Richard BLAND	ENG	71	69	75	73	288	4	6,000.00	4,065.40
	Francesco MOLINARI	ITA	72	71	73	72	288	4	6,000.00	4,065.40
	Ian GARBUTT	ENG	73	73	73	69	288	4	6,000.00	4,065.40
54	Søren HANSEN	DEN	73	72	67	77	289	5	4,178.57	2,831.26
	Paul BROADHURST	ENG	69	71	75	74	289	5	4,178.57	2,831.26
	Brian DAVIS	ENG	76	70	72	71	289	5	4,178.57	2,831.26
	Gary LOCKERBIE	ENG	71	73	73	72	289	5	4,178.57	2,831.26
	Steven O'HARA	SCO	73	73	75	68	289	5	4,178.57	2,831.26
	Tiago CRUZ	POR	70	76	71	72	289	5	4,178.57	2,831.26
	John BICKERTON	ENG	74	72	71	72	289	5	4,178.57	2,831.26
61	Edoardo MOLINARI	ITA	72	71	72	75	290	6	3,250.00	2,202.09
	Gonzalo FDEZ-CASTAÑO	ESP	70	71	73	76	290	6	3,250.00	2,202.09
	Johan AXGREN	SWE	71	74	72	73	290	6	3,250.00	2,202.09
	David LYNN	ENG	71	71	75	73	290	6	3,250.00	2,202.09
	Jonathan LOMAS	ENG	76	69	72	73	290	6	3,250.00	2,202.09
66	Scott DRUMMOND	SCO	75	69	72	75	291	7	2,812.50	1,905.66
	Hennie OTTO	RSA	73	71	74	73	291	7	2,812.50	1,905.66
68	José-Filipe LIMA	POR	75	71	77	69	292	8	2,625.00	1,778.61
69	Marcus HIGLEY	ENG	72	73	75	73	293	9	2,437.50	1,651.57
	Gary MURPHY	IRL	73	71	73	76	293	9	2,437.50	1,651.57
71	Mattias ELIASSON	SWE	74	70	73	77	294	10	2,082.50	1,411.03
	Gary EMERSON	ENG	72	72	74	76	294	10	2,082.50	1,411.03
73	Alvaro QUIROS	ESP	74	70	76	76	296	12	1,872.00	1,268.40

Total Prize Fund

€1,253,747 £849,496

Will and Defiance

1	Zach JOHNSON		289	1
2	Retief GOOSEN		291	3
	Rory SABBATINI		291	3
	Tiger WOODS		291	3
5	Jerry KELLY		292	4
	Justin ROSE		292	4
7	Stuart APPLEBY		293	5
	Padraig HARRINGTON		293	5
9	David TOMS		294	6
10	Paul CASEY		295	7
	Luke DONALD		295	7
	Vaughn TAYLOR		295	7

Major Championships not won by Tiger Woods or Phil Mickelson tend to bring out the worst in some sportswriters. It is almost like they take it personally, and look for a scapegoat. Usually it is the organisers who get the blame, with the finger pointed at the course set-up. Often it ends with one of the most patronising and awful sentences in the English language: the event got the champion it deserved.

Well, for the record, I have been lucky enough to attend over 80 Majors and there were only two where I thought the course set-up was unfair. Neither of them was the 2007 Masters Tournament, which drew way more than its fair share of criticism.

This was an event played in some of the coldest conditions seen at any Major, and that includes Open Championships. It was certainly the coldest ever Masters. An event that is often referred to as the sporting rite of spring produced the mind-boggling sight of players and spectators wearing ski hats. Third round day at Augusta National usually ends with the last group greeted by a 30 deep swell of spectators round the 18th green. On shivering Saturday, you could have picked your spot.

The weather, more than any sadistic leanings amongst the organising committee, contributed to the equal highest winning score in the tournament's history. Zach Johnson was the worthy winner who owned it at one over par 289.

It may be true that, when it comes to pure talent, Johnson would be taken to the cleaners by Tiger and Phil, but while the big hitters were finding too

many pines and dogwoods, Johnson was carrying out his masterplan from the fairway. While they were failing to take advantage of their power in being able to go for every par five in two, Johnson calmly pitched and putted his way to 11 birdies on the 16 long holes played during the tournament.

When it was over, Woods, true to character, did not look to blame the organisers. Indeed, he did not blame anyone bar himself. He looked back at finishing both his first and third rounds with successive bogeys, and admitted: "I blew it right there."

Johnson has one of those heartwarming stories that make every struggling professional stand a little taller when they hear it. For virtually all his twenties he persevered on the Hooters Tour in America, living off cheques that were in the low four figures rather than the seven digits of dollars he got for winning in Georgia. "I thought those were the best days of my life right there, eating chicken wings and everything," he said.

Now he gets to pick the menu for the Champions' Dinner at the 2008 Masters Tournament. He does so because he showed a singular quality, the ability to block out the Woods roar. On a compelling final

Luke Donald

Above David Howell

Left Four-time Masters Champion, Arnold Palmer, acknowledges spectator applause after hitting the ceremonial drive, alongside Augusta National Golf Club Chairman, Billy Payne

Retief Goosen

day when any number of players had their chance to win, Johnson was standing on the 16th tee when it came, a tidal wave of noise rushing from the 13th green that could only mean one thing: the World Number One had eagled, and was on his tail.

Johnson responded in a manner befitting a Masters Champion, a beautifully flighted six iron that pulled up 12 feet short of the flag from where he calmly rolled in the crucial birdie putt.

The great thing about Majors is that they do produce champions from left field on occasion. Champions like Larry Mize at the Masters 20 years ago, when he won a play-off against two of the titans of the age, Seve Ballesteros and Greg Norman. It is why you see the practice ground at every Major filled with people working all hours God sends in the hope of making it their turn.

Never mind slating an event because it is not won by Woods or Mickelson; let us celebrate the fact that the sport is not that predictable.

Mind you, perhaps it is just as well for Johnson's peace of mind that he was not pipped by South African Retief Goosen, who finished joint second with fellow countryman Rory Sabbatini and Woods.

It was Johnson's bogey-bogey-bogey finish on Friday that saw him tumble from the outright lead to allow Goosen into the field for the last two rounds under the rule which states that anyone within ten shots of pole position plays on. Leaders at halfway on two under par 142, two clear of Johnson, were Tim Clark and Brett Wetterich while Goosen languished, seemingly out of contention, on eight over par 152.

But the winner of two US Open Championships went on to underline all his shot making skills, somehow going round in 70 in Saturday's frigid conditions, before following the best score of the day in the third round with a joint best 69 on Sunday. It was a truly prodigious weekend effort.

So, too, was the performance of Englishman Justin Rose, who returned to Augusta National for the first time in three years, and finished tied fifth.

Out of the cold, these players emerged to show the will and defiance that is the hallmark of Major Champions. Looking at their efforts, it is perhaps worth reflecting that the 71st Masters Tournament did not get the press it deserved.

Derek Lawrenson
Daily Mail

Padraig Harrington

Over the course of 18 holes, you can see how far you've come, and how far the game can still take you.

United is proud to support The European Tour.

It's time to fly.®  **UNITED**

A STAR ALLIANCE MEMBER

www.unitedairlines.co.uk

European Tour Chief Executive George O'Grady addresses journalists from Europe and the United States and European Ryder Cup Captain Nick Faldo (seated to his right) at the International Media Dinner arranged by The European Tour and held at Augusta Country Club on the Tuesday night of Masters Tournament week

A happy young fan

Jack Nicklaus holds the record for most Green Jackets, having won the title on six occasions. Arnold Palmer and Tiger Woods have each won four, and Jimmy Demaret, Nick Faldo, Gary Player and Sam Snead have won three each.

Augusta National

Par **72**   Yards **7445**   Metres **6807**

Final Results

Pos	Name		Rd1	Rd2	Rd3	Rd4	Total		€	£
1	Zach JOHNSON	USA	71	73	76	69	289	1	975,770.04	662,941.30
2	Tiger WOODS	USA	73	74	72	72	291	3	404,763.62	274,997.70
	Retief GOOSEN	RSA	76	76	70	69	291	3	404,763.62	274,997.70
	Rory SABBATINI	RSA	73	76	73	69	291	3	404,763.62	274,997.70
5	Justin ROSE	ENG	69	75	75	73	292	4	205,995.90	139,954.28
	Jerry KELLY	USA	75	69	78	70	292	4	205,995.90	139,954.28
7	Stuart APPLEBY	AUS	75	70	73	75	293	5	174,825.09	118,776.73
	Padraig HARRINGTON	IRL	77	68	75	73	293	5	174,825.09	118,776.73
9	David TOMS	USA	70	78	74	72	294	6	157,207.40	106,807.21
10	Luke DONALD	ENG	73	74	75	73	295	7	135,523.62	92,075.18
	Vaughn TAYLOR	USA	71	72	77	75	295	7	135,523.62	92,075.18
	Paul CASEY	ENG	79	68	77	71	295	7	135,523.62	92,075.18
13	Tim CLARK	RSA	71	71	80	74	296	8	101,642.34	69,056.13
	Vijay SINGH	FIJ	73	71	79	73	296	8	101,642.34	69,056.13
	Jim FURYK	USA	75	71	76	74	296	8	101,642.34	69,056.13
	Ian POULTER	ENG	75	75	76	70	296	8	101,642.34	69,056.13
17	Stewart CINK	USA	77	75	75	70	297	9	81,314.17	55,245.11
	Henrik STENSON	SWE	72	76	77	72	297	9	81,314.17	55,245.11
	Tom PERNICE Jnr	USA	75	72	79	71	297	9	81,314.17	55,245.11
20	John ROLLINS	USA	77	74	76	71	298	10	63,153.63	42,906.78
	Lucas GLOVER	USA	74	71	79	74	298	10	63,153.63	42,906.78
	Mark CALCAVECCHIA	USA	76	71	78	73	298	10	63,153.63	42,906.78
	Mike WEIR	CAN	75	72	80	71	298	10	63,153.63	42,906.78
24	Geoff OGILVY	AUS	75	70	81	73	299	11	47,704.31	32,410.46
	Stephen AMES	CAN	76	74	77	72	299	11	47,704.31	32,410.46
	Phil MICKELSON	USA	76	73	73	77	299	11	47,704.31	32,410.46
27	Adam SCOTT	AUS	74	78	76	72	300	12	40,114.99	27,254.25
	Davis LOVE III	USA	72	77	77	74	300	12	40,114.99	27,254.25
	K J CHOI	KOR	75	75	74	76	300	12	40,114.99	27,254.25
30	Fred COUPLES	USA	76	76	78	71	301	13	32,215.37	21,887.22
	Scott VERPLANK	USA	73	77	76	75	301	13	32,215.37	21,887.22
	Dean WILSON	USA	75	72	76	78	301	13	32,215.37	21,887.22
	Robert KARLSSON	SWE	77	73	79	72	301	13	32,215.37	21,887.22
	Lee WESTWOOD	ENG	79	73	72	77	301	13	32,215.37	21,887.22
	Y E YANG	KOR	75	74	78	74	301	13	32,215.37	21,887.22
	Charles HOWELL III	USA	75	77	75	74	301	13	32,215.37	21,887.22
37	Brett WETTERICH	USA	69	73	83	77	302	14	23,852.16	16,205.23
	J J HENRY	USA	71	78	77	76	302	14	23,852.16	16,205.23
	Angel CABRERA	ARG	77	75	79	71	302	14	23,852.16	16,205.23
	Tim HERRON	USA	72	75	83	72	302	14	23,852.16	16,205.23
	Rodney PAMPLING	AUS	77	75	74	76	302	14	23,852.16	16,205.23
	Jeev Milkha SINGH	IND	72	75	76	79	302	14	23,852.16	16,205.23
43	Sandy LYLE	SCO	79	73	80	71	303	15	20,057.50	13,627.13
44	David HOWELL	ENG	70	75	82	77	304	16	16,848.30	11,446.79
	José María OLAZÁBAL	ESP	74	75	78	77	304	16	16,848.30	11,446.79
	Bradley DREDGE	WAL	75	70	76	83	304	16	16,848.30	11,446.79
	Miguel Angel JIMÉNEZ	ESP	79	73	76	76	304	16	16,848.30	11,446.79
	Shingo KATAYAMA	JPN	79	72	80	73	304	16	16,848.30	11,446.79
49	Craig STADLER	USA	74	73	79	79	305	17	13,877.62	9,428.50
	Jeff SLUMAN	USA	76	75	79	75	305	17	13,877.62	9,428.50
51	Brett QUIGLEY	USA	76	76	79	75	306	18	13,335.52	9,060.20
52	Carl PETTERSSON	SWE	76	76	79	76	307	19	12,901.85	8,765.56
	Aaron BADDELEY	AUS	79	72	76	80	307	19	12,901.85	8,765.56
54	Rich BEEM	USA	71	81	75	81	308	20	12,576.59	8,544.58
55	Niclas FASTH	SWE	77	75	77	80	309	21	12,359.75	8,397.26
	Ben CRENSHAW	USA	76	74	84	75	309	21	12,359.75	8,397.26
	Trevor IMMELMAN	RSA	74	77	81	77	309	21	12,359.75	8,397.26
58	Arron OBERHOLSER	USA	74	76	84	76	310	22	12,142.92	8,249.94
59	Billy MAYFAIR	USA	76	75	83	77	311	23	12,034.50	8,176.28
60	Fuzzy ZOELLER	USA	74	78	79	82	313	25	11,926.08	8,102.62

Total Prize Fund

€5,423,535   £3,684,767

The Course

The first year since, in 2001, Tom Fazio made the alterations to the original Bobby Jones and Dr Alister MacKenzie design, that the course had been dry for the week and the fast running greens proved the ultimate test for the world's best. Proof of that was the winning score of one over par 289 which equals the highest in the tournament's history.

Momentous Journey

			TOTAL	
1	Markus BRIER		274	-10
2	Scott HEND		279	-5
	Graeme McDOWELL		279	-5
	Andrew McLARDY		279	-5
5	Richard STERNE		280	-4
6	Raphaël JACQUELIN		281	-3
	Peter O'MALLEY		281	-3
8	Jean-François LUCQUIN		282	-2
	Prayad MARKSAENG		282	-2
10	David GRIFFITHS		283	-1

Twenty years ago in the world of entertainment, Madonna was celebrating her fourth number one record in the UK singles charts with La Isla Bonita, The Simpsons television franchise began in the United States and Oliver Stone's Vietnam war epic Platoon was claiming top honours in the Oscars.

Andrew McLardy

Graeme McDowell

In the world of sport, France won rugby union's Grand Slam in the Five Nations, Pat Cash undertook his memorable climb up the Wimbledon stands to celebrate claiming the Men's Singles title and FC Porto won football's European Cup in Vienna.

In golf, meanwhile, Europe's Big Five of Seve Ballesteros, Nick Faldo, Bernhard Langer, Sandy Lyle and Ian Woosnam were in their prime, blazing a trail across the world stage. Faldo would, of course, in July of that year, win his first Open Championship at Muirfield while in September Europe retained The Ryder Cup at Muirfield Village and in so doing won on American soil for the first time.

Elsewhere, simultaneously, two men were setting out on golfing adventures of their own that would lead both, inexorably, to the Volvo China Open two decades on.

The first was Mel Pyatt, President and CEO of Volvo Event Management, who, in 1987, guided the Swedish car company into golf. Volvo was embarking on a long and passionate association with the sport which began when it became the first and only corporate sponsor of The European Tour the following year. By the start of the 2007 season, Volvo had sponsored 43 events during which players had competed for an astounding €66,283,251 in prize money.

While all this was going on, a promising young amateur golfer in Austria was leaving school. Markus Brier was his name and he was taking the first tentative steps towards becoming one of his nation's top sportsmen.

Golf has always been a minority sport in a country more widely renowned for its skiers but even as a teenager Brier was recognised as a sportsman of special ability. All young Austrian men have to undertake Military Service but the 18 year old Brier was earmarked as a talent to be nurtured and his time in the army was spent under a sports scholarship. He went through basic training but essentially dedicated his time to playing golf as he laid the foundations for his future career.

Move the clock forward 20 years to China where two significant events unfolded at the Shanghai Silport Golf Club.

The first involved Pyatt. In 1995, he took Volvo into the world's most populous country, launching the Volvo China Tour and also the national Open of China, under Volvo's sponsorship. It was a huge step for golf in China and in the 2005 season the Volvo China Open received global recognition when it became part of The European Tour International Schedule for the first time. Then, during the 2007 event, Pyatt announced he would be retiring as President and CEO of Volvo Event Management at the end of the year. For the Englishman, it marked the end of a momentous journey.

On the course, Brier was about to make his own mark as he marched towards the title. Over the first two days it looked as if Frenchman Raphaël Jacquelin would lift the trophy as he continued a fine run of form which saw him finish second in the Estoril Open de Portugal two weeks earlier but, after opening with rounds of 68 and 67 to lead by two shots from Australian Adam Blyth at the halfway stage, he faded over the weekend and eventually finished joint sixth.

Instead, Brier stepped up to the plate, moving into pole position on Saturday with a fine round of 67. He quickly stamped his authority in the final round with two birdies in the first three holes and never looked back, closing with another excellent 67 for a ten under par total of 274 and a five shot winning margin over Australia's Scott Hend, Northern Ireland's Graeme McDowell and Andrew McLardy of South Africa.

The victory was not his first because in 2006 he had become the first Austrian to win on The European Tour when he captured the BA-CA Golf Open, presented by Telekom Austria, over his home course at Fontana Golf Club near Vienna.

There, of course, he enjoyed considerable support; in China he earned the respect of a different audience and, importantly, gained for Austria a stronger foothold on the global golfing map. Most certainly his achievement was recognised back home where his victory earned immediate congratulations from the Austrian Prime Minister Wolfgang Schüssel and placed him on the front pages of the country's newspapers as well as the back.

Twenty years earlier, Brier and Pyatt set out on separate paths on great adventures. Where these paths were to lead no-one could have known, but at the Volvo China Open they came together and their respective legacies, be it in Europe or the Far East, are sure to be felt long after the next two decades have passed.

Roddy Williams

Jean-François Lucquin

Scott Hend

Peter O'Malley

Markus Brier (left) is presented with the trophy by Mel Pyatt, President & CEO of Volvo Event Management

Peter Lawrie

> Winning here makes me feel like I am now a better player, as I had home advantage when I won in Austria last year. This is a big step for me to prove that I can also win abroad.
> **Markus Brier**

The Course

Lengthened for this year's tournament from the original Bobby Martin design of 1995 and featuring abundant water hazards and new bunkers, the Shanghai Silport course provided a stern test for the assembled field. A unique feature of the course is the 40 ancient Chinese stone statues dotted around the 18 holes, said to bring the venue good fortune.

Shanghai Silport Golf Club

Par **71**   Yards **6792**   Metres **6209**

Final Results

Pos	Name		Rd1	Rd2	Rd3	Rd4	Total		€	£
1	Markus BRIER	AUT	72	68	67	67	274	-10	249,124.95	169,590.43
2	Scott HEND	AUS	71	67	70	71	279	-5	111,464.60	75,878.91
	Graeme MCDOWELL	NIR	70	70	70	69	279	-5	111,464.60	75,878.91
	Andrew MCLARDY	RSA	72	70	67	70	279	-5	111,464.60	75,878.91
5	Richard STERNE	RSA	70	71	69	70	280	-4	63,378.02	43,144.24
6	Peter O'MALLEY	AUS	74	71	67	69	281	-3	48,579.85	33,070.46
	Raphaël JACQUELIN	FRA	68	67	75	71	281	-3	48,579.85	33,070.46
8	Jean-François LUCQUIN	FRA	73	68	71	70	282	-2	35,425.92	24,116.00
	Prayad MARKSAENG	THA	71	74	72	65	282	-2	35,425.92	24,116.00
10	David GRIFFITHS	ENG	72	71	69	71	283	-1	29,895.29	20,351.05
11	Miles TUNNICLIFF	ENG	73	74	71	66	284	0	25,759.78	17,535.83
	Brett RUMFORD	AUS	72	72	70	70	284	0	25,759.78	17,535.83
	James KINGSTON	RSA	71	72	70	71	284	0	25,759.78	17,535.83
14	Steven JEPPESEN	SWE	72	74	76	63	285	1	21,076.18	14,347.49
	Peter HANSON	SWE	72	72	70	71	285	1	21,076.18	14,347.49
	Robert-Jan DERKSEN	NED	70	72	71	72	285	1	21,076.18	14,347.49
	Unho PARK	AUS	70	74	72	69	285	1	21,076.18	14,347.49
	Garry HOUSTON	WAL	71	73	70	71	285	1	21,076.18	14,347.49
19	Scott STRANGE	AUS	74	68	73	71	286	2	17,937.18	12,210.63
	Simon WAKEFIELD	ENG	75	69	77	65	286	2	17,937.18	12,210.63
	Simon YATES	SCO	73	66	77	70	286	2	17,937.18	12,210.63
22	Grégory HAVRET	FRA	73	71	74	69	287	3	16,890.84	11,498.35
23	Mikko ILONEN	FIN	73	73	74	68	288	4	14,872.91	10,124.65
	Graeme STORM	ENG	73	74	70	71	288	4	14,872.91	10,124.65
	Terry PILKADARIS	AUS	74	70	72	72	288	4	14,872.91	10,124.65
	Andres ROMERO	ARG	71	67	73	77	288	4	14,872.91	10,124.65
	Tony CAROLAN	AUS	75	72	69	72	288	4	14,872.91	10,124.65
	Gonzalo FDEZ-CASTAÑO	ESP	71	72	71	74	288	4	14,872.91	10,124.65
	Jarmo SANDELIN	SWE	75	71	73	69	288	4	14,872.91	10,124.65
	Prom MEESAWAT	THA	72	74	68	74	288	4	14,872.91	10,124.65
31	Christopher HANELL	SWE	70	70	76	73	289	5	11,472.32	7,809.72
	Michael JONZON	SWE	70	72	71	76	289	5	11,472.32	7,809.72
	Stephen GALLACHER	SCO	73	72	70	74	289	5	11,472.32	7,809.72
	Wen-chong LIANG	CHN	76	71	73	69	289	5	11,472.32	7,809.72
	Lian-wei ZHANG	CHN	76	69	70	74	289	5	11,472.32	7,809.72
	Ter-chang WANG	TPE	73	73	71	72	289	5	11,472.32	7,809.72
	Benn BARHAM	ENG	74	71	75	69	289	5	11,472.32	7,809.72
	Yasin ALI	ENG	70	75	74	70	289	5	11,472.32	7,809.72
39	Peter LAWRIE	IRL	72	71	70	77	290	6	9,417.02	6,410.58
	Damien MCGRANE	IRL	71	69	76	74	290	6	9,417.02	6,410.58
	Gary MURPHY	IRL	74	69	73	74	290	6	9,417.02	6,410.58
	Adam BLYTH	AUS	70	67	76	77	290	6	9,417.02	6,410.58
	Thammanoon SRIROT	THA	73	72	76	69	290	6	9,417.02	6,410.58
44	Thongchai JAIDEE	THA	71	74	71	75	291	7	7,623.30	5,189.52
	Stephen DODD	WAL	74	67	74	76	291	7	7,623.30	5,189.52
	Bryan SALTUS	USA	74	71	72	74	291	7	7,623.30	5,189.52
	Marcus FRASER	AUS	75	72	77	67	291	7	7,623.30	5,189.52
	Thomas BJÖRN	DEN	70	72	73	76	291	7	7,623.30	5,189.52
	Søren HANSEN	DEN	74	72	76	69	291	7	7,623.30	5,189.52
	Gary EMERSON	ENG	72	70	79	70	291	7	7,623.30	5,189.52
51	Søren KJELDSEN	DEN	72	73	76	71	292	8	5,979.06	4,070.21
	Adam GROOM	AUS	73	72	74	73	292	8	5,979.06	4,070.21
	Marcus BOTH	AUS	74	73	73	72	292	8	5,979.06	4,070.21
	Chapchai NIRAT	THA	74	72	74	72	292	8	5,979.06	4,070.21
55	Gaurav GHEI	IND	73	73	76	71	293	9	5,231.68	3,561.43
56	Andrew BUTTERFIELD	ENG	77	70	75	72	294	10	4,434.47	3,018.74
	Maarten LAFEBER	NED	71	75	76	72	294	10	4,434.47	3,018.74
	Richard LEE	NZL	70	71	81	72	294	10	4,434.47	3,018.74
	Mahal PEARCE	NZL	73	72	71	78	294	10	4,434.47	3,018.74
	Joakim BÄCKSTRÖM	SWE	74	70	74	76	294	10	4,434.47	3,018.74
	Edward LOAR	USA	71	74	77	72	294	10	4,434.47	3,018.74
62	Gary RUSNAK	USA	69	76	76	74	295	11	3,512.70	2,391.25
	Kang-chun WU	CHN	75	71	79	70	295	11	3,512.70	2,391.25
	Ming-jie HUANG	CHN	68	76	72	79	295	11	3,512.70	2,391.25
	Gui-ming LIAO	CHN	74	71	77	73	295	11	3,512.70	2,391.25
	Zhi-feng QIU	CHN	70	75	80	70	295	11	3,512.70	2,391.25
	Wen-tang LIN	TPE	73	74	75	73	295	11	3,512.70	2,391.25
68	Kane WEBBER	AUS	72	73	74	77	296	12	2,914.79	1,984.23
	Gareth DAVIES	ENG	74	73	76	73	296	12	2,914.79	1,984.23
70	Mark PILKINGTON	WAL	72	75	74	76	297	13	2,727.95	1,857.03
71	Tom WHITEHOUSE	ENG	73	72	75	78	298	14	2,240.50	1,525.21
	Chris RODGERS	ENG	75	71	77	75	298	14	2,240.50	1,525.21
73	Ren HAN (AM)	CHN	74	72	80	73	299	15		
	José-Filipe LIMA	POR	77	69	71	82	299	15	2,236.00	1,522.14
75	Shiv KAPUR	IND	72	73	W/D		145	3		

Total Prize Fund

€1,501,482 £1,022,125

Actions Not Words

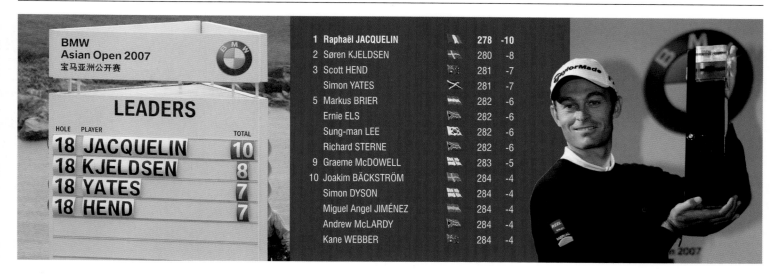

			Total	
1	Raphaël JACQUELIN		278	-10
2	Søren KJELDSEN		280	-8
3	Scott HEND		281	-7
	Simon YATES		281	-7
5	Markus BRIER		282	-6
	Ernie ELS		282	-6
	Sung-man LEE		282	-6
	Richard STERNE		282	-6
9	Graeme McDOWELL		283	-5
10	Joakim BÄCKSTRÖM		284	-4
	Simon DYSON		284	-4
	Miguel Angel JIMÉNEZ		284	-4
	Andrew McLARDY		284	-4
	Kane WEBBER		284	-4

L eading a tournament from the front is, arguably, one of the toughest tests in golf. Over the years, even great champions have succumbed in the heat of battle, illustrating perfectly not only the immense pressure that comes with attempting to win, but also proving that they are mere mortals after all.

Søren Kjeldsen

The legendary Arnold Palmer uncharacteristically threw away a seven shot lead on the back nine of the US Open Championship in 1966; Greg Norman suffered at the Masters Tournament in 1996 and, of course, there was Jean Van de Velde's infamous collapse at The 1999 Open Championship – all well documented in the annals of golfing folklore.

So when Raphaël Jacquelin failed to finish the job at The European Tour's previous stop – the Volvo China Open at Shanghai Silport Golf Club – after he led at the halfway stage, the amiable Frenchman was asked point-blank by a Chinese journalist during the BMW Asian Open at nearby Tomson Shanghai Pudong Golf Club if he could hold on to his first round lead this time.

If the player in question had been one of the more combustible members of The European Tour the reporter might have received short shrift, but a patient Jacquelin simply put on a wry smile and said: "The only win I've had up to now was in Madrid two years ago and I had the lead for three days in a row there. I'm going to keep that in my mind this week."

It was a masterstroke of a response and Jacquelin kept that happy thought with him all week as he claimed a second career title with a wire-to-wire victory.

The triumph was, in many ways, a perfect reward for the Frenchman who had claimed lesser prizes in previous BMW tournaments. Once, he won a home stereo system for carding the day's low round and has a sporty BMW Z8 parked in his garage after a hole in one.

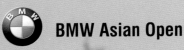

Simon Dyson

Joakim Bäckström

However, after completing a winning ten under par total of 278, BMW Consultant Marco Kaussler was delighted to congratulate Jacquelin on finally landing the big one.

"It is a fantastic moment," said the Frenchman. "It is tough to take the lead in the first round and keep it to the last. When you are in a position to win it is always difficult to finish off, but to be a winner you have to finish off. I am really happy."

While the victor had been in sparkling form prior to the start of the tournament, the attention at the beginning of the week had centred on three time Major Champion Ernie Els, who enjoyed a record breaking 13 shot victory in this tournament in 2005.

The South African's arrival in Shanghai, however, was not quite as he had planned as the Monday finish of the Verizon Heritage tournament on the US PGA Tour necessitated a late departure from South Carolina. Without the luxury of a practice round, Els was always playing catch-up after opening with a pair of 71s.

Meanwhile Jacquelin kept daylight between himself and his rivals. Not that this was ever going to be an easy affair. In Madrid he had opened with three successive 64s for a seven shot lead; in Shanghai with one round to go he was just one ahead of Australian Scott Hend, two in front of Sweden's Joakim Bäckström, Denmark's Søren Kjeldsen and Thai-based Scotsman Simon Yates with those only three back including Colin Montgomerie.

Jacquelin, however, streaked clear of the pack with an outward half of 33 on Sunday then held on as conditions turned for the worse with high winds and heavy rain buffeting the players.

As if he was not soaked enough, by the conclusion Jacquelin was showered in champagne by his compatriots on the 18th green. It had been a vintage week for the Frenchman and he had given that Chinese journalist another response only this time with his actions rather than words.

Chuah Choo Chiang
Asian Tour

Ernie Els

The Course

Course designer Shunsuke Kato, who is also the Chairman of the Japan Golf Association, succeeded in his design of combining the ancient, traditional and modern characteristics of golf courses from both the United Kingdom and the United States. Wind is always a factor around the fairways and greens and adds an extra dimension to the test.

Raphaël Jacquelin is presented with the winners trophy by Dr Christoph Stark, President & CEO of BMW Group Region China

Colin Montgomerie

i History was made at the 2004 BMW Asian Open which took place at the Tomson Shanghai Pudong Golf Club. This marked the first time a European Tour event was staged on mainland China. The 2007 BMW Asian Open was the 14th European Tour event played on Chinese soil.

Tomson Shanghai Pudong Golf Club
Par **72**   Yards **7326**   Metres **6698**

Final Results

Pos	Name		Rd1	Rd2	Rd3	Rd4	Total		€	£
1	Raphaël JACQUELIN	FRA	66	69	70	73	278	-10	283,570.25	193,317.87
2	Søren KJELDSEN	DEN	67	72	68	73	280	-8	189,044.37	128,876.90
3	Scott HEND	AUS	69	70	67	75	281	-7	95,790.87	65,303.35
	Simon YATES	SCO	74	69	64	74	281	-7	95,790.87	65,303.35
5	Ernie ELS	RSA	71	71	68	72	282	-6	56,317.54	38,393.26
	Richard STERNE	RSA	70	74	69	69	282	-6	56,317.54	38,393.26
	Markus BRIER	AUT	71	69	68	74	282	-6	56,317.54	38,393.26
	Sung-man LEE	KOR	68	70	71	73	282	-6	56,317.54	38,393.26
9	Graeme MCDOWELL	NIR	73	70	69	71	283	-5	38,112.17	25,982.15
10	Andrew MCLARDY	RSA	72	70	67	75	284	-4	29,604.99	20,182.56
	Miguel Angel JIMÉNEZ	ESP	70	69	72	73	284	-4	29,604.99	20,182.56
	Joakim BÄCKSTRÖM	SWE	70	69	68	77	284	-4	29,604.99	20,182.56
	Simon DYSON	ENG	70	70	70	74	284	-4	29,604.99	20,182.56
	Kane WEBBER	AUS	71	73	69	71	284	-4	29,604.99	20,182.56
15	Scott BARR	AUS	71	70	72	72	285	-3	23,479.82	16,006.86
	Peter O'MALLEY	AUS	73	72	68	72	285	-3	23,479.82	16,006.86
	Colin MONTGOMERIE	SCO	70	69	69	77	285	-3	23,479.82	16,006.86
	Retief GOOSEN	RSA	71	74	69	71	285	-3	23,479.82	16,006.86
19	James KINGSTON	RSA	74	71	71	70	286	-2	19,299.15	13,156.78
	Prayad MARKSAENG	THA	72	69	70	75	286	-2	19,299.15	13,156.78
	Adam BLYTH	AUS	71	73	67	75	286	-2	19,299.15	13,156.78
	Tony CAROLAN	AUS	69	74	69	74	286	-2	19,299.15	13,156.78
	David BRANSDON	AUS	76	68	68	74	286	-2	19,299.15	13,156.78
	Søren HANSEN	DEN	71	70	67	78	286	-2	19,299.15	13,156.78
	Jason KNUTZON	USA	75	70	70	71	286	-2	19,299.15	13,156.78
26	Garry HOUSTON	WAL	71	72	72	72	287	-1	15,653.21	10,671.24
	Matthew MILLAR	AUS	73	70	71	73	287	-1	15,653.21	10,671.24
	David GRIFFITHS	ENG	73	69	73	72	287	-1	15,653.21	10,671.24
	Damien MCGRANE	IRL	70	73	69	75	287	-1	15,653.21	10,671.24
	Christian CÉVAÉR	FRA	71	70	69	77	287	-1	15,653.21	10,671.24
	Peter HANSON	SWE	69	71	74	73	287	-1	15,653.21	10,671.24
	Robert-Jan DERKSEN	NED	74	72	69	72	287	-1	15,653.21	10,671.24
33	Christian L NILSSON	SWE	71	73	73	71	288	0	12,973.45	8,844.37
	Grégory HAVRET	FRA	68	75	72	73	288	0	12,973.45	8,844.37
	Shaun P WEBSTER	ENG	72	74	70	72	288	0	12,973.45	8,844.37
	Andres ROMERO	ARG	75	70	66	77	288	0	12,973.45	8,844.37
37	Brett RUMFORD	AUS	75	69	75	70	289	1	11,229.48	7,655.45
	Jarmo SANDELIN	SWE	73	70	75	71	289	1	11,229.48	7,655.45
	Frankie MINOZA	PHI	75	71	70	73	289	1	11,229.48	7,655.45
	Wen-chong LIANG	CHN	72	74	69	74	289	1	11,229.48	7,655.45
	Keith HORNE	RSA	73	69	70	77	289	1	11,229.48	7,655.45
	Mark PILKINGTON	WAL	71	72	70	76	289	1	11,229.48	7,655.45
43	Kyron SULLIVAN	WAL	75	66	72	77	290	2	9,868.33	6,727.52
	Simon WAKEFIELD	ENG	72	70	72	76	290	2	9,868.33	6,727.52
45	Jean-François LUCQUIN	FRA	71	74	71	75	291	3	8,847.47	6,031.57
	Ricardo GONZALEZ	ARG	72	73	72	74	291	3	8,847.47	6,031.57
	Adam LE VESCONTE	AUS	72	71	72	76	291	3	8,847.47	6,031.57
	Mardan MAMAT	SIN	72	73	73	73	291	3	8,847.47	6,031.57
49	Juvic PAGUNSAN	PHI	73	71	75	73	292	4	7,826.61	5,335.62
	Marcel SIEM	GER	72	69	75	76	292	4	7,826.61	5,335.62
51	Gary MURPHY	IRL	74	72	66	81	293	5	6,805.75	4,639.67
	Yasin ALI	ENG	74	72	71	76	293	5	6,805.75	4,639.67
	Keng-chi LIN	TPE	73	71	72	77	293	5	6,805.75	4,639.67
	Gonzalo FDEZ-CASTAÑO	ESP	73	72	77	71	293	5	6,805.75	4,639.67
55	Stephen GALLACHER	SCO	72	73	74	75	294	6	5,614.74	3,827.73
	Edward MICHAELS	USA	74	72	71	77	294	6	5,614.74	3,827.73
	Edward LOAR	USA	70	75	74	75	294	6	5,614.74	3,827.73
58	Marcus BOTH	AUS	71	74	74	76	295	7	4,934.17	3,363.76
	Peter LAWRIE	IRL	75	71	72	77	295	7	4,934.17	3,363.76
	Gaurav GHEI	IND	75	70	73	77	295	7	4,934.17	3,363.76
61	Chris RODGERS	ENG	73	71	75	77	296	8	4,423.73	3,015.79
	Wen-tang LIN	TPE	73	73	73	77	296	8	4,423.73	3,015.79
	Thaworn WIRATCHANT	THA	72	73	74	77	296	8	4,423.73	3,015.79
64	Gavin FLINT	AUS	68	73	76	80	297	9	4,083.45	2,783.80
65	Simon HURD	ENG	74	72	74	78	298	10	3,743.16	2,551.82
	Sven STRÜVER	GER	72	72	75	79	298	10	3,743.16	2,551.82
	Jun-won PARK	KOR	69	77	72	80	298	10	3,743.16	2,551.82
68	Wen-hong LIN	TPE	69	76	72	83	300	12	3,402.87	2,319.83
69	Lian-wei ZHANG	CHN	73	73	78	77	301	13	3,232.73	2,203.84
70	Paul CASEY	ENG	72	71	77	WD	220			

Total Prize Fund
€1,698,329 £1,157,799

Youth and Experience

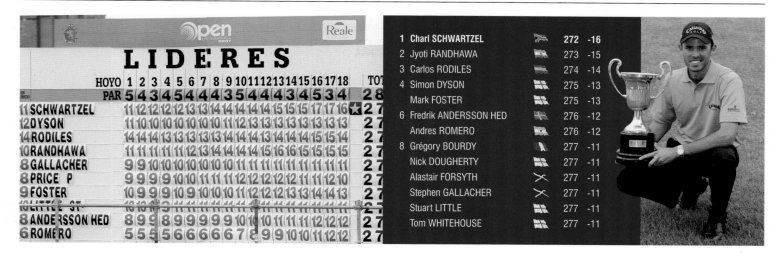

LIDERES

HOYO	1	2	3	4	5	6	7	8	9	10	11	12	13	14	15	16	17	18	TOT
PAR	5	4	3	4	5	4	4	4	3	5	4	4	4	3	4	5	3	4	28
11 SCHWARTZEL	11	12	12	12	12	13	14	14	14	14	15	15	15	17	17	16	★		27
12 DYSON	11	10	10	10	10	10	10	10	11	12	13	13	13	13	13	13	13		27
14 RODILES	14	14	14	13	13	13	13	14	14	14	14	14	14	15	15	14			27
10 RANDHAWA	11	11	11	11	11	12	13	14	14	14	15	16	16	15	15	15			27
8 GALLACHER	9	9	10	10	10	10	10	10	11	11	11	11	11	11	11	11			27
8 PRICE P	9	9	9	9	10	10	11	11	11	12	12	12	12	11	11	12	10		27
9 FOSTER	10	9	9	9	10	9	10	10	10	11	12	12	13	13	14	14	13		27
10 LITTLE ST	10	10	10	9	11	11	11	11	11	11	11	11	11	11					27
8 ANDERSSON HED	8	9	9	8	9	9	9	9	9	10	10	11	11	11	12	12			27
6 ROMERO	5	5	5	5	6	6	6	6	7	8	9	9	10	10	11	12	12		27

1	Charl SCHWARTZEL		272	-16
2	Jyoti RANDHAWA		273	-15
3	Carlos RODILES		274	-14
4	Simon DYSON		275	-13
	Mark FOSTER		275	-13
6	Fredrik ANDERSSON HED		276	-12
	Andres ROMERO		276	-12
8	Grégory BOURDY		277	-11
	Nick DOUGHERTY		277	-11
	Alastair FORSYTH		277	-11
	Stephen GALLACHER		277	-11
	Stuart LITTLE		277	-11
	Tom WHITEHOUSE		277	-11

T he Open de España is one of The European Tour's oldest tournaments, first contested in 1912 at the Polo Golf Club in Madrid. Among its illustrious list of champions is the youngest winner in Tour history, South Africa's Dale Hayes, who took the title in 1971 at El Prat at the tender age of 18 years and 290 days.

Jyoti Randhawa

Fredrik Andersson Hed

For the 81st staging of the prestigious event the nation's capital was back as host, specifically the new Centro Nacional de Golf course, opened by King Juan Carlos a year earlier, and now the headquarters of the Real Federación Española de Golf.

Once again an up and coming South African was to lift the trophy, 22 year old Charl Schwartzel this time proving that there are exceptions to George Bernard Shaw's famous words that "youth is wasted on the young."

When he was only 17 Schwartzel finished tied 15th in the South African Open and later, in 2002, he became the then third youngest player to earn a European Tour card through the Qualifying School. Since then he has twice played well enough to finish Number One on the Sunshine Tour Order of Merit and he achieved his first European Tour victory at the 2005 Dunhill Championship in his home country.

Into the top 100 on the Official World Golf Ranking thanks to three second place finishes during the 2006 season; now came the chance to climb to a career high of 40th and he was not about to squander it.

If you cannot have an old head on young shoulders, then surely the next best thing is an experienced head next to young shoulders. In caddie Ricci Roberts, Schwartzel had exactly that.

Roberts had helped Ernie Els to Open Championship and US Open Championship success amongst many others but they were no longer together and Schwartzel was delighted to

be able to link up with him. Their partnership was in only its third week, but the Johannesburg golfer said: "Ricci's helped a lot - he is very confident and that gives me a little edge."

Patience was another quality required as the event suffered rain delays on each of the first three days, necessitating the playing of the bulk of the third round, as well as the closing 18 holes, on a mercifully sunny Sunday.

There was time only for a half hour break between rounds, but it came at a opportune moment for Schwartzel who, after working his way up the leaderboard to be level with Spain's Carlos Rodiles, double-bogeyed the 18th. "It was a good thing I could have some lunch," he commented. "I was steaming. It gave me time to cool down."

Rodiles, winner of the Qualifying School the previous November, moved clear on teeing off again, but come the back nine it was Indian Jyoti Randhawa who led. Schwartzel had stayed in touch, though, and as he birdied the 13th, driving the green at the dog-leg par four, Randhawa bogeyed the 15th.

Keeping the momentum, Schwartzel hit what he described as "probably the three best shots I hit all week" on the long 16th, a perfect drive being followed by a three iron to 15 feet and a putt that found the target for eagle.

Randhawa, who had staged a remarkable recovery after being five over par 13 holes into his opening round, had already finished on 15 under par 273 when Schwartzel bogeyed the last for 16 under par 272, but it was not quite over.

119

Rodiles, returning to the form which had – like Randhawa – given him three runners-up finishes on The European Tour, hit his second shot to the 16th to six feet. Match Schwartzel's eagle and he would be level with him again, but he missed and once he did not birdie either of the last two holes, indeed bogeying the last to finish third, the issue was settled.

Given his start, Randhawa was satisfied with his second place and it completed a notable month for him and indeed for Indian golf. Jeev Milkha Singh had become the first from that country to play in the Masters Tournament at Augusta National, Gaurav Ghei had won the Pine Valley Beijing Open on the Asian Tour and Randhawa's wife Tina, who had put her Bollywood film career on hold for family reasons, had given birth to their first child.

It might have been a notable month for India, but it was a memorable week for Schwartzel.

Mark Garrod
Press Association

Stuart Little

Graeme Storm

Charl Schwartzel receives the trophy from Emma Villacieros, President Real Federación Española de Golf

Carlos Rodiles

> I have always enjoyed playing in Spain in the past and I always felt my first win outside South Africa might come here, and so it has turned out.
>
> **Charl Schwartzel**

Centro Nacional de Golf

Par **72**   Yards **7242**   Metres **6622**

Final Results

Pos	Name		Rd1	Rd2	Rd3	Rd4	Total		€	£
1	Charl SCHWARTZEL	RSA	69	68	68	67	272	-16	333,330.00	226,150.50
2	Jyoti RANDHAWA	IND	75	65	66	67	273	-15	222,220.00	150,767.00
3	Carlos RODILES	ESP	70	66	66	72	274	-14	125,200.00	84,942.98
4	Mark FOSTER	ENG	68	69	70	68	275	-13	92,400.00	62,689.54
	Simon DYSON	ENG	69	69	66	71	275	-13	92,400.00	62,689.54
6	Fredrik ANDERSSON HED	SWE	68	71	69	68	276	-12	65,000.00	44,099.79
	Andres ROMERO	ARG	70	71	69	66	276	-12	65,000.00	44,099.79
8	Grégory BOURDY	FRA	67	69	71	70	277	-11	39,700.00	26,934.79
	Stephen GALLACHER	SCO	71	68	69	69	277	-11	39,700.00	26,934.79
	Alastair FORSYTH	SCO	68	74	66	69	277	-11	39,700.00	26,934.79
	Nick DOUGHERTY	ENG	66	71	70	70	277	-11	39,700.00	26,934.79
	Tom WHITEHOUSE	ENG	71	71	67	68	277	-11	39,700.00	26,934.79
	Stuart LITTLE	ENG	67	69	70	71	277	-11	39,700.00	26,934.79
14	Phillip PRICE	WAL	73	65	70	70	278	-10	29,400.00	19,946.67
	Graeme STORM	ENG	68	72	73	65	278	-10	29,400.00	19,946.67
	Martin KAYMER	GER	71	70	67	70	278	-10	29,400.00	19,946.67
17	Bradley DREDGE	WAL	69	72	69	69	279	-9	25,866.67	17,549.45
	Johan EDFORS	SWE	71	69	70	69	279	-9	25,866.67	17,549.45
	Paul MCGINLEY	IRL	70	72	68	69	279	-9	25,866.67	17,549.45
20	David LYNN	ENG	72	69	69	70	280	-8	23,266.67	15,785.46
	Peter LAWRIE	IRL	76	65	69	70	280	-8	23,266.67	15,785.46
	Andrew TAMPION	AUS	74	67	70	69	280	-8	23,266.67	15,785.46
23	Alexander NOREN	SWE	70	71	71	69	281	-7	19,900.00	13,501.32
	Gareth DAVIES	ENG	69	70	73	69	281	-7	19,900.00	13,501.32
	Graeme MCDOWELL	NIR	71	69	71	70	281	-7	19,900.00	13,501.32
	Simon WAKEFIELD	ENG	73	69	70	69	281	-7	19,900.00	13,501.32
	Jarmo SANDELIN	SWE	70	71	71	69	281	-7	19,900.00	13,501.32
	Richard BLAND	ENG	68	71	71	71	281	-7	19,900.00	13,501.32
	Robert-Jan DERKSEN	NED	67	75	72	67	281	-7	19,900.00	13,501.32
	Carlos DEL MORAL	ESP	71	73	68	69	281	-7	19,900.00	13,501.32
31	Gary MURPHY	IRL	71	72	71	68	282	-6	15,571.43	10,564.56
	Kenneth FERRIE	ENG	69	71	71	71	282	-6	15,571.43	10,564.56
	Paul LAWRIE	SCO	74	69	66	73	282	-6	15,571.43	10,564.56
	Emanuele CANONICA	ITA	72	67	69	74	282	-6	15,571.43	10,564.56
	Niclas FASTH	SWE	68	72	71	71	282	-6	15,571.43	10,564.56
	Notah BEGAY III	USA	68	70	73	71	282	-6	15,571.43	10,564.56
	Manuel QUIROS	ESP	72	68	69	73	282	-6	15,571.43	10,564.56
38	Oliver WILSON	ENG	70	73	70	70	283	-5	13,000.00	8,819.96
	Louis OOSTHUIZEN	RSA	73	70	69	71	283	-5	13,000.00	8,819.96
	David CARTER	ENG	71	73	68	71	283	-5	13,000.00	8,819.96
	Jonathan LOMAS	ENG	70	70	73	70	283	-5	13,000.00	8,819.96
	Andrew RAITT	ENG	68	70	74	71	283	-5	13,000.00	8,819.96
43	Carlos BALMASEDA	ESP	70	74	69	71	284	-4	11,800.00	8,005.81
44	David DRYSDALE	SCO	69	73	72	71	285	-3	10,800.00	7,327.35
	David PARK	WAL	70	71	70	74	285	-3	10,800.00	7,327.35
	Gonzalo FDEZ-CASTAÑO	ESP	70	74	70	71	285	-3	10,800.00	7,327.35
	Oliver FISHER	ENG	70	71	69	72	285	-3	10,800.00	7,327.35
48	Ariel CANETE	ARG	71	73	72	70	286	-2	9,200.00	6,241.82
	Ian GARBUTT	ENG	71	73	72	70	286	-2	9,200.00	6,241.82
	Alvaro SALTO	ESP	69	73	69	75	286	-2	9,200.00	6,241.82
	Damien MCGRANE	IRL	72	70	68	76	286	-2	9,200.00	6,241.82
52	Miguel Angel JIMÉNEZ	ESP	70	73	73	71	287	-1	8,000.00	5,427.67
	Ignacio GARRIDO	ESP	71	72	72	72	287	-1	8,000.00	5,427.67
54	Gary ORR	SCO	71	72	75	70	288	0	6,800.00	4,613.52
	Marcus HIGLEY	ENG	74	70	71	73	288	0	6,800.00	4,613.52
	Terry PILKADARIS	AUS	69	74	73	72	288	0	6,800.00	4,613.52
	Andrew COLTART	SCO	70	72	74	72	288	0	6,800.00	4,613.52
58	Marcus FRASER	AUS	69	70	77	73	289	1	5,800.00	3,935.06
	Taichi TESHIMA	JPN	72	71	73	73	289	1	5,800.00	3,935.06
	Steve WEBSTER	ENG	72	69	73	75	289	1	5,800.00	3,935.06
61	Marcel SIEM	GER	73	71	75	71	290	2	5,400.00	3,663.67
62	Alvaro VELASCO	ESP	73	71	76	71	291	3	5,200.00	3,527.98
63	Terry PRICE	AUS	70	70	78	74	292	4	4,900.00	3,324.45
	François DELAMONTAGNE	FRA	71	72	75	74	292	4	4,900.00	3,324.45
65	Nicolas COLSAERTS	BEL	77	67	74	75	293	5	4,600.00	3,120.91
66	Richard MCEVOY	ENG	75	69	75	75	294	6	4,400.00	2,985.22

Total Prize Fund

€1,984,350 £1,346,298

The Course

A new course, at the home of the Real Federación Española de Golf in Madrid, which featured on The European Tour International Schedule for the first time. Designed by Thomas Vidaor, brother of European Tour Tournament Director Miguel, the course features narrow fairways and punitive rough while the water surrounding the final three holes makes for an exciting finish.

Fortune Favours The Brave

		BUCA		1	2	3	4	5	6	7	8	9	10	11	12	13	14	15	16	17	18	TOTALE	
		PAR		5	4	4	4	3	4	4	3	5	4	4	5	4	3	4	5	3	4		
9	FEDZ CASTANO			10	10	10	10	9	10	11	12	13	13	15	15	16	16	★	2	0	0		
12	BRIER			13	14	14	15	14	14	14	14	13	13	13	15	15	16	16	2	0	0		
14	MCLARDY			15	14	14	14	13	12	13	14	14	14	14	14	14	14	14	2	0	2		
12	BACKSTROM			13	13	13	13	12	12	13	14	14	14	13	12	12	11	11	2	0	5		
10	FRASER			12	11	11	11	12	12	12	13	14	14	14	14	14	14	14	2	0	2		
13	DOUGHERTY			15	15	16	16	16	16	16	17	17	16	16	16	16	15	15	2	0	1		
7	ANDERSSON HED			8	8	9	9	9	10	10	9	10	11	11	12	12	13	14	2	0	1		
9	NYSTROM			11	11	12	12	12	13	14	14	14	15	14	15	14	14	14	2	0	1		
8	MOLINARI F			9	9	9	10	10	10	9	10	11	12	12	13	13	14	15	2	0	1		
10	HAFTHORSSON			11	11	11	12	12	11	12	12	13	13	14	14	14	14	14	2	0	3		

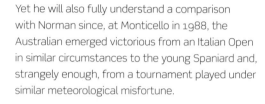

1	Gonzalo FERNANDEZ-CASTAÑO		200	-16
2	Markus BRIER		200	-16
3	Fredrik ANDERSSON HED		201	-15
	Nick DOUGHERTY		201	-15
	Francesco MOLINARI		201	-15
	Henrik NYSTROM		201	-15
7	Marcus FRASER		202	-14
	Raphaël JACQUELIN		202	-14
	Andrew McLARDY		202	-14
	Alexandre ROCHA		202	-14

I t was a never say die victory in a never say die week – a salutary lesson for everyone involved with the game of golf, that it is never over until it is over.

Martin Kaymer

Oliver Fisher

Gonzalo Fernandez-Castaño, five strokes off the lead at the start of the final round of the Telecom Italia Open at the Castello di Tolcinasco Golf and Country Club near Milan and indeed six adrift with only nine holes left to play, refused to accept the battle was lost. Then again, the 26 year old from Madrid is fast gaining the reputation for being a winner.

Seve Ballesteros and Greg Norman enjoyed a similar reputation in the 1980s, a decade during which Fernandez-Castaño began playing the game under the tutelage of his father.

Naturally enough Spanish compatriot Ballesteros is Fernandez-Castaño's hero and therefore one can perfectly understand his joy when, in 2005, he captured his maiden European Tour title in The KLM Open, since it was in The Netherlands in 1976 that Seve won his first event.

Yet he will also fully understand a comparison with Norman since, at Monticello in 1988, the Australian emerged victorious from an Italian Open in similar circumstances to the young Spaniard and, strangely enough, from a tournament played under similar meteorological misfortune.

Picture the scene at Como in 1988. Seven strokes off the lead after the first round – with storms having delayed the start by a day – and five shots adrift at halfway, Norman responded with a display of world class golf over 36 holes on the final day to claim a remarkable victory.

Fast forward to 2007 and Fernandez-Castaño was enveloped in much the same situation as this historic event – first played in 1925 – came under attack from the elements.

On a course on which fortune favours the brave, European Tour staff, Italian Golf Federation officials, an heroic greenkeeping crew and local volunteers refused to bow to the often torrential rain and storm conditions, and in the end made sure the championship finished on time on live international television.

Everyone involved in the tournament was repeatedly on dawn and dusk patrol to keep the event rolling in the face of grim skies, with a regular 72 hole outcome the target. However, with thunderstorms still a potential risk for Sunday, few protested when Tournament Director José Maria Zamora and European Tour Senior Referee Andy McFee took the tough decision to erase the few scores already on the board in a weather-interrupted second round and start again after a thunderous rain storm had completely changed the playing state of the course.

They viewed this, in addition to the decision to cut the event to 54 holes, as the best way forward. In keeping the cut to 65 and ties and going off one tee in two balls as is the preferred norm of the players on a Sunday, they were proved 100 per cent right.

As well as ensuring an ending on time, the bold decision also introduced a thrilling sprint-finish element into proceedings. The leading players rose to the challenge and the crowds loved it, particularly when local hero and defending champion Francesco Molinari posted his name on the leaderboards with a scintillating run of four birdies in a row from the ninth.

The Italian's charge, which ended in a 65, was good enough for a share of third place on 15 under par 201 with the Swedish duo of Fredrik Andersson Hed and Henrik Nystrom and England's Nick Dougherty, leaving the destination of the trophy and the €283,330 (£193,163) first prize to be contested by Austria's Markus Brier and Fernandez-Castaño.

Brier, winner of the Volvo China Open the previous month, seemed set for his third European Tour title following late birdies at the 16th and 17th, but he had reckoned without the fast finishing Spaniard who cruised home in 30 for a 65 to join the Austrian on 16 under par 200, before producing yet another birdie at the second play-off hole to triumph.

In only his 62nd tournament on The European Tour International Schedule, Fernandez-Castaño had won for the third time, capturing a trophy which has also adorned the mantelpieces of compatriots Ramon Sota (1971), Angel Gallardo (1977), José Maria Cañizares (1981) and Manuel Piñero (1985).

The man, who dedicated his first win in The 2005 KLM Open to his family and his second in the 2006 BMW Asian Open to his wife Alicia, this time praised his coaches, his support team and all his many Spanish friends.

Ironically, they responded by throwing him into a nearby swimming pool in celebration – but perhaps it was fitting that in a week where everyone was surrounded by water, the champion finished holding the trophy up to his neck in the stuff.

Gordon Richardson

Mario Pinzi, special advisor to the organising committee of the Telecom Italia Open, passed away in February 2007. As founder and owner of Promomax, a Rome based sports promotion company, Mario was co-ordinator and promoter of the Italian Golf Championship from 1974 and throughout the 1980s and 1990s. His contribution to the tournament was recognised by the Italian Golf Federation in 2002 when he was presented with the Peter Dobereiner Award by IGF president Franco Chimenti (above left).

Duffy Waldorf

Left *Tom Lehman*

Below *Phillip Archer*

Nick Dougherty

Castello di Tolcinasco Golf and Country Club

Par **72** Yards **7283** Metres **6663**

Final Results

Pos	Name		Rd1	Rd2	Rd3	Rd4	Total		€	£
1	Gonzalo FDEZ-CASTAÑO	ESP	67	68	65		200	-16	283,330.00	193,163.30
2	Markus BRIER	AUT	63	69	68		200	-16	188,880.00	128,770.99
3	Nick DOUGHERTY	ENG	67	64	70		201	-15	80,750.00	55,052.19
	Francesco MOLINARI	ITA	67	69	65		201	-15	80,750.00	55,052.19
	Henrik NYSTROM	SWE	67	68	66		201	-15	80,750.00	55,052.19
	Fredrik ANDERSSON HED	SWE	69	68	64		201	-15	80,750.00	55,052.19
7	Raphaël JACQUELIN	FRA	66	71	65		202	-14	41,395.00	28,221.49
	Andrew MCLARDY	RSA	65	65	72		202	-14	41,395.00	28,221.49
	Alexandre ROCHA	BRA	70	64	68		202	-14	41,395.00	28,221.49
	Marcus FRASER	AUS	68	66	68		202	-14	41,395.00	28,221.49
11	Simon KHAN	ENG	68	69	66		203	-13	29,296.67	19,973.32
	James HEATH	ENG	65	69	69		203	-13	29,296.67	19,973.32
	Birgir HAFTHORSSON	ISL	67	67	69		203	-13	29,296.67	19,973.32
14	Martin KAYMER	GER	69	65	70		204	-12	23,047.14	15,712.64
	Maarten LAFEBER	NED	69	66	69		204	-12	23,047.14	15,712.64
	Pelle EDBERG	SWE	70	69	65		204	-12	23,047.14	15,712.64
	Oliver FISHER	ENG	69	69	66		204	-12	23,047.14	15,712.64
	Oliver WILSON	ENG	68	68	68		204	-12	23,047.14	15,712.64
	Mark FOSTER	ENG	72	68	64		204	-12	23,047.14	15,712.64
	Phillip ARCHER	ENG	69	68	67		204	-12	23,047.14	15,712.64
21	Gary LOCKERBIE	ENG	73	65	67		205	-11	18,700.00	12,748.93
	Joakim BÄCKSTRÖM	SWE	62	70	73		205	-11	18,700.00	12,748.93
	Alvaro QUIROS	ESP	65	67	73		205	-11	18,700.00	12,748.93
	Alastair FORSYTH	SCO	68	67	70		205	-11	18,700.00	12,748.93
	Garry HOUSTON	WAL	66	70	69		205	-11	18,700.00	12,748.93
26	Mark PILKINGTON	WAL	71	68	67		206	-10	16,405.00	11,184.29
	Jeev Milkha SINGH	IND	69	65	72		206	-10	16,405.00	11,184.29
	Peter LAWRIE	IRL	68	70	68		206	-10	16,405.00	11,184.29
	Ian GARBUTT	ENG	68	71	67		206	-10	16,405.00	11,184.29
30	Anthony WALL	ENG	68	72	67		207	-9	13,672.86	9,321.62
	Søren HANSEN	DEN	69	70	68		207	-9	13,672.86	9,321.62
	Nicolas COLSAERTS	BEL	66	67	74		207	-9	13,672.86	9,321.62
	Brett RUMFORD	AUS	66	71	70		207	-9	13,672.86	9,321.62
	Edoardo MOLINARI	ITA	70	69	68		207	-9	13,672.86	9,321.62
	Charl SCHWARTZEL	RSA	67	69	71		207	-9	13,672.86	9,321.62
	Kyron SULLIVAN	WAL	70	67	70		207	-9	13,672.86	9,321.62
37	David PARK	WAL	71	68	69		208	-8	10,540.00	7,185.76
	Tom LEHMAN	USA	70	68	70		208	-8	10,540.00	7,185.76
	Steven O'HARA	SCO	69	68	71		208	-8	10,540.00	7,185.76
	David DRYSDALE	SCO	70	70	68		208	-8	10,540.00	7,185.76
	Carlos RODILES	ESP	67	67	74		208	-8	10,540.00	7,185.76
	Sven STRÜVER	GER	68	70	70		208	-8	10,540.00	7,185.76
	Grégory HAVRET	FRA	67	71	70		208	-8	10,540.00	7,185.76
	Emanuele CANONICA	ITA	70	69	69		208	-8	10,540.00	7,185.76
	Kenneth FERRIE	ENG	68	69	71		208	-8	10,540.00	7,185.76
	Gareth DAVIES	ENG	69	71	68		208	-8	10,540.00	7,185.76
47	Benn BARHAM	ENG	69	70	70		209	-7	7,310.00	4,983.67
	Richard FINCH	ENG	66	73	70		209	-7	7,310.00	4,983.67
	Jean-Baptiste GONNET	FRA	72	67	70		209	-7	7,310.00	4,983.67
	Paul BROADHURST	ENG	68	70	71		209	-7	7,310.00	4,983.67
	Sam LITTLE	ENG	71	69	69		209	-7	7,310.00	4,983.67
	Gary MURPHY	IRL	71	68	70		209	-7	7,310.00	4,983.67
	Jyoti RANDHAWA	IND	71	69	69		209	-7	7,310.00	4,983.67
	Martin ERLANDSSON	SWE	71	66	72		209	-7	7,310.00	4,983.67
	Bradley DREDGE	WAL	71	68	70		209	-7	7,310.00	4,983.67
56	Rafael CABRERA BELLO	ESP	71	69	70		210	-6	5,227.50	3,563.90
	Anders HANSEN	DEN	66	74	70		210	-6	5,227.50	3,563.90
	Andrew TAMPION	AUS	68	72	70		210	-6	5,227.50	3,563.90
	Robert ROCK	ENG	71	68	71		210	-6	5,227.50	3,563.90
60	Grégory BOURDY	FRA	73	67	71		211	-5	4,420.00	3,013.38
	Alessio BRUSCHI	ITA	72	68	71		211	-5	4,420.00	3,013.38
	Steve JONES	USA	70	69	72		211	-5	4,420.00	3,013.38
	Duffy WALDORF	USA	67	72	72		211	-5	4,420.00	3,013.38
	Steven JEPPESEN	SWE	74	66	71		211	-5	4,420.00	3,013.38
65	Michele REALE	ITA	71	68	73		212	-4	3,655.00	2,491.84
	Juan PARRON	ESP	67	71	74		212	-4	3,655.00	2,491.84
	Steve ALKER	NZL	70	69	73		212	-4	3,655.00	2,491.84
	Cesar MONASTERIO	ARG	69	70	73		212	-4	3,655.00	2,491.84
69	José Manuel CARRILES	ESP	70	70	73		213	-3	3,230.00	2,202.09
70	Jean-François REMESY	FRA	70	68	78		216	0	3,110.00	2,120.28

Total Prize Fund

€1,700,000 £1,158,993

The Course

Situated in the grounds of a beautiful 16th century castle, the Arnold Palmer designed course is the jewel in the crown of one of the most prestigious golf clubs in Italy. A relatively flat course is made challenging by the strategic placements of several ponds and streams. Admirable drainage coped well with the heavy rain all week and allowed 54 holes to be played.

(left to right) Franco Chimenti, President of the Italian Golf Federation, Gonzalo Fernandez-Castaño and Carlo Corti Galeazzi, Managing Director of Telecom Italia

I don't think I've ever played a bad Italian course and this is right up there with the best. The greens are so good; just as fast as they were in practice. It is also holding up fantastically well. They didn't play preferred lies and they didn't need to.
James Heath

Back in the Old Routine

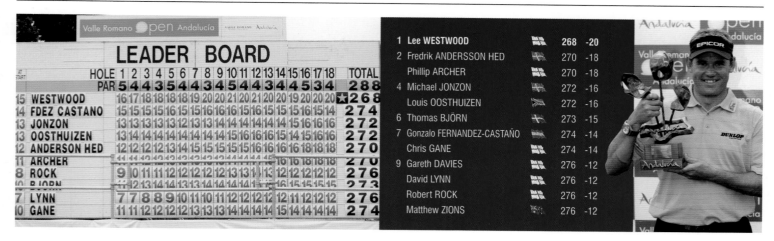

LEADER BOARD

	HOLE	1	2	3	4	5	6	7	8	9	10	11	12	13	14	15	16	17	18	TOTAL
	PAR	5	4	4	3	5	4	4	3	4	5	4	4	3	4	4	5	3	4	288
15 WESTWOOD		16	17	18	18	18	19	20	20	21	21	20	20	19	20	20	20	★		268
14 FDEZ CASTANO		15	15	15	16	15	15	16	16	15	16	15	15	15	16	15	14			274
13 JONZON		13	13	13	13	12	13	13	14	14	14	14	14	15	16	16	16			272
13 OOSTHUIZEN		13	14	14	14	14	14	14	14	15	16	16	15	14	15	16	16			272
12 ANDERSON HED		12	12	12	13	14	15	15	15	16	16	18	18	18	18					270
11 ARCHER														16	16	16	18			270
8 ROCK		9	10	11	11	12	12	12	12	13	13	13	12	12	12	12				276
10 BJORN		11	12	13	14	14	13	14	14	14	15	16	15	15	15	15				273
7 LYNN		7	7	8	8	9	10	11	10	11	12	12	12	11	12	12	12			276
10 GANE		11	11	12	12	12	12	13	13	14	14	14	15	14	14	14	14			274

1	Lee WESTWOOD		268	-20
2	Fredrik ANDERSSON HED		270	-18
	Phillip ARCHER		270	-18
4	Michael JONZON		272	-16
	Louis OOSTHUIZEN		272	-16
6	Thomas BJÖRN		273	-15
7	Gonzalo FERNANDEZ-CASTAÑO		274	-14
	Chris GANE		274	-14
9	Gareth DAVIES		276	-12
	David LYNN		276	-12
	Robert ROCK		276	-12
	Matthew ZIONS		276	-12

"I enjoy the oohs and aahs from the gallery when I hit my drives. But I'm getting pretty tired of the awws and uhhs when I miss my putts." The quote comes from the inimitable John Daly, but there is no doubt Lee Westwood would have concurred with the sentiment as he arrived in Spain for the inaugural Valle Romano Open de Andalucia.

Fredrik Andersson Hed

Perplexed by his paucity on the putting surfaces, Westwood was almost at the end of his tether, joking that, despite being one of the 88 players to make the cut in the previous week's Wachovia Championship on the US PGA Tour, he had probably finished 89th in putts per green!

Behind the smile however, there was genuine frustration at seeing all the good work from tee to green being wasted with some rather ungainly footwork on the dance floor. If a regulation two-step is turning into a three-step or even four, then you know you have problems.

So the 34 year old touched down on the Costa del Sol with a weight on his mind and even weightier luggage to boot, no fewer than five putters making their way to the picturesque Aloha Golf Club.

When Arnold Palmer once took eight putters to the Colonial Tournament in Texas, Jackie Burke was heard to remark: "That's a bagful of indecision," and it appeared Westwood's plight was similar as the first putter out of the suitcase lasted a mere 18 holes.

In truth it was lucky to survive that long considering the number of times it was flicked with disdain towards his bag, but Westwood's opening 72 barely warranted a mention after an extraordinary incident involving Joakim Haeggman.

Walking up the 18th fairway, Haeggman became the subject of over zealous attention from one of the geese lurking beside the lake. Perhaps offended by his gleaming white trousers, the goose attacked the three time European Tour winner and had to be repelled with a swift right-hander and an even swifter jog off in the opposite direction.

Valle Romano Open de Andalucía

Despite such distractions, the Swede carded a fine 67 to trail surprise leader Matthew Zions of Australia - one of only six players to come through all three stages of The 2006 European Tour Qualifying School - by two shots.

An inability to score in the 60s over the rest of the week ended Zions' interest at the business end of the tournament and, from then on, much of the limelight was shared between Spain's Gonzalo Fernandez-Castaño and Westwood - the latter seeking his first win in almost four years, the former his second in just seven days after his stunning play-off success over Markus Brier the previous Sunday in the Telecom Italia Open.

Westwood charged into contention with a course record 64 in the second round, using a standard length putter he had banished to his garage along with 200 of its unreliable brethren after the first round of the Masters Tournament at Augusta National in April.

When he took just one more blow to complete round three despite bogeys at the 17th and 18th, the former European Number One led by one from Fernandez-Castaño, who had carded rounds of 67-68-67 despite the demands of co-promoting the tournament with fellow Spaniard Miguel Angel Jiménez.

Fernandez-Castaño, who learned to play golf on the nearby par three course at Aloha and proudly stated: "I still know everybody in the clubhouse," was unable to mount a final-day challenge, leaving the Englishman seemingly cruising to his 17th European Tour International Schedule victory.

Five clear with eight to play, however, Westwood bogeyed three of his next five holes and saw his lead cut to only one shot when Phillip Archer and Fredrik Andersson Hed both eagled the par five 16th.

A renowned front runner, though, Westwood held his nerve and birdied the 16th himself to ensure an overdue return to the winner's circle. "It's great to win again, although it looked like it might be a lot easier than I made it in the end," he admitted.

"I never really thought about going so long without a win. I won so often in the late 1990s that if I had a spell where I didn't win, people were always going to highlight it and get on my case about it. But I was never going to get on my own case."

Phil Casey
PA Sport

Michael Jonzon

The Course

Designed by the renowned Spanish golf course architect, the late Javier Arana, for whom the course proved to be his last project as he died nine months before its official opening in October 1975. Not the longest course on Tour but patience is required to negotiate the narrow fairways especially when the wind gets up.

Louis Oosthuizen

Co-promoters Gonzalo Fernandez-Castaño (left) and Miguel Angel Jiménez

(left to right) Ana Gomez Gomez, Viceconsejera de Turismo, Comercio y Deporte de la Junta de Andalucía, Lee Westwood and María Eugenia Yeregui, Presidenta Valle Romano

> This is my first tournament as a promoter and I'm thrilled to play in the event as well. Andalucia has sponsored me for many years and I have had the opportunity to play all around the world. This is a way of giving back for all the support they have given me.
> *Miguel Angel Jiménez*

Aloha Golf Club

Par 72   Yards 6881   Metres 6293

Final Results

Pos	Name		Rd1	Rd2	Rd3	Rd4	Total		€	£
1	Lee WESTWOOD	ENG	72	64	65	67	268	-20	166,660.00	113,612.19
2	Phillip ARCHER	ENG	69	70	66	65	270	-18	86,855.00	59,209.09
	Fredrik ANDERSSON HED	SWE	69	71	64	66	270	-18	86,855.00	59,209.09
4	Michael JONZON	SWE	69	68	66	69	272	-16	46,200.00	31,494.56
	Louis OOSTHUIZEN	RSA	67	67	69	69	272	-16	46,200.00	31,494.56
6	Thomas BJÖRN	DEN	71	69	66	67	273	-15	35,000.00	23,859.52
7	Chris GANE	ENG	67	71	68	68	274	-14	27,500.00	18,746.76
	Gonzalo FDEZ-CASTAÑO	ESP	67	68	67	72	274	-14	27,500.00	18,746.76
9	David LYNN	ENG	70	71	68	67	276	-12	19,500.00	13,293.16
	Matthew ZIONS	AUS	65	70	70	71	276	-12	19,500.00	13,293.16
	Robert ROCK	ENG	70	73	65	68	276	-12	19,500.00	13,293.16
	Gareth DAVIES	ENG	69	71	68	68	276	-12	19,500.00	13,293.16
13	Sam WALKER	ENG	69	69	70	69	277	-11	14,740.00	10,048.26
	François DELAMONTAGNE	FRA	69	66	72	70	277	-11	14,740.00	10,048.26
	Søren HANSEN	DEN	70	68	70	69	277	-11	14,740.00	10,048.26
	Jamie DONALDSON	WAL	70	69	70	68	277	-11	14,740.00	10,048.26
	Garry HOUSTON	WAL	71	67	72	67	277	-11	14,740.00	10,048.26
18	Joakim HAEGGMAN	SWE	67	71	69	71	278	-10	12,040.00	8,207.67
	Alejandro CAÑIZARES	ESP	66	73	70	69	278	-10	12,040.00	8,207.67
	David HIGGINS	IRL	69	68	70	71	278	-10	12,040.00	8,207.67
	Richard MCEVOY	ENG	69	68	73	68	278	-10	12,040.00	8,207.67
	Paul BROADHURST	ENG	70	70	70	68	278	-10	12,040.00	8,207.67
23	Johan AXGREN	SWE	74	68	69	68	279	-9	11,000.00	7,498.70
24	Steve JONES	USA	69	67	71	73	280	-8	9,800.00	6,680.66
	Alvaro SALTO	ESP	70	69	68	73	280	-8	9,800.00	6,680.66
	Miguel Angel JIMÉNEZ	ESP	72	69	68	71	280	-8	9,800.00	6,680.66
	Carl SUNESON	ESP	69	68	71	72	280	-8	9,800.00	6,680.66
	Shaun P WEBSTER	ENG	74	67	70	69	280	-8	9,800.00	6,680.66
	David GRIFFITHS	ENG	68	72	68	72	280	-8	9,800.00	6,680.66
	Oliver FISHER	ENG	70	69	71	70	280	-8	9,800.00	6,680.66
31	Gary LOCKERBIE	ENG	67	72	70	72	281	-7	8,300.00	5,658.11
	Santiago LUNA	ESP	72	69	68	72	281	-7	8,300.00	5,658.11
	Sven STRÜVER	GER	71	71	71	68	281	-7	8,300.00	5,658.11
34	Birgir HAFTHORSSON	ISL	73	68	70	71	282	-6	7,200.00	4,908.24
	Jesus María ARRUTI	ESP	73	71	68	70	282	-6	7,200.00	4,908.24
	Notah BEGAY III	USA	71	70	71	70	282	-6	7,200.00	4,908.24
	Thomas LEVET	FRA	74	66	70	72	282	-6	7,200.00	4,908.24
	Andrew BUTTERFIELD	ENG	70	73	67	72	282	-6	7,200.00	4,908.24
	Scott STRANGE	AUS	72	71	69	70	282	-6	7,200.00	4,908.24
40	Rafael ECHENIQUE	ARG	73	71	68	71	283	-5	6,200.00	4,226.54
	Philip GOLDING	ENG	74	69	69	71	283	-5	6,200.00	4,226.54
	Ian GARBUTT	ENG	72	70	71	70	283	-5	6,200.00	4,226.54
	Sam LITTLE	ENG	71	69	74	69	283	-5	6,200.00	4,226.54
44	James HEPWORTH	ENG	72	68	71	73	284	-4	5,200.00	3,544.84
	James HEATH	ENG	75	67	72	70	284	-4	5,200.00	3,544.84
	Terry PILKADARIS	AUS	71	71	71	71	284	-4	5,200.00	3,544.84
	Sion E BEBB	WAL	70	74	70	70	284	-4	5,200.00	3,544.84
	Carlos AGUILAR	ESP	76	67	72	69	284	-4	5,200.00	3,544.84
	Paul MCGINLEY	IRL	71	72	68	73	284	-4	5,200.00	3,544.84
50	Per-Ulrik JOHANSSON	SWE	72	71	69	73	285	-3	4,200.00	2,863.14
	Wade ORMSBY	AUS	73	70	69	73	285	-3	4,200.00	2,863.14
	Peter FOWLER	AUS	73	71	70	71	285	-3	4,200.00	2,863.14
	Marcus HIGLEY	ENG	70	71	69	75	285	-3	4,200.00	2,863.14
54	Anthony WALL	ENG	72	72	71	71	286	-2	3,320.00	2,263.25
	Sebastian FERNANDEZ	ARG	70	70	72	74	286	-2	3,320.00	2,263.25
	Juan PARRON	ESP	72	71	70	73	286	-2	3,320.00	2,263.25
	Y E YANG	KOR	74	69	70	73	286	-2	3,320.00	2,263.25
	Carlos RODILES	ESP	72	69	72	73	286	-2	3,320.00	2,263.25
59	Damien MCGRANE	IRL	72	70	73	72	287	-1	2,750.00	1,874.68
	Pedro LINHART	ESP	70	70	71	74	287	-1	2,750.00	1,874.68
	Peter GUSTAFSSON	SWE	73	70	74	70	287	-1	2,750.00	1,874.68
	Adrien MÖRK	FRA	71	73	72	71	287	-1	2,750.00	1,874.68
63	Nicolas COLSAERTS	BEL	68	73	74	73	288	0	2,400.00	1,636.08
	Rafael CABRERA BELLO	ESP	69	73	72	74	288	0	2,400.00	1,636.08
	Eduardo DE LA RIVA	ESP	68	73	70	77	288	0	2,400.00	1,636.08
66	Carlos BALMASEDA	ESP	71	71	73	74	289	1	2,006.00	1,367.49
	Diego BORREGO	ESP	73	71	74	71	289	1	2,006.00	1,367.49
	Martin MARITZ	RSA	72	72	70	75	289	1	2,006.00	1,367.49
	Daniel QUIROS	ESP	72	72	74	71	289	1	2,006.00	1,367.49
	Alvaro VELASCO	ESP	72	72	73	72	289	1	2,006.00	1,367.49
71	Jorge BENEDETTI	COL	71	73	74	72	290	2	1,498.50	1,021.53
	Gary EMERSON	ENG	71	72	73	74	290	2	1,498.50	1,021.53
73	Matthew MILLAR	AUS	68	73	72	78	291	3	1,494.00	1,018.46
74	Simon DYSON	ENG	70	74	77	73	294	6	1,491.00	1,016.42

Total Prize Fund

€1,005,982   £685,778

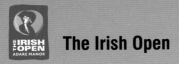

The People's Champion

1	Padraig HARRINGTON		283	-5
2	Bradley DREDGE		283	-5
3	Simon WAKEFIELD		287	-1
4	Richard GREEN		288	0
	Louis OOSTHUIZEN		288	0
	Andres ROMERO		288	0
7	Simon DYSON		290	2
	Peter HANSON		290	2
	Raphaël JACQUELIN		290	2
	Francesco MOLINARI		290	2

W hen Christy O'Connor Junior captured The Irish Open at Woodbrook in 1975, the entire country rejoiced. The championship had not taken place for 22 years and for an Irishman to emerge victorious on its revival was something very special indeed.

A year later, the event moved on to its spiritual home at Portmarnock where there were numerous great days, none more so than in 1982 when John O'Leary bestrode the winners' rostrum.

Great days indeed. But after that, nothing. Well, nothing Irish!

For a quarter of a century great players like Darren Clarke, Eamonn Darcy, Padraig Harrington, Paul McGinley, Ronan Rafferty, Des Smyth and Philip Walton gave it their best shot, but to no avail. With the exception of Walton, who lost out to Welshman Ian Woosnam in a play-off in 1989, none went particularly close.

Accordingly, when the 2007 tournament came round in the luxurious surroundings of Adare Manor Hotel and Golf Resort in County Limerick, the focus was very much on the Irish contingent once again. Could they bring an end to the drought? It had become a monkey on the backs not only of the current players but also on the shoulders of O'Leary himself who, as much as any other Irish person, desperately wanted to see an end to his 'record'.

Quite appropriately then, he was at Adare Manor when it finally happened and was able to rejoice along with thousands of Irish fans as they celebrated the end of 25 years of longing and hailed the 2007 Irish Open champion...Padraig Harrington.

The 25 year hiatus had an affect on the Irish golfers that, perhaps, even they themselves had not appreciated, and it was only when it came to finishing off the job on an emotional final day that Ireland's Number One realised just how much was involved.

"I felt more pressure out there than I would have at any other event," he admitted. "This is my most important tournament after the four Majors, the one I really wanted. It might not be the fifth hardest to win but the pressure I felt was greater even than in last year's US Open Championship or Masters Tournament. I was in contention for both but I wasn't leading and it's definitely harder to go on and win when you're out in front."

Golf is huge in Ireland and an indication of just how big came when there was a clear likelihood of Harrington winning. Then, even the following week's General Election was blown off the front pages. He is, in every way, the People's Champion, loved by his myriad of fans as much for his disposition off the golf course as for his skill and sportsmanship when walking the fairways.

The weather was none too kind over the opening two days, after which rounds of 73 and 68 had Harrington's nose in front of Joakim Bäckström, Andres Romero and Simon Wakefield before the gap opened to three shots over the field after

Simon Wakefield

Raphaël Jacquelin

Thomas Björn

Left *Bradley Dredge*

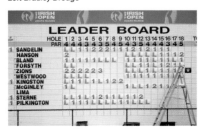

Jarmo Sandelin

Below *Paul McGinley*

a 71 on Saturday. Aside from Wakefield, his closest pursuer was now Bradley Dredge and the popular Welshman was to dog his every movement from there to the finishing line.

Dredge might well have thrown in the towel when he completed the front nine on the final day birdie-birdie-birdie only to lose ground to Harrington who went birdie-birdie-eagle. The three at the 631 yard ninth, where he followed a towering drive with a five wood from 245 yards to twelve feet, was awesome to behold and saw the Irishman four ahead going into the last nine holes.

But Dredge was not for giving up and when he conjured his own superb approach to less than a yard for birdie three on the 17th – on a hole Harrington made bogey five – they were level playing the last.

Course architect Robert Trent Jones Senior often claimed the 548 yard 18th was "the best par five I ever designed," and with the River Maigue running all the way up the left and in front of the undulating green, it certainly demanded the full attention of the entire field throughout the week.

The two leaders played it conservatively in normal time but when they returned for the first hole of the sudden-death play-off, Dredge became its latest victim, leaving Harrington to accept the crowd's adulation and initiate wild celebrations in County Limerick and all over the country.

"I never make these things easy for myself and it was the same this time," said the new champion. "Bradley played really well and my second shot in the play-off could have been just as easily in the hazard as his. But I got the break."

Looking on, a beaming John O'Leary commented: "It's appropriate that Europe's current Number One should be the first Irish player to win The Irish Open since I did so in 1982. I'm delighted for Padraig as he's a great guy. For the people who have made this a great golfing country too, it was a day out they fully deserved."

The 23,150 who thronged the wonderful Adare Manor Hotel and Golf Resort on that historic Sunday heartily concurred.

Charlie Mulqueen
Irish Examiner

CCC baselayer ionx

- **CCC BaseLayer IonX** is revolutionary in apparel technology as it delivers ionic energy to the body through a negatively charged electromagnetic field.

- **CCC BaseLayer IonX** improves performance. Ionisation improves the flow of oxygen-enriched blood to bring more energy to the muscles, which increases your average power output, improving speed and strength.

- **CCC BaseLayer IonX** accelerates recovery. The improvement in blood flow efficiently flushes out residual waste products, such as lactic acid, which is left in the muscles after high intensity activity. Recovery is accelerated, therefore training or competition can begin again sooner.

Michael Campbell wears Canterbury IonX.
www.CanterburyNZ.com

The Course

Although not an old golf course, the old trees which border the majority of the holes give the course a mature feel not present on many parkland layouts. The framed setting helps give definition to the holes and cover to the players while the eight new tees in play in 2007 augmented Robert Trent Jones Snr's superb original design.

Y E Yang

Padraig Harrington (centre) with Tom and Judy Kane, owners of Adare Manor Hotel & Golf Resort

i The play-off between Padraig Harrington and Bradley Dredge was the tenth in the event's history since 1972 – the most of any European Tour tournament. The Telecom Italia Open is next with eight.

Adare Manor Hotel and Golf Resort
Par **72**   Yards **7453**   Metres **6816**

Final Results

Pos	Name		Rd1	Rd2	Rd3	Rd4	Total		€	£
1	Padraig HARRINGTON	IRL	73	68	71	71	283	-5	416,660.00	284,141.90
2	Bradley DREDGE	WAL	75	71	69	68	283	-5	277,770.00	189,425.66
3	Simon WAKEFIELD	ENG	70	72	73	72	287	-1	156,500.00	106,725.41
4	Andres ROMERO	ARG	68	74	75	71	288	0	106,166.67	72,400.52
	Richard GREEN	AUS	71	73	72	72	288	0	106,166.67	72,400.52
	Louis OOSTHUIZEN	RSA	69	74	73	72	288	0	106,166.67	72,400.52
7	Francesco MOLINARI	ITA	71	74	73	72	290	2	60,875.00	41,513.80
	Simon DYSON	ENG	68	78	75	69	290	2	60,875.00	41,513.80
	Raphaël JACQUELIN	FRA	74	72	72	72	290	2	60,875.00	41,513.80
	Peter HANSON	SWE	68	78	73	71	290	2	60,875.00	41,513.80
11	James KINGSTON	RSA	69	78	76	69	292	4	46,000.00	31,369.77
12	Marc WARREN	SCO	76	73	73	71	293	5	35,611.11	24,285.05
	Carlos RODILES	ESP	73	72	77	71	293	5	35,611.11	24,285.05
	Alexander NOREN	SWE	74	75	75	69	293	5	35,611.11	24,285.05
	Jarmo SANDELIN	SWE	72	78	75	68	293	5	35,611.11	24,285.05
	Christian L NILSSON	SWE	69	74	76	74	293	5	35,611.11	24,285.05
	Gary MURPHY	IRL	74	72	73	74	293	5	35,611.11	24,285.05
	Damien MCGRANE	IRL	75	72	70	76	293	5	35,611.11	24,285.05
	James HEATH	ENG	74	70	77	72	293	5	35,611.11	24,285.05
	David LYNN	ENG	72	75	76	70	293	5	35,611.11	24,285.05
21	Lee WESTWOOD	ENG	71	77	72	74	294	6	25,625.00	17,475.01
	John BICKERTON	ENG	75	74	75	70	294	6	25,625.00	17,475.01
	Oliver WILSON	ENG	73	75	74	72	294	6	25,625.00	17,475.01
	Y E YANG	KOR	72	77	71	74	294	6	25,625.00	17,475.01
	Jyoti RANDHAWA	IND	76	70	73	75	294	6	25,625.00	17,475.01
	Miguel Angel JIMÉNEZ	ESP	74	73	77	70	294	6	25,625.00	17,475.01
	Sandy LYLE	SCO	72	74	76	72	294	6	25,625.00	17,475.01
	Alastair FORSYTH	SCO	72	72	74	76	294	6	25,625.00	17,475.01
	Joakim BÄCKSTRÖM	SWE	71	71	76	76	294	6	25,625.00	17,475.01
	Phillip PRICE	WAL	72	73	74	75	294	6	25,625.00	17,475.01
31	Mark PILKINGTON	WAL	73	76	76	70	295	7	20,375.00	13,894.76
	David PARK	WAL	72	78	74	71	295	7	20,375.00	13,894.76
	Michael JONZON	SWE	72	72	77	74	295	7	20,375.00	13,894.76
	Graeme MCDOWELL	NIR	74	74	77	70	295	7	20,375.00	13,894.76
35	Martin KAYMER	GER	74	77	77	68	296	8	18,500.00	12,616.10
	Mads VIBE-HASTRUP	DEN	74	74	74	74	296	8	18,500.00	12,616.10
37	Søren HANSEN	DEN	73	72	82	70	297	9	16,000.00	10,911.22
	Mark FOSTER	ENG	73	77	75	72	297	9	16,000.00	10,911.22
	Christian CÉVAÉR	FRA	75	75	73	74	297	9	16,000.00	10,911.22
	David HIGGINS	IRL	75	70	76	76	297	9	16,000.00	10,911.22
	Rafael CABRERA BELLO	ESP	79	69	78	71	297	9	16,000.00	10,911.22
	Ignacio GARRIDO	ESP	77	71	73	76	297	9	16,000.00	10,911.22
	Stephen GALLACHER	SCO	76	73	77	71	297	9	16,000.00	10,911.22
	Richard STERNE	RSA	71	79	75	72	297	9	16,000.00	10,911.22
45	Fredrik ANDERSSON HED	SWE	76	75	74	73	298	10	12,250.00	8,353.91
	Peter GUSTAFSSON	SWE	68	75	78	77	298	10	12,250.00	8,353.91
	Maarten LAFEBER	NED	75	75	72	76	298	10	12,250.00	8,353.91
	Simon KHAN	ENG	71	79	77	71	298	10	12,250.00	8,353.91
	Edward RUSH	ENG	77	73	74	74	298	10	12,250.00	8,353.91
	Søren KJELDSEN	DEN	74	75	77	72	298	10	12,250.00	8,353.91
	Ariel CANETE	ARG	72	75	78	73	298	10	12,250.00	8,353.91
52	Brett RUMFORD	AUS	80	71	73	75	299	11	9,000.00	6,137.56
	Thomas BJÖRN	DEN	75	73	75	76	299	11	9,000.00	6,137.56
	Andrew MARSHALL	ENG	76	72	72	79	299	11	9,000.00	6,137.56
	Gary LOCKERBIE	ENG	76	75	77	71	299	11	9,000.00	6,137.56
	Emanuele CANONICA	ITA	75	76	74	74	299	11	9,000.00	6,137.56
	Mattias ELIASSON	SWE	74	74	77	74	299	11	9,000.00	6,137.56
58	Paul MCGINLEY	IRL	72	76	77	75	300	12	7,250.00	4,944.15
	Sven STRÜVER	GER	73	74	79	74	300	12	7,250.00	4,944.15
	Chris GANE	ENG	76	75	75	74	300	12	7,250.00	4,944.15
61	Steven JEPPESEN	SWE	72	74	77	78	301	13	6,625.00	4,517.93
	Steven O'HARA	SCO	73	76	78	74	301	13	6,625.00	4,517.93
63	Christopher HANELL	SWE	74	77	79	73	303	15	5,875.00	4,006.46
	Alexandre ROCHA	BRA	70	81	77	75	303	15	5,875.00	4,006.46
	Thomas LEVET	FRA	74	76	77	76	303	15	5,875.00	4,006.46
	Martin ERLANDSSON	SWE	76	72	76	79	303	15	5,875.00	4,006.46
67	Jean-Baptiste GONNET	FRA	75	74	74	81	304	16	5,125.00	3,495.00
	Gary ORR	SCO	76	75	79	74	304	16	5,125.00	3,495.00
69	Shiv KAPUR	IND	77	74	79	75	305	17	4,204.25	2,867.09
	Matthew RICHARDSON	ENG	79	72	79	75	305	17	4,204.25	2,867.09
	Kenneth FERRIE	ENG	74	75	80	76	305	17	4,204.25	2,867.09
	Matthew ZIONS	AUS	71	78	80	76	305	17	4,204.25	2,867.09
73	Pat MURRAY (AM)	IRL	76	72	79	80	307	19		
74	Peter HEDBLOM	SWE	75	74	82	83	314	26	3,744.00	2,553.23
75	Sam LITTLE	ENG	80	71	DISQ					

Total Prize Fund

€2,511,241   £1,712,544

Efficiently Dynamic

1	Anders HANSEN		280	-8
2	Justin ROSE		280	-8
3	Vijay SINGH		281	-7
	Richard STERNE		281	-7
5	Angel CABRERA		282	-6
	Miguel Angel JIMÉNEZ		282	-6
7	Luke DONALD		283	-5
8	Niclas FASTH		284	-4
	Richard GREEN		284	-4
	Thongchai JAIDEE		284	-4
	Henrik STENSON		284	-4

No man may be an island but, to be fair, the scattered and somewhat dishevelled kingdom of Denmark has done its level best to demonstrate that when English Renaissance poet John Donne came up with this, his best known line, he was somewhat wide of the mark.

So many islands make up this ancient country that the Danes, to a man, all but have access to one each. So it was entirely apposite that when Anders Hansen stepped on to the 18th tee of Wentworth Club's West Course for the opening hole of a play-off against England's local hero Justin Rose, he should wear the look of a man who feels he is not only marooned on an island, but that he is on the wrong side of it as well.

It was not that the galleries who witnessed at first hand the climax of what turned out to be a vibrant final day's play in the BMW PGA Championship were even slightly impolite to their guest, it was just that Hansen knew for whom they were really rooting.

However, he had the benefit of knowing that he had won before on The European Tour and, what is more, his sole victory came in the very same PGA Championship he was now contesting. This singular fact offered all the support he required.

The knowledge that you have not only clambered atop the highest peak but have planted a flag up there is the most serious confidence enhancer available to anyone who plays sport for a living. Rose, for all his potential, has yet to secure any of the really big titles and as it turned out, Hansen, ten years older, had the experience to hold his nerve against the Englishman.

While Rose led all the way to the green, it was Hansen who holed the crucial birdie putt to bolster his European Tour curriculum vitae by precisely 100 per cent. Rose, as gracious in defeat as he had been tenacious during the chase, accepted his loss well. "Anders did what he had to do and I couldn't match him. I tip my cap to him," he said.

Hansen's victory was the sort of unpredictable outcome that makes top-level sport such compulsive viewing. His PGA Championship win in 2002 arrived like a bolt out of the bluest of blue

Miguel Angel Jiménez

Angel Cabrera

Justin Rose

Above *Ireland's Padraig Harrington (left) with The 2006 Harry Vardon Trophy and Paul Casey of England with the Golfer of the Year Trophy for 2006 during The European Tour Annual Dinner prior to the BMW PGA Championship*

Right *Marc Warren with The Sir Henry Cotton Rookie of the Year Award for 2006*

skies, a win that no-one, including himself, could see coming. "No, I didn't expect to make my first Tour victory the PGA title," he admitted.

It was different this time, but different, ironically, because the amiable Dane felt he had even less chance of winning when he flew across the Atlantic to take part.

Back in 2002 he was full of confidence, his game caressing new levels of competence when he arrived at Wentworth Club. This time he flew into town weary of golf after a flurry of mediocre performances in the United States. Like so many players before him he was discovering that, while the US PGA Tour may be dollar rich, it is largely fun free.

Hansen came back to play in this Championship partly because, as a former champion, he felt, correctly, that he was obliged to, but he came back also because he missed the different feel of competition in Europe.

This, of course, is a familiar story. Few European golfers have ever improved their games by playing more in the United States and though the attraction of the land that hosts three of the four Major Championships each year as well as all the World Golf Championship events is obvious, the bright light that seduces so many can often be the gleam of fool's golf.

Luke Donald

Right *Francesco Molinari*

Below *Vijay Singh*

What is for certain is that few, if any, American tournaments ever display themselves with quite the bravura brush strokes that are used to paint the Wentworth landscape during this week. If there is one word that sums up the whole experience it is that most significant of English words – class.

To achieve class you must try harder than ever before but you must do this in an understated way. There can be no blowing of trumpets although there may be the faint sound of a string quartet somewhere in the distance. String quartets? Actually the music that danced over the estate came on Wednesday evening and was imported from Australia.

The East Course has played host to many sounds over the years but the concert given by Australian band INXS to launch this Championship opened up a new chapter. The evening before, The European Tour had also hosted its annual dinner; the great, the good and the extremely lucky dining in a ballroom that shimmered with glamour as they reflected on a stellar 2006 season.

Lucky, too, were the privileged few who were hosted for lunch in the corporate entertainment facility that overlooked the final green. Corporate entertaining occasionally receives a bad press but it only receives this from those who are not invited to the party.

Enjoy the perfect drive.

Wentworth

BMW
PGA Championship 2008

BMW Golfsport

bmw-golfsport.com

The Ultimate
Driving Machine

Turn a bogey into a birdie...
with the Nokia golf application...

Nokia N95

NOKIA
Nseries

Nokia N73

Nokia N93i

Carl Zeiss Optics

Pro Session Golf

EUROPEAN TOUR OFFICIAL SPONSOR

www.nokia.com/golf

José Maria Olazábal

Tented Village

Marcus Fraser

Certainly, to watch master chef Albert Roux tip-tap his walking stick in frustration at some minor error as he surveyed a sensational tapas bar was to suggest the golf had a rival as a spectator sport. Apparently, a prawn was out of alignment and so spoiling the otherwise perfect symmetry of the paella on offer that day.

These dining tables were swiftly emptied, however, as Sunday afternoon wore on, the occupants drawn instead to the action as the leaderboard took on the overcrowded look of a Friday afternoon motorway. First, Vijay Singh accelerated free of the pack with a sublime 66 that catapulted his name into the frame but which ultimately left him just one stroke short of the play-off mark. This was good to see not least for the fact that Singh's continued support of The European Tour that made his name, reflects a man with his priorities well sorted.

As Singh arrived so Angel Cabrera unexpectedly departed, the Argentine's game folding over the closing holes just when he seemed to have the title all but secured. Disappointment, too, for Paul Broadhurst and his playing partner Ross Fisher, a Wentworth Academy graduate. The pair had set out in the final group on Sunday but suffered a day to forget.

By the time Rose came to the last, Hansen was already in the clubhouse, having set the mark at eight under par 280. It meant Rose needed a birdie four at the final hole to force a play-off which meant he had to get his third shot, a 109 yard wedge approach, close. Within two feet certainly ticked that box and was a shot later voted The European Tour Shot of the Month for May.

Half-an-hour later, however, Anders Hansen made the putt to secure his second BMW PGA Championship title. An unlikely brace of victories perhaps, but sensational nonetheless.

Donne's poem, by the way, goes on to suggest a man should never ask for whom the bell tolls as it may well be tolling for him. I don't know about tolling, but I suspect the bells were ringing across a lot of Danish islands that Sunday evening.

Bill Elliott
The Observer

145

The Course

Originally designed by Harry Colt in 1927, the on-going modernisation under the guise of Ernie Els continues to improve the test for the world's best golfers. Strategic placement of new hazards means course management is at a premium while the original feel to Colt's design has been retained even down to the roll-face on the new bunkers and their general shape.

Par 4 1
432m
473 y

www.bmw-sport.com

BMW PGA

Ross Fisher

INXS perform during a concert prior to the BMW PGA Championship

BBC Presenter Gary Lineker welcomes Great Britain Special Olympics athletes to the BMW PGA Championship: (left to right) Philip Rees, Matt Sims, Gary Lineker, Ruaridh Deans and Ray Percival

Stefan Krause, (left) CFO of BMW Group, presents the trophy to Anders Hansen

> The BMW PGA Championship is even bigger than The Players Championship is in America. We have three Majors over there and you have one over here, so I think this is a premium event in Europe.
> *Vijay Singh*

Wentworth Club (West Course)

Par 72   Yards **7320**   Metres **6695**

Final Results

Pos	Name		Rd1	Rd2	Rd3	Rd4	Total		€	£
1	Anders HANSEN	DEN	74	70	67	69	280	-8	725,000.00	495,848.55
2	Justin ROSE	ENG	66	70	73	71	280	-8	483,330.00	330,563.42
3	Vijay SINGH	FIJ	73	72	70	66	281	-7	244,905.00	167,497.64
	Richard STERNE	RSA	68	73	66	74	281	-7	244,905.00	167,497.64
5	Miguel Angel JIMÉNEZ	ESP	70	68	72	72	282	-6	168,345.00	115,136.03
	Angel CABRERA	ARG	70	66	76	70	282	-6	168,345.00	115,136.03
7	Luke DONALD	ENG	71	72	71	69	283	-5	130,500.00	89,252.74
8	Richard GREEN	AUS	73	73	67	71	284	-4	93,307.50	63,815.71
	Niclas FASTH	SWE	72	73	68	71	284	-4	93,307.50	63,815.71
	Henrik STENSON	SWE	70	73	72	69	284	-4	93,307.50	63,815.71
	Thongchai JAIDEE	THA	73	70	71	70	284	-4	93,307.50	63,815.71
12	Jeev Milkha SINGH	IND	77	69	67	72	285	-3	63,183.75	43,213.20
	Peter LAWRIE	IRL	76	69	71	69	285	-3	63,183.75	43,213.20
	Markus BRIER	AUT	73	68	70	74	285	-3	63,183.75	43,213.20
	Andres ROMERO	ARG	70	72	75	68	285	-3	63,183.75	43,213.20
	Marcus FRASER	AUS	67	70	70	78	285	-3	63,183.75	43,213.20
	Lee WESTWOOD	ENG	71	72	70	72	285	-3	63,183.75	43,213.20
	Paul CASEY	ENG	73	67	72	73	285	-3	63,183.75	43,213.20
	Mikko ILONEN	FIN	68	71	74	72	285	-3	63,183.75	43,213.20
20	Christian CÉVAËR	FRA	72	72	72	70	286	-2	49,916.25	34,139.17
	Nick DOUGHERTY	ENG	69	71	71	75	286	-2	49,916.25	34,139.17
	Paul BROADHURST	ENG	66	72	68	80	286	-2	49,916.25	34,139.17
	Alejandro CAÑIZARES	ESP	68	71	74	73	286	-2	49,916.25	34,139.17
24	Fredrik ANDERSSON HED	SWE	69	72	72	74	287	-1	43,935.00	30,048.42
	Padraig HARRINGTON	IRL	69	69	75	74	287	-1	43,935.00	30,048.42
	Ernie ELS	RSA	68	76	72	71	287	-1	43,935.00	30,048.42
	Simon KHAN	ENG	67	75	73	72	287	-1	43,935.00	30,048.42
	Brett TAYLOR	ENG	71	73	72	71	287	-1	43,935.00	30,048.42
29	Maarten LAFEBER	NED	73	68	75	72	288	0	40,020.00	27,370.84
30	Robert-Jan DERKSEN	NED	73	71	72	73	289	1	33,978.33	23,238.77
	Francesco MOLINARI	ITA	67	72	78	72	289	1	33,978.33	23,238.77
	Colin MONTGOMERIE	SCO	70	76	70	73	289	1	33,978.33	23,238.77
	Marc WARREN	SCO	70	75	72	72	289	1	33,978.33	23,238.77
	Steven JEPPESEN	SWE	73	72	71	73	289	1	33,978.33	23,238.77
	Ignacio GARRIDO	ESP	71	72	73	73	289	1	33,978.33	23,238.77
	Christian L NILSSON	SWE	71	73	73	72	289	1	33,978.33	23,238.77
	Martin KAYMER	GER	71	75	73	70	289	1	33,978.33	23,238.77
	Peter O'MALLEY	AUS	71	72	71	75	289	1	33,978.33	23,238.77
39	Thomas BJÖRN	DEN	74	70	73	73	290	2	28,710.00	19,635.60
	Ross FISHER	ENG	70	67	69	84	290	2	28,710.00	19,635.60
41	Jean VAN DE VELDE	FRA	77	68	70	76	291	3	25,230.00	17,255.53
	Martin ERLANDSSON	SWE	70	75	75	71	291	3	25,230.00	17,255.53
	José Maria OLAZÁBAL	ESP	70	76	73	72	291	3	25,230.00	17,255.53
	Peter HEDBLOM	SWE	72	71	75	73	291	3	25,230.00	17,255.53
	Robert KARLSSON	SWE	72	72	72	75	291	3	25,230.00	17,255.53
	James KINGSTON	RSA	70	71	74	76	291	3	25,230.00	17,255.53
47	Andrew OLDCORN	SCO	74	71	72	75	292	4	21,315.00	14,577.95
	Oliver WILSON	ENG	70	71	76	75	292	4	21,315.00	14,577.95
	Garry HOUSTON	WAL	74	71	74	73	292	4	21,315.00	14,577.95
50	Lee SLATTERY	ENG	69	71	76	77	293	5	18,270.00	12,495.38
	Ariel CANETE	ARG	72	73	73	75	293	5	18,270.00	12,495.38
	Emanuele CANONICA	ITA	72	70	77	74	293	5	18,270.00	12,495.38
	Paul MCGINLEY	IRL	74	69	76	74	293	5	18,270.00	12,495.38
54	Christopher HANELL	SWE	72	72	74	76	294	6	15,660.00	10,710.33
	Stephen DODD	WAL	72	74	70	78	294	6	15,660.00	10,710.33
56	Mattias ELIASSON	SWE	72	72	76	75	295	7	13,376.25	9,148.41
	Jarmo SANDELIN	SWE	76	70	76	73	295	7	13,376.25	9,148.41
	James HEPWORTH	ENG	71	72	75	77	295	7	13,376.25	9,148.41
	Raphaël JACQUELIN	FRA	72	74	73	76	295	7	13,376.25	9,148.41
60	Jyoti RANDHAWA	IND	68	75	76	78	297	9	11,527.50	7,883.99
	Matthew MILLAR	AUS	69	69	79	80	297	9	11,527.50	7,883.99
	Gonzalo FDEZ-CASTAÑO	ESP	72	70	78	77	297	9	11,527.50	7,883.99
	Y E YANG	KOR	68	78	73	78	297	9	11,527.50	7,883.99
64	Richard BLAND	ENG	71	71	76	80	298	10	10,005.00	6,842.71
	Miles TUNNICLIFF	ENG	71	73	75	79	298	10	10,005.00	6,842.71
	Thomas LEVET	FRA	70	76	79	73	298	10	10,005.00	6,842.71
67	Shiv KAPUR	IND	67	71	81	81	300	12	9,135.00	6,247.69
68	Rafael ECHENIQUE	ARG	70	76	76	79	301	13	8,482.50	5,801.43
	Ricardo GONZALEZ	ARG	72	73	78	78	301	13	8,482.50	5,801.43
70	Peter GUSTAFSSON	SWE	74	72	77	79	302	14	7,930.00	5,423.56
71	Louis OOSTHUIZEN	RSA	69	77	76	81	303	15	6,523.50	4,461.61
	Marcel SIEM	GER	73	72	79	79	303	15	6,523.50	4,461.61
73	Brett RUMFORD	AUS	77	69	81	77	304	16	6,519.00	4,458.53
74	Mark FOSTER	ENG	71	75	80	80	306	18	6,514.50	4,455.46
	Johan AXGREN	SWE	75	71	77	83	306	18	6,514.50	4,455.46

Total Prize Fund

€4,382,595   £2,997,384

147

The Party Starts Here

Sir Terry Matthews, owner of The Celtic Manor Resort, sprays champagne on winner Richard Sterne watched by Mardan Mamat, Søren Kjeldsen, Mads Vibe-Hastrup and Bradley Dredge

1	**Richard STERNE**		**263**	**-13**
2	Bradley DREDGE		264	-12
	Søren KJELDSEN		264	-12
	Mardan MAMAT		264	-12
	Mads VIBE-HASTRUP		264	-12
6	Mikko ILONEN		265	-11
	Gary MURPHY		265	-11
8	Paul BROADHURST		266	-10
	Alejandro CAÑIZARES		266	-10
	Nick DOUGHERTY		266	-10
	David FROST		266	-10
	Gary ORR		266	-10
	Tom WHITEHOUSE		266	-10

149

The Ryder Cup is everywhere in Wales. It is on the M4 signs to Newport welcoming visitors to 'The 2010 Host City'; it is on the new course at The Celtic Manor Resort built especially for the biennial spectacular; and now, most obviously, it is in the hearts and minds of the Principality's golfing public.

At The Celtic Manor Wales Open they proved just how much they are looking forward to the biggest sporting event ever to hit their fairways. Be sure, they will continue to play a full, active, and vocal part in the unfolding dream of The Celtic Manor Resort owner, Sir Terry Matthews.

Firstly, though, it was time for the tournament to say goodbye to the Roman Road course, a layout that has served the competition well in the three years it has been waiting for the Twenty Ten course to be created on which The Ryder Cup will be played across the Usk Valley. When the spotlight shifts in 2008, the Roman Road course will leave behind a national Open quite rude in its health and one that continues to grow in both quality and importance.

This was the most prestigious field yet in its eight year existence, with Retief Goosen making his debut. Alongside the two-time US Open Champion was eight time European Tour Order of Merit winner Colin Montgomerie, Ryder Cup player and defending champion Robert Karlsson, 2005 US Open Champion Michael Campbell and Anders Hansen, the hero of the previous week's BMW PGA Championship at Wentworth Club.

In the event, however, all the big names were put firmly in their place by a young player whose name promises to be as big as they come.

Richard Sterne is part of the South African revolution sweeping The European Tour and followed the early season successes of his fresh-faced countrymen, Anton Haig and Charl Schwartzel, by dramatically sealing his second title on The European Tour International Schedule. This was a veritable case of the form horse at last galloping into the winners' enclosure and he did so with a grandstand finish.

Coming into the week, Sterne boasted four top five finishes in his previous five events, and when he stood on the last tee a shot behind the home favourite, Bradley Dredge, it seemed he would be denied once again.

It had been a nail-biting final hour with half a dozen players vying for the €368,812 (£250,000) first prize and there was still plenty of tension left yet. Sterne coolly birdied that 18th for a 65 and a 13 under par total of 263, while, 15 minutes later, Dredge found a fairway bunker and bogeyed. When the dust had settled it meant The Celtic Manor Wales Open had its youngest champion to date.

"It's always difficult when you are knocking on the door and don't win," said the delighted 25 year old from Pretoria. "So this means a lot and what a place to do it. It was one heck of a tournament coming down the stretch. I'd like to thank Sir Terry for all he has done here at Celtic Manor and it is going to hold a special place for me for a long time. Also, the support has been absolutely fantastic. Unfortunately for the crowds, the winner was not a Welshman, but somebody has to win and, for once, it was me."

Paul Broadhurst

Gary Murphy

Left *Mikko Ilonen*

Mads Vibe-Hastrup

walesopen.com

Alejandro Cañizares

Bradley Dredge

Nobody was about to begrudge such a worthy victor but, as Sterne himself pointed out, Welsh hopes had been sky high of a first home winner and the tension was palpable when Dredge, born in Tredegar and a resident of Cardiff, stood over that wretched five footer that would have forced a play-off.

The man, who together with Stephen Dodd brought World Cup glory to Wales in 2005, was understandably "gutted" when it slipped by. "I saw what it meant to Padraig Harrington to lift his national title when he beat me in a play-off at the Irish Open a fortnight ago and I was desperate to emulate him. But Richard deserved it," said a gracious Dredge. "However I just want to thank the supporters. They gave us a great, great atmosphere to play in out there. I was proud of them."

The feeling was mutual, particularly on the Saturday evening when Dredge holed on the final green to claim a share of the third round lead with another impressive young player, Martin Kaymer of Germany, who eventually finished tied for 14th place.

The roar that greeted the eight foot putt could have come from the nearby Millennium Stadium itself and as Sir Terry Matthews stood nearby, cheering with his fellow patriots, his vision must have never appeared so near to completion.

"You wait and see what the atmosphere will be like here in three years' time," he said. "In fact, you'll see what it's like in The Celtic Manor Wales Open these next three years and thereafter. We'll have to give out ear-muffs on the first tee. The party starts here."

Jamie Corrigan
The Independent

FINE DINING, WELL-BEING, TENNIS, SHOOTING, FOURTEEN HUNDRED ACRES
OF BREATHING SPACE AND THREE STUNNING CHAMPIONSHIP GOLF COURSES.

20 10
the
*Twenty
Ten*
CELTIC MANOR RESORT

THIS IS THE TWENTY TEN. TAILOR MADE TO CHALLENGE THE BEST.

THIS IS WHERE DRAGONS PLAY

THIS IS THE FIRST COURSE IN HISTORY BUILT TO HOST THE RYDER CUP.

RYDER CUP
1927   2010
CELTIC MANOR

celtic-manor.com

The Course

The Roman Road, designed by Robert Trent Jones Snr was, in 1995, the first of the Resort's courses to open and was ranked the top inland course in Wales by Golf Monthly. Overlooking the Severn Estuary, it is named after the many Roman Roads that criss-cross it, the design shaped to avoid disrupting any remains. Long open fairways on the front nine give way to a back nine which twists and turns through trees and across lakes and streams. The Montgomerie course in addition to the course on which the 2010 Ryder Cup will be played were opened in 2007.

Mardan Mamat

i The 2007 Celtic Manor Wales Open created European Tour history with the most players tied for the lead after a round. At the end of day one, nine players; Steve Alker, Paul Broadhurst, Ricardo Gonzalez, Søren Kjeldsen, José Maniel Lara, Paul Lawrie, Steven O'Hara, Gary Orr and Brett Rumford all finished on 65(-4). The previous record was eight at the 1995 European Masters.

The Celtic Manor Resort (Roman Road Course)
Par **69**   Yards **6743**   Metres **6165**

Final Results

Pos	Name		Rd1	Rd2	Rd3	Rd4	Total		€	£
1	Richard STERNE	RSA	67	67	64	65	263	-13	368,812.50	250,000.00
2	Mardan MAMAT	SIN	71	64	67	62	264	-12	147,215.20	99,790.00
	Mads VIBE-HASTRUP	DEN	67	63	68	66	264	-12	147,215.20	99,790.00
	Søren KJELDSEN	DEN	65	70	64	65	264	-12	147,215.20	99,790.00
	Bradley DREDGE	WAL	66	66	65	67	264	-12	147,215.20	99,790.00
6	Mikko ILONEN	FIN	67	65	70	63	265	-11	71,918.44	48,750.00
	Gary MURPHY	IRL	68	65	66	66	265	-11	71,918.44	48,750.00
8	David FROST	RSA	68	64	67	67	266	-10	43,925.57	29,775.00
	Gary ORR	SCO	65	67	68	66	266	-10	43,925.57	29,775.00
	Alejandro CAÑIZARES	ESP	69	67	65	65	266	-10	43,925.57	29,775.00
	Nick DOUGHERTY	ENG	69	63	68	66	266	-10	43,925.57	29,775.00
	Tom WHITEHOUSE	ENG	71	65	66	64	266	-10	43,925.57	29,775.00
	Paul BROADHURST	ENG	65	67	67	67	266	-10	43,925.57	29,775.00
14	Grégory BOURDY	FRA	66	71	66	64	267	-9	32,529.26	22,050.00
	Andrew COLTART	SCO	69	65	67	66	267	-9	32,529.26	22,050.00
	Martin KAYMER	GER	69	63	65	70	267	-9	32,529.26	22,050.00
17	Jyoti RANDHAWA	IND	69	66	68	65	268	-8	28,619.85	19,400.00
	Oliver WILSON	ENG	66	68	68	66	268	-8	28,619.85	19,400.00
	Miles TUNNICLIFF	ENG	70	65	68	65	268	-8	28,619.85	19,400.00
20	Colin MONTGOMERIE	SCO	70	64	72	63	269	-7	25,049.75	16,980.00
	Stephen GALLACHER	SCO	67	66	67	69	269	-7	25,049.75	16,980.00
	Alastair FORSYTH	SCO	66	65	70	68	269	-7	25,049.75	16,980.00
	Steven O'HARA	SCO	65	69	66	69	269	-7	25,049.75	16,980.00
	Martin ERLANDSSON	SWE	66	69	66	68	269	-7	25,049.75	16,980.00
25	Garry HOUSTON	WAL	67	69	69	65	270	-6	22,018.11	14,925.00
	Rafael CABRERA BELLO	ESP	68	68	64	70	270	-6	22,018.11	14,925.00
	Raphaël JACQUELIN	FRA	68	68	69	65	270	-6	22,018.11	14,925.00
	Peter LAWRIE	IRL	66	69	68	67	270	-6	22,018.11	14,925.00
29	Eirik Tage JOHANSEN	NOR	69	66	66	70	271	-5	19,030.73	12,900.00
	Michael CAMPBELL	NZL	66	66	69	70	271	-5	19,030.73	12,900.00
	Paul LAWRIE	SCO	65	68	71	67	271	-5	19,030.73	12,900.00
	Matthew ZIONS	AUS	66	67	68	70	271	-5	19,030.73	12,900.00
	Benn BARHAM	ENG	70	63	69	69	271	-5	19,030.73	12,900.00
34	David GRIFFITHS	ENG	68	65	71	68	272	-4	17,039.14	11,550.00
35	Simon KHAN	ENG	67	66	68	72	273	-3	15,047.55	10,200.00
	Grégory HAVRET	FRA	69	63	71	70	273	-3	15,047.55	10,200.00
	Thomas LEVET	FRA	68	67	69	69	273	-3	15,047.55	10,200.00
	Phillip ARCHER	ENG	68	65	70	70	273	-3	15,047.55	10,200.00
	Kenneth FERRIE	ENG	71	64	65	73	273	-3	15,047.55	10,200.00
	Jesus Maria ARRUTI	ESP	69	67	69	68	273	-3	15,047.55	10,200.00
	Mattias ELIASSON	SWE	66	69	68	70	273	-3	15,047.55	10,200.00
	Anton HAIG	RSA	68	67	74	64	273	-3	15,047.55	10,200.00
43	Shiv KAPUR	IND	68	69	71	66	274	-2	11,949.53	8,100.00
	Gonzalo FDEZ-CASTAÑO	ESP	67	70	68	69	274	-2	11,949.53	8,100.00
	Ricardo GONZALEZ	ARG	65	67	73	69	274	-2	11,949.53	8,100.00
	Rafael ECHENIQUE	ARG	72	65	65	72	274	-2	11,949.53	8,100.00
	Marcus FRASER	AUS	68	69	69	68	274	-2	11,949.53	8,100.00
	Brett RUMFORD	AUS	65	66	72	71	274	-2	11,949.53	8,100.00
49	Anders HANSEN	DEN	70	65	73	67	275	-1	9,957.94	6,750.00
	Ignacio GARRIDO	ESP	68	66	70	71	275	-1	9,957.94	6,750.00
	Christian CÉVAÉR	FRA	66	69	72	68	275	-1	9,957.94	6,750.00
52	Steve ALKER	NZL	65	72	69	70	276	0	8,408.93	5,700.00
	Joakim HAEGGMAN	SWE	66	71	71	68	276	0	8,408.93	5,700.00
	José Manuel LARA	ESP	65	69	71	71	276	0	8,408.93	5,700.00
	Robert ROCK	ENG	67	70	69	70	276	0	8,408.93	5,700.00
56	Simon WAKEFIELD	ENG	69	68	68	72	277	1	6,682.88	4,530.00
	David BRANSDON	AUS	68	68	70	71	277	1	6,682.88	4,530.00
	Mark FOSTER	ENG	67	68	72	70	277	1	6,682.88	4,530.00
	Henrik NYSTROM	SWE	70	67	66	74	277	1	6,682.88	4,530.00
	James KINGSTON	RSA	66	68	72	71	277	1	6,682.88	4,530.00
61	David CARTER	ENG	68	68	73	70	279	3	5,864.12	3,975.00
	Liam BOND	WAL	66	68	75	70	279	3	5,864.12	3,975.00
63	Phillip PRICE	WAL	67	70	70	73	280	4	4,978.97	3,375.00
	Robert-Jan DERKSEN	NED	66	66	73	72	280	4	4,978.97	3,375.00
	Marcel SIEM	GER	69	68	73	70	280	4	4,978.97	3,375.00
	Simon THORNTON	IRL	69	64	73	74	280	4	4,978.97	3,375.00
	Emanuele CANONICA	ITA	69	68	75	68	280	4	4,978.97	3,375.00
	Manuel QUIROS	ESP	70	67	70	73	280	4	4,978.97	3,375.00
69	James HEATH	ENG	67	69	69	76	281	5	4,123.32	2,795.00
	Kyron SULLIVAN	WAL	68	68	72	73	281	5	4,123.32	2,795.00
71	Fredrik ANDERSSON HED	SWE	72	64	74	76	286	10	3,319.00	2,249.79

Total Prize Fund

€2,216,194   £1,502,249

Life's a Beach

Bank Austri Creditanstal

1	Richard GREEN		268	-16
2	Jean-François REMESY		268	-16
3	Chris GANE		269	-15
	Miguel Angel JIMÉNEZ		269	-15
	Michael JONZON		269	-15
6	Stephen GALLACHER		270	-14
7	Steven JEPPESEN		271	-13
	Graeme STORM		271	-13
9	Martin ERLANDSSON		273	-11
	David HIGGINS		273	-11
	Graeme McDOWELL		273	-11
	Richard McEVOY		273	-11
	Tom WHITEHOUSE		273	-11

It might not be Bondi but, nevertheless for Richard Green, life is a beach at Fontana. The striking Golf Club near the Austrian capital of Vienna has its own shoreline and golden sands but, more importantly, it also has a course which suited Green's game down to the ground.

Pelle Edberg

Jean-Francois Remesy

The Australian left-hander - who divides his time between Melbourne, where there are many famous beaches and golf courses in their own right, and Bagshot in the south-east of England, where there is not a deckchair or dune in sight - decided to dip his toe in the water at Fontana Golf Club in the summer of 2006.

The result? A course record equalling 63 in the final round for a fourth place finish only five shots adrift of the emotional home winner Markus Brier. Yes, you could safely say that Green liked Fontana a lot and when he laid out his schedule for 2007, he knew he would be giving Vienna a whirl again.

He arrived in Austria with his game in great shape and was optimistic of ending a decade's wait for a second European Tour title. Since shaking the world of golf by beating Greg Norman and Ian Woosnam in a play-off for the 1997 Dubai Desert Classic, Green had flattered to deceive.

Chances came thick and fast - and went at the same rate. The quiet man with a passion for motorsports, who had only the 2004 MasterCard Masters in his home country to show on his CV since his magnificent success in the desert, was starting to get a little desperate. Would Fontana be able to rev him up and turn the tide?

In the first round, played in high temperatures and humidity, Green was not as hot as Graeme Storm. The 1999 Amateur Champion equalled the efforts of the Australian and Frenchman Grégory Havret in 2006 by carding a 63 to take the lead. For Green, there was a place in the chasing pack after a round of 66.

Understandably, the eyes of the home gallery were all trained on Brier. The Fontana Golf Club member was to disappoint them this time, however, agonisingly missing the cut the next day by a single shot, one of 19 players to suffer such a fate.

Steven Jeppesen

Amongst them was Darren Clarke but what made it worse for the Ulsterman, attempting to make his first cut since February, was that the elements seemed to have it in for him too. A freak "monsoon", as his caddie called it, blew up for exactly the length of time it took to play his second shot into the 18th green. It was a cruel gust that blew Clarke's ball into the water, his hopes of weekend action sinking with it.

The outlook proved much brighter for Green as a 65 on Friday hauled him to the top of the leaderboard. It got even better the following day as he added a 67 to take a three shot advantage into the final round.

Green's theory that Fontana suited those who grip the club with left hand below right was borne out by another 'lefty' who came to the fore. Englishman Chris Gane seemed out of contention after an opening 75 but excellent closing rounds of 65-64-65 saw him end in a share of third place with Spain's Miguel Angel Jiménez and Michael Jonzon of Sweden.

Before that, a thunderstorm had replaced the burnishing sun on Sunday afternoon, heavy rain and lightning quickly bringing both golfers and bathers undercover, and, long before the klaxon sounded, dark clouds had started to gather for Green.

Early mistakes had seen him lose pole position, but with admirable courage he composed himself upon the resumption and battled back into contention.

Up ahead, Jean-Francois Remesy had closed with a stunning 64 to set the clubhouse total of 16 under par 268 and could only look on as Green played the long 18th, a risky hole above the beach and rocks but one that also yielded a glut of birdies, knowing a par five would end his ten year wait.

Almost inexplicably, Green three putted from the edge of the putting surface for a bogey six to fall into a play-off but on the pair's return to the 18th hole moments later, the Frenchman found the beach too much of an attraction. Or at least his ball did as an errant approach shot onto the rocks ended his challenge.

A birdie four by Green was, in the end, unnecessary but enjoyable none the less for the Australian considering what had occurred moments earlier. What really mattered to him was being, at last, a double winner on The European Tour. It had all gone swimmingly in the end.

Norman Dabell

Stephen Gallacher

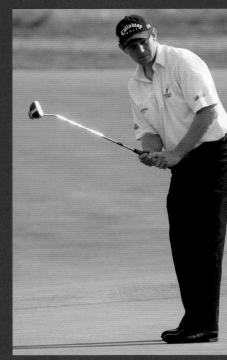

Ryder Cup Captain Nick Faldo proudly displays The Ryder Cup Trophy to Delegates at The European Tour Grass Roots Golf Initiative and Congress, whose number included; George O'Grady, Chief Executive, The European Tour (fourth from right); Richard Hills, Ryder Cup Director (far left) and Austria's Markus Brier, the 2006 BA-CA Golf Open champion (next to Faldo)

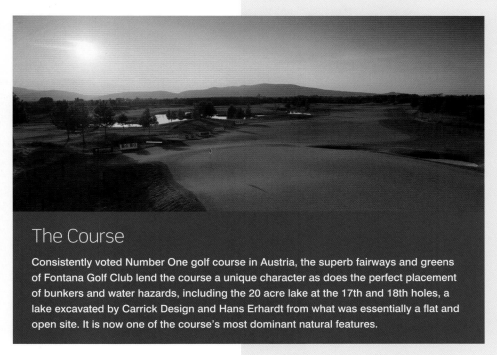

The Course

Consistently voted Number One golf course in Austria, the superb fairways and greens of Fontana Golf Club lend the course a unique character as does the perfect placement of bunkers and water hazards, including the 20 acre lake at the 17th and 18th holes, a lake excavated by Carrick Design and Hans Erhardt from what was essentially a flat and open site. It is now one of the course's most dominant natural features.

Richard Green (centre) receives the trophy for winning from Regina Prehofer, member of the board BA-CA, and Siegfried Wolf, CEO Magna and President Fontana GC

> I am relieved now. I feel I am in the prime of my career and I always felt I would win again and get the monkey off my back. My brain was pretty scrambled as I signed my card but I still felt I could win. My caddie, Stuart, told me to remember my play-off record. I won in Dubai ten years ago and I also won the Australian Masters after a play-off. Simon Dyson beat me in the KLM Open but three wins out of four isn't bad. I had to get my focus back for the play off and Stuart's words definitely helped.
>
> **Richard Green**

Fontana Golf Club

Par **71**   Yards **7071**   Metres **6466**

Final Results

Pos	Name		Rd1	Rd2	Rd3	Rd4	Total		€	£
1	Richard GREEN	AUS	66	65	67	70	268	-16	216,660.00	147,036.67
2	Jean-François REMESY	FRA	72	67	65	64	268	-16	144,440.00	98,024.45
3	Miguel Angel JIMÉNEZ	ESP	68	65	69	67	269	-15	67,166.67	45,582.77
	Michael JONZON	SWE	70	69	64	66	269	-15	67,166.67	45,582.77
	Chris GANE	ENG	75	65	64	65	269	-15	67,166.67	45,582.77
6	Stephen GALLACHER	SCO	69	68	68	65	270	-14	45,500.00	30,878.65
7	Graeme STORM	ENG	63	72	69	67	271	-13	35,750.00	24,261.80
	Steven JEPPESEN	SWE	67	66	69	69	271	-13	35,750.00	24,261.80
9	Tom WHITEHOUSE	ENG	65	71	69	68	273	-11	24,466.00	16,603.89
	Richard MCEVOY	ENG	66	71	64	72	273	-11	24,466.00	16,603.89
	Martin ERLANDSSON	SWE	64	68	73	68	273	-11	24,466.00	16,603.89
	David HIGGINS	IRL	70	71	67	65	273	-11	24,466.00	16,603.89
	Graeme MCDOWELL	NIR	71	69	69	64	273	-11	24,466.00	16,603.89
14	Johan SKÖLD	SWE	70	69	64	71	274	-10	18,720.00	12,704.36
	Jarmo SANDELIN	SWE	67	68	69	70	274	-10	18,720.00	12,704.36
	Gary ORR	SCO	71	67	66	70	274	-10	18,720.00	12,704.36
	Pelle EDBERG	SWE	67	66	73	68	274	-10	18,720.00	12,704.36
18	Patrik SJÖLAND	SWE	65	73	67	70	275	-9	16,163.33	10,969.27
	Taichi TESHIMA	JPN	71	68	70	66	275	-9	16,163.33	10,969.27
	Grégory HAVRET	FRA	71	65	72	67	275	-9	16,163.33	10,969.27
21	Birgir HAFTHORSSON	ISL	70	71	68	67	276	-8	14,105.00	9,572.38
	Euan LITTLE	SCO	68	73	66	69	276	-8	14,105.00	9,572.38
	Edward RUSH	ENG	67	74	68	67	276	-8	14,105.00	9,572.38
	Shaun P WEBSTER	ENG	65	71	68	72	276	-8	14,105.00	9,572.38
	Matthew ZIONS	AUS	68	73	68	67	276	-8	14,105.00	9,572.38
	David PARK	WAL	69	66	68	73	276	-8	14,105.00	9,572.38
27	Garry HOUSTON	WAL	72	63	70	72	277	-7	11,765.00	7,984.34
	Sam LITTLE	ENG	73	67	67	70	277	-7	11,765.00	7,984.34
	Oliver FISHER	ENG	68	72	70	67	277	-7	11,765.00	7,984.34
	Gary LOCKERBIE	ENG	66	72	68	71	277	-7	11,765.00	7,984.34
	François CALMELS	FRA	66	73	69	69	277	-7	11,765.00	7,984.34
	David FROST	RSA	68	71	68	70	277	-7	11,765.00	7,984.34
33	David BRANSDON	AUS	69	68	73	68	278	-6	10,205.00	6,925.64
	Sion E BEBB	WAL	70	68	71	69	278	-6	10,205.00	6,925.64
35	Bernd WIESBERGER	AUT	68	71	69	71	279	-5	9,490.00	6,440.40
	Paul BROADHURST	ENG	75	67	68	69	279	-5	9,490.00	6,440.40
	Santiago LUNA	ESP	68	71	70	70	279	-5	9,490.00	6,440.40
38	Carlos RODILES	ESP	68	70	71	71	280	-4	8,190.00	5,558.16
	Steve ALKER	NZL	69	73	69	69	280	-4	8,190.00	5,558.16
	Raphaël EYRAUD	FRA	71	70	70	69	280	-4	8,190.00	5,558.16
	Miles TUNNICLIFF	ENG	69	68	76	67	280	-4	8,190.00	5,558.16
	Richard FINCH	ENG	66	70	73	71	280	-4	8,190.00	5,558.16
	Mads VIBE-HASTRUP	DEN	68	70	74	68	280	-4	8,190.00	5,558.16
	Søren HANSEN	DEN	70	70	70	70	280	-4	8,190.00	5,558.16
45	Nicolas COLSAERTS	BEL	68	73	72	68	281	-3	6,760.00	4,587.69
	Hernan REY	ARG	69	73	69	70	281	-3	6,760.00	4,587.69
	Ian GARBUTT	ENG	71	67	73	70	281	-3	6,760.00	4,587.69
	Jesus Maria ARRUTI	ESP	68	69	72	70	281	-3	6,760.00	4,587.69
49	Sebastian FERNANDEZ	ARG	74	68	70	70	282	-2	5,850.00	3,970.11
	Terry PILKADARIS	AUS	71	70	71	70	282	-2	5,850.00	3,970.11
	Kyron SULLIVAN	WAL	68	72	71	71	282	-2	5,850.00	3,970.11
52	Peter FOWLER	AUS	70	72	70	71	283	-1	4,810.00	3,264.31
	Lee WESTWOOD	ENG	66	72	75	70	283	-1	4,810.00	3,264.31
	Carl SUNESON	ESP	69	72	70	72	283	-1	4,810.00	3,264.31
	Roope KAKKO	FIN	74	68	72	69	283	-1	4,810.00	3,264.31
	Alessandro TADINI	ITA	67	72	73	71	283	-1	4,810.00	3,264.31
57	Jean HUGO	RSA	72	70	69	73	284	0	3,965.00	2,690.85
	Simon NASH	AUS	73	68	68	75	284	0	3,965.00	2,690.85
59	Robert-Jan DERKSEN	NED	70	70	69	76	285	1	3,770.00	2,558.52
60	Rafael GOMEZ	ARG	70	71	75	70	286	2	3,575.00	2,426.18
	Iain PYMAN	ENG	71	70	73	72	286	2	3,575.00	2,426.18
62	Daniel DENISON	ENG	66	76	73	72	287	3	3,315.00	2,249.73
	Richard BLAND	ENG	70	71	70	76	287	3	3,315.00	2,249.73
64	Andrew BUTTERFIELD	ENG	72	70	73	73	288	4	3,120.00	2,117.39
65	Wade ORMSBY	AUS	73	69	79	69	290	6	2,860.00	1,940.94
	José Manuel CARRILES	ESP	70	72	73	75	290	6	2,860.00	1,940.94
	Matjaz GOJCIC	SLO	68	70	73	79	290	6	2,860.00	1,940.94
68	Marc CAYEUX	ZIM	70	71	76	74	291	7	2,600.00	1,764.49

Total Prize Fund

€1,295,150   £878,955

Triumph over Adversity

1	Carl SUNESON		276	-8
2	François CALMELS		279	-5
	Peter FOWLER		279	-5
	Marcus HIGLEY		279	-5
5	Mikael LUNDBERG		280	-4
6	Michael LORENZO-VERA		281	-3
7	Stuart DAVIS		283	-1
	Sébastien DELAGRANGE		283	-1
	Richard McEVOY		283	-1
10	Daniel DENISON		284	0
	Klas ERIKSSON		284	0
	Gareth PADDISON		284	0

Those who do not know the story of Carl Suneson's career may have thought the Spaniard was simply another sportsman getting carried away by the moment as he was overcome by emotion during his winner's speech at the OPEN DE SAINT-OMER presented by NEUFLIZE OBC. Anyone with an awareness of the fine details of Suneson's 18 year fight as a professional, though, could be forgiven for shedding a tear of their own.

Marcus Higley

Peter Fowler

As Suneson's eyes filled and his voice crackled upon dedicating the greatest day in his career to his family, and in particular his 94 year old grandfather who had always had great faith in his ability, his tears told a story of overcoming all the odds, and the conquest of two potentially career-threatening illnesses.

Hyperthyroidism and diabetes affect the lives of millions around the world. The majority who suffer from either can control the problem with medication and lead normal working lives, but to a professional sportsman like Suneson, the discovery of both was a hammer blow.

Having turned professional in 1989, Suneson had made four attempts to secure his place on The European Tour via the Qualifying School before he won his card in 1993, a breakthrough that promised a bright future.

Season 1994 began with Suneson, the type of player who would practice in the dark such was his dedication to golf and the nature of his work ethic, striving towards a maiden victory.

But, just as his career was gathering momentum, he began to suffer a dramatic weight loss despite a ravenous appetite, shedding 21 kilos in the space of a few months. He sought medical advice and soon discovered an overactive thyroid gland, the effects of which - fatigue, hyperactivity, apathy and depression amongst others - wrecked his immediate thoughts of winning at European golf's highest level and cast doubts over his long term ability to maintain a career on The European Tour.

To ensure the problem was permanently remedied, the Spaniard underwent radioactive iodine treatment to rid his body of all symptoms. The treatment was, and remains, a success, the only drawback being his dependence on daily hormone tablets.

With his thyroid problem under control, Suneson began to turn his thoughts to curing the rust in his golf swing. But as he prepared for a second assault on The European Tour he was diagnosed with Type One Diabetes.

"The diabetes was worse because when your energy levels go on the golf course your body just shuts down," he explained. "It's like being drunk - you have no control over your body.

"I went to see the doctor about it and he told me that it was going to be hard to play professional golf, and that I should think about another job. I'll never forget that moment. I replied: 'Are you

Richard Green of Australia during the 2007 Abu Dhabi Golf Championship,
United Arab Emirates, January 19, 2007. 73041308, David Cannon

Paula Creamer at the LPGA Kraft Nabisco Championship Rancho Mirage,
California, March 28, 2007. 73749049, Robert Laberge

Paul Casey of England during the HSBC Champions tournament, Shanghai,
November 9, 2006. 72469070, Ross Kinnaird

Performance is passion

From St Andrews to Shanghai.
From QSchool to the Claret Jug.
Your brand. Our imagery. One passion.

serious?' "He explained that because my sugar levels would go up and down so much, it would be difficult to control it in my situation. I simply stood up and walked out of his office – there was no way I was giving up."

By the time Suneson got the balance of his blood-sugar levels right and got back to full fitness, the 1997 season was under way. He worked hard and slowly recaptured the form that had allowed him to harbour hopes of winning on The European Tour. He lost his card again in 1998, and failed at the Tour School, but once again he demonstrated his determination on the fairways by winning three times on the 1999 European Challenge Tour en route to finishing Number One. Suneson returned to The European Tour, finished 60th in the Order of Merit in 2000, but then lost his card again.

It would be another six and half years of hard graft before Suneson finally achieved his ultimate goal, and when the moment came,

on Sunday June 17, 2007, he secured his first European Tour win in some style at the Aa Saint Omer Golf Club.

After opening scores of 67-70-70, he secured his triumph with a beautifully controlled final round of 69 to win by three shots from Frenchman François Calmels, Australian Peter Fowler and Marcus Higley of England. He made the breakthrough precisely 35 days before his 40th birthday.

With his scorecard signed and the trophy in hand, Suneson was nearing the end of his winner's speech when he was suddenly overwhelmed by the magnitude of his achievement. It was a wonderful moment for the man himself, his family and friends, the end of an 18 year fight in which he conquered adversity with the dignity and class of a true champion.

Michael Gibbons

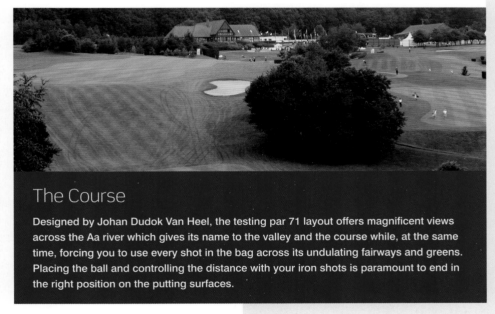

The Course

Designed by Johan Dudok Van Heel, the testing par 71 layout offers magnificent views across the Aa river which gives its name to the valley and the course while, at the same time, forcing you to use every shot in the bag across its undulating fairways and greens. Placing the ball and controlling the distance with your iron shots is paramount to end in the right position on the putting surfaces.

Carl Suneson (left) is presented with the trophy by Jean-Jacques Durand, President and owner of Aa Saint Omer GC

> My grandfather introduced my family to golf and he always said he wanted me to win on Tour. It means so much to finally achieve that and I want to dedicate this to him.
> *Carl Suneson*

Aa Saint Omer Golf Club
Par 71   Yards 6845   Metres 6259

Final Results

Pos	Name		Rd1	Rd2	Rd3	Rd4	Total		€	£
1	Carl SUNESON	ESP	67	70	70	69	276	-8	83,330.00	56,631.60
2	François CALMELS	FRA	72	69	69	69	279	-5	37,283.33	25,337.99
	Peter FOWLER	AUS	70	67	72	70	279	-5	37,283.33	25,337.99
	Marcus HIGLEY	ENG	67	70	71	71	279	-5	37,283.33	25,337.99
5	Mikael LUNDBERG	SWE	70	68	71	71	280	-4	21,200.00	14,407.66
6	Michael LORENZO-VERA	FRA	67	73	71	70	281	-3	17,500.00	11,893.11
7	Sébastien DELAGRANGE	FRA	72	68	73	70	283	-1	12,900.00	8,766.92
	Richard MCEVOY	ENG	74	66	74	69	283	-1	12,900.00	8,766.92
	Stuart DAVIS	ENG	68	70	72	73	283	-1	12,900.00	8,766.92
10	Daniel DENISON	ENG	67	74	72	71	284	0	9,266.67	6,297.69
	Klas ERIKSSON	SWE	74	70	71	69	284	0	9,266.67	6,297.69
	Gareth PADDISON	NZL	68	72	72	72	284	0	9,266.67	6,297.69
13	Gary CLARK	ENG	70	73	71	71	285	1	7,683.33	5,221.64
	Sam LITTLE	ENG	72	69	74	70	285	1	7,683.33	5,221.64
	Liam BOND	WAL	70	73	74	68	285	1	7,683.33	5,221.64
16	Wilhelm SCHAUMAN	SWE	72	70	73	71	286	2	6,271.43	4,262.10
	Jerome THEUNIS	BEL	75	70	72	69	286	2	6,271.43	4,262.10
	Simon NASH	AUS	74	69	71	72	286	2	6,271.43	4,262.10
	Julio ZAPATA	ARG	71	68	75	72	286	2	6,271.43	4,262.10
	Martin MARITZ	RSA	74	70	72	70	286	2	6,271.43	4,262.10
	Andrew OLDCORN	SCO	70	74	71	71	286	2	6,271.43	4,262.10
	Raphaël EYRAUD	FRA	67	73	73	73	286	2	6,271.43	4,262.10
23	Mickael DIEU	FRA	74	71	68	74	287	3	5,350.00	3,635.89
	Santiago LUNA	ESP	67	71	77	72	287	3	5,350.00	3,635.89
	Gustavo ROJAS	ARG	70	75	67	75	287	3	5,350.00	3,635.89
26	Manuel MERIZALDE	COL	69	72	71	76	288	4	4,600.00	3,126.19
	Thomas NIELSEN	DEN	71	74	71	72	288	4	4,600.00	3,126.19
	Jesus Maria ARRUTI	ESP	75	69	73	71	288	4	4,600.00	3,126.19
	Andrew MCARTHUR	SCO	70	73	70	75	288	4	4,600.00	3,126.19
	Birgir HAFTHORSSON	ISL	70	74	72	72	288	4	4,600.00	3,126.19
	Steve ALKER	NZL	71	68	73	76	288	4	4,600.00	3,126.19
	Sion E BEBB	WAL	69	72	75	72	288	4	4,600.00	3,126.19
33	Jan-Are LARSEN	NOR	74	71	71	73	289	5	3,760.00	2,555.32
	David HIGGINS	IRL	65	76	74	74	289	5	3,760.00	2,555.32
	Paul NILBRINK	NOR	73	72	71	73	289	5	3,760.00	2,555.32
	Richard FINCH	ENG	73	72	73	71	289	5	3,760.00	2,555.32
	Anders Schmidt HANSEN	DEN	67	75	71	76	289	5	3,760.00	2,555.32
38	Sebastian FERNANDEZ	ARG	74	70	73	73	290	6	3,100.00	2,106.78
	Robert COLES	ENG	73	70	71	76	290	6	3,100.00	2,106.78
	Cédric MENUT	FRA	73	71	73	73	290	6	3,100.00	2,106.78
	Roope KAKKO	FIN	71	73	73	73	290	6	3,100.00	2,106.78
	Ross McGOWAN	ENG	70	73	73	74	290	6	3,100.00	2,106.78
	Peter BAKER	ENG	71	73	71	75	290	6	3,100.00	2,106.78
	Philip GOLDING	ENG	71	71	74	74	290	6	3,100.00	2,106.78
	Stuart MANLEY	WAL	73	71	73	73	290	6	3,100.00	2,106.78
46	Mikko KORHONEN	FIN	71	73	78	69	291	7	2,500.00	1,699.02
	Jean-Nicolas BILLOT	FRA	70	75	73	73	291	7	2,500.00	1,699.02
	Felipe AGUILAR	CHI	72	70	77	72	291	7	2,500.00	1,699.02
	Paolo TERRENI	ITA	71	68	81	71	291	7	2,500.00	1,699.02
50	Alvaro VELASCO	ESP	73	71	71	77	292	8	2,100.00	1,427.17
	Nicolas VANHOOTEGEM	BEL	75	70	73	74	292	8	2,100.00	1,427.17
	Ally MELLOR	ENG	69	72	78	73	292	8	2,100.00	1,427.17
	Iain PYMAN	ENG	72	72	76	72	292	8	2,100.00	1,427.17
54	Adrien MÖRK	FRA	72	72	78	71	293	9	1,800.00	1,223.29
	Jamie DONALDSON	WAL	69	73	79	72	293	9	1,800.00	1,223.29
56	Julien CLÉMENT	SUI	69	71	77	77	294	10	1,405.56	955.22
	Benoit TEILLERIA	FRA	71	73	77	73	294	10	1,405.56	955.22
	Sven STRÜVER	GER	71	74	77	72	294	10	1,405.56	955.22
	Joost LUITEN	NED	70	75	75	74	294	10	1,405.56	955.22
	Carlos DEL MORAL	ESP	70	74	74	76	294	10	1,405.56	955.22
	Matthew KING	ENG	72	68	76	78	294	10	1,405.56	955.22
	Robert DINWIDDIE	ENG	71	73	75	75	294	10	1,405.56	955.22
	David BRANSDON	AUS	65	77	78	74	294	10	1,405.56	955.22
	Niki ZITNY	AUT	71	69	75	79	294	10	1,405.56	955.22
65	Hernan REY	ARG	71	72	80	72	295	11	1,050.00	713.59
	Luis CLAVERIE	ESP	74	70	76	75	295	11	1,050.00	713.59
	Johan SKÖLD	SWE	72	73	72	78	295	11	1,050.00	713.59
	Chris DOAK	SCO	73	69	78	75	295	11	1,050.00	713.59
	Julien XANTHOPOULOS	FRA	71	73	79	72	295	11	1,050.00	713.59
70	Rodolfo GONZALEZ	ARG	70	75	76	75	296	12	835.00	567.47
	Gareth WRIGHT	WAL	71	73	74	78	296	12	835.00	567.47
72	Craig WILLIAMS	WAL	73	71	78	75	297	13	742.50	504.61
	Scott STRANGE	AUS	71	74	79	73	297	13	742.50	504.61
	Andrew RAITT	ENG	71	74	77	75	297	13	742.50	504.61
	Joakim HAEGGMAN	SWE	72	72	73	80	297	13	742.50	504.61
76	Stephen BROWNE	IRL	71	72	77	78	298	14	733.50	498.49
	Phil WORTHINGTON	ENG	71	72	77	78	298	14	733.50	498.49
78	Alessio BRUSCHI	ITA	73	72	75	79	299	15	729.00	495.43
79	Kariem BARAKA	GER	71	74	80	75	300	16	724.50	492.37
	Alvaro SALTO	ESP	71	74	80	75	300	16	724.50	492.37
81	François DELAMONTAGNE	FRA	74	71	78	78	301	17	720.00	489.32

Total Prize Fund
€508,085   £345,297

Holy Smoke!

1	**Angel CABRERA**		285	5
2	Jim FURYK		286	6
	Tiger WOODS		286	6
4	Niclas FASTH		287	7
5	David TOMS		289	9
	Bubba WATSON		289	9
7	Nick DOUGHERTY		290	10
	Jerry KELLY		290	10
	Scott VERPLANK		290	10
10	Stephen AMES		291	11
	Paul CASEY		291	11
	Justin ROSE		291	11

Strictly speaking, this was another Major Championship to have passed by without a European winner. But the US Open Championship at Oakmont Country Club in Pennsylvania did provide the next best thing, for, in Angel Cabrera, not only was there an entirely worthy winner, he was also one nurtured through most of his professional career by playing on The European Tour.

That in the final shake up he beat the World Number One, Tiger Woods, and the World Number Three, Jim Furyk, by a single shot, made victory all the sweeter for the burly, barrel-chested Argentine, whose initial tournament win in America this was.

As he reflects on this memorable triumph he will come to realise that he has joined a very exclusive club. Only four other golfers have made the US Open Championship their first professional victory in America, namely Ernie Els, Retief Goosen, Jack Nicklaus and Lee Trevino. Nicklaus, furthermore, did it at Oakmont back in 1962.

However, as Cabrera remarked afterwards: "I was able to beat the best player in the world and the rest of the players here, but I wasn't able to beat the golf course. The golf course beat me."

It was a direct reference, firstly, to his winning score of five over par 285 and, secondly, to the way the United States Golf Association set up the course. During the practice rounds Oakmont was, to utilise a word much used by the players, brutal. The rough was so long and tangly that you could, as Phil Mickelson did, damage a wrist trying to remove a ball from it.

The fairways were narrow strips of grass cut so low that balls raced on and on, often into the aforementioned rough, and the greens were simply frightening. But then Oakmont greens have a history. In the 2003 US Amateur Championship held there, a competitor found the severely sloping second green in the regulation two shots and putted up three feet above the hole. The ball stopped, the player marked it, but when he went to replace his ball by the marker it would not stay there.

An official was called but he, too, could not get the ball to stay. They soon realised they would have to replace the ball somewhere on the green, not nearer the hole, where it would stay by the marker.

This was done, and the ball stayed. However, as the player removed the marker but before he had addressed his ball, it started rolling – and did not stop until it fell into the hole. The player, bemused, asked the official what was to happen now and was told: "Pick your ball up son, you have a birdie." In other words, Oakmont greens can get so quick there are times when you do not even have to hit your putts to hole them.

Justin Rose

Nick Dougherty

Paul Casey

Niclas Fasth

Course preparation has become a big issue over the last few years with players more willing to put their case than in the days when they were expected to do as they were told.

Perhaps because of the chorus of comments during Monday, Tuesday and Wednesday, the USGA kept a keen eye on the state of affairs rather than have a repeat of Shinnecock Hills in 2004 when the course got away from them completely to leave putting at best, difficult, but at times, farcical. Indeed, they even watered the putting surfaces over the last two days in Pennsylvania to avoid such scenes again.

As Woods put it when asked what his impressions were of Oakmont after four competitive rounds: "Considering they softened the golf course up for us and we still shot five over par as a winning score, that shows you how difficult this golf course really is."

The USGA always say that what they want is a "rigorous but fair" test of the field. At Oakmont things were definitely rigorous but Ian Poulter

was among those who felt it was fair. "There is no point bitching and moaning that it is a difficult golf course, because it is not supposed to be easy," said the Englishman. "You can't just say, this is unfair, let's all chuck the towel in and go home."

Mature words indeed from Poulter and a mature decision by the USGA to keep the course immensely difficult but definitely playable.

Players find many different ways to cope with the stresses and strains of such top level competition but perhaps it is best to leave the last word on the matter to the new champion who admitted to a technique which might raise a few eyebrows in the health conscious 21st century, but one which also raised a few smiles for its refreshing honesty.

"Some players have psychologists," said Cabrera. "Some have sportologists......I smoke!"

David Davies

165

BETTER THAN EVER.
MOST TRUSTED OF ALL.

2007 Worldwide Golf Ball Count

Titleist	18,688
Nearest Competitor	2,298

What a great series of highlights, the 2007 season has delivered for the new Titleist Pro V1 and Pro V1x golf balls. Titleist is the overwhelming choice across the worldwide professional tours. In fact, more players place their trust in Titleist than all other balls combined. The world's best players know that in a game that demands distance, accuracy and consistency, one ball outperforms all others. Learn why the new Pro V1 and Pro V1x are better than ever at titleist.co.uk

Titleist
#1 ball in golf.®

USGA President Walter Driver Jnr (right) watches as winner Angel Cabrera of Argentina waves to the crowd

> The European Tour will take a lot from this win. Our Tour is extremely strong and we have some great players. Angel is a European Tour player and he has been around for a long time and thoroughly deserved this. He has won big events in Europe. He has won our BMW PGA Championship at Wentworth. He is a formidable player. Nothing fazes him. He is quiet on the outside, a great ball striker and has great touch. He has everything you need.
> *Paul Casey*

Oakmont Country Club

Par 70   **Yards 7230**   **Metres 6610**

Final Results

Pos	Name		Rd1	Rd2	Rd3	Rd4	Total		€	£
1	Angel CABRERA	ARG	69	71	76	69	285	5	943,182.74	640,993.00
2	Tiger WOODS	USA	71	74	69	72	286	6	457,620.29	311,001.67
	Jim FURYK	USA	71	75	70	70	286	6	457,620.29	311,001.67
4	Niclas FASTH	SWE	71	71	75	70	287	7	243,972.18	165,805.05
5	David TOMS	USA	72	72	73	72	289	9	186,351.95	126,645.97
	Bubba WATSON	USA	70	71	74	74	289	9	186,351.95	126,645.97
7	Jerry KELLY	USA	74	71	73	72	290	10	145,403.60	98,817.21
	Scott VERPLANK	USA	73	71	74	72	290	10	145,403.60	98,817.21
	Nick DOUGHERTY	ENG	68	77	74	71	290	10	145,403.60	98,817.21
10	Paul CASEY	ENG	77	66	72	76	291	11	115,347.51	78,390.90
	Justin ROSE	ENG	71	71	73	76	291	11	115,347.51	78,390.90
	Stephen AMES	CAN	73	69	73	76	291	11	115,347.51	78,390.90
13	Aaron BADDELEY	AUS	72	70	70	80	292	12	93,349.64	63,441.01
	Lee JANZEN	USA	73	73	73	73	292	12	93,349.64	63,441.01
	Steve STRICKER	USA	75	73	68	76	292	12	93,349.64	63,441.01
	Hunter MAHAN	USA	73	74	72	73	292	12	93,349.64	63,441.01
17	Jeff BREHAUT	USA	73	75	70	75	293	13	76,754.12	52,162.59
	Carl PETTERSSON	SWE	72	72	75	74	293	13	76,754.12	52,162.59
	Tim CLARK	RSA	72	76	71	74	293	13	76,754.12	52,162.59
20	Mike WEIR	CAN	74	72	73	75	294	14	64,525.68	43,852.06
	Vijay SINGH	FIJ	71	77	70	76	294	14	64,525.68	43,852.06
	Anthony KIM	USA	74	73	80	67	294	14	64,525.68	43,852.06
23	Brandt SNEDEKER	USA	71	73	77	74	295	15	53,825.04	36,579.84
	Ken DUKE	USA	74	75	73	73	295	15	53,825.04	36,579.84
	Nick O'HERN	AUS	76	74	71	74	295	15	53,825.04	36,579.84
26	Stuart APPLEBY	AUS	74	72	71	79	296	16	42,687.25	29,010.53
	Camilo VILLEGAS	COL	73	77	75	71	296	16	42,687.25	29,010.53
	J J HENRY	USA	71	78	75	72	296	16	42,687.25	29,010.53
	Boo WEEKLEY	USA	72	75	77	72	296	16	42,687.25	29,010.53
30	D.J. BRIGMAN	USA	74	74	74	75	297	17	33,919.40	23,051.84
	Fred FUNK	USA	71	78	74	74	297	17	33,919.40	23,051.84
	Charl SCHWARTZEL	RSA	75	73	73	76	297	17	33,919.40	23,051.84
	Graeme MCDOWELL	NIR	73	72	75	77	297	17	33,919.40	23,051.84
	Pablo MARTIN	ESP	71	76	77	73	297	17	33,919.40	23,051.84
	Peter HANSON	SWE	71	74	78	74	297	17	33,919.40	23,051.84
36	Shingo KATAYAMA	JPN	72	74	79	73	298	18	27,815.66	18,903.70
	Mathew GOGGIN	AUS	77	73	74	74	298	18	27,815.66	18,903.70
	Jeev Milkha SINGH	IND	75	75	73	75	298	18	27,815.66	18,903.70
	Lee WESTWOOD	ENG	72	75	79	72	298	18	27,815.66	18,903.70
	Ian POULTER	ENG	72	77	72	77	298	18	27,815.66	18,903.70
	Tom PERNICE Jnr	USA	72	72	75	79	298	18	27,815.66	18,903.70
42	John ROLLINS	USA	75	74	74	76	299	19	23,268.17	15,813.20
	Kenneth FERRIE	ENG	74	76	77	72	299	19	23,268.17	15,813.20
	Geoff OGILVY	AUS	71	75	78	75	299	19	23,268.17	15,813.20
45	Marcus FRASER	AUS	72	78	77	73	300	20	18,725.92	12,726.25
	José María OLAZÁBAL	ESP	70	78	78	74	300	20	18,725.92	12,726.25
	Zach JOHNSON	USA	76	74	76	74	300	20	18,725.92	12,726.25
	Olin BROWNE	USA	71	75	80	74	300	20	18,725.92	12,726.25
	Chris DIMARCO	USA	76	73	73	78	300	20	18,725.92	12,726.25
	Ben CURTIS	USA	71	77	78	74	300	20	18,725.92	12,726.25
51	Dean WILSON	USA	76	74	76	75	301	21	15,182.25	10,317.95
	Charles HOWELL III	USA	76	73	77	75	301	21	15,182.25	10,317.95
	Ernie ELS	RSA	73	76	74	78	301	21	15,182.25	10,317.95
	Rory SABBATINI	RSA	73	77	78	73	301	21	15,182.25	10,317.95
55	Anders HANSEN	DEN	71	79	79	73	302	22	14,094.59	9,578.78
	Michael PUTNAM	USA	74	73	72	83	302	22	14,094.59	9,578.78
57	Chad CAMPBELL	USA	73	72	77	81	303	23	13,611.77	9,250.65
58	Bob ESTES	USA	75	75	77	77	304	24	13,003.20	8,837.06
	Michael CAMPBELL	NZL	73	77	75	79	304	24	13,003.20	8,837.06
	Harrison FRAZAR	USA	74	74	74	82	304	24	13,003.20	8,837.06
	Kevin SUTHERLAND	USA	74	76	79	75	304	24	13,003.20	8,837.06
62	Jason DUFNER	USA	71	75	79	80	305	25	12,461.24	8,468.74
63	George MCNEILL	USA	72	76	77	81	306	26	12,248.65	8,324.26

Total Prize Fund

€5,241,402   £3,562,090

The Course

The big change from the last US Open Championship at Oakmont in 1994 was the removal of some 5000 trees, done under the guidance of Grounds Chairman Banks Smith. It not only returned Oakmont to the original feel of a wide-open, links-style golf course favoured by the 1903 designer HC Fownes, but also returned the nutrients to the grass helping the greens retain their legendary roll and pace.

Last Laugh

1	Niclas FASTH		275	-13
2	Bernhard LANGER		277	-11
	José-Filipe LIMA		277	-11
4	Ricardo GONZALEZ		278	-10
	Anders HANSEN		278	-10
	Maarten LAFEBER		278	-10
7	Ernie ELS		279	-9
	Simon KHAN		279	-9
9	Benn BARHAM		280	-8
	Thomas LEVET		280	-8

169

As the dust settled on a dramatic BMW International Open it might have been Niclas Fasth who had the last laugh, but Bernhard Langer allowed himself an ironic smile when he admitted: "Every once in a while the old swing and the old talent shows up, but unfortunately not often enough."

Nevertheless, the performance of the winning 2004 European Ryder Cup Captain to storm through the field with a 67 on the final day and finish tied second with Portugal's José-Filipe Lima, two shots behind the Swede, was truly wonderful.

It was one of those trademark Langer Sundays, whipping the home crowd into a frenzy as he chased his 43rd European Tour International Schedule title, one which, if he had achieved it, would have seen him become, at 49 years and 301 days, the oldest player to win on The European Tour as well as the first player since the Tour's inception in 1972 to win from the cut-line. It would also, of course, have seen Langer finally claim the one German title which has thus far eluded him in his glittering career.

But it was not to be. Fasth, who was only 12 years old when Langer won his first Masters Tournament title at Augusta National in 1985, showed the sort of steely grit the great man himself would have been proud of to card a final round 70 and take the title.

It was the 35 year old Swede's fifth victory in his last 60 European Tour events and followed on from a fine performance in the US Open Championship the week before where he finished in fourth place, rekindling the form which saw him claim a place in The 2002 European Ryder Cup Team.

After successfully battling the brutal Oakmont rough and lightning fast putting surfaces, it was understandable that Fasth afforded himself a wry smile when he heard some of his fellow competitors in Germany commenting on the severity of the rough at Golfclub München Eichenried.

"To be honest, this feels like a holiday," he said. "Having got into a good position going into the final round, I felt like it was my tournament to win or lose and so to come through the way I did feels fantastic."

While Lima posted two late birdies to force his way onto the platform for the prizegiving ceremony, the final afternoon was largely a battle between the relative youth of Fasth and the vast experience of Langer.

The fact the German was involved at all was incredible as Langer seriously contemplated withdrawing from the tournament after an opening 76, a round plagued by a troublesome neck and back injury and one which necessitated physio Atour Frauk having to administer several massage sessions on the course.

However, dogged determination has been a watchword of Langer's career, as exemplified in his successful battle with the yips, and once again he battled back. A superb second round 66 saw him make the cut right on the mark of two under par 142 before a third round 68 moved him to the fringes of the top ten.

Into the final round Langer turned up the heat on an already sweltering Munich afternoon with a series of outrageous birdie putts, including a snaking 40 footer

Thomas Levet

Anders Hansen

Alastair Forsyth

Bernhard Langer

on the 17th which brought him within a shot of Fasth who was in the final group, 50 minutes behind.

The pair seemed destined to draw level when the Swede found tree trouble on the 15th but a brave 15 foot putt for par kept his nose in front, and when he emulated Langer's birdie two on the 17th to move two shots clear, the outcome was no longer in doubt.

After the 1997 success of Robert Karlsson and last year's victory by Henrik Stenson, Fasth became the third Swedish winner of the BMW International Open. Joint second placed Lima produced his best European Tour finish in almost precisely three years since winning the Aa St Omer Open in June 2004, while Langer took time out to praise the home crowds despite falling just short of adding a 12th title on German soil to his already impressive CV. "It was a truly wonderful atmosphere out there," he said.

While Langer occupied most of the home supporters' attention, there was praise too for young German professional Martin Kaymer who continues to make excellent progress in his rookie season on The European Tour after graduating from the 2006 Challenge Tour.

The 22 year old did not make the cut in Munich but did take away something perhaps even more valuable than prize money; namely the experience of playing two rounds with World Number Five Ernie Els, who admitted he was more than impressed with the young man.

"He is very talented and his attitude on the golf course is excellent," said the South African. "His ball flight is extremely good too and if he continues this way, he will be a future star."

Petra Himmel

OSCAR
JACOBSON
GOLF

BY APPOINTMENT TO H.M.
THE KING OF SWEDEN
SINCE 1903

FOR MORE INFORMATION CALL OSCAR JACOBSON ON +44 (0)207 402 0797 OR VISIT WWW.OSCARJACOBSON.COM

Stefan Krause (left), CFO of BMW Group, presents the trophy to Niclas Fasth

> I think it's fantastic to play in front of your home crowd. Some of the roars out there were pretty big. At times I almost got goosebumps. It was pretty unique. To be in contention every once in a while is what I still do all the work for. I like the adrenaline rush, I like to be in contention and feel the excitement.
> **Bernhard Langer**

The Course

Played for the first time in a number of years in June rather than September, the main difference was the thickness of the rough which was one of the reasons for the winning score of only 13 under par, compared to the 21 under and better scores of recent years. The extension of the lake on the 11th and a new bunker in the fairway on the 16th also made players think a little bit more turning for home.

José-Filipe Lima

Golfclub München Eichenried
Par **72**   Yards **6955**   Metres **6359**

Final Results

Pos	Name		Rd1	Rd2	Rd3	Rd4	Total		€	£
1	Niclas FASTH	SWE	67	65	73	70	275	-13	333,330.00	225,396.59
2	José-Filipe LIMA	POR	65	70	70	72	277	-11	173,710.00	117,462.10
	Bernhard LANGER	GER	76	66	68	67	277	-11	173,710.00	117,462.10
4	Anders HANSEN	DEN	68	70	72	68	278	-10	84,933.33	57,431.63
	Maarten LAFEBER	NED	71	67	73	67	278	-10	84,933.33	57,431.63
	Ricardo GONZALEZ	ARG	68	71	69	70	278	-10	84,933.33	57,431.63
7	Simon KHAN	ENG	70	71	72	66	279	-9	55,000.00	37,190.81
	Ernie ELS	RSA	67	71	74	67	279	-9	55,000.00	37,190.81
9	Thomas LEVET	FRA	68	67	72	73	280	-8	42,400.00	28,670.73
	Benn BARHAM	ENG	72	69	71	68	280	-8	42,400.00	28,670.73
11	Alastair FORSYTH	SCO	68	73	67	73	281	-7	31,228.57	21,116.65
	Simon DYSON	ENG	72	66	73	70	281	-7	31,228.57	21,116.65
	Emanuele CANONICA	ITA	69	73	70	69	281	-7	31,228.57	21,116.65
	Jyoti RANDHAWA	IND	70	69	73	69	281	-7	31,228.57	21,116.65
	Anthony WALL	ENG	72	70	73	66	281	-7	31,228.57	21,116.65
	Peter HANSON	SWE	68	66	74	73	281	-7	31,228.57	21,116.65
	Raphaël JACQUELIN	FRA	65	74	73	69	281	-7	31,228.57	21,116.65
18	Sven STRÜVER	GER	72	66	71	73	282	-6	24,450.00	16,533.01
	Jeev Milkha SINGH	IND	69	72	70	71	282	-6	24,450.00	16,533.01
	Miguel Angel JIMÉNEZ	ESP	69	69	74	70	282	-6	24,450.00	16,533.01
	Oliver WILSON	ENG	70	68	75	69	282	-6	24,450.00	16,533.01
22	Shiv KAPUR	IND	72	70	73	68	283	-5	21,700.00	14,673.46
	Steven JEPPESEN	SWE	68	74	74	67	283	-5	21,700.00	14,673.46
	Sam LITTLE	ENG	74	67	74	68	283	-5	21,700.00	14,673.46
	Andres ROMERO	ARG	67	68	75	73	283	-5	21,700.00	14,673.46
26	Nick DOUGHERTY	ENG	68	68	71	77	284	-4	18,400.00	12,442.02
	Steven O'HARA	SCO	69	70	73	72	284	-4	18,400.00	12,442.02
	David LYNN	ENG	71	66	74	73	284	-4	18,400.00	12,442.02
	Ian GARBUTT	ENG	69	71	75	69	284	-4	18,400.00	12,442.02
	Henrik STENSON	SWE	73	66	73	72	284	-4	18,400.00	12,442.02
	David FROST	RSA	67	70	70	77	284	-4	18,400.00	12,442.02
	Ross FISHER	ENG	71	71	76	66	284	-4	18,400.00	12,442.02
33	Peter FOWLER	AUS	68	73	71	73	285	-3	14,833.33	10,030.25
	Philip GOLDING	ENG	71	69	74	71	285	-3	14,833.33	10,030.25
	Phillip PRICE	WAL	73	69	68	75	285	-3	14,833.33	10,030.25
	Christian CÉVAËR	FRA	70	67	72	76	285	-3	14,833.33	10,030.25
	David GRIFFITHS	ENG	69	69	73	74	285	-3	14,833.33	10,030.25
	Rafael CABRERA BELLO	ESP	69	70	74	72	285	-3	14,833.33	10,030.25
39	Gonzalo FDEZ-CASTAÑO	ESP	66	72	72	76	286	-2	12,800.00	8,655.32
	Paul CASEY	ENG	68	70	74	74	286	-2	12,800.00	8,655.32
	Henrik NYSTRÖM	SWE	71	68	75	72	286	-2	12,800.00	8,655.32
	Peter HEDBLOM	SWE	71	70	75	70	286	-2	12,800.00	8,655.32
43	Martin ERLANDSSON	SWE	68	72	75	72	287	-1	11,600.00	7,843.88
	Mads VIBE-HASTRUP	DEN	74	66	78	69	287	-1	11,600.00	7,843.88
45	Peter GUSTAFSSON	SWE	73	65	75	75	288	0	10,600.00	7,167.68
	Terry PRICE	AUS	74	68	74	72	288	0	10,600.00	7,167.68
	Peter LAWRIE	IRL	71	67	77	73	288	0	10,600.00	7,167.68
48	Francesco MOLINARI	ITA	67	73	75	74	289	1	9,200.00	6,221.01
	Lee SLATTERY	ENG	75	66	76	72	289	1	9,200.00	6,221.01
	David HIGGINS	IRL	73	69	74	73	289	1	9,200.00	6,221.01
	Markus BRIER	AUT	71	69	74	75	289	1	9,200.00	6,221.01
52	Tom WHITEHOUSE	ENG	70	68	77	75	290	2	7,800.00	5,274.33
	Paul BROADHURST	ENG	66	73	79	72	290	2	7,800.00	5,274.33
	Alejandro CAÑIZARES	ESP	74	67	77	72	290	2	7,800.00	5,274.33
55	Edward RUSH	ENG	71	70	75	75	291	3	7,000.00	4,733.38
56	Brett RUMFORD	AUS	70	70	77	75	292	4	6,600.00	4,462.90
57	David PARK	WAL	72	70	77	74	293	5	6,200.00	4,192.42
58	Alexander NOREN	SWE	72	69	74	79	294	6	6,000.00	4,057.18
59	Juan PARRON	ESP	74	67	72	82	295	7	5,800.00	3,921.94
60	Jamie SPENCE	ENG	71	71	78	77	297	9	5,400.00	3,651.46
	Darren FICHARDT	RSA	73	69	80	75	297	9	5,400.00	3,651.46
	Marc FARRY	FRA	66	76	75	80	297	9	5,400.00	3,651.46
63	Jean-François LUCQUIN	FRA	71	71	79	77	298	10	5,000.00	3,380.98
64	Alexandre ROCHA	BRA	73	67	78	81	299	11	4,700.00	3,178.12
	Graeme STORM	ENG	71	69	78	81	299	11	4,700.00	3,178.12

Total Prize Fund
€1,979,950 £1,338,835

Le National Treasure

1	**Graeme STORM**		277	-7
2	Søren HANSEN		278	-6
3	Thomas BJÖRN		279	-5
	Simon KHAN		279	-5
	Damien McGRANE		279	-5
	Colin MONTGOMERIE		279	-5
7	Martin KAYMER		280	-4
	Jyoti RANDHAWA		280	-4
9	Ian POULTER		281	-3
10	Bradley DREDGE		282	-2
	David LYNN		282	-2

The English language has a perfect word to describe the unexpected discovery of something pleasant purely by accident: Serendipity.

Remember Wimbledon? Jamie Murray just happened to share a courtesy car to the All England Club with Jelena Jankovic. The Scot seized the moment to ask the Serbian if she had a partner for the Mixed Doubles. Two weeks later they were champions.

Serendipity came into play on The European Tour around that same time of the year, too. Graeme Storm was the central character and his chance encounter, on June 6, produced an equally profound outcome. Just 25 days later, he was the Open de France ALSTOM champion.

Having missed three consecutive cuts, the golfer from the north of England despaired of his downward spiralling form and withdrew from the US Open Championship Qualifier at Walton Heath, pondering whether he should even play in Austria that week.

However, against his better judgement, Storm elected to travel to Vienna for the BA-CA Golf Open, presented by Telekom Austria, and just happened to share a car to the golf course for Wednesday's Pro-Am with fellow Englishman, Ian Garbutt. The two passengers slipped on their spikes and lined up side-by-side to practise.

Reflecting on the sequence of events which transformed the direction of his career, Storm admitted: "It's funny how little things work out in your favour. If I hadn't arrived at the course with 'Garby' and he hadn't been next to me on the range, I don't know if I would be sitting here with my first European Tour title.

"He stopped to have a look at me and gave me a few tips about my takeaway and the fact that I wasn't rotating correctly. Those little tips gave me the self belief to pull the trigger."

Pull the trigger he did, shooting the lights out with a first round 63 and ultimately a tied seventh place in Austria. Three weeks later, Storm opened and closed the 2007 Open de France ALSTOM with rounds of 66, with 74 and 71 sandwiched in the middle, to claim the title by a stroke from Denmark's Søren Hansen.

After seven years on Tour, Storm had finally fulfilled the potential first shown almost a decade earlier when he won The 1999 Amateur Championship and played in Great Britain and Ireland's Walker Cup victory over the United States later that year.

That potential, however, was slow to develop. In three consecutive years from 2002 to 2004, his end of season position on The European Tour Order of Merit was outside the top 200. Around that time he also lost his father. Desperate, times called for desperate measures, and Storm went in search of part-time work to supplement his meagre income from golf. Fun it most certainly was not.

"I went to work in a cake factory in Hartlepool," he explained. "It was a bit of a come down, but I buckled down and spent two or three months outside in the cold, cleaning baking trays with a jet wash. Believe me, it wasn't enjoyable arriving for work at eight in the morning to find all the pipes frozen.

Damien McGrane

Simon Khan

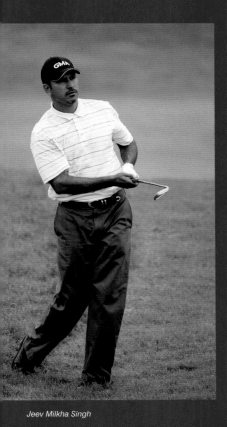

Jeev Milkha Singh

Søren Hansen

"To be honest, working in the factory showed me the other side of the coin. We all have to earn a living and it helped me to realise how fortunate I was being a professional golfer and to reset my goals. I knew where I was and where I wanted to get to."

Storm was always handily placed at the fabulous setting of Le Golf National close to the historic Palace of Versailles. South African James Kamte and Welshman Kyron Sullivan led after the first day on six under par 65, England's Simon Khan assumed the mantle of halfway leader on five under par 137 while Hansen claimed the metaphoric 'Maillot Jaune' or Yellow Jersey, as tournament leader after 54 holes on seven under par 206.

On the final day bad weather was brewing off the course but never materialised on it, much to the relief of all concerned. Over those beautifully sculpted 18 holes though, Storm's game percolated perfectly as he held off Hansen, a revitalised Thomas Björn and Colin Montgomerie, the dogged Damien McGrane and Khan to capture the title by a single shot with a seven under par total of 277.

As Patrice Clerc, President of promoters ASO, put it so aptly at the prize giving ceremony: "The European Tour promised we would not have a storm today...they were wrong!"

In a tie for 15th place was the leading French player, Grégory Havret, and he, Raphaël Jacquelin and Thomas Levet proved to be a huge hit off the course as they provided a wonderful clinic for over a thousand invited youngsters from all over France after play on Saturday evening. The happy, smiling faces told us all that the next generation could not wait to emulate their heroes.

On that week, though, the real hero was Graeme Storm. Five years earlier he was drawing a take home pay of £145 for a 40 hour week from the confectionery factory. That Sunday in France, he collected €666,660 (£448,491), some 3,093 times as much.

Just goes to prove, in fact, that you can have your cake and eat it.

Gordon Simpson

Do you see a link between Alstom and golf?

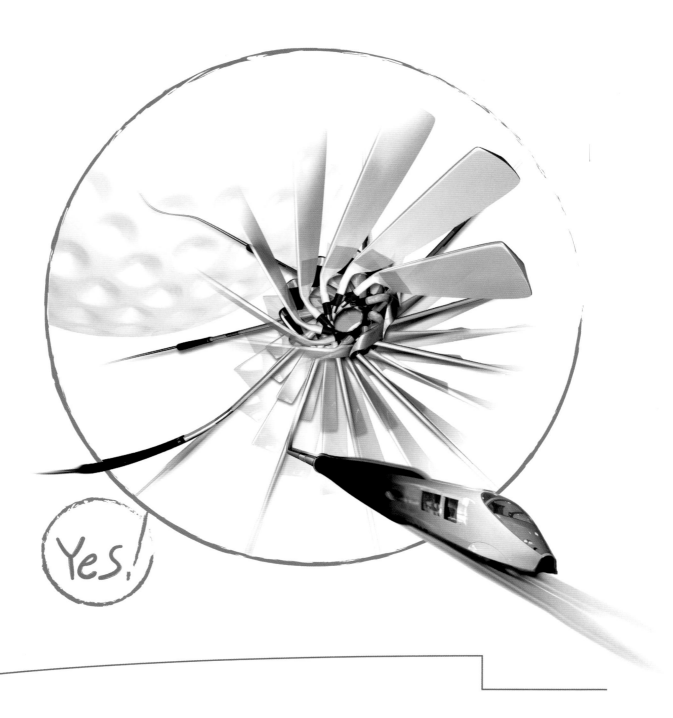

Alstom is a global leader in the world of power generation and rail infrastructure. Alstom shares with golf the values of precision, power, speed and protection of the environment. The precision of the game itself, the power of the players' swing and the speed of the ball struck by the great golf champions.

The precision of Alstom's high-tech equipment, the power of our turbines and the record-breaking speed of our trains.

Golf is also linked to the protection of the environment – Alstom is at the forefront of clean technology solutions.

Open de France
ALSTOM

we are shaping the future   **ALSTOM**

www.alstom.com
www.opendefrance.fr

Graeme Storm (left) is presented with the trophy by Patrice Clerc, Chairman and Managing Director of Amaury Sport Organisation

Seve Ballesteros made European Tour history in the 1986 Open de France. Having claimed the title in 1985 with a wire-to-wire victory, he proceeded to successfully defend the title in exactly the same fashion, making him the first player to achieve this feat.

The Course

Opened in 1990 and designed by Hubert Chesnau, the stadium style course with its many elevated viewing positions is widely regarded as one of golf's most celebrated modern layouts. Water is very much a feature, especially over the amphitheatre-like closing holes with hazards coming into play on the 13th, 15th, 16th, 17th and 18th. The water contains some of the largest carp in France who feed almost exclusively on the grass clippings from the course.

Mark Foster

Le Golf National
Par **71**   Yards **7225**   Metres **6607**

Final Results

Pos	Name		Rd1	Rd2	Rd3	Rd4	Total	€	£
1	Graeme STORM	ENG	66	74	71	66	277	-7	666,660.00	448,491.37
2	Søren HANSEN	DEN	69	71	66	72	278	-6	444,440.00	298,994.25
3	Colin MONTGOMERIE	SCO	68	70	71	70	279	-5	190,000.00	127,821.32
	Thomas BJÖRN	DEN	68	71	71	69	279	-5	190,000.00	127,821.32
	Damien MCGRANE	IRL	68	72	74	65	279	-5	190,000.00	127,821.32
	Simon KHAN	ENG	70	67	70	72	279	-5	190,000.00	127,821.32
7	Martin KAYMER	GER	70	70	69	71	280	-4	110,000.00	74,001.82
	Jyoti RANDHAWA	IND	68	72	72	68	280	-4	110,000.00	74,001.82
9	Ian POULTER	ENG	70	74	68	69	281	-3	89,600.00	60,277.84
10	David LYNN	ENG	72	69	69	72	282	-2	76,800.00	51,666.72
	Bradley DREDGE	WAL	73	71	70	68	282	-2	76,800.00	51,666.72
12	Zane SCOTLAND	ENG	68	71	72	72	283	-1	64,800.00	43,593.80
	Jeev Milkha SINGH	IND	71	72	67	73	283	-1	64,800.00	43,593.80
	Robert-Jan DERKSEN	NED	69	72	71	71	283	-1	64,800.00	43,593.80
15	Mark FOSTER	ENG	72	72	72	68	284	0	55,200.00	37,135.46
	Phillip ARCHER	ENG	72	72	69	71	284	0	55,200.00	37,135.46
	Grégory HAVRET	FRA	69	74	71	70	284	0	55,200.00	37,135.46
	José-Filipe LIMA	POR	68	72	73	71	284	0	55,200.00	37,135.46
19	Grégory BOURDY	FRA	75	71	68	71	285	1	48,800.00	32,829.90
	Pelle EDBERG	SWE	73	69	70	73	285	1	48,800.00	32,829.90
21	Søren KJELDSEN	DEN	70	75	70	71	286	2	45,800.00	30,811.67
	Maarten LAFEBER	NED	72	73	71	70	286	2	45,800.00	30,811.67
23	Richard FINCH	ENG	71	70	75	71	287	3	43,400.00	29,197.08
	Benn BARHAM	ENG	66	75	72	74	287	3	43,400.00	29,197.08
25	Nick DOUGHERTY	ENG	73	69	73	73	288	4	37,400.00	25,160.62
	David GRIFFITHS	ENG	70	74	69	75	288	4	37,400.00	25,160.62
	Richard STERNE	RSA	71	71	76	70	288	4	37,400.00	25,160.62
	Kyron SULLIVAN	WAL	65	74	77	72	288	4	37,400.00	25,160.62
	Jean-Baptiste GONNET	FRA	73	69	75	71	288	4	37,400.00	25,160.62
	Ariel CANETE	ARG	70	74	76	68	288	4	37,400.00	25,160.62
	Johan AXGREN	SWE	69	76	72	71	288	4	37,400.00	25,160.62
	Paul MCGINLEY	IRL	69	69	75	75	288	4	37,400.00	25,160.62
33	Stephen DODD	WAL	71	72	69	77	289	5	28,444.44	19,135.82
	Paul LAWRIE	SCO	71	72	75	71	289	5	28,444.44	19,135.82
	Taichi TESHIMA	JPN	72	72	76	69	289	5	28,444.44	19,135.82
	Steven JEPPESEN	SWE	66	77	68	78	289	5	28,444.44	19,135.82
	Tom WHITEHOUSE	ENG	70	69	77	73	289	5	28,444.44	19,135.82
	Michael CAMPBELL	NZL	74	71	77	67	289	5	28,444.44	19,135.82
	Stephen GALLACHER	SCO	71	73	73	72	289	5	28,444.44	19,135.82
	Markus BRIER	AUT	68	76	75	70	289	5	28,444.44	19,135.82
	Lee WESTWOOD	ENG	71	72	69	77	289	5	28,444.44	19,135.82
42	Robert ROCK	ENG	71	72	71	76	290	6	21,600.00	14,531.27
	Peter LAWRIE	IRL	69	72	71	78	290	6	21,600.00	14,531.27
	Raphaël JACQUELIN	FRA	68	73	76	73	290	6	21,600.00	14,531.27
	Sven STRÜVER	GER	72	74	74	70	290	6	21,600.00	14,531.27
	Alessandro TADINI	ITA	73	72	71	74	290	6	21,600.00	14,531.27
	Christian CÉVAËR	FRA	71	74	72	73	290	6	21,600.00	14,531.27
	Oliver WILSON	ENG	73	69	73	75	290	6	21,600.00	14,531.27
	Oliver FISHER	ENG	70	75	73	72	290	6	21,600.00	14,531.27
50	François DELAMONTAGNE	FRA	72	74	76	69	291	7	17,600.00	11,840.29
	Marcus FRASER	AUS	75	69	72	75	291	7	17,600.00	11,840.29
52	Steve WEBSTER	ENG	72	72	75	73	292	8	16,000.00	10,763.90
	Darren FICHARDT	RSA	71	71	71	79	292	8	16,000.00	10,763.90
54	Santiago LUNA	ESP	70	75	75	73	293	9	13,600.00	9,149.32
	Miguel Angel MARTIN	ESP	68	77	71	77	293	9	13,600.00	9,149.32
	Christian L NILSSON	SWE	66	76	71	80	293	9	13,600.00	9,149.32
	James KAMTE	RSA	65	78	75	75	293	9	13,600.00	9,149.32
58	Thomas LEVET	FRA	67	73	77	77	294	10	12,000.00	8,072.93
59	Simon DYSON	ENG	75	70	76	74	295	11	11,600.00	7,803.83
60	Patrik SJÖLAND	SWE	73	71	73	79	296	12	10,800.00	7,265.63
	Rafael ECHENIQUE	ARG	72	74	71	79	296	12	10,800.00	7,265.63
	Peter O'MALLEY	AUS	73	73	74	76	296	12	10,800.00	7,265.63
63	Marcus HIGLEY	ENG	70	76	74	77	297	13	9,800.00	6,592.89
	Gary LOCKERBIE	ENG	74	70	75	78	297	13	9,800.00	6,592.89
65	Juan PARRON	ESP	71	72	78	77	298	14	9,200.00	6,189.24
66	Marcel SIEM	GER	72	72	74	81	299	15	8,800.00	5,920.15

Total Prize Fund
€3,968,700 £2,669,918

Rekindling the Flame

1	Colin MONTGOMERIE	269	-11
2	Niclas FASTH	270	-10
3	Pelle EDBERG	271	-9
	Peter HANSON	271	-9
	Grégory HAVRET	271	-9
	Anthony WALL	271	-9
7	Søren HANSEN	272	-8
	Peter HEDBLOM	272	-8
	Thomas LEVET	272	-8
	Peter O'MALLEY	272	-8

ortune, they say, favours the brave and Colin Montgomerie rode his luck to the very end. That is not to say his victory in the Smurfit Kappa European Open was fashioned by luck alone. In fact, the great Scot was back to his majestic best and the elements of fortune referred to were few but fortuitous as he came from behind to beat Sweden's Niclas Fasth by a single shot in a thrilling finale.

Ricardo Gonzalez

Robert Rock

But let us not dwell on such mundane things and instead salute the return to the winners' enclosure of one of European golf's greatest ever exponents. Eight times he has ruled The European Tour Order of Merit and, entering this event, he had 30 European Tour International Schedule titles to his name.

That 30th victory was achieved in the UBS Hong Kong Open in December 2005 and, one suspects, given that he had celebrated his 44th birthday only a couple of weeks before the start of the Smurfit Kappa European Open then his 31st success will surely rank very highly on his CV when he looks back on an illustrious career.

In those intervening 19 months, some were quick to write him out of contention for future glory. Montgomerie, however, rose majestically from the ashes of desire to rekindle the flame that has burned so brightly and so often throughout his glory years.

"They don't come much better than this," said the Scot. "Winning here was not just important to me, it was very important. That is now 31 wins on Tour which puts me one ahead of Nick Faldo. That means an awful lot to me, to get ahead of somebody I have respected for a very long time."

His victory at 11 under par 269 was fashioned from rearguard action, determination and more than just a touch of class in the face of atrocious weather. It was so bad that Tournament Director David Garland and senior referee Andy McFee were forced to make radical changes to the normal layout of the Smurfit Course, even before a ball was struck.

The tees at seven holes were moved forward, the most significant coming at the 18th. Unfortunately, this great finishing par five of 578 yards was reduced to a par three of 162 yards because the landing area was unplayable. It helped bring the overall length from 7,313 yards down to 6,897 yards and the par from 72 to 70.

There was hope it could be returned to its normal length for the final two rounds but the rain was incessant and, to add to the discomfort of players and spectators, the final nine holes were fractured by two separate weather warnings lasting a total of two hours. It was over this stretch that the real battle was fought.

Denmark's Søren Hansen led by two shots going into the final round but faded as the two principal

characters surged forward. Montgomerie was first out of the traps and raced from six under par to 11 under the card after 15 holes. Behind him, though, Fasth moved from seven under to 11 under par after 11 holes. Then came the first stoppage.

Upon the resumption, Montgomerie finished with three pars, albeit with the fortune that does favour the brave. At the 17th he went perilously close to the water while at the 18th, his ball landed in the hazard but on dry land. On each occasion he capitalised with delicate chipping and putting in order to complete a brilliant final round of 65.

Meanwhile Fasth dropped shots at the 13th and 14th, birdied the 15th and parred the 16th and 17th before the siren went again. This time the stoppage was much longer and when play did eventually resume, perhaps understandably, his putt for birdie and a play-off slipped by the hole.

The Swede came to Ireland with excellent credentials. When he captured the BMW International Open two weeks before travelling to The K Club, it was his fifth victory in his last 60 European Tour events, and included in that number was a fourth place finish in the 2007 US Open Championship at Oakmont Country Club.

"It was a brave effort and I gave it a go," he said. "I felt a little unlucky as I was going strongly when we had the first break, then I came back and made those two bogeys. It was a case of nearly, but not quite."

While Montgomerie claimed the main honours, there were other awards handed out over the week, primarily for the three holes in one recorded during the tournament. Andres Romero aced the 203 yard 17th for which he received a €30,000 Renault Megane, while Peter Hanson and Mikko Ilonen holed tee shots on the 18th on Saturday and Sunday respectively, for which they each received a magnum of champagne.

Finally, Patrik Sjöland did the double, presented by local jewellers Appleby, by hitting nearest the pin at the 12th, for which he received a €16,000 Sapphire Diamond, to add to the set of diamond cuff links he received for playing the six par fives in six under par over the first two days.

Colm Smith

Pelle Edberg

Thomas Levet

Anthony Wall

Colin Montgomerie (right) is presented with the trophy by Sean Fitzpatrick, Chairman of the Smurfit Kappa Group

Graeme McDowell

> I am a competitor and when I am in contention I don't tend to fear it. Some players do, but that is why I was fearing Niclas Fasth because he doesn't fear it either. It is just great at 44 to come back and win again. I feel this is a new beginning for me and I can look forward now.
> *Colin Montgomerie*

The K Club (The Smurfit Course)

Par **70**   Yards **6897**   Metres **6309**

Final Results

Pos	Name		Rd1	Rd2	Rd3	Rd4	Total		€	£
1	Colin MONTGOMERIE	SCO	69	64	71	65	269	-11	593,580.01	400,000.00
2	Niclas FASTH	SWE	65	68	70	67	270	-10	395,710.11	266,660.00
3	Peter HANSON	SWE	68	69	66	68	271	-9	169,170.30	114,000.00
	Pelle EDBERG	SWE	67	65	73	66	271	-9	169,170.30	114,000.00
	Anthony WALL	ENG	68	72	66	65	271	-9	169,170.30	114,000.00
	Grégory HAVRET	FRA	65	70	68	68	271	-9	169,170.30	114,000.00
7	Thomas LEVET	FRA	70	67	68	67	272	-8	86,722.04	58,440.00
	Søren HANSEN	DEN	69	68	63	72	272	-8	86,722.04	58,440.00
	Peter O'MALLEY	AUS	72	68	63	69	272	-8	86,722.04	58,440.00
	Peter HEDBLOM	SWE	68	68	68	68	272	-8	86,722.04	58,440.00
11	Raphaël JACQUELIN	FRA	71	69	67	66	273	-7	59,654.79	40,200.00
	Søren KJELDSEN	DEN	66	71	69	67	273	-7	59,654.79	40,200.00
	Robert ROCK	ENG	65	71	66	71	273	-7	59,654.79	40,200.00
	Simon KHAN	ENG	67	67	71	68	273	-7	59,654.79	40,200.00
15	Mikko ILONEN	FIN	67	72	69	66	274	-6	50,216.87	33,840.00
	Phillip ARCHER	ENG	70	69	66	69	274	-6	50,216.87	33,840.00
	Per-Ulrik JOHANSSON	SWE	69	69	69	67	274	-6	50,216.87	33,840.00
18	Joakim HAEGGMAN	SWE	68	70	68	69	275	-5	41,669.32	28,080.00
	Rafael CABRERA BELLO	ESP	69	71	68	67	275	-5	41,669.32	28,080.00
	Alexander NOREN	SWE	70	71	70	64	275	-5	41,669.32	28,080.00
	Graeme MCDOWELL	NIR	69	70	65	71	275	-5	41,669.32	28,080.00
	Peter FOWLER	AUS	70	71	67	67	275	-5	41,669.32	28,080.00
	Richard GREEN	AUS	69	67	71	68	275	-5	41,669.32	28,080.00
	Ariel CANETE	ARG	67	71	72	65	275	-5	41,669.32	28,080.00
25	Ricardo GONZALEZ	ARG	73	68	64	71	276	-4	32,765.62	22,080.00
	Steve WEBSTER	ENG	70	70	65	71	276	-4	32,765.62	22,080.00
	Markus BRIER	AUT	71	68	70	67	276	-4	32,765.62	22,080.00
	Paul BROADHURST	ENG	69	67	68	72	276	-4	32,765.62	22,080.00
	David FROST	RSA	68	66	70	72	276	-4	32,765.62	22,080.00
	Marc WARREN	SCO	69	69	70	68	276	-4	32,765.62	22,080.00
	Jyoti RANDHAWA	IND	65	70	71	70	276	-4	32,765.62	22,080.00
	Martin ERLANDSSON	SWE	69	66	71	70	276	-4	32,765.62	22,080.00
	Thongchai JAIDEE	THA	71	67	70	68	276	-4	32,765.62	22,080.00
34	Johan EDFORS	SWE	69	70	68	70	277	-3	25,286.51	17,040.00
	Gonzalo FDEZ-CASTAÑO	ESP	70	69	70	68	277	-3	25,286.51	17,040.00
	Jeev Milkha SINGH	IND	67	73	69	68	277	-3	25,286.51	17,040.00
	Simon WAKEFIELD	ENG	70	69	65	73	277	-3	25,286.51	17,040.00
	Christian CÉVAËR	FRA	71	70	70	66	277	-3	25,286.51	17,040.00
	David GRIFFITHS	ENG	70	70	68	69	277	-3	25,286.51	17,040.00
	Andres ROMERO	ARG	73	67	71	66	277	-3	25,286.51	17,040.00
41	Mads VIBE-HASTRUP	DEN	68	72	71	67	278	-2	21,368.88	14,400.00
	Jean-Baptiste GONNET	FRA	69	68	67	74	278	-2	21,368.88	14,400.00
	Sven STRÜVER	GER	73	67	66	72	278	-2	21,368.88	14,400.00
	Patrik SJÖLAND	SWE	69	68	70	71	278	-2	21,368.88	14,400.00
45	Marcel SIEM	GER	68	73	71	67	279	-1	17,807.40	12,000.00
	Alastair FORSYTH	SCO	72	68	69	70	279	-1	17,807.40	12,000.00
	Robert-Jan DERKSEN	NED	73	66	72	68	279	-1	17,807.40	12,000.00
	Graeme STORM	ENG	71	67	74	67	279	-1	17,807.40	12,000.00
	David HOWELL	ENG	69	72	69	69	279	-1	17,807.40	12,000.00
	Terry PRICE	AUS	71	69	69	70	279	-1	17,807.40	12,000.00
51	Michael CAMPBELL	NZL	68	71	69	72	280	0	13,889.77	9,360.00
	Maarten LAFEBER	NED	64	72	72	72	280	0	13,889.77	9,360.00
	Padraig HARRINGTON	IRL	71	68	69	72	280	0	13,889.77	9,360.00
	Paul LAWRIE	SCO	70	69	72	69	280	0	13,889.77	9,360.00
	Stephen DODD	WAL	66	73	71	70	280	0	13,889.77	9,360.00
56	Jesus Maria ARRUTI	ESP	68	72	74	67	281	1	10,951.55	7,380.00
	David HIGGINS	IRL	73	68	68	72	281	1	10,951.55	7,380.00
	Ian GARBUTT	ENG	67	73	71	70	281	1	10,951.55	7,380.00
	Gary LOCKERBIE	ENG	71	70	69	71	281	1	10,951.55	7,380.00
60	Angel CABRERA	ARG	71	69	74	68	282	2	9,437.92	6,360.00
	Francesco MOLINARI	ITA	71	70	72	69	282	2	9,437.92	6,360.00
	Y E YANG	KOR	73	68	70	71	282	2	9,437.92	6,360.00
	Ignacio GARRIDO	ESP	69	69	66	78	282	2	9,437.92	6,360.00
64	José Manuel LARA	ESP	68	72	73	71	284	4	8,191.40	5,520.00
	Lee SLATTERY	ENG	72	68	72	72	284	4	8,191.40	5,520.00
	Mark PILKINGTON	WAL	71	70	75	68	284	4	8,191.40	5,520.00
67	Rafael ECHENIQUE	ARG	72	69	74	70	285	5	7,479.11	5,040.00
68	Thaworn WIRATCHANT	THA	68	73	69	77	287	7	7,122.96	4,800.00

Total Prize Fund

€3,548,214 £2,391,060

The Course

Created by the Arnold Palmer Design Team and opened for play in 2003, the Smurfit Course can best be described as an inland links. However, its true attributes do not stop there. Dune type mounding gives rise to excellent spectator viewing throughout as well as many dramatic landscapes, while some 14 acres of water have been worked into the design, especially through the final stretch from the 13th to the 18th.

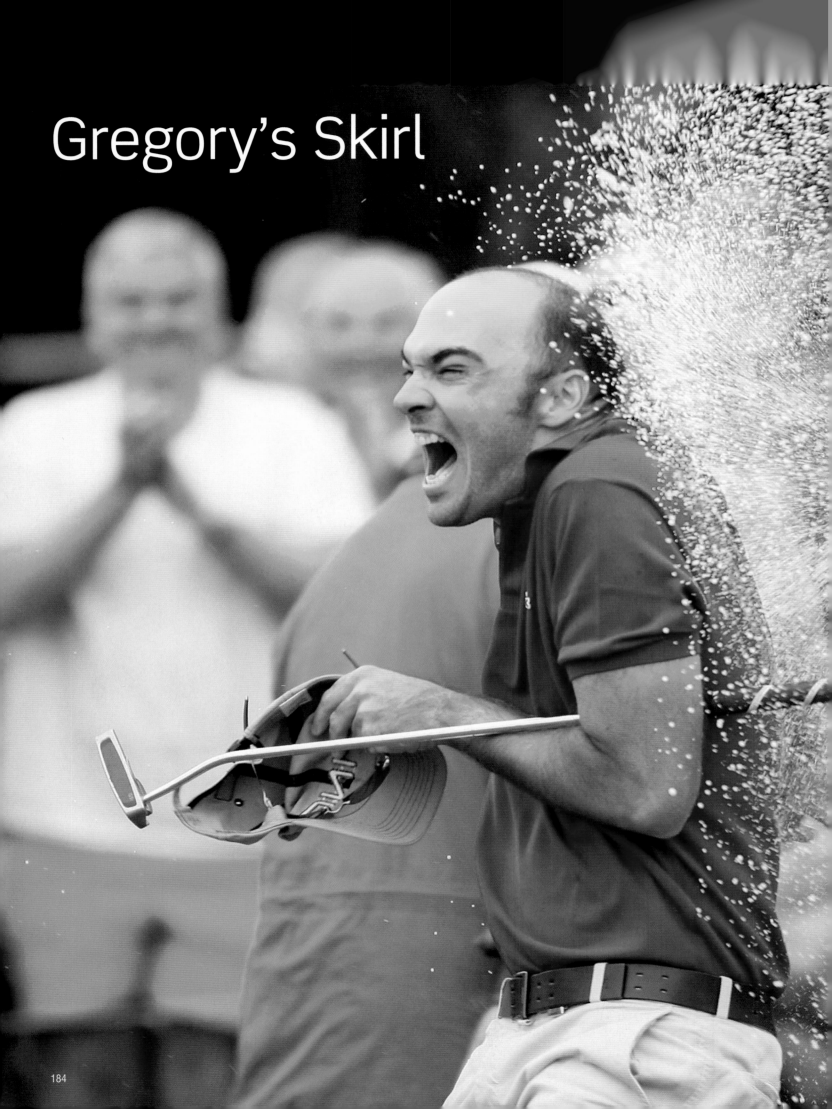

Gregory's Skirl

1	Grégory HAVRET		270	-14
2	Phil MICKELSON		270	-14
3	Ernie ELS		271	-13
4	Luke DONALD		273	-11
	Pelle EDBERG		273	-11
	Louis OOSTHUIZEN		273	-11
	Richard STERNE		273	-11
8	Mikko ILONEN		274	-10
	Ian POULTER		274	-10
	Steve WEBSTER		274	-10

185

For most Francophiles and followers of golf, the combination of Scottish turf, a play-off, and a French competitor, immediately sparks memories of Jean Van de Velde's collapse in The 1999 Open Championship at Carnoustie when he, and American Justin Leonard, eventually succumbed to the host nation's Paul Lawrie.

All golfers appreciate they can only control their own ball but sometimes, success or failure is determined by the misfortune of others. Of course, it was Van de Velde's own errors on the 72nd hole eight years ago which handed Lawrie an opportunity to lift the Claret Jug and, while Grégory Havret relished the biggest win of his career in The Barclays Scottish Open at Loch Lomond by defeating Phil Mickelson in a play-off, it had to be admitted that it was the American's mistakes as much as the Frenchman's own strengths which settled the outcome.

Watching his friend and compatriot secure the winner's cheque for €738,255 (£500,000) on the first extra hole, Van de Velde could not help thinking about the capricious nature of the game.

"Sometimes you are the one who makes the mistake and other people benefit from it, but then someone else will slip up and it's your turn to benefit - that's golf," he reflected. "Grégory is a wonderful character and a very hard working person. He's got an amazing talent and so all credit to him. He also played well the week before in Ireland and I think that gave him a big boost."

The sense of shared experience, of good fortune and bad, also echoed in Havret's thoughts. "You have some good days under pressure but I have also had some very bad days," he admitted. "In the Deutsche Bank in Germany in 2004 I was leading by two shots going into the final round but had an 82 and finished tied for 23rd. It was a nightmare.

"I then came to The Barclays Scottish Open a month later. Again I was leading after three rounds, this time alongside Marcus Fraser, but finished tied tenth after a final round 74. I was very disappointed with those experiences but I knew it was going to turn around for me one day. When it did, the feeling was awesome."

At a championship blessed with good weather, record crowds, and one of the best fields of the year, Havret, who began the week ranked 320th on the Official World Golf Ranking, found himself duelling with the Number Three, Mickelson, in an intriguing final round pairing.

The left-handed American began with a one shot advantage and maintained his edge over the front nine when the pair both reached the turn in 34.

Louis Oosthuizen

Steve Webster

Ernie Els

Luke Donald

Ian Poulter

That advantage increased when Havret dropped a shot at the tenth and, after both golfers birdied the par five 13th, the in-running bookmakers thought the championship was over and offered Mickelson at an unseemly 1/25 on to win for the first time outside the US PGA Tour.

As Van de Velde could have reminded everyone, however, nothing in golf is ever certain and there was a two shot swing on the 14th which changed the outcome of the event. Mickelson fluffed a pitch from the greenside rough and took bogey five while Havret holed an excellent putt for a birdie three.

The chase for glory was on and the momentum continued to swing back and forth between the pair as Havret played steady golf, securing fairways and greens, while Mickelson alternated brilliant putting for birdie with erratic driving for bogey.

The American held a one shot lead on the 18th tee but found the rough to the right of the fairway. He made bogey five to Havret's par four to send the pair back to the same tee for the play-off. Once

again, wayward driving cursed Mickelson as, this time, he flirted with the water on the left.

"I blocked my drive but hit a good shot out of the swamp," he said. "I had a chance but my third shot was way too hard." Havret, on the other hand, split the fairway before pushing his second into a greenside bunker. The sand wedge to five feet was well judged and he used the belly putter to perfection to secure the biggest pay day of his career.

As the bagpipes skirled, Raphaël Jacquelin and Thomas Levet ran onto the green to soak Havret in a mist of celebratory champagne. At his home in Biarritz, doubtless to say, Jean Van de Velde raised a glass for the toast.

Mike Aitken
The Scotsman

Commodities • FX • Derivatives • Equity Products • Loans • Bonds • Linkers • Emerging Markets • Fixed Income • Research • Private Equity

Whole in one

Grégory Havret (right) is presented with the trophy following his victory by Bob Diamond, President, Barclays PLC

> A few tournaments are very historic and you really want to do well in these. This is one of them. You know the field is going to be good and you know the crowd is going to be nice. You know that and you arrive here and you're not surprised. It's just amazing to play around here. We are really lucky.
>
> **Grégory Havret**

Loch Lomond
Par 71   **Yards 7139**   **Metres 6524**

Final Results

Pos	Name		Rd1	Rd2	Rd3	Rd4	Total		€	£
1	Grégory HAVRET	FRA	68	64	70	68	270	-14	738,255.02	500,000.00
2	Phil MICKELSON	USA	65	68	68	69	270	-14	492,165.09	333,330.00
3	Ernie ELS	RSA	69	66	71	65	271	-13	277,288.59	187,800.00
4	Pelle EDBERG	SWE	67	68	72	66	273	-11	174,302.01	118,050.00
	Luke DONALD	ENG	70	69	70	64	273	-11	174,302.01	118,050.00
	Richard STERNE	RSA	72	69	68	64	273	-11	174,302.01	118,050.00
	Louis OOSTHUIZEN	RSA	70	71	64	68	273	-11	174,302.01	118,050.00
8	Mikko ILONEN	FIN	66	70	70	68	274	-10	99,516.78	67,400.00
	Ian POULTER	ENG	69	67	71	67	274	-10	99,516.78	67,400.00
	Steve WEBSTER	ENG	68	67	69	70	274	-10	99,516.78	67,400.00
11	Søren KJELDSEN	DEN	67	74	69	65	275	-9	78,845.64	53,400.00
	Graeme MCDOWELL	NIR	70	71	67	67	275	-9	78,845.64	53,400.00
13	Phillip ARCHER	ENG	68	68	69	71	276	-8	66,664.43	45,150.00
	Peter HANSON	SWE	72	67	69	68	276	-8	66,664.43	45,150.00
	Robert-Jan DERKSEN	NED	69	68	73	66	276	-8	66,664.43	45,150.00
	Mark FOSTER	ENG	66	74	71	65	276	-8	66,664.43	45,150.00
17	Alessandro TADINI	ITA	72	68	69	68	277	-7	58,469.80	39,600.00
	Shaun MICHEEL	USA	67	71	70	69	277	-7	58,469.80	39,600.00
19	Richard FINCH	ENG	68	70	72	68	278	-6	47,516.78	32,181.82
	Alejandro CAÑIZARES	ESP	72	67	68	71	278	-6	47,516.78	32,181.82
	Ross FISHER	ENG	69	69	69	71	278	-6	47,516.78	32,181.82
	Lee WESTWOOD	ENG	65	74	70	69	278	-6	47,516.78	32,181.82
	Sergio GARCIA	ESP	71	65	71	71	278	-6	47,516.78	32,181.82
	José Manuel LARA	ESP	67	65	74	72	278	-6	47,516.78	32,181.82
	Ian GARBUTT	ENG	71	69	69	69	278	-6	47,516.78	32,181.82
	Darren CLARKE	NIR	71	67	74	66	278	-6	47,516.78	32,181.82
	Angel CABRERA	ARG	71	70	70	67	278	-6	47,516.78	32,181.82
	Søren HANSEN	DEN	65	73	71	69	278	-6	47,516.78	32,181.82
	Oliver FISHER	ENG	70	71	67	70	278	-6	47,516.78	32,181.82
30	Boo WEEKLEY	USA	68	66	74	71	279	-5	38,758.39	26,250.00
	Bradley DREDGE	WAL	68	72	72	67	279	-5	38,758.39	26,250.00
32	Simon KHAN	ENG	67	67	75	71	280	-4	34,882.55	23,625.00
	Jyoti RANDHAWA	IND	71	69	70	70	280	-4	34,882.55	23,625.00
	Paul BROADHURST	ENG	71	70	71	68	280	-4	34,882.55	23,625.00
	Raphaël JACQUELIN	FRA	69	73	70	68	280	-4	34,882.55	23,625.00
36	Andrew MCLARDY	RSA	71	68	75	67	281	-3	31,449.66	21,300.00
	Peter HEDBLOM	SWE	69	70	70	72	281	-3	31,449.66	21,300.00
	Kyron SULLIVAN	WAL	70	69	73	69	281	-3	31,449.66	21,300.00
39	Graeme STORM	ENG	65	72	72	73	282	-2	28,348.99	19,200.00
	Thomas LEVET	FRA	70	67	73	72	282	-2	28,348.99	19,200.00
	Andrew MARSHALL	ENG	70	71	70	71	282	-2	28,348.99	19,200.00
	Miles TUNNICLIFF	ENG	68	67	73	74	282	-2	28,348.99	19,200.00
43	Phillip PRICE	WAL	71	67	74	71	283	-1	23,919.46	16,200.00
	Ignacio GARRIDO	ESP	72	68	71	72	283	-1	23,919.46	16,200.00
	Peter LAWRIE	IRL	68	73	71	71	283	-1	23,919.46	16,200.00
	Jeev Milkha SINGH	IND	72	67	71	73	283	-1	23,919.46	16,200.00
	Patrik SJÖLAND	SWE	68	71	71	73	283	-1	23,919.46	16,200.00
	Grégory BOURDY	FRA	70	67	75	71	283	-1	23,919.46	16,200.00
49	Garry HOUSTON	WAL	69	71	71	73	284	0	19,932.89	13,500.00
	Thomas BJÖRN	DEN	69	70	73	72	284	0	19,932.89	13,500.00
	Paul MCGINLEY	IRL	68	70	74	72	284	0	19,932.89	13,500.00
52	Oliver WILSON	ENG	74	67	75	69	285	1	17,275.17	11,700.00
	Ariel CANETE	ARG	68	68	76	73	285	1	17,275.17	11,700.00
	Sam WALKER	ENG	67	69	77	72	285	1	17,275.17	11,700.00
55	Y E YANG	KOR	73	68	73	72	286	2	15,060.40	10,200.00
	Martin ERLANDSSON	SWE	72	69	72	73	286	2	15,060.40	10,200.00
57	Paul LAWRIE	SCO	68	71	74	74	287	3	13,288.59	9,000.00
	James HEPWORTH	ENG	71	70	73	73	287	3	13,288.59	9,000.00
	Matthew MILLAR	AUS	72	69	73	73	287	3	13,288.59	9,000.00
60	Lee SLATTERY	ENG	69	71	72	76	288	4	11,959.73	8,100.00
	Wade ORMSBY	AUS	70	70	78	70	288	4	11,959.73	8,100.00
	Peter O'MALLEY	AUS	70	70	75	73	288	4	11,959.73	8,100.00
63	Joakim BÄCKSTRÖM	SWE	72	68	78	72	290	6	10,852.35	7,350.00
	David DRYSDALE	SCO	70	69	75	76	290	6	10,852.35	7,350.00
65	Andres ROMERO	ARG	67	67	80	77	291	7	10,187.92	6,900.00
66	Mardan MAMAT	SIN	69	72	75	76	292	8	9,744.97	6,600.00

Total Prize Fund
€4,394,876   £2,976,530

Christian Porta (left), Chairman and CEO of Chivas, and Keith Waters, The European Tour's Director of International Policy, sign a three year deal which sees Ballantine's become an official sponsor of The Barclays Scottish Open

The Course

The beautiful Jay Morrish and Tom Weiskopf creation is rightly lauded as one of the top courses on The European Tour International Schedule as well as one of the most visually stunning, framed, as it is, by the towering hills on one side and the Loch on the other. Weiskopf describes the course, built on the ancestral home of the Clan Colquhoun, as his "lasting memorial to golf." Every hole has merits leading Ryder Cup Captain Nick Faldo to comment; "It simply cannot be faulted."

Golf as Life

1	**Padraig HARRINGTON**		**277**	**-7**
2	Sergio GARCIA		277	-7
3	Andres ROMERO		278	-6
4	Ernie ELS		279	-5
	Richard GREEN		279	-5
6	Stewart CINK		280	-4
	Hunter MAHAN		280	-4
8	K J CHOI		281	-3
	Ben CURTIS		281	-3
	Steve STRICKER		281	-3
	Mike WEIR		281	-3

191

In the end it was the grandest of dramas, a compelling story played out on one of the old game's most demanding of stages. At times, the climax of The 136th Open Championship might have veered into the realms of the Theatre of the Absurd, but the unflinching competitiveness and ambition of the two combatants left standing when events moved into overtime saved everything.

Sergio Garcia

Naturally Padraig Harrington and Sergio Garcia will never forget the week – Harrington because he won, Garcia because he so nearly did – but those of us fortunate enough to have shared Carnoustie with the men who played out this fascinating Open will also enjoy some vivid memories when the nights turn dark and cold.

Yet, though the majority of the applause rightly falls the Irishman's way, some genuine sympathy should be directed at Garcia whose efforts over the first three days greatly enhanced his reputation. However, it is the place itself that deserves the majority of trumpet calls of deep approval.

No-one is sure precisely where golf was hauled into life some 500 years ago but if that birthplace is almost certainly some ragged piece of exposed, Scottish shoreline, we may be assured that Carnoustie provided the departure lounge when the game was wrapped up for export. For it was from here some one hundred or so years ago that a most significant band of men left to make their way to the New World, taking with them their strange accents and ways.

It is thanks to this hardy group that golf is now a global phenomenon. It was upon their course designs, their teachings and their stories that golf's present high position was founded. If the Carnoustie missionaries had changed their minds and stayed at home then the game's story would be very different.

What fascinates many is the proximity of the Championship Course at Carnoustie to the Old Course at St Andrews. Separated by a narrow stretch of water, connected by the Tay Bridge, and linked by several centuries of fluctuating fortunes, these close cousins are irrevocably positioned at the game's heart. The journey between the two takes the best part of an hour by car. By helicopter – a trip Ernie Els made each day of this Open – it takes six minutes.

St Andrews is obviously more culturally rich, indeed just more obviously rich than Carnoustie. Smart people hunt for latté and the like across the water but at Carnoustie, life is more ruggedly Scottish. When The Open comes to St Andrews the town

Ernie Els and Paul Broadhurst

Andres Romero

dresses itself flamboyantly for the occasion; Carnoustie, on the other hand, heaves a sigh and hangs a haphazard string of bunting from the streetlamps.

St Andrews, one feels, is acutely aware of its significance, its cousin takes a more ambivalent attitude to fame that may be summed up in the simple phrase: "This is us." This take-it-or-leave it attitude carries its own charm but what is beyond debate is that the Championship Course at Carnoustie offers a challenge like no other.

When The Open is played on this antediluvian stretch of linksland, the oldest and most relevant Championship in the world is elevated. Fortitude, patience, skill and imagination are demanded as nowhere else. This really is golf as life, parables everywhere, triumph and disaster available on a minute-by-minute basis.

It is why The R&A, quite rightly, returned Carnoustie to their Open rota and, while some of the corporate types might bleat privately about the struggle of trying to do business in a latté-free zone, the Championship will continue to grace these bleak links in the future.

Judged however one likes, The 2007 Open was a treasure. All the usual facilities were there including

the Tented Village, a selection of huge retail marquees where eager punters gaped at the latest technology or drooled over the sort of holiday the majority can only dream about.

There, too, was the Bollinger Tent, now an Open tradition and a place where business may be conducted while enjoying the thrill of paying way over the odds for a bottle of bubbly. All this was expected; Carnoustie, however, did offer up some surprises.

Thirty yards from the Bolly Brigade, a tough looking man was putting something under some Hessian sacks. Much smoke filled the air. It turned out he was smoking the haddock that is landed a few miles up the coast – Arbroath Smokies – one of life's lasting pleasures.

Watching him place his racks of fish over a fire in a hole in the ground before covering them brought a smile to many faces. What other golf week would have the nerve and imagination to allow this? Brilliantly, though, this hard-working chap set the tone for the week.

The smile remained over the four days as a lot of fun was had by a lot of people. On the course, players came and went and some unexpected things happened.

26 COUNTRIES. 54 TOURNAMENTS.
24 TIME ZONES.
ONE OFFICIAL STARTER.

For over 30 years, Ivor Robson has been the Official Starter of The European Tour. Ensuring that the golfers tee off on time with their scorecards is an important responsibility, but one made much easier for Ivor by his Rolex. If you ask any golfer on the Tour which three familiar words they associate with Ivor, they will answer: "On the tee." **ROLEX IS OFFICIAL TIMEKEEPER TO THE EUROPEAN TOUR.**

ROLEX

K J Choi

Adam Scott

Richard Green

One of those featured Phil Mickelson who, before Saturday morning, was back home. The talented American has yet to do himself even a sliver of justice in an Open and Carnoustie proved, once again, to be a challenge too far. Tiger Woods remained for the weekend but it was a reduced Tiger this year, a shadow of the player who dominated at the Royal Liverpool Golf Club 12 months ago and a player seemingly frustrated at his own inadequacies this time round.

By the time Sunday dawned, Garcia and his belly putter were three shots clear. Next man standing was Steve Stricker, a thoroughly pleasant American who tends to earn rather than win. Then there came a clutch of class including US Open Champion Angel Cabrera, two time US PGA Tour winner so far in 2007, KJ Choi, Els and Harrington, while further European Tour interest was injected by the youth of Argentina's Andres Romero and the experience of England's Paul Broadhurst.

Garcia arrived on the first tee trying hard to appear calm but fighting to suppress his natural emotion and passion, for, ironically, the very qualities that get him into these positions are very often the ones that can then destroy him. A three stroke lead meant he remained unsure. Attack? Defend? Wait and hope?

The minds of others, however, were clear - there was no option. While Garcia deliberated, they had to grab the most straightforward plan of all and go for broke. For a while this worked for Els as he inched forward before an apparent lack of confidence kicked in and he reversed away. Choi, too, seemed strangely hesitant.

As the action progressed, it was Harrington and Romero who emerged to eyeball Garcia. Romero, a 26 year old, second youngest of six brothers and star graduate of a poor family, had the round of his life. He scooped ten birdies in total, including a truly incredible six in seven holes from the tenth, before falling a victim to the pressure of the last couple of holes.

Harrington, too, was bleak over the final hole, twice hitting into the Barry Burn. Back in Biarritz, Carnoustie's 1999 victim Jean Van de Velde grimly smiled. When Harrington, playing the 18th, passed Garcia, playing the 17th, on one of the bridges spanning this cantankerous stream neither looked at the other. No wonder. One of them was heading for the guillotine but neither knew who.

In the end Harrington's scrambled double bogey six was a testimony to his nerve. He knew this might, just might, save his Open. Garcia, meanwhile, knew that a par at the last would secure his first Major title, but when his putt for a four perversely refused to turn right, he threw his head back and howled.

The result of the four-hole play-off was a foregone conclusion. By scrambling that six, Harrington had saved everything, and by not holing that par putt, Garcia had thrown everything away. Either as winner would have made European golf proud. Actually, in the end, they both did.

Carnoustie the town, however, appeared hardly to notice. As we left on Monday afternoon, some bloke was up a ladder taking down a bit of that bunting. Nobody was whistling. But we will all be back and they, be assured, will be ready for us.

Bill Elliott
The Observer

The Course

The dreadful weather and questionable course set up in 1999 disappointed many locals who felt the jewel in their crown had not been seen at its best. All that was put right in July 2007 when the Championship Course regained its status as one of the most challenging and stimulating links courses in the world. Supremely testing closing four holes produced one of the most exciting Major finishes in decades.

Rory McIlroy

Just Champion: Padraig Harrington holds the Claret Jug aloft, flanked by Rodney James (left), Deputy Chairman of the R&A Championship Committee, and Peter Dawson (right), Chief Executive of the R&A

> I hope this has a positive aspect for European golf. Miguel Angel Jiménez came to me on the first play-off hole and said, 'The good thing is that we now have a European winner whatever happens.' I do very much believe in that side of things and hopefully it will inspire other players to emulate this.
>
> **Padraig Harrington**

Championship Course

Par **71** Yards **7421** Metres **6785**

Final Results

Pos	Name		Rd1	Rd2	Rd3	Rd4	Total		€	£
1	Padraig HARRINGTON	IRL	69	73	68	67	277	-7	1,106,617.50	750,000.00
2	Sergio GARCIA	ESP	65	71	68	73	277	-7	663,970.50	450,000.00
3	Andres ROMERO	ARG	71	70	70	67	278	-6	427,892.10	290,000.00
4	Richard GREEN	AUS	72	73	70	64	279	-5	295,098.00	200,000.00
	Ernie ELS	RSA	72	70	68	69	279	-5	295,098.00	200,000.00
6	Hunter MAHAN	USA	73	73	69	65	280	-4	214,683.80	145,500.00
	Stewart CINK	USA	69	73	68	70	280	-4	214,683.80	145,500.00
8	Steve STRICKER	USA	71	72	64	74	281	-3	139,802.68	94,750.00
	Ben CURTIS	USA	72	74	70	65	281	-3	139,802.68	94,750.00
	Mike WEIR	CAN	71	68	72	70	281	-3	139,802.68	94,750.00
	K J CHOI	KOR	69	69	72	71	281	-3	139,802.68	94,750.00
12	Justin ROSE	ENG	75	70	67	70	282	-2	86,421.56	58,571.43
	Paul BROADHURST	ENG	71	71	68	72	282	-2	86,421.56	58,571.43
	Markus BRIER	AUT	68	75	70	69	282	-2	86,421.56	58,571.43
	Tiger WOODS	USA	69	74	69	70	282	-2	86,421.56	58,571.43
	Jim FURYK	USA	70	70	71	71	282	-2	86,421.56	58,571.43
	Miguel Angel JIMÉNEZ	ESP	69	70	72	71	282	-2	86,421.56	58,571.43
	Pelle EDBERG	SWE	72	73	67	70	282	-2	86,421.56	58,571.43
19	Paul MCGINLEY	IRL	67	75	68	73	283	-1	67,872.54	46,000.00
20	Rich BEEM	USA	70	73	69	72	284	0	61,970.58	42,000.00
	Zach JOHNSON	USA	73	73	68	70	284	0	61,970.58	42,000.00
	Pat PEREZ	USA	73	70	71	70	284	0	61,970.58	42,000.00
23	Chris DIMARCO	USA	74	70	66	75	285	1	52,472.11	35,562.50
	Jonathan BYRD	USA	73	72	70	70	285	1	52,472.11	35,562.50
	Mark CALCAVECCHIA	USA	74	70	72	69	285	1	52,472.11	35,562.50
	Retief GOOSEN	RSA	74	71	73	71	285	1	52,472.11	35,562.50
27	J J HENRY	USA	70	71	71	74	286	2	41,577.20	28,178.57
	Lucas GLOVER	USA	71	72	70	73	286	2	41,577.20	28,178.57
	Vijay SINGH	FIJ	72	71	68	75	286	2	41,577.20	28,178.57
	Ian POULTER	ENG	72	73	70	70	286	2	41,577.20	28,178.57
	Paul CASEY	ENG	72	73	69	72	286	2	41,577.20	28,178.57
	Rodney PAMPLING	AUS	70	72	72	72	286	2	41,577.20	28,178.57
	Adam SCOTT	AUS	73	70	72	71	286	2	41,577.20	28,178.57
34	Angel CABRERA	ARG	68	73	72	74	287	3	35,411.76	24,000.00
35	Lee WESTWOOD	ENG	71	70	73	74	288	4	29,667.89	20,107.14
	Mark FOSTER	ENG	76	70	73	69	288	4	29,667.89	20,107.14
	Charley HOFFMAN	USA	75	69	72	72	288	4	29,667.89	20,107.14
	Shaun MICHEEL	USA	70	76	70	72	288	4	29,667.89	20,107.14
	Nick WATNEY	USA	72	71	70	75	288	4	29,667.89	20,107.14
	Boo WEEKLEY	USA	68	72	75	73	288	4	29,667.89	20,107.14
	Niclas FASTH	SWE	75	69	73	71	288	4	29,667.89	20,107.14
42	Rory MCILROY (AM)	NIR	68	75	73	72	289	5		
	Ryan MOORE	USA	72	72	74	71	289	5	24,161.15	16,375.00
	Nick DOUGHERTY	ENG	71	74	69	75	289	5	24,161.15	16,375.00
45	John SENDEN	AUS	72	74	71	73	290	6	21,394.61	14,500.00
	Arron OBERHOLSER	USA	73	71	72	74	290	6	21,394.61	14,500.00
	Ross BAIN	SCO	73	71	72	74	290	6	21,394.61	14,500.00
	Carl PETTERSSON	SWE	70	75	72	73	290	6	21,394.61	14,500.00
49	Won Joon LEE	AUS	73	73	70	75	291	7	19,181.37	13,000.00
	Jerry KELLY	USA	74	70	71	76	291	7	19,181.37	13,000.00
51	Tom LEHMAN	USA	73	73	74	73	293	9	17,890.32	12,125.00
	Kevin STADLER	USA	75	71	74	73	293	9	17,890.32	12,125.00
53	Thomas BJÖRN	DEN	70	75	74	75	294	10	16,783.70	11,375.00
	Brian DAVIS	ENG	74	72	71	77	294	10	16,783.70	11,375.00
	David HOWELL	ENG	72	74	73	75	294	10	16,783.70	11,375.00
	Grégory BOURDY	FRA	70	72	77	75	294	10	16,783.70	11,375.00
57	Anders HANSEN	DEN	72	73	74	76	295	11	15,935.29	10,800.00
	Michael CAMPBELL	NZL	68	78	72	77	295	11	15,935.29	10,800.00
	Scott VERPLANK	USA	72	73	72	78	295	11	15,935.29	10,800.00
60	Trevor IMMELMAN	RSA	71	74	77	74	296	12	15,492.65	10,500.00
	Mark O'MEARA	USA	74	72	76	74	296	12	15,492.65	10,500.00
	Toru TANIGUCHI	JPN	72	72	76	76	296	12	15,492.65	10,500.00
63	Jon BEVAN	ENG	73	73	79	72	297	13	15,123.77	10,250.00
	Luke DONALD	ENG	70	76	73	78	297	13	15,123.77	10,250.00
65	Raphaël JACQUELIN	FRA	74	69	76	79	298	14	14,828.67	10,050.00
	Sandy LYLE	SCO	73	73	73	79	298	14	14,828.67	10,050.00
67	Alastair FORSYTH	SCO	70	71	78	80	299	15	14,533.58	9,850.00
	Sean O'HAIR	USA	71	75	74	79	299	15	14,533.58	9,850.00
69	Peter HANSON	SWE	70	74	76	80	300	16	14,238.48	9,650.00
	Fredrik ANDERSSON HED	SWE	72	71	79	78	300	16	14,238.48	9,650.00

Total Prize Fund

€6,162,532 £4,176,600

No Regrets

1	**Andres ROMERO**		269	-19
2	Søren HANSEN		272	-16
	Oliver WILSON		272	-16
4	Peter O'MALLEY		274	-14
5	Peter HANSON		275	-13
	Alexander NOREN		275	-13
7	Charley HOFFMAN		276	-12
	Lee SLATTERY		276	-12
	Steve WEBSTER		276	-12
	Brett WETTERICH		276	-12

I t is funny how apparently minor decisions can turn out to have life-changing consequences. Like the record company executive whose career was over the instant he turned down The Beatles by telling their manager, Brian Epstein: "Guitar groups are on their way out." Or Abraham Lincoln's ill-fated decision to turn to the wife and say: "I'm sick of kicking around the house tonight, let's go and take in a show."

Fortunately for Andres Romero, however, he made the right choice when he decided to honour his commitment to play in The Deutsche Bank Players' Championship of Europe in Hamburg.

Understandably tired after his brilliant display in finishing third in The Open Championship at Carnoustie the week before – his fifth successive tournament appearance in a row – Romero was contemplating a well-earned break back in his native Argentina.

But the 26 year old knew all about what Gut Kaden had to offer having finished in a share of fourth place in 2006. Could he pass up the chance to claim his first European Tour International Schedule title in such a prestigious event and one which carries a five-year exemption to boot?

After a discussion with his manager, Romero decided to make the trip from the east of Scotland to the north of Germany and was given no cause to regret it with a first round 68. It was three shots off the pace set by England's Simon Khan, who revealed missing out on The Open had had its benefits too.

Watching the thrilling climax at Carnoustie, The 2004 Celtic Manor Wales Open winner noticed Padraig Harrington using a putting technique which featured one finger extended down the shaft. It was a technique Khan himself had used as a junior and, having retrieved an old putter from the garage, he honed the stroke to perfection on his living room carpet and employed it to devastating effect in the first round at Gut Kaden with six birdies and an eagle in a 65.

The living room carpet in Lee Slattery's new flat – just 300 yards from The 2008 Open Championship venue of Royal Birkdale – more closely resembled a water hazard than a putting green after a burst drain caused water to seep through the front door, but the 2004 Challenge Tour Rankings winner nevertheless added a 69 to his opening 66 to claim a share of the halfway lead.

It was becoming impossible to avoid Open connections as Slattery was joined on nine under par 135 by his good friend Zane Scotland, who shot to fame as a 16 year old qualifier in The 1999 Open Championship at Carnoustie.

LOCH	1	2	3	4	5	6	7	8
PAR	4	3	5	4	3	5	4	4
17 ROMERO	18	18	19	20	19	19	20	20
10 WETTERICH	10	10	11	11	11	11	11	11
14 SLATTERY	13	13	13	13	12	12	12	12
13 NOREN	12	13	14	14	13	14	14	14
9 HANSON	9	10	12	12	12	13	13	14

Lee Slattery

Niclas Fasth

Alexander Noren

Zane Scotland

But lurking dangerously a shot behind was Romero, who promised not to alter his attacking approach and was good to his word with a brilliant third round 63 to assume control of the event – a round only denied a share of Lee Westwood's 2006 course record by the preferred lies in operation.

"I would like to keep going this way," the affable Romero said after a round containing five birdies and two eagles. "That's the way I play. I love what I am doing so it's very easy to smile a lot on the course. We are not machines, we are human. Obviously, when you hit a bad shot you are not very happy but I try to look forward and keep going and forget the bad shot."

Two shots clear with two holes to play in Scotland seven days earlier, Romero now found himself two ahead of Scotland in Germany with a full 18 holes remaining, a lead he quickly stretched to five with four birdies in the first seven holes.

Again it was hard to avoid an Open flashback as a double bogey on the ninth, where he found the water surrounding the island green – in similar fashion to the penultimate hole at Carnoustie where he lost the Open lead – gave the chasing pack a glimmer of hope.

But Romero had plenty of time to recover and a birdie on the 11th steadied the ship despite the best efforts of Denmark's Søren Hansen - who set the clubhouse target of 16 under par 272 after a superb 64 - and England's Oliver Wilson, to pile on the pressure. In the end, the duo had to settle for a share of second place, three shots adrift.

When a long-range birdie putt on the 18th found the bottom of the cup to put the icing on the cake of his victory, Romero was drenched in champagne by fellow Argentine players and caddies. "It's a pity they threw away all that champagne, I prefer to drink it," he joked.

His views on claret may be clouded by the near miss at Carnoustie, but it looks a safe bet there will be plenty more champagne in Romero's future.

Phil Casey
PA Sport

Charley Hoffman (left) and Brett Wetterich

Doctor Clemens Boersig (left), Chairman of the Deutsche Bank Supervisory Board, presents the trophy to Andres Romero

Tino Schuster

i Bernhard Langer is the only player to win this Championship in two different countries. His first success came in 1983 at St Mellion, England. He followed that 12 years later at Gut Kaden in Germany.

Gut Kaden

Par **72**   Yards **7290**   Metres **6666**

Final Results

Pos	Name		Rd1	Rd2	Rd3	Rd4	Total		€	£
1	Andres ROMERO	ARG	68	68	63	70	269	-19	600,000.00	403,510.54
2	Søren Hansen	DEN	72	70	66	64	272	-16	312,680.00	210,282.79
	Oliver WILSON	ENG	66	70	70	66	272	-16	312,680.00	210,282.79
4	Peter O'MALLEY	AUS	69	72	68	65	274	-14	180,000.00	121,053.16
5	Alexander NOREN	SWE	67	71	65	72	275	-13	139,320.00	93,695.15
	Peter HANSON	SWE	69	70	68	68	275	-13	139,320.00	93,695.15
7	Charley HOFFMAN	USA	68	72	67	69	276	-12	87,660.00	58,952.89
	Brett WETTERICH	USA	69	70	67	70	276	-12	87,660.00	58,952.89
	Steve WEBSTER	ENG	73	67	70	66	276	-12	87,660.00	58,952.89
	Lee SLATTERY	ENG	66	69	67	74	276	-12	87,660.00	58,952.89
11	Ross FISHER	ENG	69	72	68	68	277	-11	60,300.00	40,552.81
	Zane SCOTLAND	ENG	67	68	66	76	277	-11	60,300.00	40,552.81
	Johan EDFORS	SWE	71	70	69	67	277	-11	60,300.00	40,552.81
	Rory SABBATINI	RSA	78	65	66	68	277	-11	60,300.00	40,552.81
15	Andrew MCLARDY	RSA	71	72	70	65	278	-10	48,672.00	32,732.78
	Anton HAIG	RSA	69	69	72	68	278	-10	48,672.00	32,732.78
	Miguel Angel JIMÉNEZ	ESP	69	68	71	70	278	-10	48,672.00	32,732.78
	Miles TUNNICLIFF	ENG	73	69	66	70	278	-10	48,672.00	32,732.78
	Benn BARHAM	ENG	69	70	68	71	278	-10	48,672.00	32,732.78
20	John BICKERTON	ENG	68	71	68	72	279	-9	40,200.00	27,035.21
	Sam WALKER	ENG	70	73	67	69	279	-9	40,200.00	27,035.21
	Nick O'HERN	AUS	71	69	68	71	279	-9	40,200.00	27,035.21
	Peter GUSTAFSSON	SWE	72	68	69	70	279	-9	40,200.00	27,035.21
	Robert KARLSSON	SWE	69	71	66	73	279	-9	40,200.00	27,035.21
	Charl SCHWARTZEL	RSA	71	72	65	71	279	-9	40,200.00	27,035.21
26	Retief GOOSEN	RSA	70	73	67	70	280	-8	31,058.18	20,887.17
	Taichi TESHIMA	JPN	67	74	70	69	280	-8	31,058.18	20,887.17
	Richard STERNE	RSA	69	69	70	72	280	-8	31,058.18	20,887.17
	Niclas FASTH	SWE	68	75	71	66	280	-8	31,058.18	20,887.17
	Carlos RODILES	ESP	67	72	71	70	280	-8	31,058.18	20,887.17
	Matthew MILLAR	AUS	70	71	68	71	280	-8	31,058.18	20,887.17
	Wade ORMSBY	AUS	72	69	70	69	280	-8	31,058.18	20,887.17
	Ian GARBUTT	ENG	71	69	71	69	280	-8	31,058.18	20,887.17
	David LYNN	ENG	68	73	69	70	280	-8	31,058.18	20,887.17
	Jean-Baptiste GONNET	FRA	70	72	67	71	280	-8	31,058.18	20,887.17
	Tino SCHUSTER	GER	69	72	66	73	280	-8	31,058.18	20,887.17
37	Shiv KAPUR	IND	71	67	70	73	281	-7	24,840.00	16,705.34
	Paul MCGINLEY	IRL	72	70	69	70	281	-7	24,840.00	16,705.34
	Peter LAWRIE	IRL	72	69	70	70	281	-7	24,840.00	16,705.34
40	José-Filipe LIMA	POR	70	72	71	69	282	-6	19,800.00	13,315.85
	Emanuele CANONICA	ITA	71	70	69	72	282	-6	19,800.00	13,315.85
	Alastair FORSYTH	SCO	70	73	69	70	282	-6	19,800.00	13,315.85
	Steven O'HARA	SCO	69	70	70	73	282	-6	19,800.00	13,315.85
	Christian L NILSSON	SWE	71	72	71	68	282	-6	19,800.00	13,315.85
	Mikko ILONEN	FIN	72	71	71	68	282	-6	19,800.00	13,315.85
	Anthony WALL	ENG	70	73	69	70	282	-6	19,800.00	13,315.85
	Andrew TAMPION	AUS	71	69	70	72	282	-6	19,800.00	13,315.85
	Rodney PAMPLING	AUS	71	69	70	72	282	-6	19,800.00	13,315.85
	Bradley DREDGE	WAL	69	69	73	71	282	-6	19,800.00	13,315.85
	Kyron SULLIVAN	WAL	71	72	67	72	282	-6	19,800.00	13,315.85
51	Ariel CANETE	ARG	70	71	66	76	283	-5	13,680.00	9,200.04
	Mark FOSTER	ENG	71	71	70	71	283	-5	13,680.00	9,200.04
	Jean-François LUCQUIN	FRA	71	72	67	73	283	-5	13,680.00	9,200.04
	Paul CASEY	ENG	68	70	68	77	283	-5	13,680.00	9,200.04
	David FROST	RSA	68	72	69	74	283	-5	13,680.00	9,200.04
	Damien MCGRANE	IRL	69	71	72	71	283	-5	13,680.00	9,200.04
57	Oliver FISHER	ENG	71	72	68	73	284	-4	10,980.00	7,384.24
	Ricardo GONZALEZ	ARG	67	76	70	71	284	-4	10,980.00	7,384.24
59	Terry PRICE	AUS	71	69	74	71	285	-3	9,900.00	6,657.92
	Grégory BOURDY	FRA	72	69	71	73	285	-3	9,900.00	6,657.92
	Marcel SIEM	GER	71	69	75	70	285	-3	9,900.00	6,657.92
	David GRIFFITHS	ENG	70	72	68	75	285	-3	9,900.00	6,657.92
63	Gary BIRCH JR	GER	73	70	72	71	286	-2	8,280.00	5,568.45
	Søren KJELDSEN	DEN	70	71	74	71	286	-2	8,280.00	5,568.45
	Stephen GALLACHER	SCO	68	74	72	72	286	-2	8,280.00	5,568.45
	Martin ERLANDSSON	SWE	72	67	73	74	286	-2	8,280.00	5,568.45
	Phillip PRICE	WAL	74	69	73	70	286	-2	8,280.00	5,568.45
68	Garry HOUSTON	WAL	72	70	71	74	287	-1	6,500.00	4,371.36
	Brett RUMFORD	AUS	69	73	71	74	287	-1	6,500.00	4,371.36
	Max KRAMER	GER	71	72	70	74	287	-1	6,500.00	4,371.36
	Thomas LEVET	FRA	70	71	73	73	287	-1	6,500.00	4,371.36
72	Daniel VANCSIK	ARG	70	73	74	71	288	0	5,392.50	3,626.55
	Johan AXGREN	SWE	67	76	75	70	288	0	5,392.50	3,626.55
	Mardan MAMAT	SIN	72	71	71	74	288	0	5,392.50	3,626.55
	Marc WARREN	SCO	68	73	75	72	288	0	5,392.50	3,626.55
76	Jarmo SANDELIN	SWE	69	74	71	75	289	1	5,385.00	3,621.51
77	Gary MURPHY	IRL	70	73	73	74	290	2	5,380.50	3,618.48
	Edward RUSH	ENG	71	72	71	76	290	2	5,380.50	3,618.48
79	Sion E BEBB	WAL	72	70	73	76	291	3	5,376.00	3,615.45

Total Prize Fund

€3,648,492   £2,453,674

The Course

Set in the grounds of one of the most beautiful estates in the Holstein area, lime trees, alder trees and oak trees surround the holes on the back nine while the front nine has a more open and links-like feel to it. Creeks, ponds and ditches weave around the course creating an additional challenge while the greens, although perfectly shaped, can be hard to read and demand the utmost scrutiny.

Sunshine After The Rain

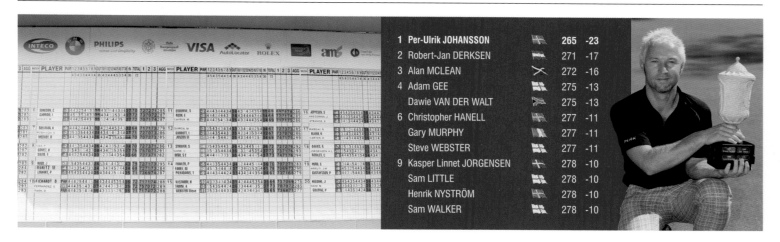

1	Per-Ulrik JOHANSSON		265	-23
2	Robert-Jan DERKSEN		271	-17
3	Alan MCLEAN		272	-16
4	Adam GEE		275	-13
	Dawie VAN DER WALT		275	-13
6	Christopher HANELL		277	-11
	Gary MURPHY		277	-11
	Steve WEBSTER		277	-11
9	Kasper Linnet JORGENSEN		278	-10
	Sam LITTLE		278	-10
	Henrik NYSTRÖM		278	-10
	Sam WALKER		278	-10

O n reflection, there was perhaps no more appropriate winner of The Russian Open Golf Championship at Le Meridien Moscow Country Club than Per-Ulrik Johansson. Let us peruse the facts.

Gary Murphy

Robert-Jan Derksen

For a start, both had last enjoyed newsworthy prominence over a decade ago; the tournament beginning its association with European golf for the first time in September 1996 when it became part of the Challenge Tour, three weeks before Johansson captured the Smurfit Kappa European Open at The K Club, the first of three wins in 11 months for the Swede which cemented his place in Europe's winning Ryder Cup Team at Valderrama in 1997.

However, since then, both had retreated from centre stage. Granted, the tournament quietly grew, but with trips to Russia increasingly prevalent in all walks of life, such a journey was no longer seen as uncommon; while Johansson's decision to base himself permanently in the United States had, as with so many others before him, not produced the outcome he had hoped for.

With success limited, so were his tournament playing opportunities, leading to the inevitable situation at the beginning of the 2007 season that saw the 40 year old Swede with nowhere to ply his trade Stateside. With a wife and two children to support, he had little option but to get pen and paper out and write to promoters back home in Europe, asking for a spot in their respective tournaments.

One such letter found its way to the desk of Hans Koeleman, the President of AMS, the Official Promoters of The 2007 Russian Open Golf Championship. Being a keen student of the game, Koeleman knew of Johansson and his pedigree and what he could bring to his tournament and, hence, wrote back offering him a starting place. It proved to be an inspired decision.

After seven years as a Challenge Tour event and three years as a dual ranking event with The European Tour, this was the second season The Russian Open Golf Championship had stood alone on The European Tour International Schedule but, with a prize fund doubled to $2 million, it was now ready to step back into the limelight. So, it turned out, was Johansson.

Winning from the front is never easy but the Swede made it look exactly that to triumph by six shots and claim his sixth European Tour title, the €244,250 (£164,282) first prize cheque, and a priceless exemption on The European Tour until the end of the 2009 season.

Having taken command of the tournament with his second round 62 – a round only denied a share of Iain Pyman's 2002 course record by the preferred lies in operation – Johansson stood four shots clear going into the final day after a third round 67.

PHILIPS   www.philips.ru

THE RUSSIA
OPEN GOLF
CHAMPIONS
2007

Hole-in-one

ambi light   HD ready

PHILIPS

sense and simpli

Above *Alan McLean*

Kyron Sullivan

Despite both his nearest challengers and playing partners – Robert-Jan Derksen of The Netherlands, who eventually took second, and Alan McLean of Scotland, who finished third – birdieing the first hole to immediately put pressure on, Johansson responded magnificently, powering clear with five birdies of his own in the next ten holes on his way to a 23 under par total of 265, a new record low winning total for the event.

Golf in Russia might still be relatively new to the general populous but the public who gathered to watch the closing holes appreciated they were witnessing something special, as Johansson's golfing master class ensured the tournament ended with as much of a bang as it had begun.

Hollywood actor and keen golfer Don Johnson was involved in many explosive situations during his time on Miami Vice but even he was slightly startled as Wednesday's Pro-Am competition – in which he played an active part - was heralded by a cacophony of bangs and crashes as a full-blown firework display took to the skies from the driving range.

Spectacular, certainly, but it did little to soothe the thumping heads of those who had been involved

in the pre-tournament tradition of toasting the event's health with a seemingly never-ending supply of neat vodka shots, or as the locals prefer to call them, 'small drops'.

The irony of that description was not lost on the tournament staff who could only look on in dismay as the first three days were hindered by the complete opposite - ie large drops - from the sky as torrential rain showers flooded the course and forced a total of 12 ¼ hours scheduled play to be lost.

But, thanks to the sterling efforts of Le Meridien Moscow Country Club greenkeeping staff – under the direction of The European Tour's Greenkeeping Consultant Eddie Adams – four rounds were made possible with the closing holes on Sunday, and the lavish presentation ceremony, taking place in glorious sunshine.

Emerging from under dark clouds and onwards to a bright future. Now which Swedish golfer does that remind you of.....?

Scott Crockett

Simon Hurd

The Course

Beautiful birch trees border every hole at Le Meridien Moscow Country Club which places the emphasis on accuracy with wood and iron. Designed by Robert Trent Jones Jnr in 1988, Russia's first 18 hole golf course has developed into a good test at 7,154 yards long it stood up well to the constant rain over the week.

Christopher Hanell plays from the floor of the 18th green scoreboard after his approach shot veered off course

Per-Ulrik Johansson (right) receives the trophy from Ivan I. Sergeyev, Director General of The Main Administration for Service to the Diplomatic Corps under the Ministry of Foreign Affairs of the Russian Federation

The unique Matrioshka Doll Trophy also presented to Per-Ulrik Johansson

> I think this was the best I have ever putted through a whole tournament. Every time I got the ball on the green I felt like I had a chance for birdie – that was a great feeling.
> *Per-Ulrik Johansson*

Le Meridien Moscow Country Club
Par 72   Yards 7154   Metres 6542

Final Results

Pos	Name		Rd1	Rd2	Rd3	Rd4	Total		€	£
1	Per-Ulrik JOHANSSON	SWE	69	62	67	67	265	-23	244,250.88	164,282.90
2	Robert-Jan DERKSEN	NED	68	69	65	69	271	-17	162,833.92	109,521.93
3	Alan MCLEAN	SCO	73	64	67	68	272	-16	91,741.55	61,705.27
4	Adam GEE	ENG	69	68	68	70	275	-13	73,276.00	49,285.36
5	Christopher HANELL	SWE	73	65	69	70	277	-11	52,465.61	35,288.32
	Gary MURPHY	IRL	67	68	70	72	277	-11	52,465.61	35,288.32
	Steve WEBSTER	ENG	73	68	71	65	277	-11	52,465.61	35,288.32
8	Sam LITTLE	ENG	67	71	69	71	278	-10	31,435.40	21,143.42
	Henrik NYSTRÖM	SWE	73	70	69	66	278	-10	31,435.40	21,143.42
	Sam WALKER	ENG	69	71	68	70	278	-10	31,435.40	21,143.42
	Kasper Linnet JORGENSEN	DEN	73	70	68	67	278	-10	31,435.40	21,143.42
12	Kyron SULLIVAN	WAL	71	71	73	64	279	-9	21,286.68	14,317.40
	Terry PILKADARIS	AUS	73	71	68	67	279	-9	21,286.68	14,317.40
	Peter GUSTAFSSON	SWE	71	69	70	69	279	-9	21,286.68	14,317.40
	Simon LILLY	ENG	70	71	67	71	279	-9	21,286.68	14,317.40
	Richard BLAND	ENG	74	71	66	68	279	-9	21,286.68	14,317.40
	Carlos RODILES	ESP	71	70	70	68	279	-9	21,286.68	14,317.40
	Philip GOLDING	ENG	70	69	70	70	279	-9	21,286.68	14,317.40
	Jesus Maria ARRUTI	ESP	70	68	72	69	279	-9	21,286.68	14,317.40
20	David CARTER	ENG	71	67	73	69	280	-8	16,816.84	11,310.99
	Simon HURD	ENG	73	70	68	69	280	-8	16,816.84	11,310.99
	Alexandre ROCHA	BRA	68	68	72	72	280	-8	16,816.84	11,310.99
	Scott STRANGE	AUS	71	71	70	68	280	-8	16,816.84	11,310.99
24	Jeppe HULDAHL	DEN	69	72	69	71	281	-7	14,581.92	9,807.78
	Gareth DAVIES	ENG	70	71	70	70	281	-7	14,581.92	9,807.78
	Matthew ZIONS	AUS	72	71	70	68	281	-7	14,581.92	9,807.78
	Joakim HAEGGMAN	SWE	71	72	69	69	281	-7	14,581.92	9,807.78
	Marcel SIEM	GER	75	64	70	72	281	-7	14,581.92	9,807.78
	Peter LAWRIE	IRL	71	69	69	72	281	-7	14,581.92	9,807.78
30	Alvaro SALTO	ESP	72	73	71	66	282	-6	11,786.97	7,927.90
	Christian L NILSSON	SWE	65	71	72	74	282	-6	11,786.97	7,927.90
	Zane SCOTLAND	ENG	70	75	69	68	282	-6	11,786.97	7,927.90
	Julien GUERRIER	FRA	68	76	70	68	282	-6	11,786.97	7,927.90
	Lee SLATTERY	ENG	71	70	73	68	282	-6	11,786.97	7,927.90
	Jean-Baptiste GONNET	FRA	66	71	71	74	282	-6	11,786.97	7,927.90
	Brett RUMFORD	AUS	72	70	67	73	282	-6	11,786.97	7,927.90
37	Prom MEESAWAT	THA	71	70	72	70	283	-5	9,818.98	6,604.24
	Lasse JENSEN	DEN	72	72	71	68	283	-5	9,818.98	6,604.24
	Chris WOOD (AM)	ENG	72	68	73	70	283	-5		
	Keith HORNE	RSA	73	68	72	70	283	-5	9,818.98	6,604.24
	Peter FOWLER	AUS	70	72	71	70	283	-5	9,818.98	6,604.24
	Jean-François REMESY	FRA	76	68	70	69	283	-5	9,818.98	6,604.24
43	Euan LITTLE	SCO	72	70	72	70	284	-4	8,500.02	5,717.10
	Tim MILFORD	ENG	75	69	70	70	284	-4	8,500.02	5,717.10
	Steven JEPPESEN	SWE	70	71	71	72	284	-4	8,500.02	5,717.10
	Martin MARITZ	RSA	72	71	73	68	284	-4	8,500.02	5,717.10
47	Edward RUSH	ENG	72	71	74	68	285	-3	7,034.50	4,731.40
	Richard MCEVOY	ENG	70	72	73	70	285	-3	7,034.50	4,731.40
	Manuel QUIROS	ESP	72	73	73	67	285	-3	7,034.50	4,731.40
	Iain PYMAN	ENG	74	68	71	72	285	-3	7,034.50	4,731.40
	Alessandro TADINI	ITA	70	70	72	73	285	-3	7,034.50	4,731.40
	Carl SUNESON	ESP	72	72	71	70	285	-3	7,034.50	4,731.40
53	Marc CAYEUX	ZIM	71	71	75	69	286	-2	5,275.87	3,548.54
	Simon ROBINSON	ENG	72	70	73	71	286	-2	5,275.87	3,548.54
	Francisco CEA	ESP	72	73	71	70	286	-2	5,275.87	3,548.54
	Ian GARBUTT	ENG	73	70	76	67	286	-2	5,275.87	3,548.54
	Sam OSBORNE	ENG	69	74	74	69	286	-2	5,275.87	3,548.54
	Richie RAMSAY	SCO	70	72	70	74	286	-2	5,275.87	3,548.54
59	Ignacio GARRIDO	ESP	73	70	72	72	287	-1	4,176.73	2,809.26
	Pedro LINHART	ESP	73	69	74	71	287	-1	4,176.73	2,809.26
	Marcus HIGLEY	ENG	70	71	74	72	287	-1	4,176.73	2,809.26
	Garry HOUSTON	WAL	75	69	70	73	287	-1	4,176.73	2,809.26
63	Darren FICHARDT	RSA	71	71	74	72	288	0	3,737.08	2,513.56
	David PARK	WAL	71	74	72	71	288	0	3,737.08	2,513.56
65	Michael JONZON	SWE	74	71	75	69	289	1	3,443.97	2,316.41
	Sebastian FERNANDEZ	ARG	73	70	72	72	289	1	3,443.97	2,316.41
67	Marc FARRY	FRA	70	69	73	78	290	2	3,224.14	2,168.55
68	Rafael GOMEZ	ARG	75	70	71	75	291	3	3,004.32	2,020.70
	Birgir HAFTHORSSON	ISL	74	71	70	76	291	3	3,004.32	2,020.70
70	Sven STRÜVER	GER	72	72	76	72	292	4	2,784.49	1,872.85
71	Chris GANE	ENG	73	71	76	73	293	5	2,674.57	1,798.91
72	Sion E BEBB	WAL	74	71	76	73	294	6	2,198.00	1,478.37
73	Jean HUGO	RSA	72	71	73	79	295	7	2,195.00	1,476.35
74	David DRYSDALE	SCO	70	73	70	W/D	213	-3		
	Dawie VAN DER WALT	RSA	72	68	DISQ		140	-4		

Total Prize Fund

€1,469,913 £988,662

Planet Invincible

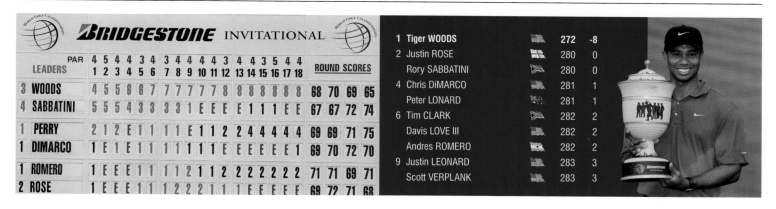

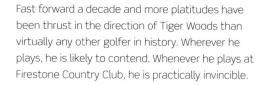

	BRIDGESTONE INVITATIONAL																			ROUND SCORES
PAR	4	5	4	4	3	4	3	4	4	4	4	3	4	4	3	5	4	4	
LEADERS	1	2	3	4	5	6	7	8	9	10	11	12	13	14	15	16	17	18	
3 WOODS	4	5	5	6	6	7	7	7	7	7	7	8	8	8	8	8	8	8	68 70 69 65
4 SABBATINI	5	5	5	4	3	3	3	3	1	E	E	E	E	1	1	1	E	E	67 67 72 74
1 PERRY	2	1	2	E	1	1	1	1	E	1	1	2	2	4	4	4	4		69 69 71 75
1 DiMARCO	1	E	1	E	1	1	1	1	1	1	1	E	E	E	E	E	E	1	69 70 72 70
1 ROMERO	1	E	E	E	1	1	1	1	2	1	1	2	2	2	2	2	2	2	71 71 69 71
2 ROSE	1	E	E	E	1	1	1	2	2	2	1	1	1	E	E	E	E	E	69 72 71 68

1	Tiger WOODS	272	-8
2	Justin ROSE	280	0
	Rory SABBATINI	280	0
4	Chris DiMARCO	281	1
	Peter LONARD	281	1
6	Tim CLARK	282	2
	Davis LOVE III	282	2
	Andres ROMERO	282	2
9	Justin LEONARD	283	3
	Scott VERPLANK	283	3

As Shakespeare put it so eloquently in Twelfth Night: 'Some are born great, some achieve greatness and some have greatness thrust upon them.' Any individual who fits one of these criteria is a rare creature; two rarer still. For a person to slide effortlessly into all three, however, borders on the unique. But, then again, there is only one Tiger Woods.

Andres Romero

Padraig Harrington

How to define greatness? Can talent alone bestow that lofty accolade? Or is it a combination of talent and nerve? Is it grace under pressure? Or is it humility in victory and magnanimity in defeat? One thing is beyond argument. Professional golf is currently witnessing a career of gargantuan proportions as the undisputed World Number One devours record after record in his pursuit of golfing immortality.

When he turned professional in 1996, cynics sneered as his late father decreed that his only son had been blessed with a God-given talent. Within a few months, his prophecy came to pass when Woods captured the first of his Jack Nicklaus record chasing haul of Majors in the 1997 Masters Tournament at Augusta National. The margin? Twelve shots.

Fast forward a decade and more platitudes have been thrust in the direction of Tiger Woods than virtually any other golfer in history. Wherever he plays, he is likely to contend. Whenever he plays at Firestone Country Club, he is practically invincible.

A matter of days after the 31 year old American captured a sixth World Golf Championships – Bridgestone Invitational title in Akron, Tom Lehman pondered the question of what makes Woods such a huge draw card, even when he is winning tournaments by almost unhealthy margins. The 2006 Ryder Cup Captain did not pause for breath. "Simple," he observed. "Greatness is always worth watching. When Michael Jordan was at his peak with the Chicago Bulls, you could guess the result, but people went along to see the best proving he was the best."

So it is with Woods and Firestone. There is nowhere on the planet he plays better than on the Ohio venue's South Course and he proved it again during the first week of August 2007, winning the tournament by eight strokes. More impressively, he did so as the only player in the field to shoot below par, eight under to be precise. Justin Rose and Rory Sabbatini tied for the other tournament – ie the one minus Woods – in second place at level par.

It was the third time that Woods had won a tournament as the only player in red numbers. In 2000 he claimed his first US Open Championship at Pebble Beach by 15 shots on 12 under par; two years later he regained that particular crown at Bethpage State Park at three under par – Phil Mickelson was second on level.

Despite his dominance, Woods continues to strive to improve and he showed that aspect of his character again on the 72nd green at Firestone. The title was in his pocket but he needed to make

Above Luke Donald

Darren Clarke

a 12 foot putt for par to ensure a bogey-free round. Never content with anything less than perfection, he duly drained the putt for a 65, the best round of a sodden final day.

In 32 rounds at Firestone, Woods is now an accumulative 80 under par and, hard though it may be for us mere mortals to comprehend, Woods has now collected six of the nine WGC events played there since 1999.

Woods possesses the finely tuned brain of a mathematician and the finely honed body of an athlete like his hero, basketball legend Jordan. Add to the concoction an unbreakable concentration, an unshakeable self-belief and a steely determination, and you have the complete package.

Rose, who arrived in Akron feeling refreshed albeit a touch rusty after a week on a Virgin Islands beach celebrating the wedding of US PGA Tour player Heath Slocum, was one of many left awestruck by Woods that final Sunday.

A birdie putt to reach the turn in 30 just slipped by, but the Englishman believed he had done enough

to challenge for the title. Not so. He said: "I hadn't looked at a leader board all through the front nine but felt sure I was in the tournament. Then I looked up and saw Tiger was seven under and I was five behind! I thought: 'Oh well, looks like we're playing for second place'. That's how it turned out."

On that final day, Woods partnered Sabbatini, who led by a shot, and Kenny Perry, who was three off the pace. Woods sprinted to the turn in 31 and led by six. Sabbatini shot 74 to tie Rose, who closed with a commendable 68. Perry signed for a 75.

Greatness has the ability to make the very good seem ordinary. Just behold Roger Federer playing tennis or Ronaldinho gliding over a football pitch to appreciate the skill of making the difficult appear easy. Yes, greatness really is worth watching.

Gordon Simpson

The Course

Originally designed by Bert Way in 1950 and updated by Robert Trent Jones a decade later, the South Course has a rich history of providing a stern challenge for the world's best and this year proved no exception with only eventual champion Tiger Woods emerging from the week in red figures. Several memorable holes exist including the daunting 667 yard 16th.

Colin Montgomerie

Tiger Woods is presented with the trophy by Tatsuya Okajima, Senior Vice President, Bridgestone Corporation

i This is the second European Tour event Tiger Woods has won on six occasions, following the WGC – CA Championship. As a result of his win in Akron, he also became the first player to win the same event for three consecutive years, on two different occasions – 1999, 2000 and 2001, then in 2005, 2006 and 2007.

Firestone Country Club

Par 70   **Yards 7400**   **Metres 6768**

Final Results

Pos	Name		Rd1	Rd2	Rd3	Rd4	Total		€	£
1	Tiger WOODS	USA	68	70	69	65	272	-8	989,225.97	665,352.39
2	Justin ROSE	ENG	69	72	71	68	280	0	465,302.59	312,962.05
	Rory SABBATINI	RSA	67	67	72	74	280	0	465,302.59	312,962.05
4	Chris DIMARCO	USA	69	70	72	70	281	1	227,155.59	152,784.62
	Peter LONARD	AUS	70	70	73	68	281	1	227,155.59	152,784.62
6	Andres ROMERO	ARG	71	71	69	71	282	2	148,017.52	99,556.43
	Tim CLARK	RSA	71	70	72	69	282	2	148,017.52	99,556.43
	Davis LOVE III	USA	74	65	74	69	282	2	148,017.52	99,556.43
9	Justin LEONARD	USA	73	67	71	72	283	3	108,082.10	72,695.91
	Scott VERPLANK	USA	70	68	73	72	283	3	108,082.10	72,695.91
11	Zach JOHNSON	USA	71	65	76	72	284	4	84,511.65	56,842.45
	Kenny PERRY	USA	69	69	71	75	284	4	84,511.65	56,842.45
	K J CHOI	KOR	71	73	69	71	284	4	84,511.65	56,842.45
14	Padraig HARRINGTON	IRL	72	69	72	72	285	5	63,444.80	42,672.91
	Rodney PAMPLING	AUS	71	73	74	67	285	5	63,444.80	42,672.91
	Stuart APPLEBY	AUS	68	74	69	74	285	5	63,444.80	42,672.91
	Mark CALCAVECCHIA	USA	68	72	76	69	285	5	63,444.80	42,672.91
	Joe DURANT	USA	74	67	71	73	285	5	63,444.80	42,672.91
	Arron OBERHOLSER	USA	68	74	72	71	285	5	63,444.80	42,672.91
20	Sergio GARCIA	ESP	71	77	71	67	286	6	55,323.38	37,210.45
	Aaron BADDELEY	AUS	70	74	67	75	286	6	55,323.38	37,210.45
22	Stephen AMES	CAN	71	73	71	72	287	7	48,545.35	32,651.55
	Anders HANSEN	DEN	71	72	71	73	287	7	48,545.35	32,651.55
	Lee WESTWOOD	ENG	68	71	79	69	287	7	48,545.35	32,651.55
	Luke DONALD	ENG	75	75	67	70	287	7	48,545.35	32,651.55
	Ernie ELS	RSA	70	77	72	68	287	7	48,545.35	32,651.55
	Niclas FASTH	SWE	75	73	70	69	287	7	48,545.35	32,651.55
	Charley HOFFMAN	USA	71	73	74	69	287	7	48,545.35	32,651.55
	Hunter MAHAN	USA	67	73	71	76	287	7	48,545.35	32,651.55
30	John ROLLINS	USA	73	75	68	72	288	8	42,500.08	28,585.51
	Carl PETTERSSON	SWE	70	79	68	71	288	8	42,500.08	28,585.51
	Richard GREEN	AUS	73	73	68	74	288	8	42,500.08	28,585.51
	Ian POULTER	ENG	71	73	74	70	288	8	42,500.08	28,585.51
	Brett WETTERICH	USA	74	75	70	69	288	8	42,500.08	28,585.51
	Boo WEEKLEY	USA	68	78	70	72	288	8	42,500.08	28,585.51
36	Adam SCOTT	AUS	75	76	70	68	289	9	39,202.66	26,367.67
	Trevor IMMELMAN	RSA	73	76	69	71	289	9	39,202.66	26,367.67
	Mark WILSON	USA	76	75	68	70	289	9	39,202.66	26,367.67
39	Charles HOWELL III	USA	72	76	70	72	290	10	37,370.76	25,135.53
	Paul MCGINLEY	IRL	72	74	73	71	290	10	37,370.76	25,135.53
41	Henrik STENSON	SWE	72	74	72	73	291	11	35,172.48	23,656.97
	Colin MONTGOMERIE	SCO	71	72	73	75	291	11	35,172.48	23,656.97
	J J HENRY	USA	73	69	74	75	291	11	35,172.48	23,656.97
	Steve STRICKER	USA	70	73	76	72	291	11	35,172.48	23,656.97
45	John SENDEN	AUS	71	69	78	74	292	12	33,706.96	22,671.27
46	Shingo KATAYAMA	JPN	71	73	75	74	293	13	32,607.82	21,931.99
	Michael CAMPBELL	NZL	71	74	72	76	293	13	32,607.82	21,931.99
	Thongchai JAIDEE	THA	73	76	73	71	293	13	32,607.82	21,931.99
	Phil MICKELSON	USA	74	72	74	73	293	13	32,607.82	21,931.99
	Jerry KELLY	USA	73	71	74	75	293	13	32,607.82	21,931.99
51	Richard STERNE	RSA	77	72	74	71	294	14	30,775.92	20,699.85
	Paul CASEY	ENG	67	73	76	78	294	14	30,775.92	20,699.85
	Jeev Milkha SINGH	IND	72	74	72	76	294	14	30,775.92	20,699.85
	Geoff OGILVY	AUS	73	71	72	78	294	14	30,775.92	20,699.85
	Troy MATTESON	USA	71	74	73	76	294	14	30,775.92	20,699.85
56	Woody AUSTIN	USA	74	77	68	76	295	15	28,944.02	19,467.72
	Nick O'HERN	AUS	72	72	75	76	295	15	28,944.02	19,467.72
	Vijay SINGH	FIJ	74	72	75	74	295	15	28,944.02	19,467.72
	Y E YANG	KOR	73	74	70	78	295	15	28,944.02	19,467.72
	Stewart CINK	USA	79	67	76	73	295	15	28,944.02	19,467.72
61	David TOMS	USA	76	74	71	75	296	16	26,928.93	18,112.37
	Retief GOOSEN	RSA	74	73	72	77	296	16	26,928.93	18,112.37
	Wen-chong LIANG	CHN	75	74	72	75	296	16	26,928.93	18,112.37
	David HOWELL	ENG	74	77	75	70	296	16	26,928.93	18,112.37
	Nick WATNEY	USA	72	72	76	76	296	16	26,928.93	18,112.37
	Vaughn TAYLOR	USA	72	77	71	76	296	16	26,928.93	18,112.37
67	Mark HENSBY	AUS	73	71	79	74	297	17	25,463.41	17,126.66
	Darren CLARKE	NIR	70	76	76	75	297	17	25,463.41	17,126.66
69	Grégory HAVRET	FRA	73	73	76	76	298	18	24,547.46	16,510.60
	Graeme STORM	ENG	75	72	76	75	298	18	24,547.46	16,510.60
	Angel CABRERA	ARG	73	76	74	75	298	18	24,547.46	16,510.60
	Robert KARLSSON	SWE	76	72	72	78	298	18	24,547.46	16,510.60
	Fred FUNK	USA	75	74	74	75	298	18	24,547.46	16,510.60
74	Brian BATEMAN	USA	77	75	72	75	299	19	23,906.29	16,079.35
	Paul GOYDOS	USA	69	76	73	81	299	19	23,906.29	16,079.35
76	José Manuel LARA	ESP	71	77	77	75	300	20	23,631.51	15,894.53
77	Chad CAMPBELL	USA	73	73	77	79	302	22	23,265.13	15,648.10
	Raphaël JACQUELIN	FRA	71	77	73	81	302	22	23,265.13	15,648.10
	Anton HAIG	RSA	77	75	71	79	302	22	23,265.13	15,648.10
80	Ben CURTIS	USA	74	79	77	73	303	23	22,898.75	15,401.68
81	Robert ALLENBY	AUS	74	76	82	80	312	32	22,715.56	15,278.46
82	José María OLAZÁBAL	ESP	77	80	78	79	314	34	22,532.37	15,155.25
83	Mike WEIR	CAN	77	RETD						
84	Jim FURYK	USA	W/D							

Total Prize Fund

€5,795,582   £3,898,102

Meeting the Challenge

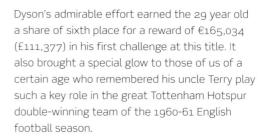

1	**Tiger WOODS**		272	-8
2	Woody AUSTIN		274	-6
3	Ernie ELS		275	-5
4	Arron OBERHOLSER		279	-1
	John SENDEN		279	-1
6	Simon DYSON		280	0
	Trevor IMMELMAN		280	0
	Geoff OGILVY		280	0
9	Kevin SUTHERLAND		281	1
	Scott VERPLANK		281	1
	Boo WEEKLEY		281	1

A familiar irritant to visiting ears got a topical twist from a local scribe in the build-up to the 89th US PGA Championship at Southern Hills Country Club. "It's been a few weeks since a European has won a Major," he cheekily informed newly-crowned Open Champion Padraig Harrington. "Will you break the drought this week?" Harrington smiled along with the rest of us, but the final Major of the season would remain in formidable, American hands.

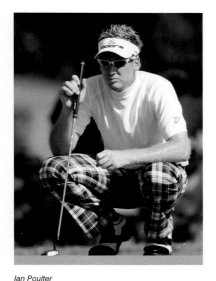

Ian Poulter

Simon Dyson

With Woody Austin and Ernie Els chasing valiantly under a torrid sun, Tiger Woods effectively slammed the door with a 12 foot birdie putt four holes from home. Ultimately, his victory margin was two strokes over his fellow American and three over the South African as the nature of an event, played in brutally hot conditions, was reflected perfectly in the sight of the champion, wrapped in a white towel, while being interviewed about his triumph.

Early in the week, Harrington pointed to "a lot of good, young European players" in the field. Best among those who answered the call was England's Simon Dyson, whose closing 64 was surpassed by only one competitor over the four days. Not surprisingly, that happened to be Woods who, in the second round, became the 23rd player to record a 63 in a Major Championship.

Dyson's admirable effort earned the 29 year old a share of sixth place for a reward of €165,034 (£111,377) in his first challenge at this title. It also brought a special glow to those of us of a certain age who remembered his uncle Terry play such a key role in the great Tottenham Hotspur double-winning team of the 1960-61 English football season.

Dyson's grand finalé owed much to precise approach play which saw him hit 13 greens in regulation, while his trusty blade wrought wondrous magic for 12 single putts and 25 in all. Having taken a break from the game after missing the cut in The Barclays Scottish Open in July, he had the good sense to arrive early in Tulsa, starting his preparation with 14 holes on the Saturday before the Championship. Of Sunday's climax, Dyson said simply: "It was one of the best days I've had for a long time."

When Woods turned professional in August 1996, Jack Nicklaus told the media: "If he can handle all the attention, all the pressure from you folks, Tiger can be as good or better than anybody who has ever played the game." Almost exactly 11 years on, he had captured his 13th Major Championship in his inexorable pursuit of the record of 18, set by The Golden Bear.

By Woods' own admission, those 18 represented a daunting challenge when he started out. But not any more. "It took Jack 20-plus years," he said. "It's one of those things where it's going to take some time and hopefully, health permitting and everything going right, I'll one day surpass it."

Notorious in the past for the so-called Blast-Furnace US Open Championship of 1958, Southern Hills gained the unwanted distinction on this

occasion of staging the hottest Major on record, with daily temperatures averaging 101 degrees. All of which prompted one wag to remark: "Farmers are feeding ice to their chickens to keep them from laying hard-boiled eggs!" Yet for the most part, European Tour challengers coped admirably because of the experience gained in tournaments in even hotter and more humid conditions in places such as Malaysia and Thailand.

This was clearly evident on the opening day when another US PGA Championship debutant, Open de France ALSTOM champion Graeme Storm, swept to the top of the leader board with a sparkling 65. 'Storm Chasers' said the headline in a local newspaper, by way of saluting the 29 year old from the north of England. There was also strong European support from Lee Westwood and Harrington on 69.

But Woods' 63 on the Friday changed everything. It would have been an all-time record 62 had a ten footer succumbed to gravity on the 18th green

but still, from outside the top 20 after an opening 71, he had surged two strokes clear of fellow countryman Scott Verplank as Championship leader at the halfway stage. Furthermore, his lead grew to three over Stephen Ames after 54 holes.

For a resurgent Els, third place gave promise of better things to come, while Darren Clarke rediscovered a long lost joy in the game when a second round 66 brought his first cut in a Major since June 2006.

But what of the wonder of Woods? Padraig Harrington offered two words of explanation, saying simply: "He believes."

Dermot Gilleece
Sunday Independent

Darren Clarke

Graeme Storm

Ernie Els

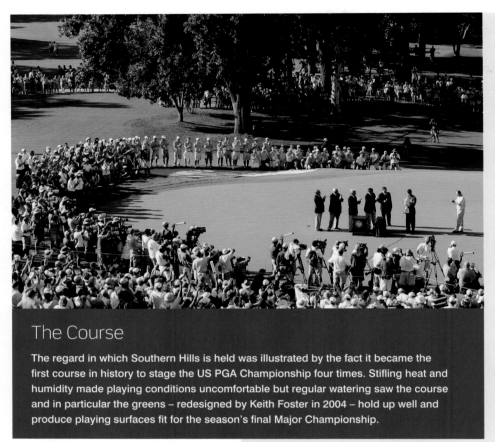

The Course

The regard in which Southern Hills is held was illustrated by the fact it became the first course in history to stage the US PGA Championship four times. Stifling heat and humidity made playing conditions uncomfortable but regular watering saw the course and in particular the greens – redesigned by Keith Foster in 2004 – hold up well and produce playing surfaces fit for the season's final Major Championship.

A fan!

Lee Westwood

For the first time in his career, Tiger Woods won an event the week before a Major Championship, having won the World Golf Championships – Bridgestone Invitational, then going on to claim his fourth US PGA Championship. Woods became the ninth player in history to achieve this feat.

Southern Hills Country Club

Par 70 Yards **7131** Metres **6520**

Final Results

Pos	Name		Rd1	Rd2	Rd3	Rd4	Total		€	£
1	Tiger WOODS	USA	71	63	69	69	272	-8	914,039.81	616,860.90
2	Woody AUSTIN	USA	68	70	69	67	274	-6	548,423.88	370,116.54
3	Ernie ELS	RSA	72	68	69	66	275	-5	345,303.93	233,036.34
4	John SENDEN	AUS	69	70	69	71	279	-1	223,431.95	150,788.22
	Arron OBERHOLSER	USA	68	72	70	69	279	-1	223,431.95	150,788.22
6	Simon DYSON	ENG	73	71	72	64	280	0	165,034.96	111,377.66
	Trevor IMMELMAN	RSA	75	70	66	69	280	0	165,034.96	111,377.66
	Geoff OGILVY	AUS	69	68	74	69	280	0	165,034.96	111,377.66
9	Scott VERPLANK	USA	70	66	74	71	281	1	123,564.64	83,390.45
	Kevin SUTHERLAND	USA	73	69	68	71	281	1	123,564.64	83,390.45
	Boo WEEKLEY	USA	76	69	65	71	281	1	123,564.64	83,390.45
12	Adam SCOTT	AUS	72	68	70	72	282	2	86,930.51	58,667.06
	Stephen AMES	CAN	68	69	69	76	282	2	86,930.51	58,667.06
	Justin ROSE	ENG	70	73	70	69	282	2	86,930.51	58,667.06
	Stuart APPLEBY	AUS	73	68	72	69	282	2	86,930.51	58,667.06
	K J CHOI	KOR	71	71	68	72	282	2	86,930.51	58,667.06
	Anders HANSEN	DEN	71	71	71	69	282	2	86,930.51	58,667.06
18	Joe DURANT	USA	71	73	70	70	284	4	59,194.96	39,949.09
	Ken DUKE	USA	73	71	69	71	284	4	59,194.96	39,949.09
	Brandt SNEDEKER	USA	74	71	69	70	284	4	59,194.96	39,949.09
	Pat PEREZ	USA	70	69	77	68	284	4	59,194.96	39,949.09
	Hunter MAHAN	USA	71	73	72	68	284	4	59,194.96	39,949.09
23	Heath SLOCUM	USA	72	70	72	71	285	5	36,996.85	24,968.18
	Camilo VILLEGAS	COL	69	71	74	71	285	5	36,996.85	24,968.18
	Nathan GREEN	AUS	75	68	67	75	285	5	36,996.85	24,968.18
	Kenny PERRY	USA	72	72	71	70	285	5	36,996.85	24,968.18
	Retief GOOSEN	RSA	70	71	74	70	285	5	36,996.85	24,968.18
	Steve STRICKER	USA	77	68	69	71	285	5	36,996.85	24,968.18
	Steve FLESCH	USA	72	73	68	72	285	5	36,996.85	24,968.18
	Peter HANSON	SWE	72	71	69	73	285	5	36,996.85	24,968.18
	Ian POULTER	ENG	71	73	70	71	285	5	36,996.85	24,968.18
32	Stewart CINK	USA	72	70	72	72	286	6	25,208.64	17,012.63
	Lee WESTWOOD	ENG	69	74	75	68	286	6	25,208.64	17,012.63
	Phil MICKELSON	USA	73	69	75	69	286	6	25,208.64	17,012.63
	John DALY	USA	67	73	73	73	286	6	25,208.64	17,012.63
	Shaun MICHEEL	USA	73	71	70	72	286	6	25,208.64	17,012.63
	Luke DONALD	ENG	72	71	70	73	286	6	25,208.64	17,012.63
	Bart BRYANT	USA	74	70	72	70	286	6	25,208.64	17,012.63
	Brett WETTERICH	USA	74	71	70	71	286	6	25,208.64	17,012.63
40	Paul CASEY	ENG	72	70	74	71	287	7	19,840.47	13,389.80
	Richard GREEN	AUS	72	73	70	72	287	7	19,840.47	13,389.80
42	Rodney PAMPLING	AUS	70	74	72	72	288	8	15,125.18	10,207.58
	Colin MONTGOMERIE	SCO	72	73	73	70	288	8	15,125.18	10,207.58
	Padraig HARRINGTON	IRL	69	73	72	74	288	8	15,125.18	10,207.58
	Niclas FASTH	SWE	71	68	79	70	288	8	15,125.18	10,207.58
	Darren CLARKE	NIR	77	66	71	74	288	8	15,125.18	10,207.58
	Charles HOWELL III	USA	75	70	72	71	288	8	15,125.18	10,207.58
	David TOMS	USA	71	74	71	72	288	8	15,125.18	10,207.58
	Sean O'HAIR	USA	70	72	70	76	288	8	15,125.18	10,207.58
50	Anthony KIM	USA	73	72	71	73	289	9	11,052.42	7,458.98
	Brian BATEMAN	USA	71	74	76	68	289	9	11,052.42	7,458.98
	Lucas GLOVER	USA	70	75	74	70	289	9	11,052.42	7,458.98
	Frank LICKLITER	USA	70	75	75	69	289	9	11,052.42	7,458.98
	Shingo KATAYAMA	JPN	76	67	72	74	289	9	11,052.42	7,458.98
	Bob TWAY	USA	71	72	71	75	289	9	11,052.42	7,458.98
	Nick O'HERN	AUS	72	72	72	73	289	9	11,052.42	7,458.98
57	Robert KARLSSON	SWE	73	71	75	71	290	10	10,446.17	7,049.84
	Chad CAMPBELL	USA	77	68	73	72	290	10	10,446.17	7,049.84
	Will MACKENZIE	USA	72	70	74	74	290	10	10,446.17	7,049.84
60	Billy MAYFAIR	USA	76	69	75	71	291	11	10,174.13	6,866.25
	Paul MCGINLEY	IRL	74	66	76	75	291	11	10,174.13	6,866.25
62	Thomas BJÖRN	DEN	73	71	76	73	293	13	9,902.10	6,682.66
	Corey PAVIN	USA	74	68	72	79	293	13	9,902.10	6,682.66
	Graeme STORM	ENG	65	76	74	78	293	13	9,902.10	6,682.66
	Brett QUIGLEY	USA	76	67	73	77	293	13	9,902.10	6,682.66
66	Troy MATTESON	USA	72	69	73	80	294	14	9,648.20	6,511.31
	Tim HERRON	USA	75	68	71	80	294	14	9,648.20	6,511.31
	Todd HAMILTON	USA	73	72	74	75	294	14	9,648.20	6,511.31
69	Tom LEHMAN	USA	73	71	74	78	296	16	9,466.84	6,388.92
	Mike SMALL	USA	73	70	78	75	296	16	9,466.84	6,388.92
71	Ryan BENZEL	USA	71	72	80	74	297	17	9,358.03	6,315.48
72	Sergio GARCIA	ESP	70	75	DISQ				1,813.57	1,223.93

Total Prize Fund

€5,007,922 £3,379,711

Stamp of Approval

LEADER BOARD

	HOLE	1	2	3	4	5	6	7	8	9	10	11	12	13	14	15	16	17
	PAR	4	3	4	3	3	4	4	4	5	4	4	4	4	4	5	3	5
4	ILONEN	5	5	5	6	5	6	5	5	6	6	6	6	6	6	7	5	5
7	KINGSTON	7	6	6	4	4	4	4	3	3	4	3	3	3	3	3	3	3
4	BROADHURST	4	4	4	4	4	5	5	5	4	4	5	5	4	4	4	4	4
7	KAYMER	7	7	7	6	5	5	5	5	6	6	6	6	6	6	7	6	6
4	DOUGHERTY	4	3	3	4	4	4	4	4	4	4	4	4	3	4	4	4	
1	ELIASSON	1	2	1	2	2	2	2	2	3	3	3	3	3	1	1	2	3
1	PAVIN	1	1	1		2	1	1	1	2	3	3	4	3	3	3	3	3
3	HEDBLOM	3	3	3	3	3	3	3	3	3	4	4	4	3	4	5	5	5
2	GONNET	2	2	2	2	2	2	2	2	2	2	2	3	3	3	3	3	4

1	Mikko ILONEN		274	-6
2	Christian CÉVAËR		276	-4
	Nick DOUGHERTY		276	-4
	Jean-Baptiste GONNET		276	-4
	Peter HEDBLOM		276	-4
	Martin KAYMER		276	-4
7	Paul BROADHURST		277	-3
	James KINGSTON		277	-3
	Corey PAVIN		277	-3
10	Mattias ELIASSON		278	-2
	David HIGGINS		278	-2

The glorious 12th at Augusta National known as Golden Bell. The famous island green 17th at Sawgrass. The Postage Stamp eighth hole at Royal Troon. There are par threes which ingrain themselves on the memory, often encapsulating the whole challenge of a golf course.

Henrik Nyström

Sam Walker

Yet you could write on a postage stamp the number of championship courses which end with a par three. Even if you use the smallest script possible, you would still have room to spare after the likes of the last at Sandy Lane and St Pierre, the 18th at St Nom-la Brétèche and Pula Golf Club in Majorca, and the finale at the Marriott Forest of Arden.

However, in your finest calligraphy, that space can now be filled with the closing hole at Arlandastad Golf on the outskirts of Stockholm, the venue for the 2007 Scandinavian Masters.

It is a lengthy 213 yards to a green boxed in by grandstands; one, to the rear, in which you can sit and dine, clinking a glass to the latest competitor who would doubtless willingly join you for something other than water and a power bar after a four and a half hour round.

Now study the shape of the green. The way the slope to the left sings a siren's song, beckoning any wayward tee shots to slide down its sinister incline. The inclination from day one was to believe

the 72nd hole would settle events and it did in dramatic fashion for eventual champion Mikko Ilonen. But more of that later.

Media interest at the start of the week centred around Australian Scott Strange, the tournament's designated first reserve. When Tom Lehman, the 2006 US Ryder Cup Captain, withdrew through injury, the 30 year old from Perth thought he would get his chance, but with Lehman having been in Stockholm on an invitation, organisers were allowed to issue another, which they gave to Swedish golfer Oskar Henningsson.

Undaunted, Strange opted to take the first bus to the course anyway on the Thursday morning, just in case. Stuck in a traffic jam, a call came. David Drysdale, off in the first group at 7.30am, was injured. A Scot was down, but a Scott would benefit – if he could get there.

However, his clubs had been delayed in transit and, as a result, he had had no practice round. He rang ahead and was relieved to find that Drysdale's

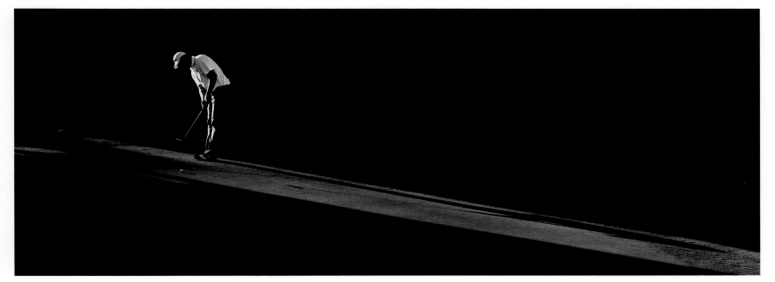

caddie, Gerry Byrne, would happily carry his now redeemed bag. Arriving in the car park at 7.21am, he had nine minutes to spare, just enough time to rush to the first tee, grab his golf shoes and a three wood and ask Byrne: "OK, where do I hit this?"

Rumour is Strange is now tempted to change his customary pre-round routine to mirror events that Thursday in Stockholm after a round played largely on instinct produced a six under par 64 and the first round lead.

As the winds picked up, Strange was not headed from lunchtime on Thursday to when the smorgasbord was unveiled again on Friday – and then it was his misfortune that brought the change, dropping a shot at the opening hole of his second round.

Henrik Nystrom flew the flag for the home country over the first two rounds, looking to add his name to those of Joakim Haeggman and Jesper Parnevik – the tournament host – as the only Swedish winners of the event. But a less impressive weekend saw him fall back leaving Peter Hedblom to engender local interest as he eventually tied for second place with Frenchmen Christian Cévaër and Jean-Baptiste Gonnet, England's Nick Dougherty and Martin Kaymer of Germany.

Kaymer shared the lead with South Africa's James Kingston into the final day, and held the advantage to the final hole. Ilonen – winner of the Enjoy Jakarta Astro Indonesia Open in February – had been three behind at the start of play, but was

making inroads. The Finn looked to have blown his chance, however, when he found water at another par three, the 16th. He donned the waterproofs and played from the hazard, but suffered a double-bogey five.

However, showing great resilience, he regrouped and approached the 18th from where he played a sublime four iron – later voted The European Tour Shot of the Month for August – to five feet. He holed the birdie putt to finish on six under par 274 while Kaymer was watching in the distance from the 18th tee.

A par for the young German and there would be a play off. But with Ilonen tuning into the television coverage from the Recorder's Hut, Kaymer's ball found the rough down the slope to the left of the green. A weak chip failed to scale the heights, and a double bogey five meant he would have to wait another day for his first title.

Finland might not strictly be part of Scandinavia, but Ilonen regarded the Scandinavian Masters as a 'home' event nevertheless. It was the first time he had made the cut in the tournament and he ended it in style.

If the final hole at Arlandastad Golf is lacking anything, perhaps it is a suitable name. In honour of Ilonen, 'A Fantastic Finnish' fits the bill perfectly.

Nick Dye
European Tour Radio

Paul Broadhurst

Christian Cévaër

Mikko Ilonen (right) receives the winner's trophy from Mia Reich Sjogren, Scandinavian Masters Chairman of the Board

> It's an unbelievable feeling because if I had to pick one tournament to win, alongside the Majors, it would be this one. The support we get from the crowds is something we don't get every week and I hope some other tournaments can learn from this. It's unbelievable for the players to be out there.
>
> **Mikko Ilonen**

The Course

Although not one of the longest courses in use on The 2007 European Tour International Schedule, the 6845 yard layout, designed by Sune Linde and Peter Chamberlein in 1982, provided a good test with strong cross winds most of the week demanding care and attention around the 12 holes which feature water hazards. Two par threes in the final three holes is unusual but the 213 yard 18th produced an excellent amphitheatre-like finish.

Michael Jonzon

Arlandastad Golf
Par **70**   Yards **6845**   Metres **6260**

Final Results

Pos	Name		Rd1	Rd2	Rd3	Rd4	Total		€	£
1	Mikko ILONEN	FIN	67	72	67	68	274	-6	266,660.00	180,498.87
2	Nick DOUGHERTY	ENG	68	69	69	70	276	-4	96,354.00	65,220.83
	Jean-Baptiste GONNET	FRA	67	70	71	68	276	-4	96,354.00	65,220.83
	Martin KAYMER	GER	67	68	68	73	276	-4	96,354.00	65,220.83
	Peter HEDBLOM	SWE	68	71	68	69	276	-4	96,354.00	65,220.83
	Christian CÉVAËR	FRA	69	69	69	69	276	-4	96,354.00	65,220.83
7	James KINGSTON	RSA	68	68	67	74	277	-3	41,280.00	27,941.92
	Corey PAVIN	USA	70	70	70	67	277	-3	41,280.00	27,941.92
	Paul BROADHURST	ENG	69	73	64	71	277	-3	41,280.00	27,941.92
10	Mattias ELIASSON	SWE	69	72	68	69	278	-2	30,720.00	20,793.99
	David HIGGINS	IRL	69	69	71	69	278	-2	30,720.00	20,793.99
12	Sam WALKER	ENG	69	74	70	72	279	-1	23,240.00	15,730.87
	Michael JONZON	SWE	71	67	74	67	279	-1	23,240.00	15,730.87
	Scott STRANGE	AUS	64	75	69	71	279	-1	23,240.00	15,730.87
	Barry LANE	ENG	70	72	69	68	279	-1	23,240.00	15,730.87
	Peter HANSON	SWE	70	72	67	70	279	-1	23,240.00	15,730.87
	Peter LAWRIE	IRL	71	70	69	69	279	-1	23,240.00	15,730.87
	Steve ALKER	NZL	74	69	68	68	279	-1	23,240.00	15,730.87
	Martin ERLANDSSON	SWE	71	72	71	65	279	-1	23,240.00	15,730.87
20	Garry HOUSTON	WAL	70	73	68	69	280	0	18,613.33	12,599.14
	Paul LAWRIE	SCO	68	72	72	68	280	0	18,613.33	12,599.14
	Edward RUSH	ENG	69	68	74	69	280	0	18,613.33	12,599.14
23	Alan MCLEAN	SCO	69	74	71	67	281	1	16,880.00	11,425.86
	Simon DYSON	ENG	69	71	72	69	281	1	16,880.00	11,425.86
	Santiago LUNA	ESP	72	70	69	70	281	1	16,880.00	11,425.86
	José Manuel LARA	ESP	70	70	73	68	281	1	16,880.00	11,425.86
27	Joakim BÄCKSTRÖM	SWE	69	69	69	75	282	2	14,720.00	9,963.79
	Stephen GALLACHER	SCO	68	72	71	71	282	2	14,720.00	9,963.79
	Henrik NYSTRÖM	SWE	67	68	73	74	282	2	14,720.00	9,963.79
	Tom WHITEHOUSE	ENG	72	69	70	71	282	2	14,720.00	9,963.79
	Oskar HENNINGSSON	SWE	72	71	71	68	282	2	14,720.00	9,963.79
32	Richard MCEVOY	ENG	71	67	76	69	283	3	12,600.00	8,528.78
	Fredrik ANDERSSON HED	SWE	70	71	72	70	283	3	12,600.00	8,528.78
	Luis CLAVERIE	ESP	69	73	72	69	283	3	12,600.00	8,528.78
	Andrew TAMPION	AUS	72	70	67	74	283	3	12,600.00	8,528.78
36	Miles TUNNICLIFF	ENG	72	70	72	70	284	4	10,720.00	7,256.24
	Per-Ulrik JOHANSSON	SWE	73	69	73	69	284	4	10,720.00	7,256.24
	Damien MCGRANE	IRL	70	70	73	71	284	4	10,720.00	7,256.24
	Johan AXGREN	SWE	73	68	76	67	284	4	10,720.00	7,256.24
	Phillip ARCHER	ENG	68	74	67	75	284	4	10,720.00	7,256.24
	David CARTER	ENG	73	68	71	72	284	4	10,720.00	7,256.24
	Brett RUMFORD	AUS	72	71	71	70	284	4	10,720.00	7,256.24
43	Dawie VAN DER WALT	RSA	67	73	72	73	285	5	8,640.00	5,848.31
	Jesper PARNEVIK	SWE	70	73	74	68	285	5	8,640.00	5,848.31
	Cesar MONASTERIO	ARG	71	69	70	75	285	5	8,640.00	5,848.31
	Jeff SLUMAN	USA	71	70	72	72	285	5	8,640.00	5,848.31
	Richard BLAND	ENG	70	72	72	71	285	5	8,640.00	5,848.31
	Ian GARBUTT	ENG	67	75	70	73	285	5	8,640.00	5,848.31
49	Gary EMERSON	ENG	73	70	75	68	286	6	6,720.00	4,548.69
	Gary MURPHY	IRL	68	75	71	72	286	6	6,720.00	4,548.69
	Wade ORMSBY	AUS	69	73	75	69	286	6	6,720.00	4,548.69
	Alejandro CAÑIZARES	ESP	76	66	70	74	286	6	6,720.00	4,548.69
	Gary LOCKERBIE	ENG	69	74	73	70	286	6	6,720.00	4,548.69
	Lee SLATTERY	ENG	70	72	73	71	286	6	6,720.00	4,548.69
55	Rafael CABRERA BELLO	ESP	67	72	72	76	287	7	5,280.00	3,573.97
	Simon KHAN	ENG	70	71	73	73	287	7	5,280.00	3,573.97
	Terry PILKADARIS	AUS	74	69	73	71	287	7	5,280.00	3,573.97
	Fredrik QVICKER (AM)	SWE	65	75	73	74	287	7		
59	Joel SJOHOLM (AM)	SWE	69	71	72	76	288	8		
	Jarmo SANDELIN	SWE	72	71	71	74	288	8	4,800.00	3,249.06
61	Lee S JAMES	ENG	67	73	74	75	289	9	4,480.00	3,032.46
	Andrew MARSHALL	ENG	72	71	77	69	289	9	4,480.00	3,032.46
	David BRANSDON	AUS	71	67	76	75	289	9	4,480.00	3,032.46
64	Stephen DODD	WAL	72	71	72	75	290	10	4,000.00	2,707.55
	John BICKERTON	ENG	72	70	74	74	290	10	4,000.00	2,707.55
	James HEATH	ENG	71	71	71	77	290	10	4,000.00	2,707.55
67	Johan EDFORS	SWE	72	71	70	78	291	11	3,520.00	2,382.64
	Shaun P WEBSTER	ENG	69	72	78	72	291	11	3,520.00	2,382.64
	Alessandro TADINI	ITA	67	74	78	72	291	11	3,520.00	2,382.64
70	Simon WAKEFIELD	ENG	69	72	77	74	292	12	3,200.00	2,166.04

Total Prize Fund

€1,594,030 £1,078,979

National Appreciation

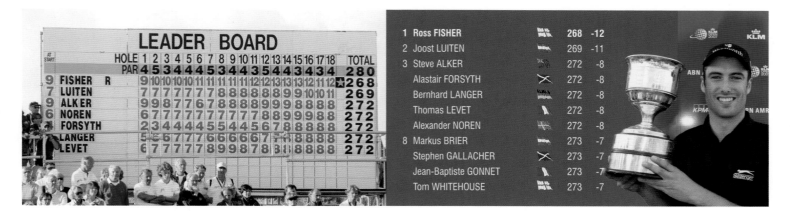

LEADER BOARD

HOLE	1	2	3	4	5	6	7	8	9	10	11	12	13	14	15	16	17	18	TOTAL
PAR	4	5	3	4	4	4	5	3	4	4	3	5	4	4	3	4	3	4	280
9 FISHER R	9	10	10	10	10	11	11	11	11	12	12	13	13	13	12	11	12	★	268
7 LUITEN	7	7	7	7	7	7	8	8	8	8	8	9	9	10	10	11			269
9 ALKER	9	9	8	7	6	7	8	8	8	8	9	9	9	8	8	8	8		272
6 NOREN	6	7	7	7	7	7	7	7	7	7	8	8	9	9	9	9	8	8	272
4 FORSYTH	2	3	4	4	4	4	5	5	4	4	5	6	7	8	8	8	8		272
LANGER	5	5	6	7	7	7	6	6	6	6	6	7	7	8	8	8	8		272
LEVET	6	7	7	7	7	8	9	9	8	7	8	8	8	8	8	8			272

1	Ross FISHER		268	-12	
2	Joost LUITEN		269	-11	
3	Steve ALKER		272	-8	
	Alastair FORSYTH		272	-8	
	Bernhard LANGER		272	-8	
	Thomas LEVET		272	-8	
	Alexander NOREN		272	-8	
8	Markus BRIER		273	-7	
	Stephen GALLACHER		273	-7	
	Jean-Baptiste GONNET		273	-7	
	Tom WHITEHOUSE		273	-7	

W hen the dust had finally settled and the rule books had been packed away, it was Ross Fisher who claimed his maiden European Tour title in The KLM Open. Not a single spectator resented his well deserved win, not least because the affable Englishman had already gone close to victory on more than one occasion this year. The home fans, however, were understandably as enthusiastic about the young man who finished second; the new hero of Dutch golf, Joost Luiten.

Alastair Forsyth

Bernhard Langer

For decades the International Golf Championship of The Netherlands, as The KLM Open has been known since its first edition in 1912, has drawn big and enthusiastic crowds despite the lack of a real Dutch contender.

There was the occasional exception, such as in 1982 – the year England's Paul Way took the title at Utrecht – when Jan Dorrestein improved his score by a shot every day, eventually carding a final round 69 to finish in a tie for eighth place.

More often, though, the growing galleries in the 1990s contented themselves with appreciating the talent of visiting victors such as Severiano Ballesteros, Scott Hoch, Miguel Angel Jiménez, Bernhard Langer, Colin Montgomerie, the late Payne Stewart and Lee Westwood.

Of course everyone also remembered the historic nine hole play-off in 1989 when José Maria Olazábal and Ronan Rafferty – Roger Chapman was eliminated on the first extra hole – battled wind, torrential rain and each other until the Spaniard triumphed minutes before darkness made further play impossible.

However, matters got interesting for the home fans when the Dutch crop did more than just make the cut. Rolf Muntz was the first to take centre stage in the 1990s and he was soon followed by Robert-Jan Derksen and Maarten Lafeber. Muntz was the first Dutch winner on The European Tour International Schedule when he pipped Ian Woosnam to the 2000 Qatar Masters, followed by Derksen, who beat none other than Ernie Els to claim the 2003 Dubai Desert Classic and went on to win in Madeira in 2005.

However well received those wins were, celebrations went wild in October 2003 when Lafeber won the Dutch Open at his beloved Hilversumsche to become the first home winner of the event since Joop Rühl in 1947 at Eindhoven.

The success of the illustrious trio gave The KLM Open another dimension. Press coverage of golf in The Netherlands got more extensive; public interest in the sport grew and continued to prosper when a young Dutchman won two of his first six tournaments on the 2007 Challenge Tour. His name? Joost Luiten.

As an amateur the 21 year old from the little town of Bleiswijk missed the cut in both the 2005 and 2006 KLM Opens, but that was soon forgotten when he trailed Englishman David Carter by a mere two strokes after the second round of the 2007 tournament. All home eyes were on him but, in searching for the eventual champion, in hindsight they should have been on Fisher, only three shots off the lead still held by Carter after opening rounds of 66 and 67. Nevertheless, Luiten's equal best of the tournament second round of 64 was one to savour.

Fisher was no stranger to being centre stage having opened the Dubai Desert Classic in February with matching 65s before playing firstly with Ernie Els and latterly with Tiger Woods over the weekend on his way to a highly respectable fifth place.

The 26 year old's previous encounter with the World Number One had come when he worked on the range at Wentworth Club in 1999, collecting the American's golf balls as he prepared to compete in the World Match Play Championship.

In Dubai, Fisher proved he was mature enough to handle the transformation of now standing alongside Woods on the first tee and a similar assuredness emanated from him in Zandvoort as a third round in succession in the 60s – this time a 68 – moved him into a share of the lead with 18 holes to play, alongside New Zealander Steve Alker and Carter on nine under par 201 with Luiten two shots back after a 71.

Into the latter stages of the final round it seemed to be Fisher's day. He had distanced himself from the field over a flawless 15 holes which featured birdies at the second, sixth, 11th and 13th. A fine final round 66 saw Luiten take the clubhouse lead on 11 under par 269 but even then the Dutchman only received congratulations in the clubhouse for claiming second place.

However, out of nowhere, Fisher inexplicably three putted both the 16th and 17th holes for back-to-back bogeys. All of a sudden, he and Luiten were tied. But the Englishman pulled himself together superbly, hit a sublime approach to the 18th and sank the six foot birdie putt for a 67 and a total of 12 under par 268.

Still the drama was not over. Before signing his card, Tournament Director Miguel Vidaor informed the puzzled Fisher there might be a rules issue. An on-course radio reporter had spotted he had lifted some bramble branches in the rough to the right of the par five 12th prior to playing his shot.

After a lengthy study of television pictures and a trip back out to the 12th to recreate events, Vidaor was eventually satisfied that Fisher had not improved his lie, his area of intended stance or swing or his line of play, Rule 13-2 had not been breached and, finally, he could celebrate as the champion.

The Dutch fans were happy for Fisher, for the integrity of golf, and for Luiten who had won their hearts with his swashbuckling play. One thing is for certain, expectations will be even higher when The KLM Open returns to Kennemer in 2008.

Jan Kees van der Velden
Golfers Magazine and GOLFjournaal

Jean-Baptiste Gonnet

Alexander Noren

John Bickerton

Kennemer Golf and Country Club

Par 70   **Yards 6626**   **Metres 6057**

Final Results

Pos	Name		Rd1	Rd2	Rd3	Rd4	Total		€	£
1	Ross FISHER	ENG	66	67	68	67	268	-12	266,660.00	181,449.50
2	Joost LUITEN	NED	68	64	71	66	269	-11	177,770.00	120,964.07
3	Alexander NOREN	SWE	65	67	72	68	272	-8	70,400.00	47,903.87
	Alastair FORSYTH	SCO	66	71	69	66	272	-8	70,400.00	47,903.87
	Bernhard LANGER	GER	67	71	67	67	272	-8	70,400.00	47,903.87
	Steve ALKER	NZL	66	66	69	71	272	-8	70,400.00	47,903.87
	Thomas LEVET	FRA	65	70	68	69	272	-8	70,400.00	47,903.87
8	Tom WHITEHOUSE	ENG	68	67	71	67	273	-7	34,320.00	23,353.13
	Markus BRIER	AUT	67	68	70	68	273	-7	34,320.00	23,353.13
	Stephen GALLACHER	SCO	70	68	66	69	273	-7	34,320.00	23,353.13
	Jean-Baptiste GONNET	FRA	64	71	70	68	273	-7	34,320.00	23,353.13
12	John BICKERTON	ENG	68	67	69	70	274	-6	24,768.00	16,853.45
	Richard FINCH	ENG	68	67	72	67	274	-6	24,768.00	16,853.45
	Michael CAMPBELL	NZL	65	71	69	69	274	-6	24,768.00	16,853.45
	Simon KHAN	ENG	67	69	69	69	274	-6	24,768.00	16,853.45
	David LYNN	ENG	65	70	70	69	274	-6	24,768.00	16,853.45
17	Phillip PRICE	WAL	68	68	67	72	275	-5	19,653.33	13,373.16
	Garry HOUSTON	WAL	68	68	72	67	275	-5	19,653.33	13,373.16
	Martin ERLANDSSON	SWE	69	71	71	64	275	-5	19,653.33	13,373.16
	Brett RUMFORD	AUS	69	70	69	67	275	-5	19,653.33	13,373.16
	David HIGGINS	IRL	68	67	68	72	275	-5	19,653.33	13,373.16
	Chris RILEY	USA	66	69	71	69	275	-5	19,653.33	13,373.16
23	Alejandro CAÑIZARES	ESP	69	67	69	71	276	-4	16,880.00	11,486.04
	David CARTER	ENG	65	65	71	75	276	-4	16,880.00	11,486.04
	Henrik NYSTRÖM	SWE	66	67	72	71	276	-4	16,880.00	11,486.04
	Peter GUSTAFSSON	SWE	70	70	69	67	276	-4	16,880.00	11,486.04
27	Sam WALKER	ENG	69	64	75	69	277	-3	13,568.00	9,232.38
	Simon DYSON	ENG	67	73	66	71	277	-3	13,568.00	9,232.38
	Lee SLATTERY	ENG	66	73	70	68	277	-3	13,568.00	9,232.38
	Mark PILKINGTON	WAL	71	68	68	70	277	-3	13,568.00	9,232.38
	Simon WAKEFIELD	ENG	68	68	73	68	277	-3	13,568.00	9,232.38
	Andrew MCLARDY	RSA	70	70	69	68	277	-3	13,568.00	9,232.38
	David BRANSDON	AUS	68	69	70	70	277	-3	13,568.00	9,232.38
	Gary MURPHY	IRL	67	71	70	69	277	-3	13,568.00	9,232.38
	James HEPWORTH	ENG	70	69	66	72	277	-3	13,568.00	9,232.38
	Paul LAWRIE	SCO	66	69	69	73	277	-3	13,568.00	9,232.38
37	Marc CAYEUX	ZIM	69	70	69	70	278	-2	10,080.00	6,858.96
	Johan AXGREN	SWE	67	71	69	71	278	-2	10,080.00	6,858.96
	Maarten LAFEBER	NED	67	69	71	71	278	-2	10,080.00	6,858.96
	Steve WEBSTER	ENG	65	71	72	70	278	-2	10,080.00	6,858.96
	Marcus HIGLEY	ENG	72	67	72	67	278	-2	10,080.00	6,858.96
	Taichi TESHIMA	JPN	64	72	71	71	278	-2	10,080.00	6,858.96
	Andrew COLTART	SCO	65	73	71	69	278	-2	10,080.00	6,858.96
	Nick DOUGHERTY	ENG	69	67	69	73	278	-2	10,080.00	6,858.96
	Shiv KAPUR	IND	68	71	68	71	278	-2	10,080.00	6,858.96
46	Kenneth FERRIE	ENG	66	74	68	71	279	-1	8,480.00	5,770.24
47	Nicolas COLSAERTS	BEL	67	73	68	72	280	0	7,520.00	5,117.00
	Emanuele CANONICA	ITA	67	70	71	72	280	0	7,520.00	5,117.00
	Luis CLAVERIE	ESP	67	70	73	70	280	0	7,520.00	5,117.00
	Sven STRÜVER	GER	66	72	68	74	280	0	7,520.00	5,117.00
	Mads VIBE-HASTRUP	DEN	69	70	70	71	280	0	7,520.00	5,117.00
52	Fredrik ANDERSSON HED	SWE	69	68	76	68	281	1	5,760.00	3,919.41
	Steven O'HARA	SCO	68	69	69	75	281	1	5,760.00	3,919.41
	James HEATH	ENG	70	69	71	71	281	1	5,760.00	3,919.41
	Christian CÉVAÉR	FRA	71	66	75	69	281	1	5,760.00	3,919.41
	James KINGSTON	RSA	70	67	71	73	281	1	5,760.00	3,919.41
	Joakim BÄCKSTRÖM	SWE	69	68	73	71	281	1	5,760.00	3,919.41
58	Martin MARITZ	RSA	70	70	71	71	282	2	4,480.00	3,048.43
	Robert ROCK	ENG	69	69	72	72	282	2	4,480.00	3,048.43
	Rafael ECHENIQUE	ARG	69	68	71	74	282	2	4,480.00	3,048.43
	David GRIFFITHS	ENG	71	64	72	75	282	2	4,480.00	3,048.43
	Thongchai JAIDEE	THA	71	68	70	73	282	2	4,480.00	3,048.43
63	Andrew MARSHALL	ENG	66	73	71	73	283	3	3,920.00	2,667.37
	Marcel SIEM	GER	68	72	73	70	283	3	3,920.00	2,667.37
65	Ian GARBUTT	ENG	73	67	70	75	285	5	3,440.00	2,340.76
	David DRYSDALE	SCO	70	68	75	72	285	5	3,440.00	2,340.76
	Anton HAIG	RSA	69	69	73	73	285	5	3,440.00	2,340.76
	Matthew MILLAR	AUS	68	71	72	74	285	5	3,440.00	2,340.76
69	Shaun P WEBSTER	ENG	71	66	74	76	287	7	3,040.00	2,068.58
70	Anthony WALL	ENG	69	69	71	80	289	9	2,575.67	1,752.62
	Wade ORMSBY	AUS	69	70	75	75	289	9	2,575.67	1,752.62
	David PARK	WAL	70	69	77	73	289	9	2,575.67	1,752.62

Joost Luiten (left) and Stephen Gallacher

Ross Fisher (right) is presented with the trophy by Peter F. Hartman, KLM President & CEO

Kennemer Golf and Country Club played host to The KLM Open in 1989 and staged the longest play-off in European Tour history. Roger Chapman, José Maria Olazábal and Ronan Rafferty finished the regulation 72 holes on 277(-3). The first extra hole saw Chapman depart after a bogey five. The remaining two players proceeded to go another eight holes, before Olazábal triumphed on the ninth hole.

Total Prize Fund

€1,604,797 £1,091,988

The Course

Founded in 1910, one of the most celebrated links courses in The Netherlands ensures every part of a golfer's game is tested, from low and high shots to lob shots zand bump and runs depending on the lie or the weather. It is quite tight in places so driving has to be accurate while the small greens mean you have to ensure your approach shots are in the right place to give a realistic attempt at a birdie.

Devil in Focus

1	Marc WARREN		280	-12
2	Simon WAKEFIELD		280	-12
3	Martin ERLANDSSON		281	-11
	Søren HANSEN		281	-11
5	Fredrik ANDERSSON HED		282	-10
	Graeme STORM		282	-10
7	Ricardo GONZALEZ		283	-9
	Steven O'HARA		283	-9
9	Thomas LEVET		284	-8
	Oliver FISHER		284	-8
	Francesco MOLINARI		284	-8
	Colin MONTGOMERIE		284	-8
	Lee WESTWOOD		284	-8

It began with a tiff between friends but ended with a nation celebrating. When Marc Warren arrived on the practice range on Tuesday before the Johnnie Walker Championship at Gleneagles he was not smiling. A heavy cold, allied to nine missed cuts in 13 outings, had left The 2006 Sir Henry Cotton Rookie of the Year frustrated to the point of questioning his coach Bob Torrance's advice as well as his own capacity to successfully adopt a couple of swing changes.

Five days later, however, the smile was back on the face of the 26 year old Scot as he held the championship trophy high above his head after overcoming England's Simon Wakefield at the second extra hole of a sudden-death play-off.

This was a week when the international resort nestling in the rolling Perthshire hills looked, and sounded, at its best. On the eve of the tournament, Scotland's world renowned violinist Nicola Benedetti played to invited guests at the sumptuous Gala Dinner while, thankfully, when play got underway, the rain that has dogged this British summer was confined to only a few spots on Friday which delighted both organisers and the near 40,000 spectators who watched the action unfold.

After Scotland's big month of golf in July, the fans were still keen to watch The European Tour's finest, and keener still to witness a home victory.

Up to that point only six Scots had won an official European Tour event in their homeland; Brian Barnes, Ken Brown, Stephen Gallacher, Paul Lawrie, Sandy Lyle and Colin Montgomerie. A seventh was eagerly anticipated, especially over the PGA Centenary Course, which, in 2014, will stage The Ryder Cup when the biennial contest is played in Scotland for only the second time.

The Jack Nicklaus-designed 18 holes is a continually developing layout under the direction of architect, Perthshire's own David McLay-Kidd, and will have a further four years to mature after a number of alterations are completed in time for The 2010 Junior Ryder Cup.

This week, however, most of the talk amongst fans was about whether Paul Casey would retain the title or whether anyone, including four men who had played alongside the Englishman in The Ryder Cup - Darren Clarke, Thomas Levet, Lee Westwood or Montgomerie - could wrench it away from him.

Simon Wakefield

Martin Erlandsson

Fredrik Andersson Hed

David Lynn

As it turned out, Levet, Montgomerie and Westwood came close, all finishing in a share of ninth place on Sunday, while Championship Chairman Montgomerie's 69 on Thursday matched his opening round in his debut in The Scottish Open at Gleneagles in 1988, the season, of course, which launched The European Tour Yearbook.

However, after an eight under par first round of 65, Warren always was going to be the man to beat. The player who holed the winning putt in the 2001 Walker Cup at Sea Island, Georgia, still finds it difficult to focus when he is not in contention but when he is, he becomes the very devil to beat.

Robert Karlsson, Denny Lucas and Peter Whiteford will testify to that for they all lost to him in play-offs; Karlsson in the 2006 Scandinavian Masters on The European Tour with Lucas and Whiteford, respectively, succumbing in the Rolex Trophy and the Ireland Ryder Cup Challenge on the European Challenge Tour in 2005.

By the end of a windy second day, a 68 from Levet, thankfully recovered from an inner ear infection that blighted his 2006 season, and a 69 from Wakefield were sufficient to earn them a share of the lead on nine under par 137. But Warren trailed by only one shot, despite irritating sniffles as his cold of earlier in the week finally petered out.

However, worse was to follow early the next day when he surrendered four shots to par after only five holes. If that had happened a couple of years earlier he would have disappeared from view, but he has learned resilience to add to his undoubted ability and he covered the last 11 holes in four under par. This, he concluded later, was the key to his ultimate triumph.

With Sweden's Fredrik Andersson Hed and Wakefield the overnight leaders, Warren again started the fourth round poorly, but playing alongside the 2000 European Number One Westwood, he rallied once more, finally holing resolutely from eight feet at the 18th to force the play-off before holing from four feet at the second extra hole to win.

"Bob Torrance told me before I went out that I was the kind of player he wants to work with," said Warren, who had patched up his differences with his coach in a clear-the-air phone call on the eve of the tournament. "Hopefully, I've made him proud tonight."

He did, just as another Torrance devotee, Padraig Harrington, did six weeks earlier at Carnoustie.

Jock MacVicar
Daily Express

KEEP WALKING™

JOHNNIE WALKER®

Barry Lane

Marc Warren (left) is presented with the trophy by Andrew Morgan, President Diageo

i Thomas Levet matched a European Tour record at the Johnnie Walker Championship at Gleneagles by beginning his tournament with a hole-in-one. Starting from the tenth hole, the Frenchman aced his tee shot with a five iron. Coincidentally, the only other previous occasion this has happened in European Tour history was by Paul Lawrie in this event in 2000.

The Gleneagles Hotel (PGA Centenary Course)
Par 73   Yards 7320   Metres 6695

Final Results

Pos	Name		Rd1	Rd2	Rd3	Rd4	Total		€	£
1	Marc WARREN	SCO	65	73	73	69	280	-12	343,692.77	233,330.00
2	Simon WAKEFIELD	ENG	68	69	73	70	280	-12	229,123.60	155,550.00
3	Martin ERLANDSSON	SWE	71	72	72	66	281	-11	116,101.07	78,820.00
	Søren HANSEN	DEN	69	72	72	68	281	-11	116,101.07	78,820.00
5	Fredrik ANDERSSON HED	SWE	73	71	66	72	282	-10	79,806.60	54,180.00
	Graeme STORM	ENG	70	70	73	69	282	-10	79,806.60	54,180.00
7	Steven O'HARA	SCO	71	73	71	68	283	-9	56,710.11	38,500.00
	Ricardo GONZALEZ	ARG	70	71	75	67	283	-9	56,710.11	38,500.00
9	Francesco MOLINARI	ITA	76	70	72	66	284	-8	38,810.34	26,348.00
	Colin MONTGOMERIE	SCO	69	74	71	70	284	-8	38,810.34	26,348.00
	Thomas LEVET	FRA	69	68	76	71	284	-8	38,810.34	26,348.00
	Lee WESTWOOD	ENG	74	69	69	72	284	-8	38,810.34	26,348.00
	Oliver FISHER	ENG	73	72	72	67	284	-8	38,810.34	26,348.00
14	Barry LANE	ENG	70	71	75	69	285	-7	29,695.48	20,160.00
	James KINGSTON	RSA	70	73	71	71	285	-7	29,695.48	20,160.00
	Alan MCLEAN	SCO	72	71	74	68	285	-7	29,695.48	20,160.00
	David LYNN	ENG	72	68	74	71	285	-7	29,695.48	20,160.00
18	Jesus Maria ARRUTI	ESP	74	72	72	68	286	-6	25,639.85	17,406.67
	Alastair FORSYTH	SCO	69	71	72	74	286	-6	25,639.85	17,406.67
	Wade ORMSBY	AUS	71	69	75	71	286	-6	25,639.85	17,406.67
21	Nicolas COLSAERTS	BEL	66	75	74	72	287	-5	22,684.05	15,400.00
	Santiago LUNA	ESP	73	69	75	70	287	-5	22,684.05	15,400.00
	Mark FOSTER	ENG	74	72	72	69	287	-5	22,684.05	15,400.00
	Marcus HIGLEY	ENG	69	74	72	72	287	-5	22,684.05	15,400.00
	Robert DINWIDDIE	ENG	72	71	72	72	287	-5	22,684.05	15,400.00
26	Phillip ARCHER	ENG	68	71	73	76	288	-4	18,972.11	12,880.00
	Carlos RODILES	ESP	73	71	73	71	288	-4	18,972.11	12,880.00
	Anthony WALL	ENG	73	71	72	72	288	-4	18,972.11	12,880.00
	Sion E BEBB	WAL	71	72	74	71	288	-4	18,972.11	12,880.00
	Shiv KAPUR	IND	68	74	76	70	288	-4	18,972.11	12,880.00
	Joost LUITEN	NED	68	75	77	68	288	-4	18,972.11	12,880.00
	Ariel CANETE	ARG	73	72	68	75	288	-4	18,972.11	12,880.00
33	Alexandre ROCHA	BRA	71	75	73	70	289	-3	15,507.64	10,528.00
	Brett RUMFORD	AUS	72	73	75	69	289	-3	15,507.64	10,528.00
	Stephen GALLACHER	SCO	71	72	70	76	289	-3	15,507.64	10,528.00
	Luis CLAVERIE	ESP	70	73	73	73	289	-3	15,507.64	10,528.00
	Søren KJELDSEN	DEN	71	72	75	71	289	-3	15,507.64	10,528.00
38	José Manuel CARRILES	ESP	74	70	75	71	290	-2	13,404.21	9,100.00
	Garry HOUSTON	WAL	73	72	72	73	290	-2	13,404.21	9,100.00
	Paul LAWRIE	SCO	69	77	73	71	290	-2	13,404.21	9,100.00
	Miles TUNNICLIFF	ENG	67	74	74	75	290	-2	13,404.21	9,100.00
	Patrik SJÖLAND	SWE	75	71	74	70	290	-2	13,404.21	9,100.00
43	Dean ROBERTSON	SCO	69	75	75	72	291	-1	10,929.59	7,420.00
	Mads VIBE-HASTRUP	DEN	71	74	74	72	291	-1	10,929.59	7,420.00
	Mark PILKINGTON	WAL	68	76	73	74	291	-1	10,929.59	7,420.00
	Mark LOFTUS	SCO	70	74	71	76	291	-1	10,929.59	7,420.00
	Ignacio GARRIDO	ESP	71	74	72	74	291	-1	10,929.59	7,420.00
	Phillip PRICE	WAL	68	76	75	72	291	-1	10,929.59	7,420.00
	Jean-François REMESY	FRA	72	74	72	73	291	-1	10,929.59	7,420.00
50	Darren FICHARDT	RSA	73	71	75	73	292	0	8,867.40	6,020.00
	David GRIFFITHS	ENG	71	73	75	73	292	0	8,867.40	6,020.00
	Zane SCOTLAND	ENG	68	73	75	76	292	0	8,867.40	6,020.00
53	Peter LAWRIE	IRL	72	74	77	70	293	1	7,630.09	5,180.00
	Jeev Milkha SINGH	IND	67	74	74	78	293	1	7,630.09	5,180.00
	Ian GARBUTT	ENG	70	74	76	73	293	1	7,630.09	5,180.00
56	Stephen DODD	WAL	72	74	74	74	294	2	6,341.22	4,305.00
	Darren CLARKE	NIR	73	71	76	74	294	2	6,341.22	4,305.00
	Richard FINCH	ENG	71	72	79	72	294	2	6,341.22	4,305.00
	Grégory BOURDY	FRA	69	75	74	76	294	2	6,341.22	4,305.00
60	Paul CASEY	ENG	71	71	73	80	295	3	5,567.90	3,780.00
	Greig HUTCHEON	SCO	69	75	76	75	295	3	5,567.90	3,780.00
	Matthew MILLAR	AUS	77	67	76	75	295	3	5,567.90	3,780.00
63	Emanuele CANONICA	ITA	71	74	77	74	296	4	5,155.47	3,500.00
64	Peter O'MALLEY	AUS	73	71	81	74	299	7	4,743.03	3,220.00
	Richard BLAND	ENG	69	75	78	77	299	7	4,743.03	3,220.00
	Chinarat PHADUNGSIL	THA	73	73	77	76	299	7	4,743.03	3,220.00
67	James HEPWORTH	ENG	68	75	82	75	300	8	4,330.59	2,940.00
68	Terry PILKADARIS	AUS	69	76	81	78	304	12	4,124.37	2,800.00
69	Terry PRICE	AUS	71	75	80	80	306	14	3,918.15	2,660.00

Total Prize Fund
€2,058,415   £1,397,440

The Course

The venue for The 2014 Ryder Cup is widely acclaimed as a modern golfing classic. Designed by Jack Nicklaus, the 18 time Major winner described the course as: "The finest parcel of land in the world I have ever been given to work with." Fittingly, the opening hole begins by playing towards Glendevon while the remaining holes over lush fairways give stunning views of the distant mountains of the Grampian and Trossach ranges.

Mountain High

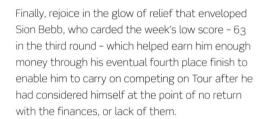

1	Brett RUMFORD		268	-16
2	Phillip ARCHER		268	-16
3	Bradley DREDGE		269	-15
4	Sion E BEBB		270	-14
5	Oliver WILSON		272	-12
6	Gonzalo FERNANDEZ-CASTAÑO		273	-11
	Lee WESTWOOD		273	-11
8	Eduardo ROMERO		274	-10
	Miles TUNNICLIFF		274	-10
	Anthony WALL		274	-10

M any moments during the Omega European Masters at Crans-sur-Sierre were as spectacular as the Alpine setting where the late afternoon sun, which turned the snow-capped peaks a delightful shade of pink, formed a backdrop to the memorable events on the course.

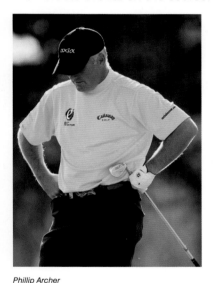

Phillip Archer

Gonzalo Fernandez-Castaño

Top of the list was unquestionably Brett Rumford's chip in on the first extra hole of the play-off with Phillip Archer; a sublime shot by the Australian and a fitting climax to so many of the delights that had gone before.

Included in that was Alessandro Tadini's second round hole in one, a six iron to the 192 yard third hole that won him a gold ingot worth £12,000.

Imagine, too, the joy of 16 year old American Tadd Fujikawa at his final shot on his European Tour debut. Despite knowing he was missing the cut, he nevertheless holed his second shot on the monster ninth hole in the second round – he had started at the tenth - with a three wood that went 285 yards straight into the cup and won him a watch from sponsors Omega.

Finally, rejoice in the glow of relief that enveloped Sion Bebb, who carded the week's low score – 63 in the third round – which helped earn him enough money through his eventual fourth place finish to enable him to carry on competing on Tour after he had considered himself at the point of no return with the finances, or lack of them.

Every day seemed to throw up something new, not least a two hour delay to the start of the opening round because of frost. The days leading to the tournament had been bitterly cold but once the sun burned away the clouds, glorious weather embraced the tournament.

No one enjoyed the first round more than England's Oliver Wilson, although he had to return the following morning, along with 43 other players, to complete his opening 18 holes. When play was suspended as darkness fell he was left with a ten foot eagle putt on the 15th green.

To putt, or not to putt, that was the question? He deliberated for a few seconds and decided to mark his ball. He holed it on his return on Friday morning and proceeded to birdie the 17th to post a six under par 65, one better than defending champion, Bradley Dredge.

Wilson was loving gathering the experience of being at the top of the leader board, fully aware that he was not only vying for a place in Great Britain and Ireland's Seve Trophy team in three weeks time but also trying for some early Ryder Cup points in this, the first qualifying event for the 2008 contest against the United States.

Subsequent rounds of 66 and 70 saw him enter the final round in third place, one behind joint leaders Dredge and Rumford, who had to take painkillers on the 16th tee to combat a troublesome neck injury.

It appeared to be yet another problem for Rumford who was having, by his own admission, a disappointing year. The affable Australian might not have won since 2004 but he had been a consistent performer on The European Tour International Schedule as finishes of 61st and 51st respectively on the Order of Merit in 2005 and 2006 attested.

Going into the week in Crans Montana, the 30 year old from Perth was 106th on the Order of Merit and without a top ten finish since the Blue Chip New Zealand Open in Auckland at the beginning of December 2006. Little wonder his normally cheery demeanour had been replaced by genuine concern.

Rumford was used to flying high on Tour, none more so than when he won 50,000 miles in a private jet for topping the Red Bull Final Five competition during the week of the 2004 Nissan Irish Open at County Louth Golf Club – also his last Tour victory. Now, without some drastic change in fortune, he was in danger of being grounded.

Conscientiously, he worked hard with his coach and on the range and it came to fruition in dramatic fashion as his 30 foot pitch from the back left of the green at the first play-off hole dropped into the cup to pip a gallant Phillip Archer, whose 65 matched the best round of the final day and tied had Rumford on 16 under par 268.

Archer's consolation, along with third placed Dredge and fifth placed Wilson, was the fact they all would book a berth in the Seve Trophy while, with all the pressure of a poor season now firmly behind him, it was little wonder that Rumford allowed the tears to flow in a moment of quiet reflection before he stepped up to receive the impressive trophy and the famous red jacket.

James Mossop
The Sunday Telegraph

Bradley Dredge

Eduardo Romero

The Course

Greg Norman once said about Crans-sur-Sierre: "This is by far the most spectacular tournament site in the world," and, anyone who visits the breathtaking Alpine location immediately empathises with his view. Being so high up in the mountains, the greater distances travelled by the ball have to be factored into calculations while the undulating greens, redesigned by Seve Ballesteros in 1999, demand respect.

Ian Garbutt

Brett Rumford (right) is presented with the trophy from the President of Omega, Stephen Urquhart

Garry Houston

> This has proved very emotional and I had to have five minutes in a back room when it all hit me. I've been trying hard, grinding week in week out for not much but at last it's all come together this week.
> **Brett Rumford**

Crans-sur-Sierre

Par **71**   Yards **6857**   Metres **6239**

Final Results

Pos	Name		Rd1	Rd2	Rd3	Rd4	Total		€	£
1	Brett RUMFORD	AUS	68	66	66	68	268	-16	333,330.00	225,488.07
2	Phillip ARCHER	ENG	69	66	68	65	268	-16	222,220.00	150,325.38
3	Bradley DREDGE	WAL	66	66	68	69	269	-15	125,200.00	84,694.17
4	Sion E BEBB	WAL	71	68	63	68	270	-14	100,000.00	67,647.10
5	Oliver WILSON	ENG	65	66	70	71	272	-12	84,800.00	57,364.74
6	Lee WESTWOOD	ENG	71	67	65	70	273	-11	65,000.00	43,970.61
	Gonzalo FDEZ-CASTAÑO	ESP	70	67	65	71	273	-11	65,000.00	43,970.61
8	Anthony WALL	ENG	69	68	68	69	274	-10	44,933.33	30,396.10
	Miles TUNNICLIFF	ENG	71	65	70	68	274	-10	44,933.33	30,396.10
	Eduardo ROMERO	ARG	68	69	72	65	274	-10	44,933.33	30,396.10
11	Graeme MCDOWELL	NIR	73	69	67	66	275	-9	36,800.00	24,894.13
12	Robert KARLSSON	SWE	69	69	69	69	276	-8	34,400.00	23,270.60
13	Juan PARRON	ESP	72	71	68	66	277	-7	31,400.00	21,241.19
	Richard MCEVOY	ENG	71	70	71	65	277	-7	31,400.00	21,241.19
15	Richard BLAND	ENG	73	68	67	70	278	-6	28,200.00	19,076.48
	Joakim BÄCKSTRÖM	SWE	71	68	69	70	278	-6	28,200.00	19,076.48
	David FROST	RSA	72	70	68	68	278	-6	28,200.00	19,076.48
18	Steven O'HARA	SCO	74	70	70	65	279	-5	25,300.00	17,114.72
	Mikko ILONEN	FIN	68	75	70	66	279	-5	25,300.00	17,114.72
20	Tino SCHUSTER	GER	71	65	74	70	280	-4	22,640.00	15,315.30
	Graeme STORM	ENG	69	69	71	71	280	-4	22,640.00	15,315.30
	Rafael ECHENIQUE	ARG	69	70	71	70	280	-4	22,640.00	15,315.30
	Johan EDFORS	SWE	73	70	69	68	280	-4	22,640.00	15,315.30
	Manuel QUIROS	ESP	74	70	70	66	280	-4	22,640.00	15,315.30
25	Alessandro TADINI	ITA	72	69	68	72	281	-3	19,300.00	13,055.89
	Ariel CANETE	ARG	72	69	68	72	281	-3	19,300.00	13,055.89
	Daniel VANCSIK	ARG	71	70	72	68	281	-3	19,300.00	13,055.89
	Andrew MARSHALL	ENG	74	68	72	67	281	-3	19,300.00	13,055.89
	Marcel SIEM	GER	71	70	70	70	281	-3	19,300.00	13,055.89
	Jean-François REMESY	FRA	77	67	70	67	281	-3	19,300.00	13,055.89
31	David CARTER	ENG	73	69	70	70	282	-2	15,800.00	10,688.24
	Edward RUSH	ENG	72	72	64	74	282	-2	15,800.00	10,688.24
	Jeev Milkha SINGH	IND	74	68	72	68	282	-2	15,800.00	10,688.24
	Henrik NYSTRÖM	SWE	74	69	68	71	282	-2	15,800.00	10,688.24
	Mattias ELIASSON	SWE	72	69	67	74	282	-2	15,800.00	10,688.24
	Pelle EDBERG	SWE	71	73	69	69	282	-2	15,800.00	10,688.24
37	Carl SUNESON	ESP	74	70	69	70	283	-1	12,200.00	8,252.95
	Simon WAKEFIELD	ENG	74	69	73	67	283	-1	12,200.00	8,252.95
	Paul CASEY	ENG	71	68	72	72	283	-1	12,200.00	8,252.95
	Tom WHITEHOUSE	ENG	73	71	68	71	283	-1	12,200.00	8,252.95
	Richard FINCH	ENG	70	72	64	77	283	-1	12,200.00	8,252.95
	Zane SCOTLAND	ENG	69	69	71	74	283	-1	12,200.00	8,252.95
	Barry LANE	ENG	78	65	70	70	283	-1	12,200.00	8,252.95
	Alexandre ROCHA	BRA	71	70	73	69	283	-1	12,200.00	8,252.95
	Peter O'MALLEY	AUS	73	70	68	72	283	-1	12,200.00	8,252.95
	Kyron SULLIVAN	WAL	72	69	69	72	283	-1	12,200.00	8,252.95
	Garry HOUSTON	WAL	72	70	73	68	283	-1	12,200.00	8,252.95
48	Søren KJELDSEN	DEN	76	68	69	71	284	0	9,200.00	6,223.53
	Pablo MARTIN	ESP	71	73	71	69	284	0	9,200.00	6,223.53
	Julien CLÉMENT	SUI	74	70	72	68	284	0	9,200.00	6,223.53
	Carlos RODILES	ESP	69	75	66	74	284	0	9,200.00	6,223.53
52	Oscar FLOREN	SWE	69	67	76	73	285	1	8,000.00	5,411.77
	Marcus FRASER	AUS	68	71	74	72	285	1	8,000.00	5,411.77
	Pierre RELECOM (AM)	BEL	70	74	71	70	285	1		
55	Jamie SPENCE	ENG	70	71	72	73	286	2	7,400.00	5,005.89
56	Ian GARBUTT	ENG	70	72	72	73	287	3	6,600.00	4,464.71
	Jonathan LOMAS	ENG	74	70	74	69	287	3	6,600.00	4,464.71
	Ricardo GONZALEZ	ARG	75	69	69	74	287	3	6,600.00	4,464.71
59	Lee SLATTERY	ENG	72	72	75	69	288	4	5,800.00	3,923.53
	Sven STRÜVER	GER	74	68	73	73	288	4	5,800.00	3,923.53
	Steve ALKER	NZL	75	66	74	73	288	4	5,800.00	3,923.53
62	Francesco MOLINARI	ITA	74	70	70	75	289	5	5,100.00	3,450.00
	Andrew COLTART	SCO	70	72	72	75	289	5	5,100.00	3,450.00
	Patrik SJÖLAND	SWE	70	72	72	75	289	5	5,100.00	3,450.00
	Terry PRICE	AUS	75	68	74	72	289	5	5,100.00	3,450.00
66	Alexander NOREN	SWE	72	71	76	71	290	6	4,400.00	2,976.47
	Ignacio GARRIDO	ESP	74	69	71	76	290	6	4,400.00	2,976.47
	Shiv KAPUR	IND	72	72	76	70	290	6	4,400.00	2,976.47
69	Sam LITTLE	ENG	78	66	73	74	291	7	4,000.00	2,705.88
70	José Manuel LARA	ESP	71	71	75	75	292	8	3,800.00	2,570.59
71	Eirik Tage JOHANSEN	NOR	75	69	68	81	293	9	3,650.00	2,469.12
72	Alessandro NAPOLEONI	ITA	71	69	78	77	295	11	3,000.00	2,029.41

Total Prize Fund

€2,003,000   £1,354,971

Winners Only

1	Søren HANSEN		271	-17
2	Phillip ARCHER		275	-13
	Alastair FORSYTH		275	-13
4	Thomas BJÖRN		276	-12
	Bradley DREDGE		276	-12
6	Simon KHAN		277	-11
	Søren KJELDSEN		277	-11
	Lee WESTWOOD		277	-11
9	Paul LAWRIE		278	-10
	Richard STERNE		278	-10

I n and around Cologne, via the medium of numerous posters adorning giant billboards and images of players on sleek, expensive Mercedes-Benz cars, it was billed as a tournament for 'Winners Only.'

The cream of European Tour talent was in town – and the marquee names amongst the elite field of 78 teeing up at Golf Club Gut Lärchenhof for the Mercedes-Benz Championship proved that its marketing push was no idle boast.

Almost 20 years after he won the first of his four German Masters titles – the title which preceded the Mercedes-Benz Championship on The European Tour International Schedule – tournament host Bernhard Langer and his brother Erwin had attracted a list of competitors befitting the stature of such a tournament.

'Winners Only' is a statement of fact, illustrating that those playing have the necessary ability, skill, strength and character to succeed in their chosen sport. Those who assembled at Gut Lärchenhof exhibited all such qualities in abundance, making the question of who would emerge victorious after four days, a difficult one to predict.

Bernhard Langer, as the winner of 67 events worldwide, is a man who knows a champion when he sees one – and even though Lee Westwood had carded a brilliant 11 under par 61 to hold a four shot lead on the first day, it was another who had caught the eye of the two time Masters Tournament winner.

After playing with Søren Hansen for the first two days, during which the Dane carded 65 and 68

to overtake Westwood at the top, Langer was sufficiently moved to comment on the quiet and unassuming 33 year old's talent.

"I was extremely impressed with his game," said Langer. "The guy hits a lot of fantastic shots and his short game is immaculate, so I wouldn't be surprised if he is at the top of the leader board at the end of the week."

Initially, they were words Hansen took to heart gladly. "To hear comments like that, and to play with players like Bernhard, who has achieved so much in the game, is a massive pat on the back," he said. "It's so good for my morale and confidence."

Yet they were also words which proved prophetic, as Hansen took on and dealt with the challenge of all-comers, including England's Phillip Archer and Alastair Forsyth of Scotland who eventually shared second place, fellow Dane Thomas Björn who shared fourth with Bradley Dredge of Wales, Langer and Westwood.

Not that Hansen had it all his own way, for there was a scare of sorts. Leading by three shots over the final three holes on Saturday, a run of three consecutive bogeys to finish afforded the field a view of a rare chink in his armour, as Hansen slipped back to be tied for the lead with Björn on 12 under par.

Alastair Forsyth

Graeme McDowell

Left *Bernhard Langer pitches to the centre circle during half time in the RheinEnergie Stadion in Cologne where Germany played Romania in a friendly football international*

Thomas Björn

Paul Lawrie

But, going into the final round, it was quickly obvious that, in Hansen, here was one Viking raider who was not to be denied a pillaging foray into the country with which his own nation shares a border.

A closing 67, helped by two fantastic eagles on the back nine – a chip in on the 13th and a six foot putt on the 15th after a towering three-wood approach flew 239 yards and skipped the greenside bunker – moved him well clear of the chasing pack. A solitary bogey on the 17th was his only blemish, as a steady par at the last secured a 17 under par total of 271 and a four shot triumph.

"In the past I have looked a little bit too much over my shoulder at what the others were doing, but today I just stuck with what I had and I hit some really good shots to stay on top all the time," he said.

It was Hansen's first win since he claimed The 2002 Irish Open at Fota Island. "I wouldn't say it has been a monkey on my back but I have been close," he admitted. "I have had a lot of second places, but I have kept hanging in there."

However, with increased experience – 2007 being his ninth successive season on The European Tour – as well as the hard work he has been putting into improving his golf, Hansen has now found his status among the elite of The European Tour.

"I beat 77 other players in this tournament, all the best players of the year, and I feel really, really proud of that. It is the best golf I have ever played – and I'm going to enjoy this one for a very long time."

Among 'Winners Only', Hansen, deservedly, became the only winner.

Graeme Hamlett

Since Golf came along, gentlemen no longer duel with pistols.

www.mercedes-benz-championship.de

Mercedes-Benz

Simon Khan

'' I had a really good feeling coming into the event. I've been knocking on the door this summer and I just felt this might be the week for me. ''
Søren Hansen

Søren Hansen (left) is presented with the trophy by Doctor Olaf Göttgens, Vice President of Brand Communications Mercedes-Benz Passenger Cars

The Course

The only golf course in Germany designed by Jack Nicklaus is a stern test if you stray too often into the punitive rough but also provides an opportunity to score well if you keep the ball on the short grass. Part of the reason for that is the exquisite putting surfaces which were widely praised and described by Lee Westwood as: "Immaculate and as good as I've putted on for a long, long time."

Golf Club Gut Lärchenhof
Par 72 **Yards 7289** **Metres 6662**

Final Results

Pos	Name		Rd1	Rd2	Rd3	Rd4	Total		€	£
1	Søren HANSEN	DEN	65	68	71	67	271	-17	320,000.00	217,277.65
2	Phillip ARCHER	ENG	71	70	66	68	275	-13	171,250.00	116,277.49
	Alastair FORSYTH	SCO	76	67	62	70	275	-13	171,250.00	116,277.49
4	Thomas BJÖRN	DEN	71	67	66	72	276	-12	91,025.00	61,805.31
	Bradley DREDGE	WAL	68	71	70	67	276	-12	91,025.00	61,805.31
6	Søren KJELDSEN	DEN	73	67	72	65	277	-11	59,333.33	40,286.90
	Simon KHAN	ENG	67	70	69	71	277	-11	59,333.33	40,286.90
	Lee WESTWOOD	ENG	61	73	72	71	277	-11	59,333.33	40,286.90
9	Paul LAWRIE	SCO	68	70	71	69	278	-10	42,000.00	28,517.69
	Richard STERNE	RSA	67	73	68	70	278	-10	42,000.00	28,517.69
11	Graeme MCDOWELL	NIR	69	72	69	69	279	-9	35,600.00	24,172.14
	Niclas FASTH	SWE	67	71	69	72	279	-9	35,600.00	24,172.14
13	Robert KARLSSON	SWE	70	71	70	69	280	-8	30,733.33	20,867.71
	Johan EDFORS	SWE	70	71	72	67	280	-8	30,733.33	20,867.71
	Mikko ILONEN	FIN	68	70	72	70	280	-8	30,733.33	20,867.71
16	John BICKERTON	ENG	71	69	71	70	281	-7	25,960.00	17,626.65
	Per-Ulrik JOHANSSON	SWE	74	69	69	69	281	-7	25,960.00	17,626.65
	Fredrik ANDERSSON HED	SWE	69	70	73	69	281	-7	25,960.00	17,626.65
	Gonzalo FDEZ-CASTAÑO	ESP	67	73	72	69	281	-7	25,960.00	17,626.65
	Jeev Milkha SINGH	IND	72	70	72	67	281	-7	25,960.00	17,626.65
21	Andrew MCLARDY	RSA	70	69	70	73	282	-6	21,700.00	14,734.14
	Y E YANG	KOR	70	73	72	67	282	-6	21,700.00	14,734.14
	Retief GOOSEN	RSA	72	71	69	70	282	-6	21,700.00	14,734.14
	Miguel Angel JIMÉNEZ	ESP	68	70	72	72	282	-6	21,700.00	14,734.14
	Richard GREEN	AUS	73	67	66	76	282	-6	21,700.00	14,734.14
	Thongchai JAIDEE	THA	71	72	71	68	282	-6	21,700.00	14,734.14
27	John DALY	USA	67	71	76	69	283	-5	18,400.00	12,493.46
	Ian POULTER	ENG	72	70	71	70	283	-5	18,400.00	12,493.46
	Bernhard LANGER	GER	69	68	70	76	283	-5	18,400.00	12,493.46
	Peter HANSON	SWE	69	74	70	70	283	-5	18,400.00	12,493.46
	Alex CEJKA	GER	70	73	68	72	283	-5	18,400.00	12,493.46
32	Martin KAYMER	GER	70	72	71	71	284	-4	15,520.00	10,537.97
	Nick DOUGHERTY	ENG	66	75	69	74	284	-4	15,520.00	10,537.97
	Ross FISHER	ENG	74	70	68	72	284	-4	15,520.00	10,537.97
	Markus BRIER	AUT	74	69	72	69	284	-4	15,520.00	10,537.97
	Alejandro CAÑIZARES	ESP	70	69	73	72	284	-4	15,520.00	10,537.97
37	Simon DYSON	ENG	66	71	73	75	285	-3	13,600.00	9,234.30
	Marcel SIEM	GER	71	73	70	71	285	-3	13,600.00	9,234.30
	Pelle EDBERG	SWE	70	72	70	73	285	-3	13,600.00	9,234.30
	Carl SUNESON	ESP	69	72	70	74	285	-3	13,600.00	9,234.30
41	Marc WARREN	SCO	71	69	70	76	286	-2	11,800.00	8,012.11
	Pablo MARTIN	ESP	70	69	72	75	286	-2	11,800.00	8,012.11
	Emanuele CANONICA	ITA	72	68	75	71	286	-2	11,800.00	8,012.11
	Andres ROMERO	ARG	68	71	76	71	286	-2	11,800.00	8,012.11
	Simon WAKEFIELD	ENG	70	70	74	72	286	-2	11,800.00	8,012.11
46	Mark FOSTER	ENG	76	70	71	70	287	-1	9,800.00	6,654.13
	Anders HANSEN	DEN	72	72	70	73	287	-1	9,800.00	6,654.13
	Paul MCGINLEY	IRL	70	79	67	71	287	-1	9,800.00	6,654.13
	Colin MONTGOMERIE	SCO	69	69	73	76	287	-1	9,800.00	6,654.13
	Peter HEDBLOM	SWE	74	73	73	67	287	-1	9,800.00	6,654.13
51	Raphaël JACQUELIN	FRA	76	73	73	66	288	0	8,600.00	5,839.34
52	Sven STRÜVER	GER	71	72	76	70	289	1	8,000.00	5,431.94
	Francesco MOLINARI	ITA	73	67	75	74	289	1	8,000.00	5,431.94
54	Scott DRUMMOND	SCO	72	72	71	75	290	2	7,000.00	4,752.95
	Jean-François REMESY	FRA	73	70	75	72	290	2	7,000.00	4,752.95
	Stephen DODD	WAL	73	71	72	74	290	2	7,000.00	4,752.95
57	Ariel CANETE	ARG	71	70	76	74	291	3	5,900.00	4,006.06
	Peter O'MALLEY	AUS	70	76	72	73	291	3	5,900.00	4,006.06
	Robert-Jan DERKSEN	NED	68	74	73	76	291	3	5,900.00	4,006.06
	Jyoti RANDHAWA	IND	74	71	74	72	291	3	5,900.00	4,006.06
61	Ricardo GONZALEZ	ARG	77	67	73	75	292	4	5,300.00	3,598.66
	Oliver WILSON	ENG	70	76	72	74	292	4	5,300.00	3,598.66
63	Grégory HAVRET	FRA	73	79	71	70	293	5	4,900.00	3,327.06
	Angel CABRERA	ARG	74	73	73	73	293	5	4,900.00	3,327.06
65	Kenneth FERRIE	ENG	69	73	78	74	294	6	4,400.00	2,987.57
	Michael CAMPBELL	NZL	77	73	72	72	294	6	4,400.00	2,987.57
	Ignacio GARRIDO	ESP	77	71	71	75	294	6	4,400.00	2,987.57
68	Anton HAIG	RSA	70	76	77	72	295	7	3,737.50	2,537.74
	Daniel VANCSIK	ARG	73	75	72	75	295	7	3,737.50	2,537.74
	Graeme STORM	ENG	71	78	70	76	295	7	3,737.50	2,537.74
	Phillip PRICE	WAL	70	71	76	78	295	7	3,737.50	2,537.74
72	David HOWELL	ENG	73	71	73	79	296	8	3,275.00	2,223.70
	Mardan MAMAT	SIN	70	76	73	77	296	8	3,275.00	2,223.70
74	Louis OOSTHUIZEN	RSA	75	73	72	77	297	9	2,975.00	2,020.00
	Jean VAN DE VELDE	FRA	76	69	76	76	297	9	2,975.00	2,020.00
76	Darren CLARKE	NIR	69	75	77	77	298	10	2,750.00	1,867.23
77	José Manuel LARA	ESP	72	76	77	74	299	11	2,600.00	1,765.38
78	Charl SCHWARTZEL	RSA	73	77	74	79	303	15	2,450.00	1,663.53

Total Prize Fund

€2,000,000 £1,357,985

Past, Present and Future

1	**Lee WESTWOOD**		**273**	**-15**
2	Ian POULTER		278	-10
3	Mark FOSTER		279	-9
4	Fredrik ANDERSSON HED		281	-7
	Michael CAMPBELL		281	-7
	Niclas FASTH		281	-7
	Miguel Angel JIMÉNEZ		281	-7
	Søren KJELDSEN		281	-7
	Zane SCOTLAND		281	-7
	Sam WALKER		281	-7

THE QUINN GROUP / CLUB ISM VIEWING GALLERY

A nostalgic look into the past; a clear view of the present and a thrilling glimpse of the future were all vividly embraced during The Quinn Direct British Masters on the Brabazon Course at The Belfry.

Sandy Lyle prompted memories of yesteryear; Lee Westwood provided proof of the force he still is in world golf, while teenager Rory McIlroy showed why Northern Ireland might have unearthed another jewel and potentially its brightest.

Lyle, who won the British Masters in 1988 – when the average house price was less than £50,000, petrol cost 30 pence a gallon and The European Tour Yearbook made its first appearance on the shelves – was at The Belfry to mark the 20th anniversary of that triumph, but there would be no similar ending this time.

Ironically, like his imperious triumph at Woburn – where he held off an illustrious chasing pack led by Nick Faldo, Mark McNulty and José Maria Olazábal to win by two shots – Lyle started well with a tidy round of 69, the only problem being he signed for a 68, leading to the Scot's disqualification.

There were no such concerns for Westwood, however, who was back at his majestic best, showing the drive that took him to a career high of fourth on the Official World Golf Ranking at the beginning of the new millennium. "I've been there once and my aim is to get back there again – I don't just want to be a top 50 player," he said after his five stroke victory over Ian Poulter.

Westwood's 29 worldwide triumphs have come on the back of a cheery personality and a laidback countenance – qualities which have masked one of the fiercest resolves in the game. The greater the pressure, the surer his putting stroke and despite a win in May in the Valle Romano Open de Andalucia, it had been four years since his name adorned a trophy in Great Britain. After coming close in recent weeks, he would not be denied despite being under close scrutiny not only from himself, but also a Ryder Cup ally on one side and a lifelong friend on the other.

The eventual margin of victory disguised just how close the battle had been between himself, Poulter, and a fellow Worksop Golf Club member, Mark Foster, until a sensational closing stretch allowed Westwood the most enjoyable of walks up the 18th fairway.

The 34 year old was applauded all the way from tee to green and his smile throughout the 473 yard saunter illuminated the early evening gloom. Waiting on the green was the adoration and respect of a huge gallery, his 18th European Tour International Schedule title, and a cheque for €434,727 (£300,000).

"A win has been coming for a few weeks now and doing it in front of so many of my supporters is

Søren Kjeldsen

Sam Walker

Mark Foster

Geoff Cousins from Jaguar (right) presents Stephen Dodd with the keys to an XType for being nearest the pin on the par three 12th on the final day

Rory McIlroy

particularly pleasing," said Westwood, who had rounds of 68-70-70 and a stunning final 65 in his 15 under par winning aggregate of 273.

With three holes to play, any one of the leading triumvirate were potential winners, but less than half an hour later it was all over bar the card marking as Westwood calmly rolled in a birdie putt on the 16th and then watched a long, snake of a putt find the cup for an eagle three on the 17th. "I'm not sure who made the loudest noise when that went it – the gallery or me," he admitted.

"I have had some very special moments in my career at The Belfry and this one is right up there," added the Englishman, who had recorded three top ten finishes in the weeks leading up to his historic triumph over the famous Ryder Cup venue.

While Westwood very much epitomised the present, the future, during a chilly week in the Midlands of England, was personified by Rory McIlroy, a slip of a lad but a massive talent nonetheless. It was his professional debut after a

glittering amateur career, which at one point had taken him to the pinnacle of number one amateur in the world.

Just as he had achieved during the 136th Open Championship at Carnoustie – when his opening 68 was the only bogey-free card of the first day – McIlroy's first card in the paid ranks was a flawless 69. The wind nearly blew him over in the second round, but a 78 did not blow away his chance of making the cut. His first cheque, for finishing in a share of 42nd place, was €15,128 (£10,440) – not bad for four days work, but a mere drop in the ocean compared with the riches which will surely come the way of this extraordinary 18 year old.

The lion's share of the spoils from The Belfry, however, went to Westwood, already one of the best players ever in Europe, and now determined to become one of its greatest.

Martin Hardy

Carbon neutral and conscientious about global warming.
Not only is our equipment energy efficient,
but we could also reduce your print costs by 30%.
To help put our customers first, we ensure our
products put the planet first.

For a free guide to making your office more environmentally friendly go to
www.ricoh.co.uk/greentodo

putting you first | www.ricoh.co.uk/greentodo

RICOH

Ian Poulter

Lee Westwood (left) is presented with the trophy by Colin Morgan, General Manager of Quinn Direct Insurance

> This is right up there with winning The Ryder Cup here in 2002. I don't think I've ever been clapped the entire length of the final hole before, which is very, very special. It's been a long time since I won in Britain – and it feels great.
> **Lee Westwood**

The Course

Legendary in the world of golf, The Brabazon Course is regarded as a truly great championship course and has tested many of the world's best over the years and this year was no exception. The four time host of The Ryder Cup was in superb shape from tee to green, leading BBC commentator Ken Brown to offer the opinion that the course was in the best condition he had seen it in 30 years.

The Belfry (The Brabazon Course)

Par **72**   Yards **7228**   Metres **6607**

Final Results

Pos	Name		Rd1	Rd2	Rd3	Rd4	Total		€	£
1	Lee WESTWOOD	ENG	68	70	70	65	273	-15	434,727.00	300,000.00
2	Ian POULTER	ENG	67	71	70	70	278	-10	289,818.00	200,000.00
3	Mark FOSTER	ENG	71	66	69	73	279	-9	163,283.46	112,680.00
4	Søren KJELDSEN	DEN	66	72	74	69	281	-7	83,765.68	57,805.71
	Miguel Angel JIMÉNEZ	ESP	71	69	70	71	281	-7	83,765.68	57,805.71
	Michael CAMPBELL	NZL	73	69	69	70	281	-7	83,765.68	57,805.71
	Zane SCOTLAND	ENG	69	73	70	69	281	-7	83,765.68	57,805.71
	Sam WALKER	ENG	71	67	75	68	281	-7	83,765.68	57,805.71
	Fredrik ANDERSSON HED	SWE	67	73	68	73	281	-7	83,765.68	57,805.71
	Niclas FASTH	SWE	75	66	67	73	281	-7	83,765.68	57,805.71
11	Benn BARHAM	ENG	70	75	67	70	282	-6	43,690.06	30,150.00
	Nick DOUGHERTY	ENG	72	68	75	67	282	-6	43,690.06	30,150.00
	Grégory BOURDY	FRA	70	73	65	74	282	-6	43,690.06	30,150.00
	Francesco MOLINARI	ITA	68	72	69	73	282	-6	43,690.06	30,150.00
15	Stephen DODD	WAL	68	79	69	67	283	-5	35,995.40	24,840.00
	Raphaël JACQUELIN	FRA	66	76	69	72	283	-5	35,995.40	24,840.00
	Jarmo SANDELIN	SWE	65	79	67	72	283	-5	35,995.40	24,840.00
	Mads VIBE-HASTRUP	DEN	74	71	67	71	283	-5	35,995.40	24,840.00
19	Peter HEDBLOM	SWE	71	70	71	72	284	-4	31,822.02	21,960.00
	Colin MONTGOMERIE	SCO	70	70	70	74	284	-4	31,822.02	21,960.00
21	Robert KARLSSON	SWE	71	75	70	69	285	-3	29,083.24	20,070.00
	Jyoti RANDHAWA	IND	70	72	73	70	285	-3	29,083.24	20,070.00
	James KINGSTON	RSA	71	74	68	72	285	-3	29,083.24	20,070.00
	Martin KAYMER	GER	72	73	72	68	285	-3	29,083.24	20,070.00
25	David LYNN	ENG	72	70	71	73	286	-2	26,344.46	18,180.00
	Jean VAN DE VELDE	FRA	69	75	70	72	286	-2	26,344.46	18,180.00
	Robert-Jan DERKSEN	NED	69	68	74	75	286	-2	26,344.46	18,180.00
28	Phillip ARCHER	ENG	68	72	73	74	287	-1	23,214.42	16,020.00
	Martin ERLANDSSON	SWE	63	75	70	79	287	-1	23,214.42	16,020.00
	Paul MCGINLEY	IRL	70	75	72	70	287	-1	23,214.42	16,020.00
	Louis OOSTHUIZEN	RSA	69	75	71	72	287	-1	23,214.42	16,020.00
	Richard STERNE	RSA	65	77	71	74	287	-1	23,214.42	16,020.00
33	Daniel VANCSIK	ARG	72	71	73	72	288	0	19,888.76	13,725.00
	Thongchai JAIDEE	THA	70	74	73	71	288	0	19,888.76	13,725.00
	Andrew MARSHALL	ENG	73	72	69	74	288	0	19,888.76	13,725.00
	Phillip PRICE	WAL	71	72	72	73	288	0	19,888.76	13,725.00
37	Carlos RODILES	ESP	72	73	71	73	289	1	17,476.03	12,060.00
	Jean-Baptiste GONNET	FRA	74	72	71	72	289	1	17,476.03	12,060.00
	Marcus FRASER	AUS	70	72	72	75	289	1	17,476.03	12,060.00
	Oliver WILSON	ENG	70	74	75	70	289	1	17,476.03	12,060.00
	Bradley DREDGE	WAL	71	70	72	76	289	1	17,476.03	12,060.00
42	Simon WAKEFIELD	ENG	71	76	69	74	290	2	15,128.50	10,440.00
	Marc WARREN	SCO	70	74	70	76	290	2	15,128.50	10,440.00
	Anthony WALL	ENG	73	74	72	71	290	2	15,128.50	10,440.00
	Rory MCILROY	NIR	69	78	70	73	290	2	15,128.50	10,440.00
46	Peter HANSON	SWE	69	75	73	74	291	3	12,259.30	8,460.00
	Damien MCGRANE	IRL	78	68	69	75	291	3	12,259.30	8,460.00
	Kenneth FERRIE	ENG	69	74	76	72	291	3	12,259.30	8,460.00
	Jean-François LUCQUIN	FRA	70	74	74	73	291	3	12,259.30	8,460.00
	Juan PARRON	ESP	75	72	72	72	291	3	12,259.30	8,460.00
	David PARK	WAL	72	74	69	76	291	3	12,259.30	8,460.00
	Simon KHAN	ENG	67	74	79	71	291	3	12,259.30	8,460.00
53	Ignacio GARRIDO	ESP	69	78	70	75	292	4	9,390.10	6,480.00
	Johan EDFORS	SWE	71	75	72	74	292	4	9,390.10	6,480.00
	Peter O'MALLEY	AUS	73	72	73	74	292	4	9,390.10	6,480.00
	Taichi TESHIMA	JPN	70	74	73	75	292	4	9,390.10	6,480.00
57	Marcel SIEM	GER	69	76	73	75	293	5	7,955.50	5,490.00
	Gonzalo FDEZ-CASTAÑO	ESP	72	73	77	71	293	5	7,955.50	5,490.00
59	Henrik NYSTRÖM	SWE	67	76	75	76	294	6	7,433.83	5,130.00
	Grégory HAVRET	FRA	73	74	77	70	294	6	7,433.83	5,130.00
61	Garry HOUSTON	WAL	70	76	76	73	295	7	6,912.16	4,770.00
	Marcus HIGLEY	ENG	74	73	76	72	295	7	6,912.16	4,770.00
63	Stephen GALLACHER	SCO	69	75	79	74	297	9	6,260.07	4,320.00
	Christopher HANELL	SWE	73	74	72	78	297	9	6,260.07	4,320.00
	Steven O'HARA	SCO	74	73	75	75	297	9	6,260.07	4,320.00
66	Andrew TAMPION	AUS	70	75	76	78	299	11	5,738.40	3,960.00
67	Carl SUNESON	ESP	73	73	76	80	302	14	5,477.56	3,780.00
68	Darren FICHARDT	RSA	71	76	79	78	304	16	5,216.72	3,600.00

Total Prize Fund

€2,598,653   £1,793,300

Trailblazing Teams

INDIVIDUAL PLAYER PERFORMANCES

Continental Europe		Pld	W	L	H	Pts
Thomas BJÖRN		3	0	3	0	0
Markus BRIER		5	2	1	2	3
Gonzalo FERNANDEZ-CASTAÑO		5	2	3	0	2
Søren HANSEN		5	1	3	1	1½
Peter HANSON		5	3	2	0	3
Grégory HAVRET		5	3	2	0	3
Mikko ILONEN		4	2	1	1	2½
Raphaël JACQUELIN		5	3	2	0	3
Miguel Angel JIMÉNEZ		4	0	4	0	0
Robert KARLSSON		5	3	2	0	3

Great Britain & Ireland		Pld	W	L	H	Pts
Phillip ARCHER		5	3	0	2	4
Paul CASEY		4	2	2	0	2
Nick DOUGHERTY		5	2	2	1	2½
Bradley DREDGE		5	4	0	1	4½
Simon DYSON		5	3	2	0	3
Justin ROSE		5	3	2	0	3
Colin MONTGOMERIE		4	1	3	0	1
Graeme STORM		5	2	3	0	2
Marc WARREN		3	1	2	0	1
Oliver WILSON		5	2	3	0	2

Players win tournaments but, in team golf, there is also the added input of a captain. So it was in the Seve Trophy at The Heritage Golf & Spa Resort Killenard, Co Laois – a spectacular five-star development in the heart of the Irish midlands – where two men with 11 Major Championships between them oversaw their respective teams on terrain that one of them had transformed from flat farmland into a wonderful tapestry of hillocks and lakes.

In truth, Seve Ballesteros and Nick Faldo are probably the most iconic figures in European golf. Both trailblazers but in quite different ways, their competitive edges were brought to the beautifully manicured course – where Simon Dyson, for one, reckoned the tees had as fine a surface as many greens he had encountered during the season – for the fifth edition of the contest.

The signature of designer Ballesteros is attached to the course where the charismatic Spaniard has a home away from home close to the second fairway. It was an appropriate venue, therefore, to stage the Seve Trophy, a contest which was his vision and one where Europe's top players could hone their match play qualities in alternate years to those of The Ryder Cup.

Yet, it was his opposite number, Nick Faldo, Captain of the Great Britain and Ireland team against Ballesteros' Continental Europe side, who attracted most focus in this Seve Trophy. The reason? The Englishman was dipping his toes into team captaincy for the first time, a year ahead of assuming a similar role for The 2008 Ryder Cup at Valhalla.

Those players who did make it to Killenard were seen very much as the future of European golf, with possible Ryder Cup players on either side. One

of them, Justin Rose, numbered 13 in the Official World Golf Ranking, had even turned down an invitation to the wedding of Ian Poulter, one of his best friends on Tour, so he could play on the Great Britain and Ireland side. Faldo appreciated such commitment.

On the Tuesday evening prior to the four day match, Faldo held a get together for players from both teams, with a look ahead to The Ryder Cup. Furthermore, on the Wednesday evening and on the eve of competition, the relaxed atmosphere continued when Ballesteros hosted a dinner party in his house. By Thursday, however, players – and captains – had moved into tournament mode. This was a match everyone wanted to win.

"I'm on a learning curve," opined Faldo, on the eve of the contest. Indeed, just as he had done in his own playing days, the Englishman had learned to cope with whatever adversity had been thrown his way. An early body blow had come a week before the match when Padraig Harrington, The Open Champion, had been forced to withdraw citing fatigue and a recurring injury problem.

That learning curve took on a new twist on the evening after the first day's Fourballs session, at which stage Continental Europe had edged into a

Colin Montgomerie

Graeme Storm

Left Seve Ballesteros

Simon Dyson (above) and Oliver Wilson

Mikko Ilonen (left) and Markus Brier

Bradley Dredge

3-2 lead. On that Thursday night, Marc Warren, the Scot who, along with Dyson, had been handed a 'wild card' by Faldo, was practising his swing with a five-iron in his hotel when he accidentally hit the overhead chandelier in his room. The crystal shattered, leading to cuts on his forehead and abdomen which necessitated butterfly stitches, while he required shards of glass to be removed from his arms at a local hospital.

Despite the drama, Warren pronounced himself fit to partner Colin Montgomerie in Friday's second Fourball session, but nevertheless finished up losing to the all-French pairing of Grégory Havret and Raphaël Jacquelin on a day when Great Britain and Ireland nevertheless managed to level matters at 5-5 heading into the weekend.

By close of play on Saturday, though, Continental Europe had reclaimed the initiative. In the morning Greensomes session, they had threatened to take a stranglehold when winning three and halving the other match, but Faldo's men rallied in the afternoon Foursomes session - winning three - to leave matters delicately poised at 9 ½ - 8 ½ in favour of Continental Europe going into the final day's ten singles.

Nobody could have envisaged how Great Britain and Ireland would dominate those singles so much so that when the dust had settled, the trophy remained in the same hands that had been custodians in 2002, 2003 and 2005, winning by 16 ½ - 11 ½.

Stalwarts such as Paul Casey and Colin Montgomerie played their part with victories while debutants such as Phillip Archer halved his match with Markus Brier to not only move Great Britain and Ireland over the winning line but to also finish the week unbeaten and with four points out of five, only a half point behind the week's top points scorer, Bradley Dredge.

"It was a privilege to do something like this," said Archer. What is more, Faldo, who had never even met his fellow Englishman prior to the Seve Trophy, now had his telephone number. The countdown to The Ryder Cup had started.

Philip Reid
The Irish Times

NEW
ultralite
ProQuip's lightest ever rain suit.

Ultralite, the multi-award winning waterproof is back with a new high performance fabric, and is ProQuip's lightest ever rain suit.

What makes the new fabric unique is its dense but lightweight weave. Similar to a duck's feathers, this results in water and spray running straight off, ensuring the garment remains light and easy to play in.

PRO QUIP

Ahead of the game

ProQuip is proud
to supply

www.proquipgolf.com

Paul Casey

Søren Hansen

Seve Ballesteros (right) with Tom Keane, Owner of The Heritage Golf and Spa Resort

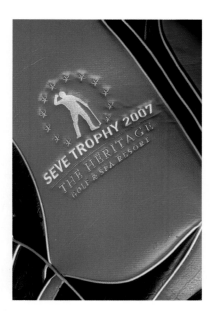

> I thought it was a great week. All 20 players did their bit. My wild cards both had a great week. Simon Dyson was a real bubbly, bouncing character and Marc Warren did a great job. The whole experience has been really, really worth doing.
> **Nick Faldo**

The Heritage Golf & Spa Resort

Par 72   Yards 7319   Metres 6694

Total Prize Fund

€2,000,000   £1,393,116

Final Results

CONTINENTAL EUROPE		GREAT BRITAIN & IRELAND	
Captain: Seve Ballesteros		**Captain: Nick Faldo**	
Thursday September 27: Fourballs			
Peter Hanson & Robert Karlsson (3 & 1)	1	Colin Montgomerie & Marc Warren	0
Miguel Angel Jiménez & Gonzalo Fernandez-Castaño	0	Bradley Dredge & Phillip Archer (2 & 1)	1
Raphaël Jacquelin & Grégory Havret (4 & 3)	1	Paul Casey & Simon Dyson	0
Thomas Björn & Søren Hansen	0	Nick Dougherty & Graeme Storm (1 hole)	1
Markus Brier & Mikko Ilonen (3 & 2)	1	Justin Rose & Oliver Wilson	0
	3		**2**
Friday September 28: Fourballs			
Peter Hanson & Robert Karlsson	0	Bradley Dredge & Phillip Archer (5 & 4)	1
Raphaël Jacquelin & Grégory Havret (5 & 3)	1	Colin Montgomerie & Marc Warren	0
Thomas Björn & Søren Hansen	0	Oliver Wilson & Simon Dyson (3 & 2)	1
Markus Brier & Mikko Ilonen (1 hole)	1	Nick Dougherty & Graeme Storm	0
Miguel Angel Jiménez & Gonzalo Fernandez-Castaño	0	Justin Rose & Paul Casey (1 hole)	1
	5		**5**
Saturday September 29: Morning Greensomes			
Gonzalo Fernandez-Castaño & Robert Karlsson (3 & 1)	1	Justin Rose & Paul Casey	0
Raphaël Jacquelin & Grégory Havret (2 & 1)	1	Nick Dougherty & Graeme Storm	0
Peter Hanson & Søren Hansen (1 hole)	1	Oliver Wilson & Simon Dyson	0
Markus Brier & Mikko Ilonen	½	Bradley Dredge & Phillip Archer	½
	8 ½		**5 ½**
Saturday September 29: Afternoon Foursomes			
Raphaël Jacquelin & Grégory Havret	0	Justin Rose & Nick Dougherty (2 & 1)	1
Gonzalo Fernandez-Castaño & Robert Karlsson (3 & 2)	1	Colin Montgomerie & Graeme Storm	0
Peter Hanson & Søren Hansen	0	Oliver Wilson & Simon Dyson (3 & 2)	1
Markus Brier & Miguel Angel Jiménez	0	Bradley Dredge & Phillip Archer (2 holes)	1
	9½		**8½**
Sunday September 30: Singles			
Robert Karlsson	0	Colin Montgomerie (1 hole)	1
Raphaël Jacquelin	0	Paul Casey (3 & 2)	1
Grégory Havret	0	Marc Warren (1 hole)	1
Søren Hansen	½	Nick Dougherty	½
Thomas Björn	0	Graeme Storm (6 & 5)	1
Mikko Ilonen	0	Simon Dyson (2 & 1)	1
Markus Brier	½	Phillip Archer	½
Gonzalo Fernandez-Castaño	0	Bradley Dredge (2 holes)	1
Peter Hanson (2 holes)	1	Oliver Wilson	0
Miguel Angel Jiménez	0	Justin Rose (2 & 1)	1
CONTINENTAL EUROPE	**11½**	**GREAT BRITAIN & IRELAND**	**16½**

The Course

Nestling in the quaint village of Killenard in the heart of Ireland, the Seve Ballesteros and Jeff Howes designed course is a true gem and was presented in immaculate condition for the fifth staging of the Seve Trophy. With the Slieve Bloom mountains as a backdrop, the course features five lakes and a stream, 98 bunkers and more than 7000 trees, all factors which demand accuracy and patience at all times.

The Caring Professional

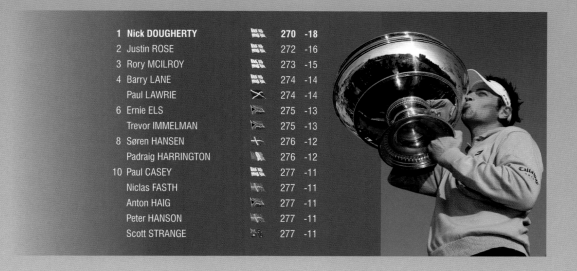

1	**Nick DOUGHERTY**		**270**	**-18**
2	Justin ROSE		272	-16
3	Rory MCILROY		273	-15
4	Barry LANE		274	-14
	Paul LAWRIE		274	-14
6	Ernie ELS		275	-13
	Trevor IMMELMAN		275	-13
8	Søren HANSEN		276	-12
	Padraig HARRINGTON		276	-12
10	Paul CASEY		277	-11
	Niclas FASTH		277	-11
	Anton HAIG		277	-11
	Peter HANSON		277	-11
	Scott STRANGE		277	-11

Nick Dougherty has always had a winning smile but, up until he captured the cavernous silver trophy at the Alfred Dunhill Links Championship, he had only the one victory to go with it. Namely, the Caltex Masters, presented by Carlsberg, in Singapore in 2005.

Yet there were plenty of occasions when he had come close, with none more painful than the Telecom Italia Open in May where he was three ahead with nine to play before slipping back to share third.

Dougherty, like everyone else, saw the Italian slide and others like it as "squandered opportunities". At the same time, though, he could see that he was amassing a wealth of great experience. "It's because of what I've done," he said at the conclusion of events in St Andrews, "that I could do what I did today."

The Alfred Dunhill Links Championship is an event in which competitors want for nothing – save when it comes to the weather. There have been wet and wind-tossed years in which the golfers have cowered under their waterproofs all week but this year they revelled in one gloriously sunlit day after another.

For the best of first round spectacles, everyone hurried to Carnoustie where the greens were at their stunning best. In particular, people wanted to watch Padraig Harrington at the 18th, the hole where he was twice in the Barry Burn at the 72nd in the 136th Open Championship in July.

This time around, however, he raised his hands aloft as he stayed above ground with his tee shot,

a three wood. He then hit a nine iron to 15 feet and made off with a birdie three on his way to an opening 70. It gave him food for thought. "In years to come," he suggested, wryly, "I don't think it will be today's birdie that I remember most!"

England's Steve Webster led the way on the opening day after a splendid 65 at Carnoustie, one clear of Hennie Otto and Scott Strange, while the South African and the Australian's respective 66s on the Championship Course were matched at St Andrews by Denmark's Søren Hansen and the tournament's inaugural winner Paul Lawrie of Scotland. In a harbinger of things to come, however, Dougherty began with four birdies in five holes and was among those to bed down with a 67 on the cliff top gem that is Kingsbarns.

By Friday night, after a 66 at Carnoustie, Dougherty was in a three-way tie at the top with Peter O'Malley and Otto. This was the day when O'Malley had to rely on his landlady in Crail to do rather more than make his breakfast. When the Australian discovered he had left his clubs at his lodgings, he rang the good lady and she obliged by driving his golf bag as far as Leuchars – something which saved the player a crucial half hour.

Saturday night saw Dougherty with a three shot lead which left him with mixed feelings. After carding a 66 at St Andrews he said: "I don't feel particularly

Rory McIlroy

Gonzalo Fernandez-Castaño (left) and Beltran Gomez-Acebo

Left *Peter Hanson*

Anton Haig (left) and Springbok legend Schalk Burger

Kenneth Ferrie

Sandy Lyle (left) and Sir Bobby Charlton

Nick Dougherty (left) and Peter Dawson, Chief Executive of the R&A

ALFRED DUNHILL
LINKS CHAMPIONSHIP

EADING PROS	PAR	HOLE	LEADING TEAMS	PAR
UGHERTY	-18	18	COE	-3
SE	-16	18	DE KOCK	-3
LROY	-15	18	BURGER	-3
WRIE	-14	18	ALGKVIST	-3
NE	-14	18	G ACEBO	-3

stressed by being in front." Come next morning, though, the butterflies were beginning to circle.

He began with two bogeys but Ron Cuthbert, his physical trainer, had impressed on him that if he did make that kind of a start, he should not get things out of perspective. "I was prepared for it," said Dougherty, later.

Cuthbert's advice apart, Dougherty was blessed in having Peter Dawson by way of an amateur partner. Dawson, the Chief Executive of the R&A, knows precisely what makes golfers tick. He sensed when to talk and he sensed when a bit of silence would not go amiss.

Meanwhile, it was typical of Dougherty's nature that he continued to encourage Dawson in the duo's quest for the amateur prize. Their eventual 24 under par total of 264 for 16th place was respectable but fell well short of the 36 under par winning total of 250 posted by Scott Strange and his amateur partner, 22 year old Sydney university student Robert Coe.

Back in the quest for the main prize, Dougherty responded to his bogey, bogey start in precisely the right fashion with three successive birdies from the fifth. Thereafter, he holed more than the occasional testing par putt to keep himself ahead of his pursuers – notably Ernie Els and Justin Rose.

Heading towards the denouement, Els faded before Rose. At a time when he was one behind, the South African hit through the 16th green before putting back into the bunker, which was within a whisker of his line, on his way to a triple bogey seven. He knew then his chance had gone.

Rose remained one shot off the lead until the 17th where his second braked within inches of the Road Hole bunker. He was better off there than in it but, with no chance of getting close to the pin, he walked from the green with a three putt bogey five.

Meanwhile, 18 year old Rory McIlroy had a rush of birdies in his closing 68 which enabled him to finish third and virtually secure his European Tour card for 2008. In the end, his 15 under par total of 273 saw him finish one shot behind Rose and three behind champion Dougherty.

After all the near misses, it was easy to understand Dougherty's emotions at the end. "I felt very nervous going out to be honest," he said. "It means so much to win and as much as I really wanted for it not to mean that much, it's difficult, as it is in my nature to care."

Lewine Mair
The Daily Telegraph

Oliver Wilson
getting energised on
The European Tour

Robert Coe (left) and Scott Strange

Thomas Björn (left) and Hugh Grant

i By playing in the 2007 Alfred Dunhill Links Championship, Sam Torrance extended his European Tour record of playing a European Tour event every year since the Tour began in 1972 – spanning 36 years. The Scottish event was his 702nd official event in all.

The Course

The Home of Golf is rarely seen in a better light with glorious sunshine and blue skies blessing all three venues. Kingsbarns continued to enhance its reputation as one of the best new courses in the world while the greens at Carnoustie drew praise from all quarters. The beautifully manicured Old Course at St Andrews never looked better than on Sunday and provided the perfect platform for a thrilling final day.

Nick Dougherty (right) is presented with the trophy by Julian Diment, Marketing Director of Alfred Dunhill

Old Course, St Andrews
Par **72**   Yards **7279**   Metres **6655**
Carnoustie
Par **72**   Yards **7412**   Metres **6780**
Kingsbarns
Par **72**   Yards **7106**   Metres **6498**

Final Results

Pos	Name		Rd1	Rd2	Rd3	Rd4	Total		€	£
1	Nick DOUGHERTY	ENG	67	66	66	71	270	-18	562,624.90	392,368.40
2	Justin ROSE	ENG	68	69	66	69	272	-16	375,080.90	261,577.28
3	Rory MCILROY	NIR	71	67	67	68	273	-15	211,321.90	147,373.56
4	Paul LAWRIE	SCO	66	73	64	71	274	-14	155,959.60	108,764.51
	Barry LANE	ENG	69	70	68	67	274	-14	155,959.60	108,764.51
6	Trevor IMMELMAN	RSA	73	65	67	70	275	-13	109,711.90	76,511.87
	Ernie ELS	RSA	67	67	70	71	275	-13	109,711.90	76,511.87
8	Padraig HARRINGTON	IRL	70	66	67	73	276	-12	80,005.27	55,794.79
	Søren HANSEN	DEN	66	70	71	69	276	-12	80,005.27	55,794.79
10	Scott STRANGE	AUS	66	70	69	72	277	-11	58,738.04	40,963.26
	Paul CASEY	ENG	74	68	68	67	277	-11	58,738.04	40,963.26
	Anton HAIG	RSA	68	66	75	68	277	-11	58,738.04	40,963.26
	Peter HANSON	SWE	68	68	69	72	277	-11	58,738.04	40,963.26
	Niclas FASTH	SWE	67	70	67	73	277	-11	58,738.04	40,963.26
15	Martin KAYMER	GER	69	68	70	71	278	-10	43,251.79	30,163.32
	Gonzalo FDEZ-CASTAÑO	ESP	67	67	73	71	278	-10	43,251.79	30,163.32
	Miguel Angel JIMÉNEZ	ESP	68	68	73	69	278	-10	43,251.79	30,163.32
	Graeme STORM	ENG	74	66	68	70	278	-10	43,251.79	30,163.32
	Rafael ECHENIQUE	ARG	67	67	72	72	278	-10	43,251.79	30,163.32
	Brett RUMFORD	AUS	70	68	72	68	278	-10	43,251.79	30,163.32
	Phillip ARCHER	ENG	68	68	71	71	278	-10	43,251.79	30,163.32
	Steve WEBSTER	ENG	65	70	68	75	278	-10	43,251.79	30,163.32
23	Peter O'MALLEY	AUS	69	64	69	77	279	-9	33,082.35	23,071.27
	Zane SCOTLAND	ENG	72	72	67	68	279	-9	33,082.35	23,071.27
	Luke DONALD	ENG	67	70	69	73	279	-9	33,082.35	23,071.27
	John BICKERTON	ENG	70	70	69	70	279	-9	33,082.35	23,071.27
	Gary ORR	SCO	70	70	69	70	279	-9	33,082.35	23,071.27
	Gary MURPHY	IRL	71	67	72	69	279	-9	33,082.35	23,071.27
	Jeev Milkha SINGH	IND	67	68	72	72	279	-9	33,082.35	23,071.27
	Paul MCGINLEY	IRL	70	71	67	71	279	-9	33,082.35	23,071.27
	Robert-Jan DERKSEN	NED	70	71	70	68	279	-9	33,082.35	23,071.27
32	Richard STERNE	RSA	73	67	70	70	280	-8	26,584.03	18,539.41
	Jean-François REMESY	FRA	71	67	69	73	280	-8	26,584.03	18,539.41
	Jean VAN DE VELDE	FRA	71	69	67	73	280	-8	26,584.03	18,539.41
	Anthony WALL	ENG	73	69	65	73	280	-8	26,584.03	18,539.41
36	Kenneth FERRIE	ENG	69	65	75	72	281	-7	21,942.37	15,302.37
	David LYNN	ENG	67	76	68	70	281	-7	21,942.37	15,302.37
	James HEPWORTH	ENG	74	70	67	70	281	-7	21,942.37	15,302.37
	Graeme MCDOWELL	NIR	70	68	70	73	281	-7	21,942.37	15,302.37
	Hennie OTTO	RSA	66	67	74	74	281	-7	21,942.37	15,302.37
	Alejandro CAÑIZARES	ESP	70	69	72	70	281	-7	21,942.37	15,302.37
	Peter HEDBLOM	SWE	69	74	67	71	281	-7	21,942.37	15,302.37
	Martin ERLANDSSON	SWE	71	68	71	71	281	-7	21,942.37	15,302.37
	Rhys DAVIES	WAL	71	70	68	72	281	-7	21,942.37	15,302.37
45	Alexander NOREN	SWE	68	73	67	74	282	-6	17,553.90	12,241.90
	Henrik STENSON	SWE	68	69	69	76	282	-6	17,553.90	12,241.90
	Thomas AIKEN	RSA	71	66	69	76	282	-6	17,553.90	12,241.90
	Alessandro TADINI	ITA	69	72	68	73	282	-6	17,553.90	12,241.90
49	Scott DRUMMOND	SCO	73	69	69	72	283	-5	14,178.15	9,887.69
	Ross FISHER	ENG	73	66	68	76	283	-5	14,178.15	9,887.69
	Mikko ILONEN	FIN	67	73	71	72	283	-5	14,178.15	9,887.69
	Grégory BOURDY	FRA	72	67	71	73	283	-5	14,178.15	9,887.69
	Nathan GREEN	AUS	68	74	67	74	283	-5	14,178.15	9,887.69
	Christopher HANELL	SWE	70	71	70	72	283	-5	14,178.15	9,887.69
55	Daniel VANCSIK	ARG	70	70	71	73	284	-4	10,886.79	7,592.33
	Matthew MILLAR	AUS	69	74	68	73	284	-4	10,886.79	7,592.33
	Simon DYSON	ENG	73	70	68	73	284	-4	10,886.79	7,592.33
	Thomas LEVET	FRA	70	65	75	74	284	-4	10,886.79	7,592.33
59	Steven O'HARA	SCO	70	70	69	76	285	-3	9,789.67	6,827.21
	Richard FINCH	ENG	70	71	70	74	285	-3	9,789.67	6,827.21
61	Gary LOCKERBIE	ENG	70	73	69		212	-4	6,911.98	4,820.34
	Simon KHAN	ENG	73	71	68		212	-4	6,911.98	4,820.34
	Lee WESTWOOD	ENG	70	74	68		212	-4	6,911.98	4,820.34
	Kurt BARNES	AUS	71	71	70		212	-4	6,911.98	4,820.34
	Mattias ELIASSON	SWE	78	65	69		212	-4	6,911.98	4,820.34
	Robert KARLSSON	SWE	69	70	73		212	-4	6,911.98	4,820.34
	Francesco MOLINARI	ITA	73	70	69		212	-4	6,911.98	4,820.34
	Darren CLARKE	NIR	72	66	74		212	-4	6,911.98	4,820.34
	Michael CAMPBELL	NZL	71	71	70		212	-4	6,911.98	4,820.34
	Prom MEESAWAT	THA	69	72	71		212	-4	6,911.98	4,820.34
	Jonathan MOORE	USA	68	70	74		212	-4	6,911.98	4,820.34

Total Prize Fund

€3,376,087   £2,354,446

Team Results

Pos	Name	Rd1	Rd2	Rd3	Rd4	Total		€
1	Scott Strange and Robert Coe	62	64	64	60	250	-36	35,164.06
2	Rory Mcilroy and Mike De Kock	65	62	65	60	252	-34	21,098.44
3	Anton Haig and Schalk Burger	62	64	66	63	255	-33	12,307.42
	Niclas Fasth and Bjorn Algkvist	64	64	61	66	255	-33	12,307.42
5	Gonzalo Fdez-Castaño and Beltran Gomez-Acebo	65	62	66	64	257	-31	7,032.81

Magnificent Seven

4

552 yard par 5

HSBC ◇

rld m play

1 **Ernie ELS**
2 Angel CABRERA
3 Hunter MAHAN
 Henrik STENSON
5 Paul CASEY
 Anders HANSEN
 Søren HANSEN
 Andres ROMERO
9 Woody AUSTIN
 Niclas FASTH
 Retief GOOSEN
 Padraig HARRINGTON
 Jerry KELLY
 Colin MONTGOMERIE
 Justin ROSE
 Rory SABBATINI

259

There is no place like home as the old saying goes, especially if, like Ernie Els, you can pop out your front door and return shortly afterwards with £1 million in your pocket.

When, in 1991, Seve Ballesteros equalled Gary Player's record of five World Match Play Championship victories, it seemed unlikely that anyone would better the legendary duo's achievements, yet for Els, his convincing 6 and 4 victory over US Open Champion Angel Cabrera on a glorious October Sunday in the south of England, completed another "Magnificent Seven" only a few miles down the road from the Ascot Racecourse where Frankie Dettori created history by riding seven successful winners on the same card in 1996.

In all he has played 30 matches, winning 25 of them. He has appeared in eight finals losing just once, to Vijay Singh in 1997, all of which means that from this single event, the Els bank balance has benefitted to the tune of £3,750,000.

No wonder then, that Wentworth Club is much more than just a British base for the popular South African. His lovely home lies beside the 16th fairway of the West Course, an historic building which he has re-designed for the 21st century. He has been adopted as the Club's international touring professional and his children go to the local school.

No wonder, too, that Els, moments after being handed the gleaming Mark McCormack Trophy, should greet his latest triumph by declaring. "I wish I could pick Wentworth up and take it round the world with me – I just love it here. Never in my wildest imagination could I have seen myself winning this prestigious title seven times. It's a dream come true."

The victory also ended a long absence from the winners circle for Els, who underwent knee surgery in 2005 and who last tasted victory in the South African Airways Open in December 2006.

"This is brilliant for me and such a blessed relief," he added. "I have played some good golf for the past two years but I haven't had any luck. So to get

Paul Casey of England holds the HSBC World Match Play Championship trophy surrounded by the other 2007 players

Angel Cabrera

Henrik Stenson

DJ Spooney and children from the Golf Roots programme - a dynamic new initiative run by the Golf Foundation designed to bring golf to inner city children - watch Ernie Els tee off at Wentworth Club

such an important win and to play the way I did this week in such a world class field is so satisfying."

Els, who beat Colin Montgomerie and Andres Romero by 6 and 5 and Henrik Stenson by 3 and 2 on his way to the final, saved his best golf for the showdown with Cabrera, bagging no fewer than 13 birdies in 32 holes and indeed he was never behind against an opponent who had himself collected 31 birdies in dispatching Retief Goosen 6 and 5, defending champion Paul Casey 4 and 3 and Hunter Mahan 2 and 1.

Three up at lunch, the key moment for Els came at the third hole in the afternoon when he almost drove into the trees and caught a branch with his intended recovery, before managing a superb up and down to save par. Cabrera, on the fringe of the green in two, mishit his chip and saw his four foot par putt slide by to lose a hole he had seemed certain to win.

"That was huge because it gave me a good cushion against any possible comeback," admitted the South African.

Cabrera did manage to cut the deficit to two holes with winning birdies at the sixth and ninth, but when Els holed a 15 foot birdie putt on the tenth it

was virtually all over, the end eventually coming at the short 14th.

Cabrera, who had beaten Els 2 and 1 in the first round last year, was full of praise for his conqueror. "I played my best today, but it wasn't enough," he said. "Ernie played great and showed why he is so hard to beat in his own back yard. He truly is 'The King of Wentworth'.

Stenson, winner of the World Golf Championships – Accenture Match Play in Arizona in February, showed a welcome return to form in his march to the semi-finals while British golf fans found out why the Americans fully expect Hunter Mahan to be one of their major stars of the next decade as he reached the last four with a disarming mixture of class and character.

In the end, however it was Ernie – who Els? – who prevailed. Considering his previous six World Match Play Championship crowns have come in two batches of three, should we think of pencilling him in already for 2008 and 2009?

John Whitbread
Surrey Herald

Wentworth Club. Nurturing the future of British Golf.

Talent spotting: Ross Fisher, age 13, with Bernard Gallacher at Wentworth Club

Ross Fisher, winner of The KLM Open 2007 - his first European Tour title - joined Wentworth's Foundation in 1994 aged 13. After a string of achievements, he turned pro in 2004 and won his place on The European Tour through the 2005 Challenge Tour and is now a Wentworth Touring Professional.

Wentworth

WWW.WENTWORTHCLUB.COM
+44 (0)1344 842201

Padraig Harrington and Angel Cabrera, Major Champions in 2007, who became the 30th and 31st recipients of Honorary Life Membership of The European Tour, and received their solid silver Membership cards from George O'Grady, Chief Executive of The European Tour, during the HSBC World Match Play Championship Official Dinner at Wentworth Club. Left to Right: George O'Grady, Padraig Harrington, Angel Cabrera, Retief Goosen, Ernie Els and Colin Montgomerie

The Course

Although exactly the same course as the one used for the BMW PGA Championship, the West Course at Wentworth Club plays longer and has different characteristics in October than it does in May. Another reason for that is the fact it is match play rather than stroke play as defending champion Paul Casey explained: "You look at the shots differently, keep the ball in play and try and make the other guy make mistakes."

Right *Justin Rose of England poses in an England Rugby Union jersey prior to the HSBC World Match Play Championship*

Ernie Els (right) is presented with the trophy by Dyfrig John, Director & Chief Executive, HSBC Bank plc

Wentworth Club (West Course)
Par **72**   Yards **7320**   Metres **6695**

Final Results

FIRST ROUND (seedings in parentheses)

Paul Casey (Eng) (1) beat Jerry Kelly (USA) (16) 3 and 2
Angel Cabrera (Arg) (9) beat Retief Goosen (RSA) (8) 6 and 5
Hunter Mahan (USA) (12) beat Justin Rose (Eng) (5) 5 and 4
Søren Hansen (Den) (13) beat Rory Sabbatini (RSA) (4) 4 and 3
Anders Hansen (Den) (14) beat Padraig Harrington (Ire) (3) 4 and 2
Henrik Stenson (Swe) (6) beat Woody Austin (USA) (11) 1 hole
Andres Romero (Arg) (10) beat Niclas Fasth (Swe) (7) 3 and 2
Ernie Els (RSA) (2) beat Colin Montgomerie (Scot) (15) 6 and 5

QUARTER - FINALS

Cabrera beat Casey 4 and 3
Mahan beat Søren Hansen 6 and 4
Stenson beat Anders Hansen 7 and 6
Els beat Romero 6 and 5

SEMI - FINALS

Cabrera beat Mahan 2 and 1
Els beat Stenson 3 and 2

FINAL (36 holes)

Els beat Cabrera 6 and 4

Prize Fund Breakdown

Pos	Name	€	£	€ (Order of Merit)	£
1	Ernie ELS (RSA)	1,443,830.00	1,000,000.00	587,147.91	406,660.00
2	Angel CABRERA (ARG)	577,532.00	400,000.00	391,436.75	271,110.00
3	Hunter MAHAN (USA)	173,259.00	120,000.00	198,341.81	137,372.00
	Henrik STENSON (SWE)	173,259.00	120,000.00	198,341.81	137,372.00
5	Paul CASEY (ENG)	115,506.00	80,000.00	116,609.49	80,764.00
	Anders HANSEN (DEN)	115,506.00	80,000.00	116,609.49	80,764.00
	Søren HANSEN (DEN)	115,506.00	80,000.00	116,609.49	80,764.00
	Andres ROMERO (ARG)	115,506.00	80,000.00	116,609.49	80,764.00
9	Woody AUSTIN (USA)	86,629.00	60,000.00	60,858.88	42,151.00
	Niclas FASTH (SWE)	86,629.00	60,000.00	60,858.88	42,151.00
	Retief GOOSEN (RSA)	86,629.00	60,000.00	60,858.88	42,151.00
	Padraig HARRINGTON (IRL)	86,629.00	60,000.00	60,858.88	42,151.00
	Jerry KELLY (USA)	86,629.00	60,000.00	60,858.88	42,151.00
	Colin MONTGOMERIE (SCO)	86,629.00	60,000.00	60,858.88	42,151.00
	Justin ROSE (ENG)	86,629.00	60,000.00	60,858.88	42,151.00
	Rory SABBATINI (RSA)	86,629.00	60,000.00	60,858.88	42,151.00

Total Prize Fund
€3,522,945 £2,440,000

> It's very satisfying to win any tournament but I've always been a fan of this kind of match play event. I've played some good golf these last two years and although it might seem that I'm a very patient guy, in fact I am quite impatient when it comes to getting results.
> *Ernie Els*

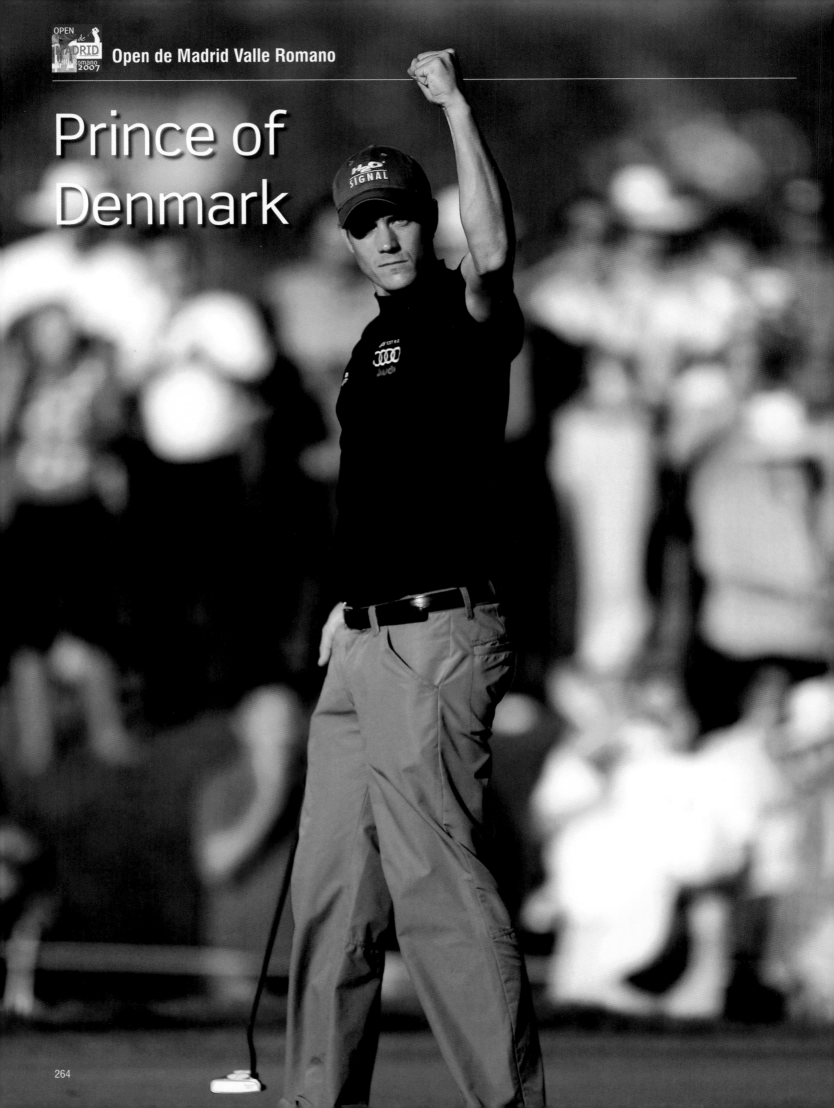

Prince of Denmark

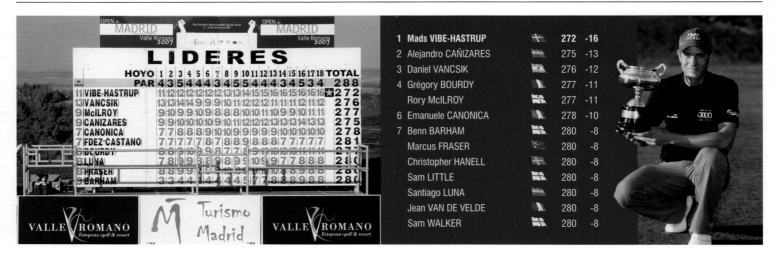

				TOTAL	
1	Mads VIBE-HASTRUP			272	-16
2	Alejandro CAÑIZARES			275	-13
3	Daniel VANCSIK			276	-12
4	Grégory BOURDY			277	-11
	Rory McILROY			277	-11
6	Emanuele CANONICA			278	-10
7	Benn BARHAM			280	-8
	Marcus FRASER			280	-8
	Christopher HANELL			280	-8
	Sam LITTLE			280	-8
	Santiago LUNA			280	-8
	Jean VAN DE VELDE			280	-8
	Sam WALKER			280	-8

H istory has a great knack of repeating itself in golf and October 2007 in Madrid was no exception. In the autumn of 2002, the Open de Madrid was won by a Dane wielding a long handled putter. Five years later, and once again with the leaves on the trees turning russet, the tournament, now fully titled the Open de Madrid Valle Romano, was won by, yes, a Dane wielding a long-handled putter!

Grégory Bourdy

Daniel Vancsik

Mads Vibe-Hastrup was the man this time who became the 17th first-time winner on The 2007 European Tour International Schedule. The 28 year old from Helsingor was delighted to have followed in the footsteps of one of the first professionals to bring his country to the fore on The European Tour, the previous Danish winner in Madrid, Steen Tinning.

However, while Tinning's victory proved to be his swansong as a debilitating back injury took its toll, one hopes that Vibe-Hastrup's career has only just begun in earnest.

Certainly Denmark's remarkable production line of winners had just sent another along the conveyor belt as Vibe-Hastrup, after a few years of trying to establish himself, had finally joined Thomas Björn, Anders and Søren Hansen, Søren Kjeldsen and Tinning on the Roll of Honour.

Before the tall, slim Dane could clutch his trophy, however, he had to defy portents that were suggesting an entirely different outcome.

As he took to the Real Sociedad Hípica Española Club de Campo course on the Sunday afternoon, he was two strokes adrift of the big-hitting Argentine, Daniel Vancsik, attempting to win his second event in only his second full year on Tour. Vancsik had dominated the Madeira Islands Open BPI in March and was poised to do the same in Madrid.

Indeed it seemed the world over that Argentina was in the ascendancy. At Wentworth Club, Angel Cabrera was just a final away from adding the HSBC World Match Play Championship to his CV while, later that night, Argentina were to play South Africa in the semi-final of the Rugby World Cup.

Of the three scenarios, Vancsik's chances looked the best. He had led for three rounds, equalling the course record seven under par 65 on the first day, before sharing the lead the following day with the home favourite Alejandro Cañizares. Indeed he would have had a healthier advantage than two shots going into the last day had he not found the water at the short 14th on the Saturday afternoon.

While Vancsik strived for his second win and Vibe-Hastrup attempted to follow in Tinning's footsteps, the youngster in a share of third place going into the final day was looking for a piece of history of his own.

Rory McIlroy, just 18 years old, had finished third the previous week in the Alfred Dunhill Links Championship at St Andrews and was on the brink of not only becoming The European

Tour's youngest winner but also following fellow Ulsterman David Feherty, who won the Open de Madrid in 1992, into the record books.

McIlroy, exciting the galleries in much the same way as Sergio Garcia had done a few years earlier, was trying to better Garcia's record, too. It was only McIlroy's third event as a professional while Garcia had taken four tournaments after leaving the amateur ranks, to win the 1999 Irish Open.

The baby-faced youngster from Holywood in Northern Ireland battled gamely but his final round 70 was good enough only for a share of fourth place with Frenchman Grégory Bourdy leaving the main battle for the spoils to be contested between Cañizares, Vancsik and Vibe-Hastrup.

Vancsik's hopes disappeared on one hole, the fifth, where he ran up a quintuple bogey nine and it proved to be the first of a hat-trick of

disappointments on the day for Argentina who saw Cabrera beaten by Ernie Els at Wentworth Club and the Pumas beaten by the Springboks in Paris.

It left Vibe-Hastrup's only rival in the end as Cañizares, son of José Maria, the 1989 Ryder Cup hero whose putt on the 18th at The Belfry ensured a 14-14 tie with the United States to keep the trophy in Europe. No such telling finalé came from Cañizares junior, though, as his closing 68 saw him finish three shots shy.

With his Spanish opponent unable to force him off the top of the leader board, Vibe-Hastrup became the latest golfing Prince of Denmark.

Norman Dabell

Alejandro Cañizares

Emanuele Canonica

Mads Vibe-Hastrup (left) of Denmark is presented with the trophy by Santiago Fisas, Minister of Culture and Tourism for the Region of Madrid

> It's very difficult to follow performances like Anders and Søren's so I am very pleased to have done what I've done. My mantra of the day was to play my own game.
> **Mads Vibe-Hastrup**

The Course

Opened in 1997, the Real Sociedad Hípica Española Club de Campo occupies a prime location to the north of Spain's capital city. Robert Von Hagge's undulating 7167 yard layout places a premium on accuracy off the tee, while the sloping greens demand a player's utmost attention. The signature 14th hole, a stunning 183 yard par three, is a wonderful risk / reward hole, with a lake running all the way along the green's right hand side and snaking around the back of the putting surface.

Real Sociedad Hípica Española Club de Campo
Par **72**   Yards **7167**   Metres **6552**

Final Results

Pos	Name		Rd1	Rd2	Rd3	Rd4	Total		€	£
1	Mads VIBE-HASTRUP	DEN	69	69	67	67	272	-16	150,000.00	103,890.35
2	Alejandro CAÑIZARES	ESP	69	66	72	68	275	-13	100,000.00	69,260.23
3	Daniel VANCSIK	ARG	65	70	68	73	276	-12	56,340.00	39,021.21
4	Grégory BOURDY	FRA	71	69	68	69	277	-11	41,580.00	28,798.40
	Rory MCILROY	NIR	73	68	66	70	277	-11	41,580.00	28,798.40
6	Emanuele CANONICA	ITA	68	70	71	69	278	-10	31,500.00	21,816.97
7	Benn BARHAM	ENG	71	71	71	67	280	-8	19,170.00	13,277.19
	Christopher HANELL	SWE	70	73	66	71	280	-8	19,170.00	13,277.19
	Santiago LUNA	ESP	75	67	66	72	280	-8	19,170.00	13,277.19
	Jean VAN DE VELDE	FRA	71	66	71	72	280	-8	19,170.00	13,277.19
	Sam LITTLE	ENG	72	71	68	69	280	-8	19,170.00	13,277.19
	Marcus FRASER	AUS	75	68	65	72	280	-8	19,170.00	13,277.19
	Sam WALKER	ENG	71	72	70	67	280	-8	19,170.00	13,277.19
14	Gonzalo FDEZ-CASTAÑO	ESP	71	69	69	72	281	-7	12,960.00	8,976.13
	Sven STRÜVER	GER	69	74	68	70	281	-7	12,960.00	8,976.13
	Damien MCGRANE	IRL	71	74	67	69	281	-7	12,960.00	8,976.13
	Fredrik ANDERSSON HED	SWE	75	70	68	68	281	-7	12,960.00	8,976.13
18	Henrik NYSTRÖM	SWE	74	71	69	68	282	-6	10,836.00	7,505.04
	Thomas BJÖRN	DEN	74	68	71	69	282	-6	10,836.00	7,505.04
	José Manuel LARA	ESP	72	70	68	72	282	-6	10,836.00	7,505.04
	Ariel CANETE	ARG	75	70	67	70	282	-6	10,836.00	7,505.04
	Shiv KAPUR	IND	72	70	69	71	282	-6	10,836.00	7,505.04
23	Manuel QUIROS	ESP	72	67	69	75	283	-5	9,765.00	6,763.26
	Carlos RODILES	ESP	71	73	66	73	283	-5	9,765.00	6,763.26
25	Andrew MARSHALL	ENG	70	74	70	70	284	-4	8,550.00	5,921.75
	Anthony WALL	ENG	75	68	72	69	284	-4	8,550.00	5,921.75
	Richard BLAND	ENG	72	74	70	68	284	-4	8,550.00	5,921.75
	Gary LOCKERBIE	ENG	68	68	73	75	284	-4	8,550.00	5,921.75
	Martin KAYMER	GER	67	75	68	74	284	-4	8,550.00	5,921.75
	José-Filipe LIMA	POR	72	76	72	70	284	-4	8,550.00	5,921.75
	Robert ROCK	ENG	72	74	72	66	284	-4	8,550.00	5,921.75
32	Graeme MCDOWELL	NIR	74	73	68	70	285	-3	6,600.00	4,571.18
	Pablo MARTIN	ESP	74	71	65	75	285	-3	6,600.00	4,571.18
	James KINGSTON	RSA	76	65	73	71	285	-3	6,600.00	4,571.18
	David LYNN	ENG	76	71	71	67	285	-3	6,600.00	4,571.18
	John BICKERTON	ENG	74	69	72	70	285	-3	6,600.00	4,571.18
	David CARTER	ENG	71	73	69	72	285	-3	6,600.00	4,571.18
	Michael JONZON	SWE	74	70	72	69	285	-3	6,600.00	4,571.18
	Francis VALERA	ESP	70	67	73	75	285	-3	6,600.00	4,571.18
	Christian L NILSSON	SWE	73	70	70	72	285	-3	6,600.00	4,571.18
41	Joakim BÄCKSTRÖM	SWE	73	70	69	74	286	-2	5,130.00	3,553.05
	Martin ERLANDSSON	SWE	73	74	69	70	286	-2	5,130.00	3,553.05
	Miguel Angel MARTIN	ESP	77	68	73	68	286	-2	5,130.00	3,553.05
	Birgir HAFTHORSSON	ISL	75	72	68	71	286	-2	5,130.00	3,553.05
	Steven O'HARA	SCO	67	79	66	74	286	-2	5,130.00	3,553.05
	Peter GUSTAFSSON	SWE	70	70	73	73	286	-2	5,130.00	3,553.05
	Matthew MILLAR	AUS	72	73	67	74	286	-2	5,130.00	3,553.05
48	Rhys DAVIES	WAL	76	70	72	69	287	-1	4,140.00	2,867.37
	Eirik Tage JOHANSEN	NOR	72	70	72	73	287	-1	4,140.00	2,867.37
	Rafael CABRERA BELLO	ESP	72	72	75	68	287	-1	4,140.00	2,867.37
	Marcel SIEM	GER	73	71	72	71	287	-1	4,140.00	2,867.37
52	Jean-François REMESY	FRA	71	69	70	78	288	0	3,510.00	2,431.03
	Steve ALKER	NZL	72	75	69	72	288	0	3,510.00	2,431.03
	Andrew TAMPION	AUS	71	73	73	71	288	0	3,510.00	2,431.03
55	Terry PILKADARIS	AUS	74	69	73	73	289	1	3,060.00	2,119.36
	Johan AXGREN	SWE	75	72	73	69	289	1	3,060.00	2,119.36
57	David PARK	WAL	73	71	71	76	291	3	2,745.00	1,901.19
	Kyron SULLIVAN	WAL	73	74	72	72	291	3	2,745.00	1,901.19
59	Lee SLATTERY	ENG	73	72	73	74	292	4	2,385.00	1,651.86
	Jarmo SANDELIN	SWE	74	73	69	76	292	4	2,385.00	1,651.86
	Zane SCOTLAND	ENG	74	73	72	73	292	4	2,385.00	1,651.86
	David DRYSDALE	SCO	72	73	77	70	292	4	2,385.00	1,651.86
	Carlos BALMASEDA	ESP	79	68	76	69	292	4	2,385.00	1,651.86
	Stuart LITTLE	ENG	71	76	71	74	292	4	2,385.00	1,651.86
65	Peter LAWRIE	IRL	71	75	72	75	293	5	2,070.00	1,433.69
66	Carl SUNESON	ESP	75	68	76	75	294	6	1,935.00	1,340.19
	Patrik SJÖLAND	SWE	72	75	78	69	294	6	1,935.00	1,340.19
68	Cesar MONASTERIO	ARG	73	73	70	79	295	7	1,800.00	1,246.68
69	Pedro LINHART	ESP	76	71	77	72	296	8	1,710.00	1,184.35
70	Mathew RICHARDSON	ENG	72	72	78	75	297	9	1,640.00	1,135.87
71	Agustin DOMINGO	ESP	75	72	76	78	301	13	1,350.00	935.01
72	Matthew ZIONS	AUS	71	75	W/D		146	2		

Total Prize Fund
€901,350   £624,277

Mother's Pride

1	**Steve WEBSTER**		**263**	**-25**
2	Robert KARLSSON		265	-23
3	Fredrik ANDERSSON HED		269	-19
	Peter HANSON		269	-19
	Daniel VANCSIK		269	-19
	Lee WESTWOOD		269	-19
7	Ross FISHER		271	-17
	Martin KAYMER		271	-17
	Charl SCHWARTZEL		271	-17
	Sam WALKER		271	-17

olf is a game of the heart and soul. It trawls deep into the emotions as the tears of many fine champions have shown. Like Ben Crenshaw at Augusta National in 1995; Tiger Woods at Hoylake in the summer of 2006; and Steve Webster at the climax to the inaugural Portugal Masters at the Oceânico Victoria Golf Club in Vilamoura.

Devastated by the loss of his beloved mother, Val, to cancer in May, the 32 year old Englishman believed he would struggle to hold onto his European Tour card in 2007 as a result. "But to win this season is just ... I can't believe it," said Webster who, in his moment of victory, paid tribute to his mother in a way which extended far beyond words.

The tears began as soon as the winning putt dropped, continued in the arms of caddie John Mulrooney on the way to the recorder's hut, and were still unquenchable in there in the embrace of his father Terry. After finally signing his card, Webster said: "I must phone my Nan." Yet, when they were connected, neither he nor his grandmother could utter one syllable - but then they did not really need to.

"The emotions really hit me," he admitted. "I was thinking about my mum all the time and I know she was watching out for me today. Even though it was hard to keep my mind on the golf, in a funny way, I think it helped me."

Certainly his scoring reflected that for, although high on emotion, Webster still managed to post the lowest score against par on The European Tour International Schedule in 2007 - closing with a 64 for a 25 under par total of 263 at a tournament which excelled on two counts.

For a start, Vilamoura was bathed in heavenly sunshine for the entire week, truly a blessing in a year where most of us have shivered in waterproofs at tournaments the world over, and secondly, with the ocean breezes barely rising above a whisper, little or no rough and relatively yielding greens, the spectators were treated to a veritable banquet of birdies and eagles.

It was a glorious throwback to the days when par was there to be beaten and greenkeepers cut grass instead of growing it. Okay, one could not feast like this every week, but it was distinctly refreshing for a change.

Talented young German Martin Kaymer set the ball rolling with his spectacular 61 early on Thursday,

Peter Hanson

Alexander Noren

Peter Lawrie

Robert Karlsson

Ross Fisher

equalling the low rounds of the year carded by Chapchai Nirat in the TCL Classic in March and Lee Westwood in the Mercedes-Benz Championship in September.

Remarkably, Kaymer had carded even lower in the past, shooting a 13 under par 59 in 2005 as a fledgling professional in a Satellite EPD Tour event in his homeland. Yet expectation weighed heavily on him during the second round at Vilamoura and he had to settle for a level par 72 on his way to a share of seventh.

Argentina's Daniel Vancsik led through 36 holes with Sweden's Martin Erlandsson, England's Ross Fisher, Spain's Alvaro Quiros and Webster tied second, the latter thoroughly enjoying two rounds of 66 in the relaxed company of fellow Midlander Sam Walker, his regular practice partner and good friend.

Into the weekend, Webster remained relentless in his march towards a second career victory to follow that of the Telecom Italia Open in 2005. Even when two bogeys early in his back nine on Saturday threatened to slow him, a hat-trick of birdies from the 15th got him within one stroke of Vancsik entering the final round.

Oceânico Victoria Golf Club's perilous par five 12th would prove pivotal for both men on Sunday,

Webster rolling home an eight foot eagle putt at the very moment Vancsik pulled his tee shot into the hazard, setting up a stinging bogey six.

Webster then birdied the 13th, 16th and 17th, giving himself such a comfortable cushion that he could afford to settle for a 'safe' bogey at the 18th after pushing his drive into the rough. His superlative closing round of 64 was the best by a tournament winner in 2007 and good enough to beat Sweden's Robert Karlsson, who closed with a 65, by two shots.

Webster might have been comfortable at the finish but it was not easy for a man who had had to claw his way out of the despair in mid-season. "This means so much to me," he said.

"Four months ago I was near the bottom of the Order of Merit and didn't really know if I could turn it around. Losing my mum really knocked me about. It was tough but I had a good week at Loch Lomond where I finished tied for eighth place and that helped me turn the corner."

Karl MacGinty
Irish Independent

Portugal

To be continued… at an unforgettable dinner

www.visitportugal.com

TURISMO DE
PORTUGAL

Martin Kaymer

Steve Webster (right) receives the trophy from Manuel Pinho, the Portugal Minister of Economy and Innovation

> It's one of those courses, there's so many birdies out there, you have to keep your foot on the pedal really. It's in great condition and the weather has been amazing all week.
>
> *Steve Webster*

The Course

Designed by the Arnold Palmer Course Design Company in 2004, the course's first public appearance came when it hosted the World Cup in 2005 before staging the inaugural Portugal Masters in 2007. A huge amount of care went into preserving the wetlands and foliage of the area so the course, in particular the back nine, plays around stunning water features. Was recognised as the best golf course in the country in 2006 by the Portuguese Tourist Board.

Oceânico Victoria Golf Club
Par **72**   Yards **7177**   Metres **6560**

Final Results

Pos	Name		Rd1	Rd2	Rd3	Rd4	Total		€	£
1	Steve WEBSTER	ENG	66	66	67	64	263	-25	500,000.00	348,279.15
2	Robert KARLSSON	SWE	67	68	65	65	265	-23	333,330.00	232,183.78
3	Fredrik ANDERSSON HED	SWE	66	73	64	66	269	-19	142,500.00	99,259.56
	Peter HANSON	SWE	69	65	67	68	269	-19	142,500.00	99,259.56
	Lee WESTWOOD	ENG	65	69	67	68	269	-19	142,500.00	99,259.56
	Daniel VANCSIK	ARG	64	66	68	71	269	-19	142,500.00	99,259.56
7	Charl SCHWARTZEL	RSA	66	67	66	72	271	-17	73,050.00	50,883.58
	Sam WALKER	ENG	66	68	67	70	271	-17	73,050.00	50,883.58
	Martin KAYMER	GER	61	72	69	69	271	-17	73,050.00	50,883.58
	Ross FISHER	ENG	68	64	68	71	271	-17	73,050.00	50,883.58
11	Alvaro QUIROS	ESP	66	66	70	70	272	-16	55,200.00	38,450.02
12	Alexander NOREN	SWE	68	69	67	69	273	-15	47,475.00	33,069.11
	Thongchai JAIDEE	THA	71	67	66	69	273	-15	47,475.00	33,069.11
	Robert-Jan DERKSEN	NED	69	70	69	65	273	-15	47,475.00	33,069.11
	Bradley DREDGE	WAL	68	72	67	66	273	-15	47,475.00	33,069.11
16	James KINGSTON	RSA	68	69	70	67	274	-14	38,940.00	27,123.98
	James HEPWORTH	ENG	67	68	70	69	274	-14	38,940.00	27,123.98
	Peter HEDBLOM	SWE	67	71	67	69	274	-14	38,940.00	27,123.98
	Peter LAWRIE	IRL	67	71	68	68	274	-14	38,940.00	27,123.98
	Brett RUMFORD	AUS	67	71	66	70	274	-14	38,940.00	27,123.98
21	Nick DOUGHERTY	ENG	66	73	68	68	275	-13	30,750.00	21,419.17
	Retief GOOSEN	RSA	65	72	69	69	275	-13	30,750.00	21,419.17
	Andres ROMERO	ARG	69	71	69	66	275	-13	30,750.00	21,419.17
	José-Filipe LIMA	POR	69	68	65	73	275	-13	30,750.00	21,419.17
	Ariel CANETE	ARG	66	70	69	70	275	-13	30,750.00	21,419.17
	Pablo MARTIN	ESP	69	70	67	69	275	-13	30,750.00	21,419.17
	Oliver WILSON	ENG	68	70	68	69	275	-13	30,750.00	21,419.17
	Anthony WALL	ENG	71	68	70	66	275	-13	30,750.00	21,419.17
	Justin ROSE	ENG	69	70	66	70	275	-13	30,750.00	21,419.17
	Mattias ELIASSON	SWE	69	72	65	69	275	-13	30,750.00	21,419.17
31	Gary MURPHY	IRL	68	71	68	69	276	-12	24,900.00	17,344.30
	Paul BROADHURST	ENG	72	66	70	68	276	-12	24,900.00	17,344.30
	Francesco MOLINARI	ITA	66	72	72	66	276	-12	24,900.00	17,344.30
34	Søren HANSEN	DEN	72	65	70	70	277	-11	21,600.00	15,045.66
	Sam LITTLE	ENG	67	69	70	71	277	-11	21,600.00	15,045.66
	Jean-François LUCQUIN	FRA	66	73	74	64	277	-11	21,600.00	15,045.66
	Stephen DODD	WAL	69	71	71	66	277	-11	21,600.00	15,045.66
	Martin ERLANDSSON	SWE	64	68	71	74	277	-11	21,600.00	15,045.66
	Marc WARREN	SCO	71	70	69	67	277	-11	21,600.00	15,045.66
40	Rafael ECHENIQUE	ARG	67	71	72	68	278	-10	18,000.00	12,538.05
	Steven JEPPESEN	SWE	70	69	72	67	278	-10	18,000.00	12,538.05
	Christian L NILSSON	SWE	70	67	70	71	278	-10	18,000.00	12,538.05
	Jeev Milkha SINGH	IND	70	67	70	71	278	-10	18,000.00	12,538.05
	Alessandro TADINI	ITA	69	71	70	68	278	-10	18,000.00	12,538.05
	David LYNN	ENG	70	69	71	68	278	-10	18,000.00	12,538.05
46	Simon KHAN	ENG	71	70	71	67	279	-9	13,800.00	9,612.50
	Thomas BJÖRN	DEN	70	70	68	71	279	-9	13,800.00	9,612.50
	Jarmo SANDELIN	SWE	67	72	73	67	279	-9	13,800.00	9,612.50
	Miles TUNNICLIFF	ENG	69	72	70	68	279	-9	13,800.00	9,612.50
	Emanuele CANONICA	ITA	66	70	73	70	279	-9	13,800.00	9,612.50
	Barry LANE	ENG	67	71	71	70	279	-9	13,800.00	9,612.50
	Santiago LUNA	ESP	69	71	68	71	279	-9	13,800.00	9,612.50
	Mads VIBE-HASTRUP	DEN	67	68	69	75	279	-9	13,800.00	9,612.50
54	Grégory HAVRET	FRA	71	70	71	68	280	-8	10,800.00	7,522.83
	Carl SUNESON	ESP	69	70	73	68	280	-8	10,800.00	7,522.83
56	Terry PRICE	AUS	67	73	70	71	281	-7	9,225.00	6,425.75
	Lee SLATTERY	ENG	70	69	73	69	281	-7	9,225.00	6,425.75
	Richard FINCH	ENG	72	68	71	70	281	-7	9,225.00	6,425.75
	Rory MCILROY	NIR	71	69	73	68	281	-7	9,225.00	6,425.75
60	Peter GUSTAFSSON	SWE	69	71	66	76	282	-6	8,100.00	5,642.12
	Marcel SIEM	GER	70	71	70	71	282	-6	8,100.00	5,642.12
	Andrew MCLARDY	RSA	66	72	68	76	282	-6	8,100.00	5,642.12
63	Grégory BOURDY	FRA	65	74	71	73	283	-5	7,500.00	5,224.19
64	Shiv KAPUR	IND	67	70	70	77	284	-4	6,900.00	4,806.25
	Mark FOSTER	ENG	70	71	72	71	284	-4	6,900.00	4,806.25
	Damien MCGRANE	IRL	69	72	71	72	284	-4	6,900.00	4,806.25
67	Phillip ARCHER	ENG	67	72	73	73	285	-3	6,150.00	4,283.83
	Paul LAWRIE	SCO	68	72	76	69	285	-3	6,150.00	4,283.83
69	Tiago CRUZ	POR	71	70	71	74	286	-2	5,700.00	3,970.38
70	David PARK	WAL	71	68	73	75	287	-1	5,470.00	3,810.17
71	Raphaël JACQUELIN	FRA	68	67	81	73	289	1	4,500.00	3,134.51
72	David FROST	RSA	67	69	76	79	291	3	4,497.00	3,132.42
73	Miguel Angel JIMÉNEZ	ESP	71	69	75	77	292	4	4,494.00	3,130.33

Total Prize Fund

€3,013,491   £2,099,072

Customary Greeting

1	**Grégory BOURDY**		268	-12
2	Sam LITTLE		270	-10
3	Robert-Jan DERKSEN		271	-9
4	Alastair FORSYTH		273	-7
5	Johan EDFORS		274	-6
	Peter LAWRIE		274	-6
7	Richard FINCH		275	-5
	José Manuel LARA		275	-5
	Jean-François LUCQUIN		275	-5
	Alexander NOREN		275	-5

Question one: What connection is there between Rafael Nadal and the Mallorca Classic? Easy. The island's favourite son - from nearby Manacor - played alongside Sergio Garcia in the Pro-Am and acquitted himself very favourably. Slightly better, in fact, than the pre-tournament favourite did in the event, Garcia finishing in a tie for 16th place, nine shots adrift of the impressive champion, Frenchman Grégory Bourdy, who claimed his maiden European Tour title with a degree of style and panache.

Question two: What does Roger Federer have in connection with the Mallorca Classic? Harder. No, he did not emulate Ivan Lendl and play in a professional golf event, although it almost goes without saying that he is a good player. Neither did he arrive as a supporter of the event as he had done at the HSBC Champions when watching pal Tiger Woods. The answer to the link between Federer, and indeed Nadal, and the Mallorca Classic, is, Stuart Burridge.

Here's why. Palma de Mallorca played host to the 'Battle of the Surfaces' in May when the world's greatest grass court player (Federer) and tennis' top clay proponent (Nadal) played on a court made half-and-half of each surface, a unique contest eventually won by the Spaniard. However, there was a problem with the lawn laid in the Palma Arena. To the rescue at less than a day's notice came one Stuart Burridge, the greenkeeper at Pula Golf Club, who performed similar heroics keeping the turf playable during the week of the Mallorca Classic.

A heavy thunderstorm brought an abrupt halt to the opening day's play, and the subsequent rain felt relentless. Indeed, things got so bad that two members of the television production team decided their buggy could negotiate the 'puddle' in the tunnel between the two halves of the course. When the motor cut out and left them stranded, they climbed onto the seats to evade the rising waters as two saviours waded in to push the buggy clear. The tidemark the next morning was well above hip height.

Not that it was the first time the golf club had suffered as a result of the elements. Earlier in the month a tornado had struck the island. The lake by the ninth flooded the adjacent fairway and a call came through later in the day asking why were there carp in the bunkers on the 14th? Scooping them into wheelie bins later in the day eventually appeased the members!

Therefore, it was a remarkable job the greenkeeping team did to make the course playable for the remainder of the Mallorca Classic, and to make sure the disruption did not prevent the tournament ending on time. It was

remarkable, too, that three players near the top of the leader board after round one - Niclas Fasth, Andrew McLardy and Gary Murphy - were the same three who initially dominated proceedings in 2006. This time, however, all three faltered, including the defending champion Fasth.

The first round continued into day two, the second round into the third day, and the third circuit into Sunday morning. The weather improved, but it left little time for tournament staff to position the new pin placings as Dutchman Robert-Jan Derksen and Bourdy shared a nine under par aggregate of 201 and the lead going into the final round.

He might not be used to winning on The European Tour but Bourdy's performance made light of that fact as he bounded to a closing 67, got lucky when narrowly avoiding the water with his approach shot at the 16th, and subsequently became the 18th first time winner of The 2007

Sergio Garcia

Richard Finch

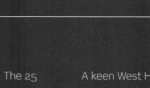

Jean-François Lucquin

Sam Little

European Tour season, a record number. The 25 year old from Bordeaux received the customary greeting from his fellow Frenchmen with the champagne free flowing on the 18th green as he sealed a two stroke victory.

Yet, given the position of the tournament in the calendar, the celebrations did not end with the man who secured a last gasp place in the Volvo Masters, for the man in second spot secured perhaps an even bigger prize, namely his career.

England's Sam Little began the week in 136th place on the Order of Merit. He had had both a wonderful but disruptive time during the Johnnie Walker Championship at Gleneagles in August. His wife, Maria, gave birth to twin daughters eight weeks prematurely and although he continued to play in the weeks following the birth, he did not play well. He seemed destined for a return to the Qualifying School before a share of seventh place in the Open de Madrid Valle Romano a fortnight before lifted his confidence and with his runners-up performance at Pula Golf Club, he ensured he no longer needed to fit San Roque into his schedule.

A keen West Ham fan, Little likened his great escape to their survival in the English Premiership at the end of the 2006/2007 season. Indeed, survival was the name of the game, too, for compatriot Richard Finch and Jarmo Sandelin of Sweden who ensured their playing privileges for the 2008 season via the Order of Merit at the last possible moment through their respective finishes.

Finally, though, spare a thought for young Englishman Lee Slattery. His missed cut in the Mallorca Classic cost him his card as he finished a mere €77 (£53) behind Sandelin. Another perfect example of the fine line between glory and sheer frustration.

Nick Dye
European Tour Radio

Un Oasis de lujo en Palma
A luxury Oasis in Palma
Eine Oasis des luxus in Palma

Grupotel Valparaíso Palace
H O T E L
★★★★★

The Course

Located in the north east of the island, the course was founded in 1995 but has undergone extensive redesign over the past three years under the watchful eye of two time Masters Tournament Champion José Maria Olazábal. Not the longest of venues used on The 2007 European Tour International Schedule, but care is nevertheless required on a course where greens are visible from the tee on 14 holes. Ever present wind means care is always required on club selection.

Grégory Bourdy (right) is presented with the trophy by Joan Sastre, General Manager of Tourist Promotion from the Balearic Government

Robert-Jan Derksen

> I did think it was in the water at the 16th so I was very relieved when I saw it bounce in the rough in front of the green. It was a bit lucky but sometimes these little things go your way and perhaps that signifies that it is your day. To get my first win on Tour feels absolutely fantastic.
>
> **Grégory Bourdy**

Pula Golf Club

Par **70**   Yards **6850**   Metres **6263**

Final Results

Pos	Name		Rd1	Rd2	Rd3	Rd4	Total		€	£
1	Grégory BOURDY	FRA	69	68	64	67	268	-12	333,330.00	232,098.09
2	Sam LITTLE	ENG	66	69	68	67	270	-10	222,220.00	154,732.06
3	Robert-Jan DERKSEN	NED	66	65	70	70	271	-9	125,200.00	87,176.92
4	Alastair FORSYTH	SCO	68	69	70	66	273	-7	100,000.00	69,630.12
5	Peter LAWRIE	IRL	66	68	68	72	274	-6	77,400.00	53,893.72
	Johan EDFORS	SWE	68	71	68	67	274	-6	77,400.00	53,893.72
7	Jean-François LUCQUIN	FRA	66	65	71	73	275	-5	48,700.00	33,909.87
	José Manuel LARA	ESP	71	70	68	66	275	-5	48,700.00	33,909.87
	Richard FINCH	ENG	68	69	66	72	275	-5	48,700.00	33,909.87
	Alexander NOREN	SWE	71	69	64	71	275	-5	48,700.00	33,909.87
11	Thongchai JAIDEE	THA	71	64	75	66	276	-4	32,680.00	22,755.12
	Graeme MCDOWELL	NIR	71	67	70	68	276	-4	32,680.00	22,755.12
	Mattias ELIASSON	SWE	69	72	65	70	276	-4	32,680.00	22,755.12
	Christian CÉVAÉR	FRA	71	70	67	68	276	-4	32,680.00	22,755.12
	Thomas BJÖRN	DEN	71	67	68	70	276	-4	32,680.00	22,755.12
16	Sergio GARCIA	ESP	68	67	69	73	277	-3	27,600.00	19,217.91
	Graeme STORM	ENG	67	73	67	70	277	-3	27,600.00	19,217.91
18	Mark FOSTER	ENG	67	75	65	71	278	-2	24,866.67	17,314.69
	Miguel Angel JIMÉNEZ	ESP	73	69	68	68	278	-2	24,866.67	17,314.69
	Carl SUNESON	ESP	72	64	70	72	278	-2	24,866.67	17,314.69
21	Francesco MOLINARI	ITA	68	68	72	71	279	-1	21,700.00	15,109.74
	Paul LAWRIE	SCO	69	68	72	70	279	-1	21,700.00	15,109.74
	Barry LANE	ENG	68	68	73	70	279	-1	21,700.00	15,109.74
	Y E YANG	KOR	68	72	72	67	279	-1	21,700.00	15,109.74
	Rafael CABRERA BELLO	ESP	68	74	72	65	279	-1	21,700.00	15,109.74
	Matthew MILLAR	AUS	71	67	71	70	279	-1	21,700.00	15,109.74
27	Gonzalo FDEZ-CASTAÑO	ESP	71	69	68	72	280	0	17,800.00	12,394.16
	Jean-François REMESY	FRA	69	68	73	70	280	0	17,800.00	12,394.16
	Anthony WALL	ENG	72	69	69	70	280	0	17,800.00	12,394.16
	Andrew MCLARDY	RSA	66	73	70	71	280	0	17,800.00	12,394.16
	Markus BRIER	AUT	70	69	69	72	280	0	17,800.00	12,394.16
	Niclas FASTH	SWE	65	70	79	66	280	0	17,800.00	12,394.16
	Marcel SIEM	GER	68	68	70	74	280	0	17,800.00	12,394.16
34	Paul MCGINLEY	IRL	71	72	66	72	281	1	14,600.00	10,166.00
	Damien MCGRANE	IRL	71	70	70	70	281	1	14,600.00	10,166.00
	Søren KJELDSEN	DEN	69	69	73	70	281	1	14,600.00	10,166.00
	Mads VIBE-HASTRUP	DEN	68	66	74	73	281	1	14,600.00	10,166.00
	Wade ORMSBY	AUS	70	70	69	72	281	1	14,600.00	10,166.00
39	Robert ROCK	ENG	69	68	70	75	282	2	12,600.00	8,773.40
	Carlos RODILES	ESP	74	68	69	71	282	2	12,600.00	8,773.40
	Thomas LEVET	FRA	70	71	69	72	282	2	12,600.00	8,773.40
	Gary ORR	SCO	70	69	72	71	282	2	12,600.00	8,773.40
	Benn BARHAM	ENG	70	72	71	69	282	2	12,600.00	8,773.40
44	Simon WAKEFIELD	ENG	69	71	70	73	283	3	10,400.00	7,241.53
	Francis VALERA	ESP	69	73	70	71	283	3	10,400.00	7,241.53
	Pedro LINHART	ESP	68	74	70	71	283	3	10,400.00	7,241.53
	Peter O'MALLEY	AUS	70	73	68	72	283	3	10,400.00	7,241.53
	Richard BLAND	ENG	72	69	71	71	283	3	10,400.00	7,241.53
	Phillip ARCHER	ENG	70	72	71	70	283	3	10,400.00	7,241.53
50	Miles TUNNICLIFF	ENG	71	72	69	72	284	4	8,600.00	5,988.19
	Jarmo SANDELIN	SWE	70	73	71	70	284	4	8,600.00	5,988.19
	Peter GUSTAFSSON	SWE	71	71	72	70	284	4	8,600.00	5,988.19
53	Jyoti RANDHAWA	IND	68	69	75	73	285	5	6,833.33	4,758.06
	Jesus Maria ARRUTI	ESP	70	69	74	72	285	5	6,833.33	4,758.06
	Ian GARBUTT	ENG	69	69	73	74	285	5	6,833.33	4,758.06
	Phillip PRICE	WAL	69	72	72	72	285	5	6,833.33	4,758.06
	Alessandro TADINI	ITA	68	73	73	71	285	5	6,833.33	4,758.06
	Gary MURPHY	IRL	66	74	68	77	285	5	6,833.33	4,758.06
59	Emanuele CANONICA	ITA	69	69	73	75	286	6	5,600.00	3,899.29
	Brett RUMFORD	AUS	71	72	70	73	286	6	5,600.00	3,899.29
	Steven O'HARA	SCO	73	68	75	70	286	6	5,600.00	3,899.29
62	Luis CLAVERIE	ESP	67	70	74	76	287	7	5,000.00	3,481.51
	Alvaro SALTO	ESP	71	71	72	73	287	7	5,000.00	3,481.51
	Andrew MARSHALL	ENG	69	74	72	72	287	7	5,000.00	3,481.51
65	Joakim BÄCKSTRÖM	SWE	67	73	71	77	288	8	4,200.00	2,924.47
	Marcus HIGLEY	ENG	73	67	76	72	288	8	4,200.00	2,924.47
	Stephen DODD	WAL	74	68	74	72	288	8	4,200.00	2,924.47
	Andrew COLTART	SCO	69	74	70	75	288	8	4,200.00	2,924.47
	Christopher HANELL	SWE	72	71	71	74	288	8	4,200.00	2,924.47
70	Ariel CANETE	ARG	69	71	75	74	289	9	3,650.00	2,541.50
71	James HEPWORTH	ENG	67	74	75	78	294	14	3,000.00	2,088.90

Total Prize Fund

€2,003,000   £1,394,691

Raising the Standards

1	**Justin ROSE**		283	-1
2	Simon DYSON		283	-1
	Søren KJELDSEN		283	-1
4	Padraig HARRINGTON		285	1
	Graeme McDOWELL		285	1
6	Martin KAYMER		288	4
7	Miguel Angel JIMÉNEZ		289	5
8	Ian POULTER		290	6
9	Thomas BJÖRN		291	7
	Jyoti RANDHAWA		291	7

From Nick Faldo, the first winner in 1988, to Justin Rose in 2007, the Volvo Masters has produced some very special champions. It is fitting because the tournament – played for the 20th time and for the 15th time at Club de Golf Valderrama – has been championed by two very special men over all those years.

Don Jaime Ortiz-Patiño, the driving force behind Valderrama's success, and Mel Pyatt, President & CEO of Volvo Event Management, are a truly remarkable duo who, together, helped move standards forward not only at the Volvo Masters but across The European Tour as a whole.

It was Pyatt who was chosen by Volvo to oversee their involvement in golf from 1988, a decision put into perspective by Colin Montgomerie, the only man to play in all 20 editions of the tournament. "Every player must be thankful to Volvo and Mel Pyatt for their visionary approach," said the Scot. "Once the Volvo Masters was established at Valderrama, every other tournament on the circuit had to raise its standards."

Little wonder then that the pair rejoiced at perhaps one of the most thrilling Volvo Masters finishes in history to help celebrate the tournament's 20th anniversary, a denouement which also produced a champion linked to the man who started the ball rolling.

For while Rose is unquestionably continuing his rise to the top of the game – the victory not only sealed his position as The European Tour's Number One for 2007 but also saw him move up to seventh on the Official World Golf Ranking – Faldo now holds the honour of being European Ryder Cup Captain and very possibly leading a Team containing Rose at Valhalla Golf Club in Kentucky in September, 2008.

Back in 1988, Faldo won the inaugural Volvo Masters from Seve Ballesteros, Sandy Lyle and Ian Woosnam in places second to fourth. Players such as the illustrious quartet were the reason Rose, like so many, got into golf in the first place.

Rose, who as an amateur stunned the world of golf by finishing tied fourth in The 1998 Open Championship at Royal Birkdale ten days before his 18th birthday, has had his ups and downs since then, but winning the MasterCard Masters in Australia – the third event of The 2007 European Tour International Schedule – proved a turning point.

Subsequent runners-up finishes at Wentworth Club, Firestone Country Club and St Andrews, in addition to cool and consistent showings in all four of the season's Major Championships, put him in contention for the Order of Merit heading for Valderrama and the equation was simple. Ernie Els led but was not playing, competing instead in Singapore. Open Champion Padraig Harrington and Rose were second and third respectively. Each needed to finish in the top three and ahead of the other to claim the Harry Vardon Trophy.

Rose suffered from food poisoning on Thursday morning and though deathly pale in appearance, a hole-in-one at the third brought colour to his cheeks and was a welcome boost on his way to an opening 70. Harrington started poorly but gritted his teeth as the heroic Irishman does so well in

Simon Dyson

Padraig Harrington

Søren Kjeldsen

Graeme McDowell

Robert Karlsson

a crisis and came home in four under par for a battling 71.

The windy conditions which lasted the week made life difficult for all competitors but, nevertheless, the pair ascended to the top of the leaderboard on day two, Rose leading by four from Harrington after a stunning 68 – the only player from the 55-strong field to break 70 on the Friday.

The Englishman's advantage remained the same after day three and still four ahead with eight to play on Sunday it looked all over before it almost all disappeared. Bunkered twice at the 11th on his way to a double-bogey seven, Rose followed that with dropped shots at both the 13th and 14th holes. Suddenly, the drama was at its peak.

Dane Søren Kjeldsen had birdied four of the first seven holes to move into contention while England's Simon Dyson almost holed his second at the 16th before his birdie there, and at the 17th, put him firmly in the mix. Elsewhere, Northern Ireland's Graeme McDowell holed a seven iron from 176 yards for an albatross two at the 17th to catapult himself into the frame, albeit briefly.

Harrington could not find the birdies he needed at either the 17th or the 18th and had to make do with a share of fourth place with McDowell, whose rollercoaster finish saw him end with a double-bogey six at the 18th after an errant drive found the cork trees.

After his earlier trauma, Rose settled with a par at the 16th and a birdie at the 17th. However all three of the main protagonists – Dyson, Kjeldsen and Rose – bogeyed the 72nd hole leading to a three-way play-off.

After all registered par fours on their immediate return to the 18th, all had birdie chances at the second extra hole – the 389 yard tenth – but Rose, from 12 feet, was the only one to find the bottom of the cup, the ball dropping to signal a rush of relief.

"There must be an easy way to do these things but that wasn't it," admitted the 27 year old. "However, there is no giving up at Valderrama, just as at any Major Championship. To be Europe's Number One is awesome. The best thing is that I hoped to do it this way, as a champion."

Andy Farrell
Independent on Sunday

VOLVO MASTERS

20 YEARS
• 1988 - 2007 •

A Score to be Proud of – It's Par for the Course

2007 marked a major milestone for Volvo and European golf. The most far-reaching and long-lasting partnership between a blue-chip brand and gilt-edged golf celebrated its 20th anniversary year in style.

Ever since 1988, when Ian Woosnam won the first Volvo PGA Championship at Wentworth and Nick Faldo the Volvo Masters at Valderrama, with the irrepressible Seve Ballesteros winning the inaugural Volvo Order of Merit, quality, integrity and longevity have become the watchwords for European golf.

As Volvo and The European Tour celebrate a generation of partnership in golf, the pioneering phase - initially in Europe then as the first global brand to lead where others have followed into China - long since having made way for assurance and continuance, the next chapter of golf's success story is about to be written.

With the future of the Volvo Masters confirmed until 2010 and the Volvo China Open through to 2015, the most enduring corporate commitment in world golf going forward has, for Volvo and The European Tour, become par for the course.

Volvo Event Management | Hunderenveldlaan, 10 | BE-1082 Brussels | Belgium | Tel. +32 2 482 56 83 | Fax +32 2 468 12 20
E-mail info.sponsorship@volvo.com | www.volvomasters.com

A SCORE TO BE PROUD OF

VOLVO

Don Jaime Ortiz-Patiño (centre), the Past President of Valderrama, with George O'Grady (centre left), Chief Executive of The European Tour, and Richard Hills (centre right), The European Ryder Cup Director and the Trustees of Golf Environment Europe who held their year-end conference during the week of the Volvo Masters

i England's Justin Rose won The European Tour Order of Merit for 2007 having played just 12 European Tour Order of Merit events. Only Peter Oosterhuis, in 1972, who claimed the Number One crown from 11 starts, has won The Order of Merit title in fewer tournaments.

The Course

One of the best known golf courses in the world and its manicured fairways and greens presented the perfect platform for the 20th anniversary staging of the Volvo Masters. Designed by Robert Trent Jones, the course has two prevailing winds; the warm poniente from the land and the cooler levanter from the sea. Depending on which one is blowing, it adds variety to a golf course that is already rich in shot values. Strategic play is required on every shot to avoid the water hazards, the cork trees, or running out of position on the demanding greens.

From left to right: Mel Pyatt, President & CEO of Volvo Event Management, Justin Rose and George O'Grady, Chief Executive of The European Tour with the Harry Vardon Trophy and the Volvo Masters trophy after Rose won the Order of Merit and the Volvo Masters at Valderrama

Club de Golf Valderrama
Par 71   Yards **6952**   Metres **6356**

Final Results

Pos	Name		Rd1	Rd2	Rd3	Rd4	Total		€	£
1	Justin ROSE	ENG	70	68	71	74	283	-1	666,660.00	467,644.52
2	Søren KJELDSEN	DEN	73	70	73	67	283	-1	347,420.00	243,706.03
	Simon DYSON	ENG	74	70	69	70	283	-1	347,420.00	243,706.03
4	Padraig HARRINGTON	IRL	71	71	71	72	285	1	184,800.00	129,632.36
	Graeme MCDOWELL	NIR	68	75	74	68	285	1	184,800.00	129,632.36
6	Martin KAYMER	GER	72	78	66	72	288	4	140,000.00	98,206.33
7	Miguel Angel JIMÉNEZ	ESP	73	70	77	69	289	5	120,000.00	84,176.86
8	Ian POULTER	ENG	76	71	69	74	290	6	100,000.00	70,147.38
9	Thomas BJÖRN	DEN	76	73	70	72	291	7	84,800.00	59,484.98
	Jyoti RANDHAWA	IND	73	70	74	74	291	7	84,800.00	59,484.98
11	Robert KARLSSON	SWE	77	70	71	74	292	8	74,600.00	52,329.95
12	Paul MCGINLEY	IRL	69	75	74	75	293	9	66,900.00	46,928.60
	Anthony WALL	ENG	73	74	72	74	293	9	66,900.00	46,928.60
14	Alex CEJKA	GER	78	70	70	76	294	10	59,900.00	42,018.28
	Ross FISHER	ENG	71	80	71	72	294	10	59,900.00	42,018.28
	Peter HANSON	SWE	75	72	74	73	294	10	59,900.00	42,018.28
17	Colin MONTGOMERIE	SCO	72	73	71	79	295	11	52,500.00	36,827.37
	Raphaël JACQUELIN	FRA	71	73	79	72	295	11	52,500.00	36,827.37
	Francesco MOLINARI	ITA	75	71	76	73	295	11	52,500.00	36,827.37
	Markus BRIER	AUT	76	72	74	73	295	11	52,500.00	36,827.37
21	Oliver WILSON	ENG	74	75	71	76	296	12	48,700.00	34,161.77
22	Gonzalo FDEZ-CASTAÑO	ESP	74	75	76	73	298	14	46,100.00	32,337.94
	Niclas FASTH	SWE	75	70	76	77	298	14	46,100.00	32,337.94
	Peter HEDBLOM	SWE	77	72	78	71	298	14	46,100.00	32,337.94
25	Nick DOUGHERTY	ENG	75	76	73	76	300	16	38,800.00	27,217.18
	Paul CASEY	ENG	80	73	72	75	300	16	38,800.00	27,217.18
	Jeev Milkha SINGH	IND	76	74	74	76	300	16	38,800.00	27,217.18
	Søren HANSEN	DEN	75	74	70	81	300	16	38,800.00	27,217.18
	Andres ROMERO	ARG	76	76	78	70	300	16	38,800.00	27,217.18
	Brett RUMFORD	AUS	73	74	75	78	300	16	38,800.00	27,217.18
	Peter O'MALLEY	AUS	70	75	75	80	300	16	38,800.00	27,217.18
	Anders HANSEN	DEN	72	77	75	76	300	16	38,800.00	27,217.18
	Simon WAKEFIELD	ENG	75	74	77	74	300	16	38,800.00	27,217.18
34	Luke DONALD	ENG	72	75	76	78	301	17	32,250.00	22,622.53
	Sergio GARCIA	ESP	77	72	73	79	301	17	32,250.00	22,622.53
	Grégory BOURDY	FRA	75	72	77	77	301	17	32,250.00	22,622.53
	Richard STERNE	RSA	75	70	78	78	301	17	32,250.00	22,622.53
38	Robert-Jan DERKSEN	NED	73	77	81	71	302	18	28,650.00	20,097.22
	Alastair FORSYTH	SCO	75	73	77	77	302	18	28,650.00	20,097.22
	Henrik STENSON	SWE	76	78	71	77	302	18	28,650.00	20,097.22
	Yong-eun YANG	KOR	74	74	78	76	302	18	28,650.00	20,097.22
42	Mark FOSTER	ENG	76	78	76	74	304	20	25,500.00	17,887.58
	Pelle EDBERG	SWE	79	73	74	78	304	20	25,500.00	17,887.58
	Marc WARREN	SCO	82	75	71	76	304	20	25,500.00	17,887.58
45	Phillip ARCHER	ENG	76	78	74	77	305	21	23,700.00	16,624.93
46	Steve WEBSTER	ENG	79	74	78	75	306	22	22,800.00	15,993.60
47	Graeme STORM	ENG	81	74	77	75	307	23	21,000.00	14,730.95
	Simon KHAN	ENG	75	79	79	74	307	23	21,000.00	14,730.95
	Fredrik ANDERSSON HED	SWE	81	74	80	72	307	23	21,000.00	14,730.95
50	Thongchai JAIDEE	THA	73	78	80	77	308	24	18,333.33	12,860.35
	Bradley DREDGE	WAL	75	72	83	78	308	24	18,333.33	12,860.35
	Mikko ILONEN	FIN	83	72	78	75	308	24	18,333.33	12,860.35
53	Grégory HAVRET	FRA	83	73	76	77	309	25	16,800.00	11,784.76
54	Sandy LYLE	SCO	84	81	72	78	315	31	16,300.00	11,434.02
55	Ronan RAFFERTY	NIR	83	89	W/D				15,800.00	11,083.29

Total Prize Fund
€3,928,500 £2,755,740

Good Timing

The 2007 Omega Mission Hills World Cup launched a new and exciting era in the history of this prestigious event, first played as the Canada Cup in 1953.

Tradition and romance have become bywords in the annals of a competition which has enjoyed such winning partnerships as Kel Nagle and Peter Thomson, Ben Hogan and Sam Snead, Jack Nicklaus and Arnold Palmer, Seve Ballesteros and Manuel Piñero, Fred Couples and Davis Love III, Padraig Harrington and Paul McGinley, David Duval and Tiger Woods, Ernie Els and Retief Goosen and Paul Casey and Luke Donald to name but a few.

Now the tradition will continue through to 2018, and most probably beyond, at Mission Hills following the signing of an agreement which brought the prestige watch manufacturer Omega together with the Club which introduced the game of golf to China by first hosting the World Cup in 1995.

For the International Federation of PGA Tours, now the custodians of what is recognised throughout sport as 'The Olympics of Golf', this was indeed a proud and momentous announcement. John Jay Hopkins, the noted Canadian industrialist, brought a dream that the game of golf could promote goodwill between nations to reality when the event was first played in 1953 in Montreal and called the Canada

Cup. This founded the International Golf Association and they grew the event as the game gathered popularity around the world so that its international image was reflected in a change of name in 1967 to The World Cup.

Forty years on that image burns even brighter and, coincidentally, the 53rd edition of the event unfolded less than a year before the staging in Beijing of the Olympic Games at which Omega has a unique role as Official Timekeeper.

Stephen Urquhart, President of Omega, stated: "Omega has an unparalleled position in China and recently celebrated 111 years presence in this significant market. The Omega Mission Hills World Cup seals our commitment to the world of golf and represents an exciting opportunity to further develop our activities in this sport."

Dr David Chu, Group Chairman, Mission Hills Group, said: "Being the largest golf facility in the world, we are proud that the Omega Mission Hills World Cup will be held here for the next 12 years. We are making history in the fine chronicle of golf. China

Zhang Lian-wei (left) and Liang Wen-chong

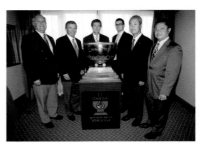

The return of the World Cup trophy to active service was endorsed by the International Federation of PGA Tours at Carnoustie in Scotland during The 136th Open Championship in July. Pictured with the impressive trophy are (left to right): Johan Immelman, Commissioner, Sunshine Tour; Tim Finchem, Commissioner, PGA Tour; George O'Grady, Chief Executive, The European Tour; Ben Sellenger, CEO, PGA Tour of Australasia; Kosaku Shimada, Chairman, Japan Golf Tour and Kyi Hla Han, Executive Chairman, Asian Tour

***Below** Ben Hogan and Sam Snead*

Colin Montgomerie (left) and Marc Warren

MISSION HILLS
—GOLF CLUB·CHINA—
觀瀾湖高爾夫球會

216 洞
Holes
World's No.1

Guinness World Records™

World's No.1

Omega celebrated its status as the title sponsor of one of the oldest and most prestigious global golf team events with the launch, at the Omega European Masters, of the Double Eagle Co-Axial Chronograph "OMEGA Mission Hills World Cup". Left to right: Dr David Chu (Mission Hills Group Chairman); George O'Grady (Chief Executive of The European Tour); Stephen Urquhart (President of Omega) and Henrique Lavie (Commissioner of the Tour De Las Americas)

> Golf is a game for good neighbours. It has the spice of competition while imposing the highest moral restraints. It offers a contest but demands in return the last full measure of discipline.
> **John Jay Hopkins, Founder of The World Cup**

The Course

The Olazábal course, designed by the two time Masters Tournament Champion, delivers a fair but stern test. There are many shots from elevated tees or, conversely, playing approaches to elevated greens. The bunkering is another feature of the course and there is also water to consider on several holes, especially to the left of the 18th. In general the fairways are generous but the par threes are all strong holes – not too long but all challenging.

Arnold Palmer and Jack Nicklaus receive the trophy after their World Cup victory at Saint-Nom-La-Bretèche in 1963

has a population of 1.4 billion with 400 million youths. I believe hosting the World Cup of Golf in China together with partners like Omega, the IGA, the China Golf Association and the International Federation of PGA Tours, under The European Tour's guidance, will go beyond just influencing sports and commercial development. It will create an impact so big it will truly turn golf into a global sport!"

George O'Grady, Chief Executive of The European Tour and on behalf of the International Federation of PGA Tours, said: "We already have an excellent relationship with Omega through their sponsorship of the Omega European Masters on The European Tour International Schedule and this will be considerably enhanced through their link-up with Mission Hills who have been at the forefront of promoting golf in China since they first staged the World Cup in 1995."

The recent successes of England (Paul Casey and Luke Donald), Wales (Stephen Dodd and Bradley Dredge) and Germany (Bernhard Langer and Marcel Siem) has indicated a European dominance of the World Cup. In fact the United States have won a record 23 times and Argentina, Australia, Canada, England, Germany, Ireland, Japan, South Africa, Spain, Sweden, Taiwan, the United States and Wales have all celebrated glory. That is the beauty of a competition which thrives on tradition and proud partnerships such as Mission Hills and Omega.

Mitchell Platts

Stephen Dodd (left) and Bradley Dredge

Champions of The Future

O nce again victories by Spaniards Alvaro Quiros and Carl Suneson and Argentina's Daniel Vancsik on The 2007 European Tour International Schedule demonstrated the capacity of The European Tour Qualifying School to develop champions of the future.

Quiros's fairytale first start on The European Tour as a fully paid-up card-carrying Member resulted in victory in the Alfred Dunhill Championship in South Africa following an astonishing year when he progressed from the Peugeot Tour in Spain to full playing rights on the European Challenge Tour augmented by his 34th place finish in the Qualifying School at San Roque.

Vancsik used the Qualifying School to regain his playing rights following a disappointing first year on The European Tour International Schedule in 2006 then after finishing 31st at San Roque powered into the winner's circle with an euphoric maiden victory in the Madeira Islands Open BPI.

Vancsik said: "It was very important for me because if I hadn't qualified at the School I wouldn't be where I am now. I wouldn't have been able to win in Madeira and that changed everything for me. I didn't think that when I finished the last round at San Roque, because I played very badly for the last six holes and thought that I had missed out on my card by a shot. But the weather helped

me because that affected everyone and they all finished by dropping shots. You never know in the Qualifying School – you have to play well for six rounds and that's tough, but I got through it and because of that I won in Madeira."

Suneson produced a final round back nine stamped with class and authority to secure his first European Tour title at the OPEN DE SAINT-OMER presented by NEUFLIZE OBC in Lumbres, France.

All of this, of course, came only one year after Sweden's Johan Edfors emerged from the Qualifying School to win three times on The 2006 European Tour International Schedule and Spain's Gonzalo Fernandez-Castaño, a graduate from 2004, followed up his win in The KLM Open in 2005 by firmly establishing himself with victory at the 2006 BMW Asian Open, and in 2007 at the Telecom Italia Open.

Ireland's Paul McGinley and Olazábal are among the finest illustrations of players starting out on the road to glory at the Qualifying School. McGinley

Above Carlos Rodiles (left) and Alexandre Rocha with the trophy after both finishing on scores of 15 under par at The European Tour Qualifying School 2006 - Rocha claimed the Number One card thanks to a better last round

Alvaro Quiros

Daniel Vancsik

played in the 1991 Walker Cup – helping Liam White beat Phil Mickleson and Bob May – then gained his card at his first visit to the Qualifying School that year. The rest, as they say, is history. McGinley holed the winning putt in The 2002 Ryder Cup and with his win in the 2005 Volvo Masters took his earnings to approaching ten million euros. He has also represented Ireland in 12 World Cups, winning with Padraig Harrington in 1997, not to mention playing in seven Alfred Dunhill Cups, two Seve Trophys and of course, three Ryder Cups. Olazábal, after his electrifying start in 1986, has won no fewer than 30 tournaments worldwide and in 2006 he teed-up in his seventh Ryder Cup.

No fewer than 27 players have moved on from the School to win the very next year on The European Tour – Gordon Brand Jnr, Paul Way, Greg Turner, José Maria Olazábal, Vijay Singh, Paul Broadhurst, Mike McLean, Per-Ulrik Johanssson, Ian Palmer, Andrew Oldcorn, Padraig Harrington, Niclas Fasth, Roger Chapman, Ian Poulter, Grégory Havret, Jorge Berendt, Arjun Atwal, Adam Mednick, Philip Golding, Robert-Jan Derksen, Christopher Hanell, Joakim Bäckström, Fernandez-Castaño, Edfors, Quiros, Vancsik and Suneson.

Carl Suneson

Few events can rival the drama and the tension of The European Tour Qualifying School. The pressure, with the ultimate dream of Membership of The European Tour at stake, warmed-up in 2007 at the First Stage, held at six venues across England, France, Germany and Italy, and the Second Stage, held at Arcos Gardens, PGA Golf de Catalunya, Golf Costa Ballena and Sherry Golf Club in Spain with 156 players eventually contesting the Final Stage at the San Roque Club, Cadiz, Spain.

Uniquely, the Qualifying School is one tournament where the goal is not necessarily to triumph but simply to finish in the upper echelons. The higher you finish can maximise playing opportunities but, in reality, anyone finishing the six rounds with a card unlocks the way to that road to glory.

Mitchell Platts

Final Results (2006)

Pos	Name	Ctry	PQ	R1	R2	R3	R4	R5	R6	Agg	Par	€
1	Carlos RODILES	ESP	275	70	64	69	75	70	69	417	-15	19,452.42
2	Alexandre ROCHA	BRA	EX	74	72	65	66	69	71	417	-15	19,452.42
3	David DRYSDALE	SCO	EX	73	68	69	68	73	71	422	-10	12,718.89
4	Fredrik ANDERSSON HED	SWE	285	71	70	70	72	70	71	424	-8	9,905.77
5	Oliver FISHER (AM)	ENG	282	68	70	68	74	74	71	425	-7	
6	Sven STRÜVER	GER	EX	76	65	78	68	69	70	426	-6	7,761.02
7	Patrik SJÖLAND	SWE	EX	68	73	70	70	70	75	426	-6	7,761.02
8	Notah BEGAY III	USA	280	72	69	71	67	71	76	426	-6	7,761.02
9	Carl SUNESON	ESP	EX	71	69	74	72	73	69	428	-4	6,082.62
10	Julien FORET	FRA	EX	74	71	70	71	69	73	428	-4	6,082.62
11	Warren BENNETT	ENG	EX	69	67	72	71	76	73	428	-4	6,082.62
12	Sam LITTLE	ENG	EX	73	67	71	72	70	75	428	-4	6,082.62
13	Santiago LUNA	ESP	EX	72	70	70	71	73	73	429	-3	4,870.59
14	Sion E BEBB	WAL	EX	74	76	67	70	68	74	429	-3	4,870.59
15	Wade ORMSBY	AUS	EX	74	72	71	69	69	74	429	-3	4,870.59
16	Eirik Tage JOHANSEN	NOR	279	65	71	72	72	74	75	429	-3	4,870.59
17	Jesus Maria ARRUTI	ESP	EX	71	71	71	72	75	70	430	-2	3,636.11
18	Alex CEJKA	GER	EX	73	71	74	70	70	72	430	-2	3,636.11
19	Taichi TESHIMA	JPN	EX	72	70	75	70	71	72	430	-2	3,636.11
20	Steve ALKER	NZL	EX	76	73	69	72	67	73	430	-2	3,636.11
21	Matthew ZIONS	AUS	282	75	70	72	68	72	73	430	-2	3,636.11
22	Henrik NYSTROM	SWE	EX	70	71	69	71	76	73	430	-2	3,636.11
23	Richard MCEVOY	ENG	282	73	69	73	67	74	74	430	-2	3,636.11
24	Andrew RAITT	ENG	283	73	74	70	74	71	69	431	-1	2,728.33
25	Birgir HAFTHORSSON	ISL	282	69	72	75	71	75	69	431	-1	2,728.33
26	François CALMELS	FRA	280	72	74	73	71	71	70	431	-1	2,728.33
27	Andrew TAMPION	AUS	278	71	71	75	69	71	74	431	-1	2,728.33
28	Pelle EDBERG	SWE	278	76	69	68	74	69	75	431	-1	2,728.33
29	Matthew RICHARDSON	ENG	274	73	71	68	74	69	76	431	-1	2,728.33
30	Edward RUSH	ENG	275	70	69	71	76	75	71	432	0	2,473.95
31	Daniel VANCSIK	ARG	EX	75	73	70	72	69	73	432	0	2,473.95
32	Manuel QUIROS	ESP	274	70	73	78	68	70	73	432	0	2,473.95
33	José Manuel CARRILES	ESP	282	74	71	70	72	72	73	432	0	2,473.95
34	Alvaro QUIROS	ESP	EX	73	69	73	73	70	74	432	0	2,473.95
35	Luis CLAVERIE	ESP	276	69	69	71	73	74	76	432	0	2,473.95
36	Magnus A CARLSSON	SWE	268	76	70	67	73	76	71	433	1	1,047.44
37	Simon NASH	AUS	EX	71	78	68	74	69	73	433	1	1,047.44
38	Leif WESTERBERG	SWE	EX	73	71	69	73	74	73	433	1	1,047.44
39	Euan LITTLE	SCO	276	74	74	73	67	71	74	433	1	1,047.44
40	Antti AHOKAS	FIN	273	68	72	76	71	71	75	433	1	1,047.44
41	Marc CAYEUX	ZIM	EX	70	71	72	74	69	77	433	1	1,047.44
42	Paolo TERRENI	ITA	274	74	72	71	73	73	71	434	2	1,047.44
43	Michael JONZON	SWE	EX	74	76	71	68	74	71	434	2	1,047.44
44	Mikko KORHONEN	FIN	278	74	72	72	71	73	72	434	2	1,047.44
45	Tim DYKES	WAL	277	73	74	72	70	74	72	435	3	1,047.44
46	George MURRAY (AM)	SCO	284	77	71	69	72	74	72	435	3	
47	Jorge BENEDETTI	COL	279	74	71	75	71	69	75	435	3	1,047.44
48	Nicolas COLSAERTS	BEL	EX	73	71	72	71	72	76	435	3	1,047.44
49	Jean HUGO	RSA	EX	76	72	68	75	71	74	436	4	1,047.44
50	Stuart DAVIS	ENG	284	76	69	71	70	76	74	436	4	1,047.44
51	Gareth WRIGHT	WAL	EX	73	72	70	68	77	76	436	4	1,047.44
52	Keith HORNE	RSA	EX	71	75	70	69	72	80	437	5	1,047.44
53	Ariel CANETE	ARG	EX	71	72	73	72	77	73	438	6	1,047.44
54	Amandeep JOHL	IND	EX	74	71	73	72	74	74	438	6	1,047.44
55	Matthew KING	ENG	282	73	67	71	72	72	83	438	6	1,047.44
56	Raphaël DE SOUSA	SUI	261	75	74	71	69	79	71	439	7	1,047.44
57	Ivó GINER	ESP	EX	73	68	70	76	73	79	439	7	1,047.44
58	Gareth PADDISON	NZL	EX	76	73	70	72	73	75	439	7	1,047.44
59	Liam BOND	WAL	277	75	69	71	75	74	75	439	7	1,047.44
60	Raphael EYRAUD	FRA	271	73	72	70	74	75	75	439	7	1,047.44
61	Peter FOWLER	AUS	EX	76	73	68	73	72	77	439	7	1,047.44
62	Thomas NIELSEN	DEN	278	75	75	71	70	71	78	440	8	1,047.44
63	Heman REY	ARG	EX	71	74	73	70	74	78	440	8	1,047.44
64	Sebastian FERNANDEZ	ARG	EX	80	71	70	70	76	74	441	9	1,047.44
65	Ally MELLOR	ENG	278	80	68	72	69	77	75	441	9	1,047.44
66	Manuel MERIZALDE	COL	284	75	75	69	72	73	77	441	9	1,047.44
67	Pedro LINHART	ESP	EX	70	75	72	73	74	77	441	9	1,047.44
68	David DIXON	ENG	275	79	68	70	71	76	77	441	9	1,047.44
69	Andrew OLDCORN	SCO	EX	75	70	73	73	72	78	441	9	1,047.44
70	Miguel Angel MARTIN	ESP	EX	73	73	72	73	72	78	441	9	1,047.44
71	Fredrik WIDMARK	SWE	EX	79	73	69	70	73	78	442	10	1,047.44
72	Lee S JAMES	ENG	EX	71	77	68	72	74	81	443	11	1,047.44
73	Scott HENDERSON	SCO	279	74	70	72	73	74	80	444	12	1,047.44
74	Peter BAKER	ENG	EX	74	73	69	75	75	78	444	12	1,047.44
75	Inder VAN WEERELT	NED	284	75	71	71	73	76	78	444	12	1,047.44
76	Jan-Are LARSEN	NOR	EX	77	70	73	78	70	80	448	12	1,047.44
77	Robert DINWIDDIE	ENG	273	76	72	73	70	79	76	446	14	1,047.44
78	David HIGGINS	IRL	EX	72	70	73	75	76	81	447	15	1,047.44
79	Daniel DENISON	ENG	280	71	71	73	72	77	84	448	16	1,047.44
80	Mads VIBE-HASTRUP	DEN	EX	73	76	70	71	76	W/D			

The first 35 players became eligible for Category 11 Membership on The 2007 European Tour International Schedule

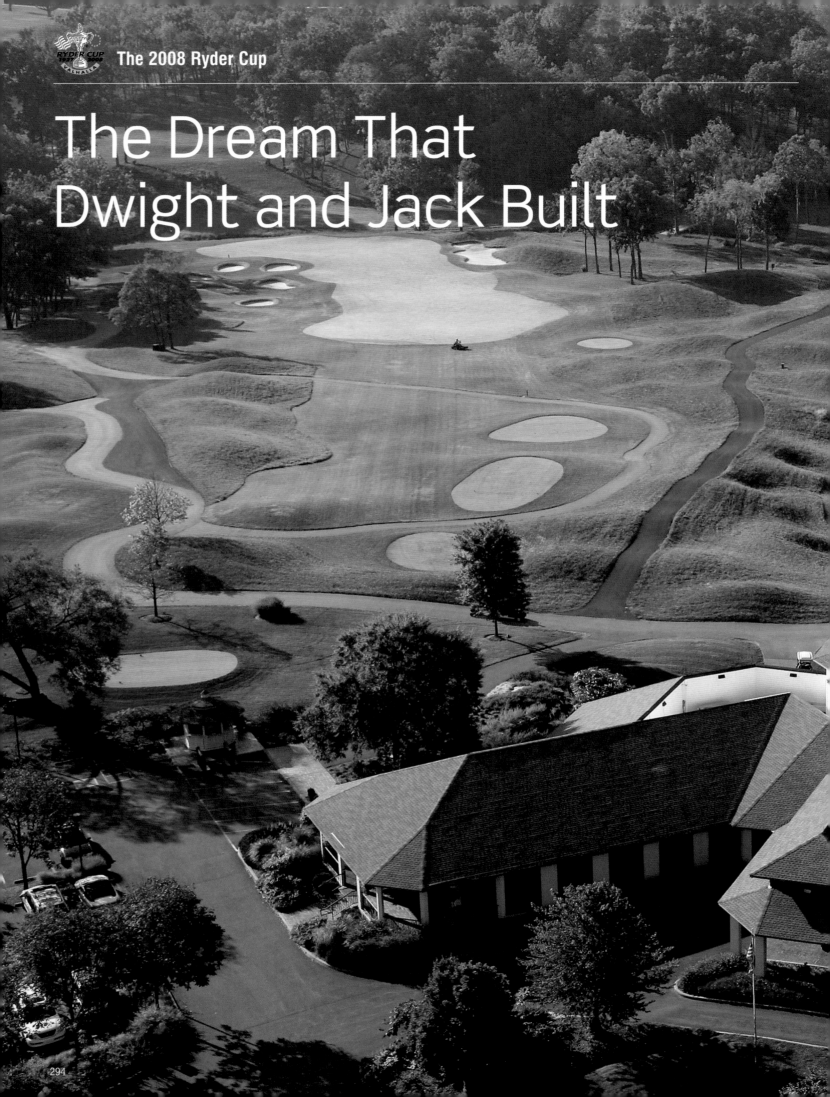

The Dream That Dwight and Jack Built

One thing is certain; there has never been a course in Ryder Cup history that stretches as far as 7,496 yards, which will be the case when the 37th edition of the biennial match unfolds at Valhalla Golf Club from September 19-21, 2008. What can also be stated without fear of contradiction is that there has not been a club, since The Ryder Cup began in 1927, which has been named after a hall in Norse mythology where the souls of Viking heroes feasted and celebrated with the Gods.

The Vikings can be traced back as far as the eighth century, but Valhalla cannot claim such history. Nevertheless it has, since its own birth in 1986, contributed to the history of the game of golf. In 1996 Mark Brooks won the US PGA Championship at Valhalla after a play-off, and in the Millennium year it was the turn of Tiger Woods to win the US PGA Championship which proved to be the third leg of his unique achievement of holding all of the four Major Championships at the same time. For the record, he won the US Open Championship at Pebble Beach and the Open Championship at St Andrews in 2000 prior to the US PGA Championship, then the Masters Tournament at Augusta National in 2001. It meant that Valhalla will always have a place in golf's record books alongside those three other legendary golfing venues.

Then again, that is fair enough since Valhalla just happened to be designed by the man whose record Woods seeks to beat. Jack Nicklaus, winner of 18 Major Championships, sculpted the course at Valhalla and, more recently, he returned in partnership with the PGA of America to ensure an

even more spectator-friendly venue for The 2008 Ryder Cup, not to mention a challenging course for those who eventually fill the European and United States Teams.

That modification programme began in the summer of 2006 and included not only extensive changes, especially at the 14th, 15th and 16th, to improve spectator viewing but also significant alterations to the course. Not only has the grass been replaced on all 18 greens, but Nicklaus has also overseen the reconstruction of the sixth, eighth, 11th and 16th greens in addition to new bunkers being added on the first, second, fifth, 12th, 15th, 16th and 17th holes.

Joe Steranka, Chief Executive Officer of the PGA of America, said: "Valhalla has already achieved much attention in its short history, and now it is ready to be showcased to the world at The 2008 Ryder Cup."

Valhalla Golf Club started as the dream of Louisville businessman and golf enthusiast Dwight Gahm (pronounced game). Just as Samuel Ryder's dream of The Ryder Cup becoming an international

Right The winning 2006 European Ryder Cup Team captained by Ian Woosnam

Dwight Gahm

Jack Nicklaus salutes the huge galleries on the 18th hole at Valhalla

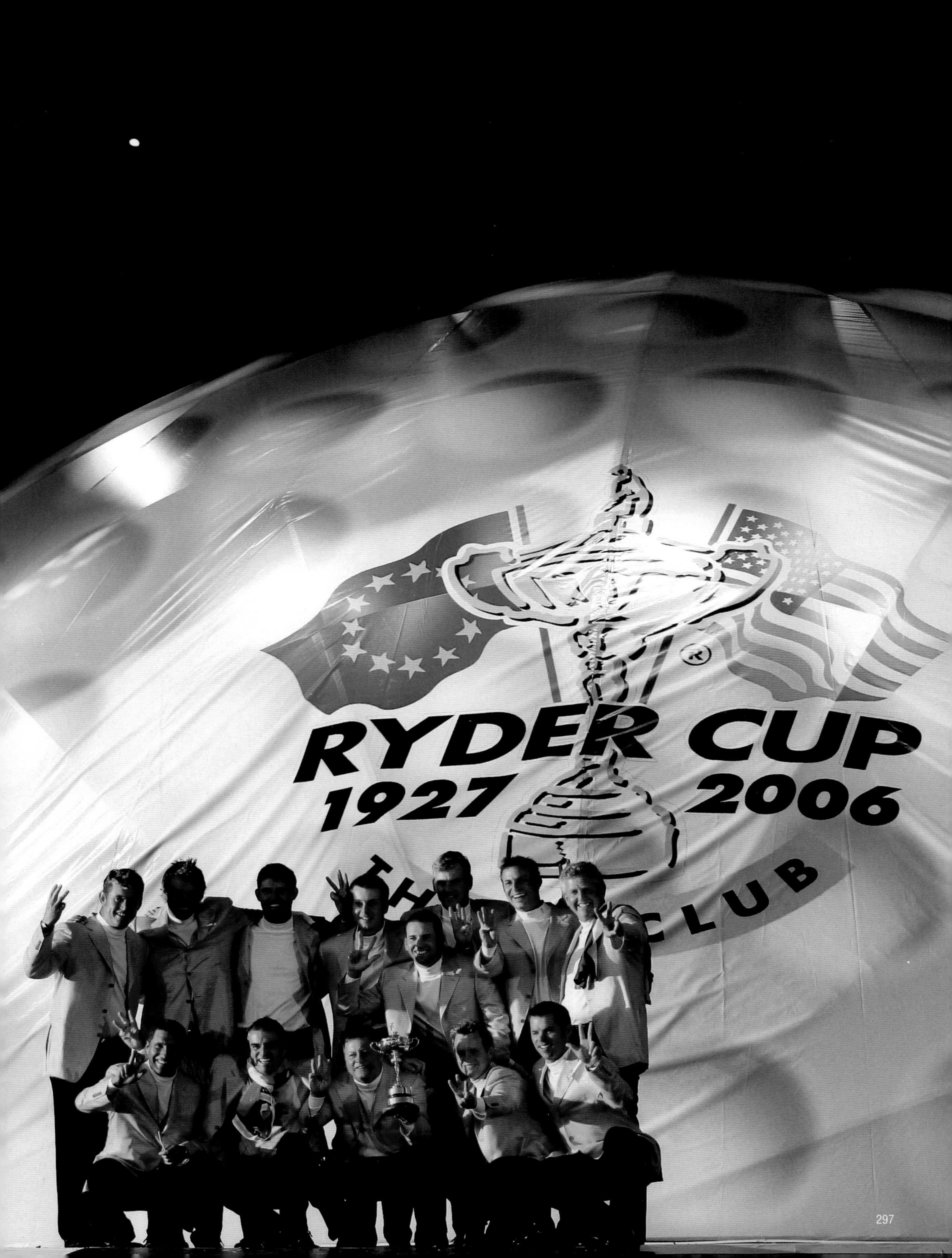
RYDER CUP
1927
2006
CLUB

Club Car

It's the world's greatest game.
Let your guests play it in style.

Why settle for just any golf car when you can treat your guests to an extraordinary golf experience? Club Car is all about style, performance and comfort. With industry–leading technology for superior reliability and efficiency, Club Car continues to set the standard for technological innovation.

Club Car/Ingersoll Rand   Greenbank House   Swan Lane, Hindley Green Wigan   WN2 4AR
+44.1942.503141   www.clubcar.com

Valhalla - Card of the Course

Hole	Yards	Metres	Par
1	448	410	4
2	505	462	4
3	206	188	3
4	375	343	4
5	463	423	4
6	500	457	4
7	601	550	5
8	180	165	3
9	416	380	4
Out	**3,694**	**3,378**	**35**
10	594	543	5
11	208	190	3
12	464	424	4
13	352	322	4
14	215	197	3
15	434	397	4
16	511	467	4
17	477	436	4
18	547	500	5
In	**3,802**	**3,476**	**36**
Total	**7,496**	**6,854**	**71**

Right Recent Winning European Ryder Cup Captains (Clockwise from top left)

Tony Jacklin - 1985 (Pictured), 1987
Bernard Gallacher - 1995
Seve Ballesteros - 1997
Sam Torrance - 2002
Bernhard Langer - 2004
Ian Woosnam - 2006

contest turned into reality, so Gahm's vision of Valhalla becoming a venue to host such events has been realised.

It was in 1981 that Gahm commissioned Nicklaus to design the course on 486 acres of rolling Kentucky countryside some 20 minutes east of Louisville on Shelbyville Road in eastern Jefferson County. The thick woodlands and the lush, bluegrass-covered river bottom whetted the designer's taste buds; as did the thought of tee boxes tucked onto ledges above riverbanks containing the lazy waters of Floyd's Fork. Nicklaus described the site as "a golf designer's dream because there is a variety of terrain, vegetation and water to work with. Everything necessary for an excellent golf course is here; room for wide, tree-lined fairways and spectacular golf holes."

Gahm is now aged 88. He has been called a dreamer; a visionary. In Kentucky they know him as 'Mr Golf'. Why not? What he put down at Valhalla, with a little bit of help from Mr Nicklaus, was a golf course not a country club. His ambition was for a course to hold Major Championship golf; not

to be an excuse for a housing development. He determined to transform an abandoned Kentucky horse farm into a golf course, simply a course, but a great course, as against a money making project. This was to be Gahm's legacy which is why Nicklaus received the call. All Gahm requested was that the course that Jack built was worthy of hosting Major Championships and, perhaps, The Ryder Cup, and that a noon start time was reserved for him everyday so that if the opportunity arose, he could play with his sons Gordy, Phil and Walt.

In 1993, some seven years after Valhalla Golf Club opened its doors, the PGA of America agreed to purchase 25 per cent of the Club. Then after the successful conclusion of the 1996 US PGA Championship, the PGA of America assumed 50 per cent ownership and, following the victory by Woods in 2000, they purchased the remaining 50 per cent. That ensured Gahm's legacy to the game since, just as according to legend the warriors of Odin marched through the doors of Valhalla shoulder to shoulder armed with swords and spears to do battle, so will two forces in golf now stand shoulder to shoulder as Europe seeks to win The Ryder Cup

US Open   US PGA Championship   All World Golf Championships
PGA European Tour   The Ryder Cup   The Solheim Cup

THERE'S ONLY ONE PLACE YOU'LL SEE THEM ALL

SKY SPORTS

www.sky.com

for a fourth successive time against the United States. This time, of course, it will be golf clubs that will do the talking or, more specifically, those belonging to the 24 world class golfers who will line up under the leadership of Captains Paul Azinger and Nick Faldo.

Europe, of course, won their third Ryder Cup in a row, and indeed their fifth in six contests, on the course that Arnold Palmer built at The K Club in Ireland. This time the action will take place on the course that Jack built and, make no mistake, he has been doing everything possible to ensure that this course provides the ultimate challenge to today's golfers.

That came through loud and clear when he discussed the changes to the 11th hole. Nicklaus, on-site, admitted: "Where the green was, made that hole too benign. How the green got there, I'm not sure. Probably my mistake!"

Honesty has always been a byword in Nicklaus' vocabulary, and there is no question that he has swallowed his own pride to make changes to his original design to cater for the changes in the modern game. "The technology of golf has changed so the courses have to change, too," he said. "The game has changed dramatically." So for The 2008 Ryder Cup the course will stretch to 7,496 yards compared to 7,167 yards in 2000 when Woods won the US PGA Championship.

Nicklaus acknowledges that the biggest challenge when he designed Valhalla was that he had two very distinctive and different pieces of property with which to work. The front nine meandered through a flood plain, and flooded quite often by Floyd's Fork, so that situation had to be accommodated, and in Nicklaus's opinion it has a Scottish feel to it. In contrast the back nine winds through trees and has a traditional

North American feel about it. Nicklaus regards it as a thinking man's course - you need to be long and straight but you also need to be a good strategist.

Strategy might be the key word when the players of both Teams start producing the shots; but for Dwight Gahm and Jack Nicklaus this will be the realisation of a dream. The Bluegrass State may have more than 250 courses but all eyes will be on only one in 2008 when Valhalla Golf Club plays host to The Ryder Cup. "It was my vision to take the course to worldwide recognition," said Gahm.

The Ryder Cup will truly see to that.

Mitchell Platts

European Captain Nick Faldo (left) allows his American counterpart, Paul Azinger, the briefest of touches of The Ryder Cup

6, 7, 5, 6, 7, 7, 9, 7, 5, 6, 6, 7, 8, 6, 7, 6, 8, 5, but happy.

We all get those days.
Where you seriously consider
packing it all in and taking up
darts or something.
But even a bad round here
has its positives.
Stunning championship courses.
Very reasonable green fees.
No pretentious nonsense.
A good walk through our
beautiful countryside.
And best of all, in Wales
tomorrow's always another day.

golfasitshouldbe.com

Wales
Cymru

The new course built for staging The Ryder Cup at The Celtic Manor Resort in 2010 has been named after the date that shaped its existence. The Twenty Ten Course – the first ever to be designed and built specifically for The Ryder Cup – has been given a title which reflects the fact that the spectacular new layout will forever be associated with hosting The Ryder Cup, one of the world's most captivating sporting events.

Ryder Cup Future Venues

2008	Valhalla Golf Club, Louisville, Kentucky, USA
2010	The Celtic Manor Resort, Newport, South Wales
2012	Medinah Country Club, Medinah, Illinois, USA
2014	The Gleneagles Hotel, Perthshire, Scotland
2016	Hazeltine National Golf Club, Chaska, Minnesota, USA
2018	TBC
2020	Whistling Straits, Kohler, Wisconsin, USA

Ryder Cup results 1985-2006

1985	The Belfry, Sutton Coldfield, West Midlands, England
	Europe 16½ - USA 11½
1987	Muirfield Village, Columbus, Ohio, USA
	Europe 15 - USA 13
1989	The Belfry, Sutton Coldfield, West Midlands, England
	Europe 14 - USA 14 (Europe retained Cup)
1991	The Ocean Course, Kiawah Island Resort, Kiawah Island, USA
	Europe 13½ - USA 14½
1993	The Belfry, Sutton Coldfield, West Midlands, England
	Europe 13 - USA 15
1995	Oak Hill Country Club, Rochester, New York, USA
	Europe 14½ - USA 13½
1997	Club de Golf Valderrama, Sotogrande, Spain
	Europe 14½ - USA 13½
1999	The Country Club, Brookline, Massachusetts, USA
	Europe 13½ - USA 14½
2002	The Belfry, Sutton Coldfield, West Midlands, England
	Europe 15½ - USA 12½
2004	Oakland Hills Country Club, Bloomfield Township, Michigan, USA
	Europe 18½ - USA 9½
2006	The K Club, Straffan, Co. Kildare, Ireland
	Europe 18½ - USA 9½

Valhalla
Hole-by-hole

By Keith Reese, PGA Head Golf Professional

Graphics produced by bestapproach.com

Hole 1 (Cut the Corner)
Par 4 448 Yards 410 Metres

A deceptive par four with a slight dog-leg to the left. From the tee, the first appears mostly tame; however the approach to the green has been made dramatically different with the addition of two greenside bunkers one front right and one back left. The new bunker front right has filled the area which was once the low portion of green in the front right and the bluegrass low to the right of the green. This bunker is a visually intimidating sight for approach shots to the front left and back right hole locations. The left bunker is positioned to gobble up errant shots to the back portion of the green.

Hole 2 (The Ridge)
Par 4 505 Yards 462 Metres

A slight dog-leg to the left which challenges the players from the tee with a finger of Floyd's Fork, a waterway which meanders through the front nine, bordering the left side of the fairway and a bunker squeezing the fairway to the right. In 2006 Jack Nicklaus made a few enhancements to the green. The slopes in the green have been softened to be more receptive to longer approach shots, and the green has been made smaller. The two existing bunkers to the left have been reworked and deepened. A new bunker has been added right of the green. Floyd's Fork is there to catch shots missing the green to the left.

Hole 3 (Floyd's Fork)
Par 3 206 Yards 188 Metres

A challenging par three with Floyd's Fork winding between the tee and the green then sweeping around to the right of the green. The third hole remained relatively unchanged through the 2006 renovation with the exception of softening some of the existing slopes in the green and adding a small portion of green to the back left which will allow for more hole locations on or near the back left of the green. The green is guarded by a large bunker to the left and a bunker to the right. The real danger is misreading the wind and having the ball pushed to the right and down the slope into Floyd's Fork.

Hole 3

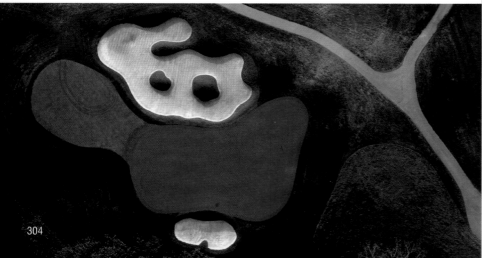

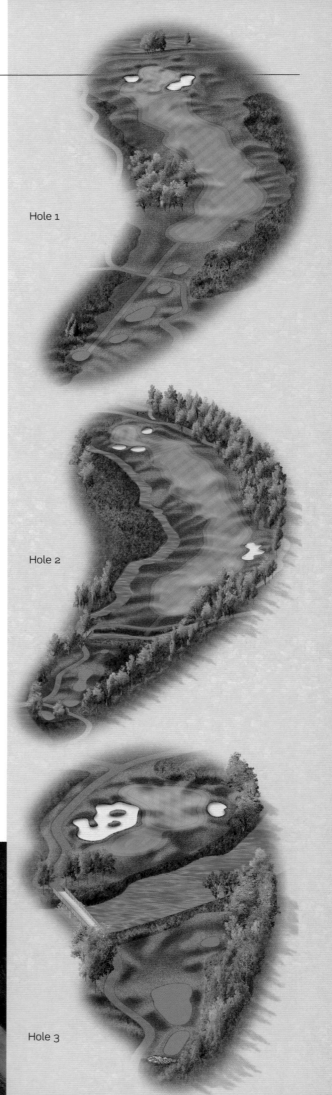

Hole 1

Hole 2

Hole 3

Hole 4

Hole 5

Hole 6

Hole 4 (Short n' Sweet)
Par 4 375 Yards 343 Metres

The tee shot was difficult before with a deep bunker left side of the fairway and another fairway bunker lying in wait on the right, and the addition of a new tee 20 yards further back has further strengthened the hole. The aggressive play is to take the tee shot over the left bunker which has a carry of 260 yards. Although a relatively short par four by today's standards, as its name implies, this hole will still be a test for all players. Distance control is the key for approaches to this green, shots going long will surely reach a watery grave in Floyd's Fork.

Hole 5 (Fade Away)
Par 4 463 Yards 423 Metres

A slightly new look with Mr. Nicklaus having added a new fairway bunker on the players' right hand side which now complements the three bunkers which line the left of the landing area off the tee. This dog-leg right, as its name implies, requires a fade from the tee or a 290 yards carry will be needed to fly the new right hand bunker. The green has a bunker positioned to grab errant shots to the right or short and a closely mown collection area left of the green. This green allows for a back right hole location which is one of the most difficult hole locations on the course.

Hole 6 (The Bear)
Par 4 500 Yards 457 Metres

One of the more dramatic enhancements of the 2006 renovation project. The sixth measured 420 yards with the second shot over Floyd's Fork. With the increase in length, the second shot is a real eye opener. The green has been moved back nearly 80 yards leaving players with an approach shot of 180 to 200 yards after a well positioned tee shot. The green has been totally redesigned with plenty of trouble. A deep bunker guards the left side of the green and a closely mown collection area will grab shots to the right.

Hole 6

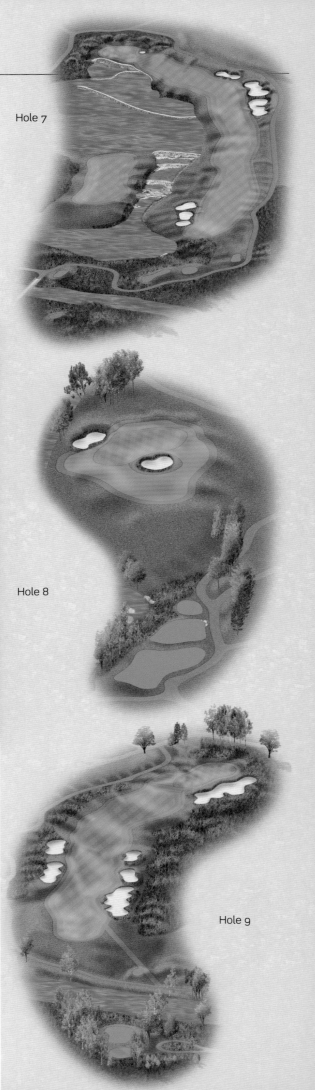

Hole 7

Hole 8

Hole 9

Hole 7 (Player's Pick)
Par 5 601 Yards 550 Metres

A definite risk and reward approach. This hole features a split fairway. The route to the left shortens the hole by more than 50 yards, but the landing area is only 26 yards wide with the fairway surrounded by bluegrass rough in addition to a water hazard. The approach from the island fairway sets a carry of 210 to 230 yards all over water. The fairway to the right is the longer but safer route, although it has been made more challenging by narrowing the fairway. The fairway bunkers on the right have been enlarged and moved closer to the fairway. The water hazard has been expanded to the very edge of the green and will surely drown any approach shot missing to the left.

Hole 7

Hole 8 (Thor's Hammer)
Par 3 180 Yards 165 Metres

The tee area has been redesigned with 25 yards added to the length of the hole. The green is extremely challenging with the front protected by two bunkers, another one at the back and one more to the left where Floyd's Fork also waits for the wayward shot. The green features multiple shelves to allow for the most challenging of pin positions.

Hole 9 (The Rise)
Par 4 416 Yards 380 Metres

An uphill hole which remained mostly unchanged through the renovation. The tee shot is challenging with three fairway bunkers bordering the right side of the fairway and two more to the left. The uphill approach to the green makes judging the yardage very difficult and the presence of one of the largest and deepest bunkers looming just right of the green further applies the pressure.

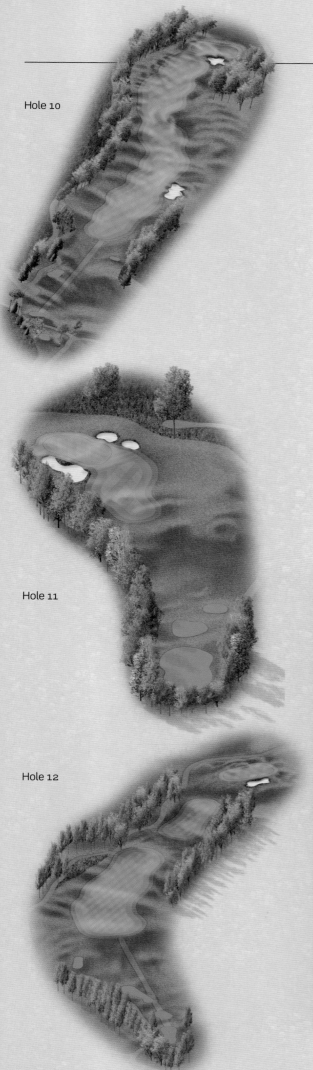

Hole 10

Hole 11

Hole 12

Hole 10 (Turns)
Par 5 594 Yards 543 Metres

A double dog-leg with a fairway bunker on the right side of the driving zone and deep rough to the left. The undulating two-tiered green is protected by a large, deep bunker guarding the front. Distance control on the approach is a must as shots missing long will make par extremely difficult and shots coming up short will find the front bunker. The 2006 renovation added a new Championship tee which increased the length of the hole by 30 yards.

Hole 11 (On the Edge)
Par 3 208 Yards 190 Metres

The new green, completely rebuilt during the renovations, has been moved back some 30 yards and to the left of the previous green position and sits out on the edge of the hillside. It features a slight false front with two bunkers bordering the front and left of the green. Accuracy is a must; shots carrying too far to the left will bound down the hillside making getting up and down a very difficult task.

Hole 12 (Odin's Revenge)
Par 4 464 Yards 424 Metres

This hole has a difficult-to-find driving area which leaves players with a 160 to 180 yard approach to an elevated green. The subtly recontoured green is extremely well guarded with one of the deepest bunkers on the course to the right and gnarly bluegrass rough to the left.

Hole 12

Hole 13

Hole 13

Hole 14

Hole 15

Hole 13 (The Island)
Par 4 352 Yards 322 Metres

The driving zone of the hole is surrounded by five small bunkers to the left and one large bunker to the right. The "Island" green is one of the most spectacular on the course, built up nearly 20 feet on large boulders, and nearly completely surrounded by water. Accuracy with controlled spin is a must. If the forward tee is used on this hole it will tempt players to drive the green which would make for a truly exciting match play decision.

Hole 14 (Two Tears)
Par 3 215 Yards 197 Metres

The longest of the par threes at 215 yards, it features a two-tiered green with a large bunker guarding the front. The renovation project has included recontouring the rear portion of the green and the addition of two greenside bunkers on the left of the green, one just behind the lower tier and one just behind the upper tier of the green. The hole places demand on club selection, and anything long will leave a tough recovery.

Hole 15 (On the Rocks)
Par 4 434 Yards 397 Metres

One of the most scenic holes at Valhalla with Brush Run Creek skirting the entire right side of the hole. The landing area from the tee is framed by a small bunker to the left and a larger bunker to the right; however the challenge of this hole is the approach. The green, just like the fairway, is skirted by Brush Run Creek leaving very little room for error to the right. The green has seen the addition of a bunker, which fills what used to be a closely mown collection area to the left, and has been re-contoured on both the left and right sides allowing for additional pin placements, some of which may be close to the rocks and the water.

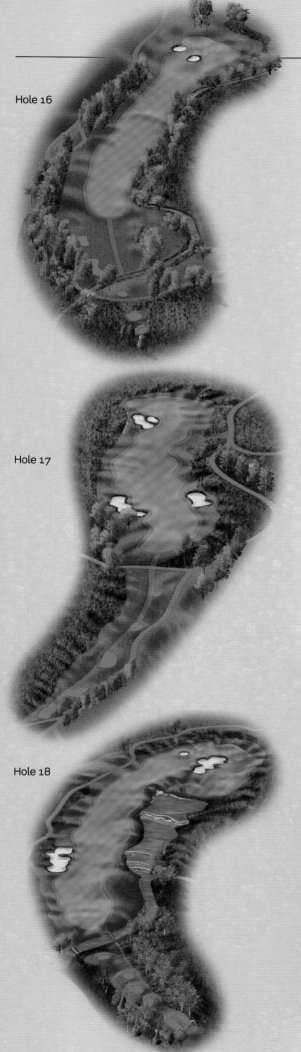

Hole 16

Hole 17

Hole 18

Hole 16 (Down the Stretch)
Par 4 511 Yards 467 Metres

Turning back towards the clubhouse, this is the longest of the par fours. A slight dog-leg to the right with Brush Run Creek guarding the right side and a tree covered slope with deep rough on the left. One of the most difficult holes on the golf course and amazingly enough has yet to be tested at its full length in a Major Championship. The approach has been changed in dramatic fashion with a completely new green and the lowering of the 17th tee area which creates an amphitheatre for spectacular viewing. Three greenside bunkers now exist, where once there were none.

Hole 17 (No Mercy)
Par 4 477 Yards 436 Metres

An uphill hole which was one of the major projects during the course renovation. The tee has been lowered six to eight feet creating the spectacular viewing area for the sixteenth green. The existing left fairway bunker has been complemented by the addition of a right fairway bunker making the landing area an even more difficult target. The new teeing area has added 50 yards in length to the hole. The green has remained virtually the same with some minor recontouring of slopes.

Hole 18 (Gahm Over)
Par 5 547 Yards 500 Metres

A great finishing hole time and time again with play-off finishes in the 78th & 82nd US PGA Championships as well as the down to the wire finish in the 65th Senior US PGA Championship. This hole has a large fairway bunker to the left of the landing zone and a spectacular water feature on the right, and has remained mostly unchanged with the exception of a new greenside bunker just off the left of the green. The existing bunker guarding the entire front portion of the green is a classic feature that guards the green which now has slopes running from the upper portion of the green down to the left and right lower levels.

Hole 18

SCOTLAND THE PERFECT STAGE

For more information on how Scotland can provide the perfect stage for your event, log onto **EventScotland.org**

EventScotland™

NICK FALDO MBE – The 2008 European Team Captain

Viewed how one likes, it has been some trip to get here for Nicholas Alexander Faldo MBE. And us. As it happens, the timing of his career as a professional golfer almost exactly mirrors your correspondent's own schedule as a golf writer. On the whole, however, it may have to be conceded that his curriculum vitae has ended up just that little bit more impressive.

Certainly the finest British golfer of his generation, and quite probably the best ever, Faldo turned out to be that rarest of combinations – talented, hard working and a natural winner. The title of his recent autobiography – Life Swings – offers us his own, apt, summation of his extraordinary yomp towards the peaks of the grand, old game.

Nowhere, however, has he swung more eagerly than in The Ryder Cup arena. To suggest that Faldo took instinctively well to the contest would be to seriously undervalue his contribution to Europe's cause. Indeed, so swiftly did he arrive on the scene – his appearance at Royal Lytham & St Annes in 1977 made him, at 20, the youngest ever participant before the 19 year old Sergio Garcia played at Brookline in 1999 – that he managed to play for what turned out to be the last of the Great Britain and Ireland squads.

His total of 11 appearances is, of course, a record. He also holds the points won record (25) and has played more Ryder Cup rounds (46) than anyone else. His playing statistics read: won 23, lost 19, halved 4, and are not so much swinging as phenomenal.

Now here he is as Captain. It is particularly fitting that Faldo's tenancy should embrace the contest when it is played in the United States, a country that seems to have suited his particular take on life. The Americans, for their part, have always granted the respect his ability has deserved and to this has been added a genuine affection as, over the last few years, he has revealed himself to them as an informed, relaxed and witty commentator on television with viewers of CBS and the Golf Channel now benefiting from his authoritative views.

It was perhaps perversely inevitable that after a career studded with often tetchy relationships where much of the media was concerned that he should make a second name for himself as a gifted communicator in this arena. To be fair, there were times when his exasperation at some of the criticism he had had to read was fully merited but, to

be equally fair to the media, he never quite seemed to weigh these pinpricks against the avalanche of praise that often poured over him from reporters only too pleased to join him on his ride to six Major Championship triumphs.

However, that was then and this is now. What we know for sure is that the European players will have a Captain in Valhalla who will leave nothing to chance. His attention to detail is legendary and it is no surprise that one of the traits he dislikes in others is an inability to deliver on a promise. There is no doubt that whatever Faldo promises his players for September 2008, it will indeed be brought to bear.

Where he may help them most, however, will come if he can find a way to communicate deeply his own sense of purpose and commitment to those players. That they will turn up already filled with respect for him is a given, while his ability to point them in the right direction after arranging them in the correct order is surely beyond debate.

This singularity of purpose was swiftly exhibited by Faldo when, as a teenager, he set a tentative toe on the game's lowest foothill. In his case, his first tournament proper was a monthly medal at Welwyn Garden City Golf Club in southern England. Playing off a handicap of five, he returned a gross 72 to sweep the board. At least that was what happened until some jobsworth discovered he had teed off 15 minutes earlier than juniors were supposed to play.

Following an astonishing display of official pettiness on the part of the golf club, Faldo found himself disqualified, a low-rent decision sadly representative of the attitude prevalent at many golf clubs in the 1970s. It was also, however, entirely typical of Faldo's own nature that this was not only the first Monthly Medal he entered, it also turned out to be the last. It is not sure if he forgives, but he certainly never forgets.

It is certain, however, after all these years that he never, ever has given less than he has had available to him on any given day.

Pertinent to this is my own recollection of his physical state immediately after The 1989 Ryder Cup at The Belfry. On the final day he had battled Lanny Wadkins to the last only for the American to prevail by a single hole. When he came into the Media Centre half an hour later, Faldo looked totally exhausted.

"You look absolutely knackered," I said when we spoke briefly. He stared back for a minute and then slowly answered. "That's because I am," each word uttered in isolation for a couple of seconds. "Are you surprised?" he went on. "This IS the bloody Ryder Cup you know."

Will Nick Faldo be a brilliant Captain? I suspect we already know the answer.

Bill Elliott
The Observer

PAUL AZINGER – The 2008 United States Team Captain

Heroes, as it turns out, do not just emerge from shadows, they also march briskly forward from adversity. Foremost from this latter bracket is Paul Azinger. It is not heroic, of course, to be diagnosed with cancer but the way in which this tall and elegant American dealt with the bad news that greeted him soon after his one Major triumph – the 1993 US PGA Championship – and his subsequent recreation of himself as a man and a golfer, edges him significantly towards the highest plateau of superlatives.

The non-Hodgkin's lymphoma of the right shoulder that blighted his life 14 years ago naturally remains a vivid memory for 'Zinger' and his family but the other fact is, like so many sufferers before him and since, he has emerged from this dark trial a stronger, more focused man. And, quite probably, a better one.

Ask him what he felt as he lay on a cold table awaiting the X-ray that was to confirm whether or not the cancer had spread out from his shoulder – it thankfully had not – and he will tell you: "As I lay there, my Major Championship, my other victories before that, everything I had accomplished in life became meaningless to me. All I wanted to do was to live. But then another reality hit me even harder. I'm going to die eventually anyway, whether from cancer or something else I'm definitely going to die. It's just a question of when."

At first this comment may seem a trite confirmation of the blindingly obvious but it is not, and the reason it is not is because this realisation that time is brief, that life is microscopically finite, comes only to those who have faced the real prospect of possible and imminent death. After that moment, almost everything else is put into a unique perspective.

Which brings us on to the glorious triviality that is The Ryder Cup and Azinger's selection as skipper of a United States Team that will be desperate to halt the tide of European domination so firmly established in recent years. Whether he will be successful in this objective remains to be seen, but there can be no doubt that he is at least made of the right stuff to take on the challenge.

He has already obtained a radical alteration to the American Team's selection process, doubling his Captain's picks to four, extending the pressure on himself to come up with the right answers to this larger question, and laying down a template that he believes will contribute hugely to the home Team's cause at Valhalla Golf Club in 2008.

What he also brings to the table is a genuine affection for the old contest, a love affair that was consummated during his own Ryder Cup campaigns of which there were four between 1989 and 2002. The attraction when he first played at The Belfry in 1989 was instant. It was also cloaked in real drama and not a little conflict.

Out first in the Sunday singles his opponent was Seve Ballesteros, talismanic leader of The European Team and a genius still embracing his silkiest skills. By the time the pair arrived at the 18th Azinger was a hole up, but his drive disappeared into the weeds and he had to take a drop, one whose legitimacy was challenged by Ballesteros.

To his credit, Azinger stood tall against the great intimidator before pulling off an unlikely recovery to win a point for his Team, a crucial victory in a match that ended in a tie overall. The pair have since made up, the Spaniard recognising a genuine opponent, Azinger acknowledging that, in Ballesteros, he had a rival worthy of the battle.

Now he gets to pit his wits against another occasionally stern European, Nick Faldo. It was Faldo who frustrated Azinger with his 18 par final round in the 1987 Open Championship at Muirfield. The American ended the day frustrated at his inability to buy a putt in Scotland and aghast that he had allowed the Englishman to overtake him for this most glittering of prizes.

When Faldo shook his hand at the end and offered that most chilling of British understatements: "Hard luck, old boy," Azinger bristled mightily. Several years later he was still bristling. Here, too, however, the two men have been reconciled. So much so that their partnership as co-commentators for ABC television was widely recognised as one of the most entertaining in sport before Faldo moved to pastures new.

Now they meet again on the field of play and Azinger has already offered the thought that "there will be some serious fun," between the pair. This, of course, is as it should be. There is, however, unlikely to be any serious rancour. Apart from anything else, Paul Azinger learned the hard way, 14 years ago, what is really important in this life.

If he can drip feed this wisdom into his Team during this Ryder Cup then it just might be that American golf has unveiled a saviour.

Bill Elliott
The Observer

Globetrotting Glory

R ightly, and properly, the main focus of attention in terms of the achievements by European Tour Members on The 2007 European Tour International Schedule centred around the sensational Major Championship victories of Angel Cabrera in the US Open Championship and Padraig Harrington in The 136th Open Championship.

Mark McNulty

Left *Angel Cabrera and Padraig Harrington at the PGA Grand Slam of Golf*

Arnold Palmer and Vijay Singh

However, it was not purely in the realms of The European Tour that Members triumphed in the Major arena during another memorable year of success around the globe.

While Cabrera's win came in June and Harrington's in July, it was in August that 54 year old Mark McNulty joined the select "Major Championship" club with his first Senior Major Championship victory in the JELD-WEN Tradition on the US Champions Tour.

The Zimbabwean-born Irishman, who led after the first and third rounds, produced a sublime putting display on the greens to post a final round 68 at the Crosswater Golf Club in Oregon for a 16 under par total of 272 and a six shot winning margin over American David Edwards.

"Guys who putt well through the ages are born with it," said McNulty, a winner of 16 titles on The European Tour. "Admittedly you have times when you go through poor putting rounds and tournaments, but it always comes back because you have it, because it's inbred, it's inside."

Runner-up Edwards agreed. "I can attest, he is a very good putter," he said. "I played with him the last three days and he played very solidly. He didn't miss very many."

Significantly both Cabrera and Harrington added to their magnificent CVs during their year of Major Championship glory.

Cabrera grabbed the headlines in October when he defeated Harrington at the third extra hole of a sudden-death play-off to win the PGA Grand Slam of Golf at the Mid-Ocean Club in Bermuda. The Argentine spectacularly eagled the 18th hole in regulation play to tie his fellow Major Champion on four under par 136, before a birdie at the same hole at the third time of asking was enough to take the title. US PGA Champion Jim Furyk was third while Masters Tournament winner Zach Johnson was fourth.

Later in the month Cabrera won the Argentina Masters Tournament Personal Cup at Olivos Golf Club in his native Argentina. Cabrera again eagled the last hold then beat fellow European Tour Member Ricardo Gonzalez at the first play-off hole. Daniel Vancsik, another European Tour Member, finished third and Federico Cabrera, the 18 year old son of Angel, won the Ivar Brostrom Cup for the best amateur in the field. Furthermore Cabrera moved on the next week to win the Barclays Singapore Open at Sentosa Golf Club.

There was a special resonance in the Emerald Isle when their favourite son, Padraig Harrington, ended the 2006 season in spectacular style, going head to head with World Number One Tiger Woods before beating the American at the second play-off hole to win the Dunlop Phoenix tournament at the Phoenix Country Club in Miyazaki.

Little did we realise it was only a portent of things to come as Harrington went on to lift the Irish PGA Championship in July at The European Club for the third time in the last four years, beating club professional Brendan McGovern in a play-off after the duo had ended regulation play on five under par 279.

If a few pints of Guinness were raised that night, they were only a speck on the country's bar bill a week later when Harrington triumphed in another play-off, this time at Carnoustie over Sergio Garcia to win The Open Championship. Moreover he won the Hassan II Trophy in Morroco on the Royal Dar Es-Salam course in Rabat.

Elsewhere, plaudits were also handed out to Fiji's Vijay Singh, Australia's Adam Scott and Sweden's Daniel Chopra on the US PGA Tour, England's Mark James and Bernhard Langer of Germany, who joined McNulty in the Seniors' winners' circle, and Challenge Tour Member Miguel Carballo, who won on the Nationwide Tour.

Singh claimed two victories, the first coming in the season-opening Mercedes-Benz Championship in January where matching weekend rounds of 70 were enough for a 14 under par total of 278 and a two shot triumph at the Plantation Course in Kapaula; while the second came in March where a three under par final round 67 saw the 44 year old come from three shots behind overnight to post a winning eight under par total of 272 in the Arnold Palmer Invitational, presented by MasterCard, at Bay Hill.

Every win is special but the latter had particular resonance for the Fijian as it saw him tie English-born Harry Cooper as the most prolific non-American winner on the US PGA Tour with 31 titles to his credit. "I always thought Gary Player was way out there but apparently not," said Singh. "It feels great but I am not done yet – I want to win as many as I can."

Singh later won the Kolon-Hana Bank Korea Open at the Woo Jeong Hills Country Club in Seoul with a with a six under par total of 278.

Scott had his moment of glory in April at the Redstone Golf Club in Humble, Texas, when a final round 66 saw him win the Shell Houston Open by three shots from fellow countryman Stuart Appleby and American Bubba Watson on 17 under par 271, while Chopra captured the Ginn sur Mer Classic at the Tesoro Resort, Florida, with a 19 under par 273.

While the Texan tournament might have only been Scott's fifth tournament of the season, he was put in the shade in terms of speed out of the blocks by James and Carballo who both, like Singh, won on their respective first outings of 2007.

James' victory came in the Allianz Championship on the US Champions Tour in February, where four birdies in the first eight holes of the final round on The Old Course at Broken Sound, Florida, helped The 1999 European Ryder Cup Captain to a two stroke

Mark James

victory on 15 under par 201, two clear of American Jay Haas. "It is a nice surprise and gives me a lot of confidence," he said.

Two weeks earlier, Carballo achieved a similar feat, the 27 year old Argentine – who won the Abierto Movistar de Guatemala on the 2006 Challenge Tour – carding a final round 65 at the Panama Golf Club to take the Movistar Panama Championship, the first counting event of the 2007 Nationwide Tour season, with a six under par total of 274.

Completing the bounty in the United States was The 2004 European Ryder Cup Captain Langer who showed his class with a stunning maiden victory on the US Champions Tour in only his fourth appearance.

The 50 year old German was at his imperious best at Augusta Pines Golf Club in Texas, romping to an eight shot victory in the Administaff Small Business

Miguel Carballo

Bernhard Langer

The Royal Trophy - The victorious European Team

Classic following rounds of 62-65-64 for a 25 under par total of 191, which tied the all-time 54 hole US Champions Tour record set by Loren Roberts in the 2006 MasterCard Championship.

Aside from the United States, the most bountiful harvest in terms of silverware at the start of the year was gathered in South Africa where three European Tour Members triumphed on no less than four separate occasions in their home country, towards the end of the Sunshine Tour's 2006-2007 season.

Leading the way was Louis Oosthuizen who won the Dimension Data Pro-Am at the beginning of January with an 11 under par total of 277 at the Gary Player Country Club, to be closely followed by Jean Hugo who took the Nashua Masters title at the Wild Coast Sun Country Club after a play-off with Challenge Tour Member Titch Moore after both players had ended the regulation 72 holes on 11 under par 269.

Towards the end of February, another two victories were struck in successive weeks for The European Tour as, firstly Richard Sterne won the Vodacom Championship before Oosthuizen won again, this time in the Telkom PGA Championship.

Indeed Oosthuizen could have been celebrating a hat-trick of successes for he finished tied with Sterne on 14 under par 272 in the former event at Pretoria Country Club, before the winner of The Celtic Manor Wales Open on The European Tour claimed the glory with a birdie four at the second play-off hole, the par five 18th.

Oosthuizen, however had his revenge a mere seven days later at the Johannesburg Country Club when a closing 65 was good enough for a 22 under par total of 266 and a one shot victory over Sterne, who closed with a 71 for 267 and he did enjoy a third success when in October he beat Zimbabwean Marc Cayeux and Brazil's Adilson da Silva in a play-off for the Platinum Classic on the Sunshine Tour in Mooinooi after all three finished tied on 11 under par 205.

While Oosthuizen celebrated the tournament victory, there was further joy for European Tour Member Charl Schwartzel who, in finishing in a tie for third place, secured the Sunshine Tour Order of Merit for the third consecutive time, a feat which has only been achieved once before, by Mark McNulty, from 1985 to 1987.

HEREDEROS DEL

MARQUÉS DE RISCAL

Available at Majestic Wine Warehouses

Schwartzel opted out of playing in the World Golf Championships - Accenture Match Play in Arizona to try and carve his name in the record books in his homeland and was naturally delighted with the outcome. "I'm happy with my decision to stay on," he said. "I've achieved what I wanted to achieve."

It was not only in the Sunshine Tour's official season where European Tour Members prospered as six wins were garnered from the winter season too.

Jean Hugo

Rafael Gomez

Louis Oosthuizen

Leading the way in May was Hennie Otto whose 15 under par total of 201 was good enough for a three shot victory in the Vodacom Origins of Golf Tour Gauteng at Pretoria Country Club; while the following month, Warren Abery took the Nashua Golf Challenge at the Gary Player Country Club with a nine under par total of 207.

James Kamte was next to triumph, in September in the Seekers Travel Pro-Am at the Dainfern Country Club, where a 13 under par total of 203 was good enough for a one shot victory over Albert Pistorius; before Titch Moore made up for his Nashua Masters play-off disappointment with victory in the Vodacom Origins of Golf Tour Final at St Francis Links, the stocky 31 year old winning by three shots from Ulrich van den Berg with a seven under par total of 209.

Completing the winter of content in South Africa in October were Cayeux - whose 14 under par total of 202 gave him a three shot winning margin in the Bearing Man Highveld Classic at the Witbank Golf Club - and Challenge Tour Member Keith Horne who fired a final round 63 at the Windhoek Country Club to cruise to a five shot victory in the MTC Nambia PGA Championship.

"It has been nine years since I won so this will take a while to sink in," said Horne. "The way I played over the last three days, not dropping a shot, has been just fantastic."

European Tour influence and success was, however, not confined to the United States and South Africa in 2007 as victories were enjoyed in other destinations as far flung as Thailand, Argentina, China and India in addition to those by Cabrera in Bermuda, Harrington in Morocco and Singh in Korea.

Leading the way in the match play sphere was Seve Ballesteros's European Team who comprehensively beat their Asian Tour rivals 12 ½ - 3 ½ at Amata Spring Country Club in Bangkok in January to retain the Royal Trophy.

Returning to the stroke play genre in April, the way was led by Argentina's Rafael Gomez who triumphed in his home country to win the inaugural Angel Cabrera Classic, coming from five shots behind at the start of the final round at the Jockey Club in Cordoba to win with a stunning course record 62.

While Gomez was naturally thrilled with his success, the man who gave his name to the tournament admitted he was equally delighted with the week. "It has been a great event and a very exciting final day," said the US Open Champion. "We will be back at the Jockey Club for this tournament for the next two years."

The next milestone success came for Thailand's Thaworn Wiratchant, who edged his fellow countryman Chinarat Phadungsil and Scotland's Simon Yates in a play-off to win the Midea China Classic at the Royal Orchid International Golf Club in Guangzhou in September after the trio finished on 21 under par 263.

As well as being Wiratchant's first success since November 2005, his ninth victory on the Asian Tour saw him also surpass compatriot Thongchai Jaidee as the most prolific winner in Asian Tour history.

Meanwhile India's Jyoti Randhawa enjoyed success in his home country when he defended the Hero Honda Indian Open title at Delhi Golf Club and in the process became only the second player in history behind Australian Peter Thomson to win the tournament three times.

"I was thinking about that," said Randhawa, who posted a final round 69 for a 13 under par total of 275 to celebrate a three shot victory. "Any time you equal a legendary name like Peter Thomson, you know you've done something good in life."

If one is talking of celebrations, then perhaps no other country in the world does it better than the Irish, although the South Americans might disagree.

Whatever, the South Africans might have rejoiced when Retief Goosen won the Nelson Mandela Invitational in partnership with Bobby Lincoln at the end of the 2006 season, the Australians might have raised a beer when, two weeks later, Nick O'Hern won the Cadbury's Schweppes Australian PGA Championship and the Indian golfing public would have been naturally delighted to see Jeev Milkha Singh win back to back tournaments in Japan at the end of 2006, namely the Casio World Open and the Golf Nippon Series JT Cup, but for Harrington and Cabrera 2007 was a "Major" year of Globetrotting Glory for all followers of The European Tour to toast.

Scott Crockett

King of Confidence

Carl Mason

C onfidence is one of those attributes all professional sportsmen covet, yet by its very spectral nature you cannot see it, hold it or know when it will arrive or leave – it is such an elusive state of being.

Gordon J Brand

However, there is no question that when it is prevalent throughout body and mind, confidence is manifested through achievement and in 2007, no more so was it evident than in the remarkable accomplishments of England's Carl Mason.

The 54 year old sent records tumbling and set new standards of excellence with the outstanding quality of his golf, becoming the most prolific winner in Europe in 2007 after his unrivalled five tournament victories – the Ryder Cup Wales Seniors Open at Conwy (Caernarvonshire) Golf Club, Wales; Bad Ragaz PGA Seniors Open at Golf Club Bad Ragaz, Switzerland; European Senior Masters at the Duke's Course, Woburn Golf Club,

England; the PGA Seniors Championship at The Stoke By Nayland Golf Club, England; and the OKI Castellón Open de España Senior at Club de Campo del Mediterráneo, Spain.

Those wins swept him to a third John Jacobs Trophy – his other European Seniors Tour Order of Merit triumphs coming in 2003 and 2004 – and he completed the season as the first man to pass €400,000, with his record earnings of €412,376, beating his previous best total of €354,743 set in 2004.

Not only that, but he also became the leading money winner in European Seniors Tour history

Guillermo Encina

Right Simon Owen

Stewart Ginn

when he overtook the previous holder, England's Tommy Horton, at the pinnacle, which Mason now tops with €1,642,960.

The scale of that staggering success is put into context by the fact that, in 25 years on The European Tour, Mason earned €1,684,040 and won five titles worldwide. In less than a fifth of that time as a senior golfer, he is close to surpassing that sum and has 19 victories to his name.

Why has he been able to perform so well since turning 50, and especially in 2007? He is in no doubt: "It's having the confidence to win," he said. "It makes all the difference to everything – the way you approach playing, the way you feel on the course and play when you're in a position to win."

Although he won the Ryder Cup Wales Seniors Open in June, Mason's purple patch began with his win in the Bad Ragaz PGA Seniors Open in August.

A runners-up spot to Scotland's Bill Longmuir in The Midas English Seniors Open at St Mellion International Hotel Golf and Country Club, England, was duly followed by consecutive tournament victories, as he retained the European Senior

Bobby Lincoln

Denis Watson

Costantino Rocca

Bill Longmuir

Masters and then captured the PGA Seniors Championship after four consecutive rounds of 67.

The last two successes gave Mason satisfaction for different reasons; his inner fortitude to snatch a win from the jaws of defeat with two late birdies in the former, and then a metronomic level of consistency to lead from the front in the latter.

After some welcome rest with the subsequent breaks in the schedule, Mason duly set a new record earnings when the €48,750 he claimed in October for win number five of 2007 - the OKI Castellón Open de España Senior, took his winnings to €401,747 with one event left to play.

When he finished tied eighth and won €10,629 at the season's grand finale, The Kingdom of Bahrain Trophy - Seniors Tour Championship at the Buckinghamshire Golf Club, England, his third John Jacobs Trophy and final tally of €412,376, was assured.

"I am delighted. My goal was to win the Order of Merit again this season, and it really has been a wonderful year for me," he said. "The European Seniors Tour is fantastic and I'm very grateful for all that it's done for my career. All the players are. It's

strong, competitive and we get to play great golf courses around the world."

That statement was borne out by the many other fine champions who tasted glory on the 2007 schedule, in a variety of fabulous locations.

England's Gordon J Brand started the 2007 season in exactly the same winning manner he finished the 2006 one, after storming through the field to capture the DGM Barbados Open title at Royal Westmoreland, Barbados, in March.

Although the season's opener may have had a touch of déjà-vu about it, the remainder of the year certainly could not be described in that fashion. Not when it boasted two first time winners, Italy's Costantino Rocca and South Africa's Bobby Lincoln; not when England's greatest golfer Nick Faldo turned 50 and made his debut at The Senior Open Championship at Muirfield; and definitely not when Mason rewrote the record books in such scintillating fashion.

The campaign might have begun in March with Brand's Caribbean success, but it was not until May that it got underway in earnest and it was another

**Turf Equipment &
Irrigation Solutions**

One great result.

visit www.toro.com

TORO® **Count on it.**

Juan Quiros

Emilio Rodriguez

Denis Durnian

Englishman, Nick Job, who won. He defeated compatriot Martin Poxon at the first hole of a sudden-death play-off at the Gloria Golf Resort, Turkey, to capture The Gloria Classic.

A week later, New Zealand's Simon Owen confirmed his return to form by capturing the Sharp Italian Seniors Open via a four-man play-off at the magnificent Circolo Golf Venezia, Italy,

A total of 29 European Seniors Tour Members then travelled to the United States and the Ocean Course, Kiawah Island, South Carolina, for the first Major of the season, the 68th US Senior PGA Championship. Denis Watson of Zimbabwe secured a two stroke win with a 72 hole aggregate of nine under par 279 to become the first international player to win the Championship since Gary Player in 1990.

As the Tour returned to European soil, Italian Ryder Cup star Rocca celebrated his first win as a senior golfer when he closed with a final round of one under par 71 to capture the AIB Irish Seniors Open, in association with Greenstar and Fáilte

Ireland, at the PGA National, Palmerston House, Co.Kildare, Ireland.

He was duly followed by another debutant into the Senior winners' ranks when Lincoln won the Jersey Seniors Classic at La Moye Golf Club, Jersey. The 53 year old from Johannesburg posted rounds of 71-67-67 for an 11 under par aggregate of 205 and a two shot victory over Bill Longmuir.

After Mason's first win of the season in Wales, at the next event Scotland's Sam Torrance, the man who pipped him to the Order of Merit in 2005 and 2006, held his nerve to produce a magnificent up-and-down on the final hole to secure a one stroke victory over Spain's José Rivero in the Bendinat London Seniors Masters at The London Golf Club, England, for his second success in three editions of the tournament. Added delight came for Torrance given it was also his first win in partnership with his son Daniel on the bag. "It is extra special to do it with my son," he said.

Torrance came close to emulating the victory two weeks later in the US Senior Open at

Sam Torrance

COPTHORNE
TARA HOTEL
LONDON, KENSINGTON

Ross Drummond

José Rivero

Des Smyth

Whistling Straights, Wisconsin, USA, but American Brad Bryant held off the challenge of the Scot and the rest of the field to win by three shots from Ben Crenshaw.

The season continued the following week and, as the Tour de France was nearing the completion of its first Alpine stage, the European Seniors Tour crowned its own king of the mountains.

In the imposing shadow of Mont Blanc, Spain's Juan Quiros captured the Open de France Senior de Divonne at Golf du Domaine de Divonne, France, by one shot from England's Tony Allen. Instead of pulling on a yellow jersey, however, Quiros left with a cheque for €48,750.

Having turned 50 on July 18, six-time Major Champion Faldo was eligible to tee up at The Senior Open Championship, presented by Aberdeen Asset Management, at Muirfield, Scotland – the scene of two of his three Open Championship victories – to make his eagerly awaited senior debut.

He duly found the experience to his liking – firing an opening round of 67 to finish co-leader – but after suffering with his putting over the next two rounds, he could only watch in admiration as another golfing legend – American Tom Watson – emerged the victor.

Watson proved his talent for links golf remains as brilliant as ever after he won a record equalling third Senior Open by one shot from Australia's Stewart Ginn and compatriot Mark O'Meara. He overcame a double bogey finish to capture his second triumph at Muirfield – to go alongside the 1980 Open Championship – and his 13th Major victory overall of a stellar career with his 284 level par return.

The Tour duly returned to its home turf at Wentworth Club, England, and the Edinburgh Course for the Wentworth Senior Masters, where Ireland's Des Smyth closed in three under par 69 to win in front of record crowds.

The 2006 European Ryder Cup Vice-Captain captured the Green Jacket by two shots from former Open Champion Bob Charles, the 71 year old New Zealander beating his age with a round of 70 on the final day. "So many great players have won here before and it is very special to add my name. I lost the PGA Championship in a play-off to Rodger Davis in 1986, so this makes up for that," said 54 year old.

European Seniors Tour

Above left Tom Watson

Victor and Sergio Garcia

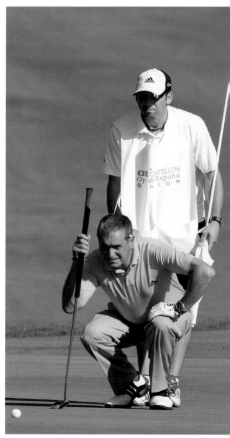

From that juncture in the season, so began Mason's superb summer, punctured only by Longmuir in The Midas English Seniors Open, which Mason had won three years consecutively.

Starting the final round one behind Mason, Longmuir fired a closing 69 to deprive his principal rival by a two shot margin. "I thought I'd forgotten how to win," said the Scot. "It's a long time since 2005. What made it harder was that I was up against Carl. He won last week at Bad Ragaz and has had four great years in this event, so I'm really proud that I held him off."

Following Mason's two subsequent wins in England and a fortnight's break in the schedule, Scotland's John Chillas ended a three year wait for his third European Seniors Tour title when he beat England's Glenn Ralph at the fourth hole of a sudden-death play-off to win the Scandinavian Senior Open at Royal Copenhagen Golf Club, Denmark.

"It is good to know that I can still come up with the goods when it really matters," said Chillas, who would have dearly loved to triumph the following week too in his native country, but it was Spain's José Rivero who closed with a battling two under par 70 to claim his third European Seniors Tour title in the Charles Church Scottish Seniors Open

at the Marriott Dalmahoy Hotel and Country Club, Edinburgh, Scotland.

The 56 year old former Ryder Cup player said: "It's great honour to win here in Scotland. I did well in a couple of Scottish Opens and to win here means a lot to me."

An exceptionally strong field, including nine of the top ten in the Order of Merit standings, descended on Rivero's home country of Spain three weeks later to tee up at the Club de Campo del Mediterráneo for the OKI Castellón Open de España Senior, all seeking victory in the Tour's penultimate tournament of 2007.

Sergio Garcia returned to caddie for his father Victor on their home course where Mason won once more and Rocca, who came within one match of being a Ryder Cup colleague of Sergio Garcia, finished in the top ten before going on to win the season-ending Kingdom of Bahrain Trophy - Seniors Tour Championship at the Buckinghamshire Golf Club in England. With that Rocca secured second place in the European Seniors Tour Order of Merit behind the undisputed Number One for 2007 - Carl Mason.

Graeme Hamlett

Nick Job

Right *Bob Cameron*

John Chillas

> Just to have this feeling you get when you've got the chance to win is wonderful. The nerves start jingling, but I've found the secret of what happens, how to be able to control it, and go on from there. It's been absolutely wonderful, because I used to panic a little bit under pressure, didn't trust myself and let things slip away on the main Tour. I've done the complete opposite as a senior. Now, I don't worry and it's all down to confidence.
>
> *Carl Mason*

European Seniors Tour
Order of Merit 2007

Pos	Name	Country	Played	€	£
1	Carl MASON	(ENG)	(17)	412376.47	286820.70
2	Costantino ROCCA	(ITA)	(14)	277782.58	193206.45
3	Juan QUIROS	(ESP)	(16)	235922.87	164091.72
4	Stewart GINN	(AUS)	(14)	224017.14	155810.91
5	Bob CAMERON	(ENG)	(18)	178795.54	124357.88
6	Ross DRUMMOND	(SCO)	(14)	172001.63	119632.50
7	Nick JOB	(ENG)	(18)	168519.15	117210.33
8	Sam TORRANCE	(SCO)	(15)	164036.67	114092.62
9	José RIVERO	(ESP)	(17)	163730.87	113879.93
10	Gordon J BRAND	(ENG)	(19)	139481.91	97014.02
11	Luis CARBONETTI	(ARG)	(17)	131533.87	91485.92
12	Doug JOHNSON	(USA)	(18)	130607.19	90841.38
13	Bill LONGMUIR	(SCO)	(18)	128404.81	89309.55
14	Des SMYTH	(IRL)	(6)	122880.75	85467.40
15	John CHILLAS	(SCO)	(18)	113705.40	79085.65
16	Guillermo ENCINA	(CHI)	(18)	102188.77	71075.48
17	Bobby LINCOLN	(RSA)	(17)	97838.68	68049.86
18	Tony ALLEN	(ENG)	(17)	95982.76	66759.00
19	Giuseppe CALI	(ITA)	(19)	93444.63	64993.66
20	Tony JOHNSTONE	(ZIM)	(16)	93044.98	64715.69
21	Horacio CARBONETTI	(ARG)	(14)	92459.41	64308.41
22	David MERRIMAN	(AUS)	(17)	91333.58	63525.36
23	Glenn RALPH	(ENG)	(18)	90648.69	63049.00
24	Simon OWEN	(NZL)	(16)	86058.42	59856.32
25	John BLAND	(RSA)	(11)	85620.06	59551.42
26	Bruce HEUCHAN	(CAN)	(15)	75684.18	52640.71
27	Martin POXON	(ENG)	(18)	74961.58	52138.12
28	David GOOD	(AUS)	(17)	74426.09	51765.67
29	Eamonn DARCY	(IRL)	(13)	72389.45	50349.12
30	David J RUSSELL	(ENG)	(19)	67757.42	47127.40
31	Adan SOWA	(ARG)	(15)	62124.56	43209.57
32	Delroy CAMBRIDGE	(JAM)	(18)	61072.60	42477.90
33	Kevin SPURGEON	(ENG)	(17)	60760.49	42260.82
34	Emilio RODRIGUEZ	(ESP)	(17)	58512.89	40697.54
35	Pete OAKLEY	(USA)	(19)	57043.27	39675.37
36	Philippe DUGENY	(FRA)	(17)	55647.03	38704.25
37	Denis O'SULLIVAN	(IRL)	(17)	55591.25	38665.45
38	Jim RHODES	(ENG)	(17)	54688.40	38037.49
39	Bob CHARLES	(NZL)	(7)	54245.15	37729.19
40	Katsuyoshi TOMORI	(JPN)	(5)	53942.35	37518.59
41	Angel FERNANDEZ	(CHI)	(15)	53146.33	36964.93
42	Martin GRAY	(SCO)	(18)	50428.10	35074.31
43	Jimmy HEGGARTY	(NIR)	(17)	41998.07	29210.97
44	Ian MOSEY	(ENG)	(17)	41234.82	28680.10
45	John BENDA	(USA)	(14)	39268.19	27312.25
46	Gery WATINE	(FRA)	(17)	39071.91	27175.73
47	Noel RATCLIFFE	(AUS)	(13)	36790.85	25589.18
48	Andrew MURRAY	(ENG)	(12)	36048.28	25072.71
49	Jerry BRUNER	(USA)	(17)	34745.05	24166.26
50	Tommy HORTON	(ENG)	(17)	34317.34	23868.78
51	Terry GALE	(AUS)	(13)	33734.76	23463.58
52	Denis WATSON	(ZIM)	(5)	32042.45	22286.52
53	Bertus SMIT	(RSA)	(17)	31666.53	22025.06
54	Peter TERAVAINEN	(USA)	(11)	30424.43	21161.14
55	John MASHEGO	(RSA)	(15)	28780.33	20017.62
56	Jean Pierre SALLAT	(FRA)	(9)	28020.86	19489.38
57	Steve MARTIN	(SCO)	(15)	27636.78	19222.25
58	Manuel PIÑERO	(ESP)	(14)	26789.14	18632.68
59	Seiji EBIHARA	(JPN)	(5)	26210.61	18230.30
60	Bob LARRATT	(ENG)	(14)	25694.39	17871.25
61	Mike MILLER	(SCO)	(17)	24245.36	16863.41
62	Jim LAPSLEY	(NZL)	(16)	23617.45	16426.67
63	Maurice BEMBRIDGE	(ENG)	(16)	21930.83	15253.58
64	Denis DURNIAN	(ENG)	(13)	19042.04	13244.34
65	Ray CARRASCO	(USA)	(12)	18918.94	13158.71
66	Gavan LEVENSON	(RSA)	(10)	17310.89	12040.27
67	Tim RASTALL	(ENG)	(15)	14317.76	9958.45
68	Martin FOSTER	(ENG)	(6)	13276.88	9234.49
69	David CREAMER	(ENG)	(14)	12959.73	9013.90
70	Ronald STELTEN	(USA)	(7)	11922.73	8292.63
71	Bob LENDZION	(USA)	(11)	11894.94	8273.30
72	Bill MALLEY	(USA)	(12)	11494.42	7994.73
73	Mike CLAYTON	(AUS)	(6)	11023.71	7667.33
74	Tony CHARNLEY	(ENG)	(16)	10817.33	7523.79
75	Terry DILL	(USA)	(9)	10179.20	7079.95
76	Mike FERGUSON	(AUS)	(12)	9654.31	6714.87
77	Neil COLES	(ENG)	(5)	9099.89	6329.26
78	Antonio GARRIDO	(ESP)	(13)	8489.57	5904.76
79	Peter O'HAGAN	(IRL)	(3)	6777.00	4713.62
80	Gordon TOWNHILL	(ENG)	(5)	6767.88	4707.27
81	Eddie POLLAND	(NIR)	(11)	5651.02	3930.46
82	Ian PALMER	(RSA)	(6)	5428.46	3775.66
83	Jeff HALL	(ENG)	(6)	5202.02	3618.17
84	Victor GARCIA	(ESP)	(12)	5058.70	3518.48
85	Bill MCCOLL	(SCO)	(6)	4278.43	2975.78
86	Bill HARDWICK	(CAN)	(8)	4191.77	2915.51
87	Neville CLARKE	(RSA)	(6)	3151.86	2192.22
88	Juan ANGLADA	(ESP)	(3)	2971.43	2066.72
89	Anders JOHNSSON	(SWE)	(3)	2314.89	1610.08
90	Torsten GIEDEON	(GER)	(3)	2210.22	1537.28
91	Robin MANN	(ENG)	(5)	1933.37	1344.72
92	Terry HANSON	(ENG)	(3)	1066.79	741.99
93	Michael G WOLSELEY	(NIR)	(3)	474.47	330.01
94	Philip HARRISON	(ENG)	(1)	379.54	263.99

Simply the Best

Michael Lorenzo-Vera

The 2007 European Challenge Tour season was quite simply the best in the Tour's 19 year history as the race for the Number One spot on the Rankings lasted from the first tee shot of the season until the final putt of the year, when a hugely talented young Frenchman named Michael Lorenzo-Vera added a fantasy finish to a dream season and in doing so earned the Rolex award as the leading player.

Felipe Aguilar

Ross McGowan

Between the season's opening act in the 101° Campeonato Abierto VISA de la Republica presented by Jeep at the Pilar Golf Club in Buenos Aires, Argentina, won by Rafael Echenique in his home country, and the curtain coming down dramatically in the Apulia San Domenico Grand Final, the Challenge Tour produced eight double winners and a battle for the Rankings which reached boiling point with Lorenzo-Vera's electrifying victory at the breathtaking San Domenico Golf in Savalletri, Italy.

After the traditional early season jostling at the Rankings' summit, Edoardo Molinari of Italy pulled away from the pack to spend almost the entire first half of the year in the Number One spot. But, as the chasing pack closed the gap, a gripping battle developed between Felipe Aguilar of Chile, the English duo of Robert Dinwiddie and

Ross McGowan, Joost Luiten of The Netherlands, Lorenzo-Vera and Molinari.

Molinari's early season victories in the Club Colombia Masters at the Country Club de Bogota in the nation's capital in February and the Tusker Kenya Open at Karen Golf Club in Nairobi five weeks later were the basis for the 2005 US Amateur champion's early season surge to the top.

He forged further ahead in his homeland by taking sixth place behind Northern Ireland's Michael Hoey in the Tessali-Metaponto Open di Puglia e Basilicata at the Riva dei Tessali and Metaponto Golf Club in Puglia, but the first real challenger to Molinari's dominance was emerging in the form of Luiten, a player whose natural aggressiveness and refusal to back down made him a joy to watch.

European Challenge Tour

Leif Westerberg

The Dutchman drew on both these qualities to storm to victory at both the A.G.F. Allianz Golf Open de Toulouse and the Vodafone Challenge within the space of a month. Anyone who witnessed his dynamic final round thrusts at the Golf de Toulouse-Seilh in Seilh, France, and the Golf and Country Club An der Elfrather Mühle in Dusseldorf, Germany, will testify to his combative brilliance.

Luiten, who drove The Netherlands to victory in amateur golf's World Cup, the Eisenhower Trophy, in 2006 and was the Spanish Amateur champion in 2005, recorded a brilliant last day score of eight under par 64 to win by a stroke from Nicolas Vanhootegem in France and followed that with a mesmeric fourth round performance in Germany, where an 11 under par 61 secured his second title.

Vanhootegem's disappointment at losing out would, however, be short lived. Just a week after finishing second in France, the Belgian roared to victory in front of an ecstatic home crowd in the Telenet Trophy at the Royal Waterloo Golf Club in La Marache, and was followed into the 2007 winners' enclosure a week later by England's Ben Mason,

who collected the Open Mahou de Madrid title at the Casino Club de Golf Retamares in Spain's capital city.

Seven days before Luiten's second win of the season in Germany, McGowan had lifted his maiden professional title with a play-off victory over Lorenzo-Vera in the Oceânico Developments Pro-Am Challenge at the Marriott Worsley Park Hotel and Country Club in Manchester, England.

The 2006 English Amateur champion possesses an experienced head on his young shoulders and did not take long to craft his second victory in the Estoril Challenge de Portugal at Quinta da Marinha, Portugal, to propel himself towards the business end of the Rankings and identify himself as a contender for Number One honours.

In between McGowan's victory in Portugal and Dinwiddie's first professional win in the Scottish Challenge presented by Bank of Scotland Corporate at the Macdonald Cardrona Hotel and Country Club, Scotland, there were victories for New Zealand's Gareth Paddison in the A.G.F. Allianz

Jamie Donaldson

Open des Volcans – Challenge de France at Golf des Volcans in Clermont Ferrand, France; Anders Schmidt Hansen of Denmark in the MAN NÖ Open at the Golfclub Adamstal in Ramsau, Austria; Ireland's Colm Moriarty in the FIRSTPLUS Wales Challenge at the Vale Hotel Golf and Spa Resort, Wales, and Sweden's Magnus A Carlsson in the Challenge of Ireland presented by Glasson at the Glasson Golf Hotel and Country Club in Athlone, Co.Westmeath, Ireland.

After putting his way to victory in Scotland, Dinwiddie, who had played in the 2005 Walker Cup and collected the 2005 Scottish and Welsh Amateur Open Stroke Play Championships as well as the English edition in 2006, immediately headed for Switzerland where his superb all-round game helped him record his second win just seven days after his first, taking the glory in the unique Rolex Trophy, where a 36 man field competed in a prestigious four round Pro-Am tournament over the exclusive Golf Club de Génève.

Robert Dinwiddie

Magnus A Carlsson

The European Tour
Golf Collection

Stuart Manley

Joost Luiten

That same week in August, Martin Wiegele of Austria triumphed in the Lexus Open in the Miklagard Golf Club in Kløfta, Norway, as the top 20 on the Rankings began to take shape and the countdown to the season's finalé began.

With a string of top ten finishes, including sixth place in the dual ranking OPEN DE SAINT OMER presented by NEUFLIZE OBC at the Aa Saint Omer Golf Club, Lumbres, France – won by Spain's Carl Suneson – Lorenzo-Vera led the way going into the POSTBANK Challenge presented by Marcel Siem. He would, however, be displaced as Number One by Aguilar, who ended a climactic final round at the Golfclub Mülheim an der Ruhr, Mülheim, Germany, by emerging the victor from a thrilling three-way sudden-death play-off with Scotland's Andrew McArthur and Englishman Paul Waring.

Aguilar had hitherto enjoyed a tremendously consistent year but, up to that point, had yet to make it to the winners' podium. The Chilean made a great start to the season with a third place

European Challenge Tour

Peter Baker

Left Fabrizio Zanotti

Mikael Lundberg

finish in the Abierto Mexicano Corona at the Club de Golf de la Hacienda in Mexico City – won by Paraguay's Fabrizio Zanotti – and a fifth place finish in the Kai Fieberg Costa Rica Open over the Cariari Country Club in San Jose, where Argentina's Miguel Rodriguez took the spoils.

A further two second place finishes in Belgium and Wales had thrown Aguilar into the race at the top of the Rankings, but his win in Germany saw him move to pole position for the first time. He would forge further ahead with a second play-off win, this time against Germany's Tobias Dier, just three weeks later in the OKI Mahou Challenge de España over the Golf Campo de Layos in Toledo, Spain.

Sandwiched between Aguilar's two wins was another of 2007's double champions, Englishman Iain Pyman, whose victories at the Odense Golf Club in Denmark in the ECCO Tour Championship and at the Waxholm Golf Club in Stockholm, Sweden, in the Telia Challenge Waxholm, ensured a place on The 2008 European Tour as part of the Challenge Tour's top 20, an achievment also enjoyed by Spain's Alvaro Velasco and Julia Zapata of Argentina who, although they did not win in 2007, were consistent enough over the season to finish in 17th and 15th places respectively on the Rankings.

Peter Whiteford

While the Challenge Tour's primary function is to unearth and educate The European Tour's next generation of star players, it also affords players who are rebuilding their careers an opportunity to rejoin European golf's main circuit.

François Delamontagne of France, Welshman Jamie Donaldson – winner of the Abierto Telefonica de Guatemala at the Hacienda Nueva Country Club, San Jose Pinula, Guatemala – Australian Peter Fowler, Norway's Jan-Are Larsen, Mikael Lundberg of Sweden – who triumphed at the season's penultimate event, the Toscana Open Italian Federation Cup at Le Pavoniere Golf and Country Club in Tuscany, Italy – Welshman Stuart Manley, who finished tenth on the Rankings, and Pyman, all took advantage of that opportunity and will feature once again on The European Tour in 2008.

The most experienced player to enjoy success on the 2007 Challenge Tour, however, was England's Peter Baker. Three times a European Tour champion and perhaps best remembered for his superb Ryder Cup performance when winning three points out of four at The Belfry in 1993, Baker took the decision to play on the Challenge Tour to re-launch his career and soon found himself back in contention, thriving on the competition afforded by some of European golf's most talented young players.

Iain Pyman

Julio Zapata

Edoardo Molinari

Jan-Are Larsen

Peter Fowler

The Englishman's triumphs in the Credit Suisse Challenge at Wylihof Golf in Luterbach, Switzerland, and then on his 40th birthday in the Open A.G.F. Allianz Côtes d'Armor Bretagne at the Golf Blue Green de Pléneuf in Val André, France, where he defeated McGowan in a play-off, proved he still possesses the old magic.

Another man to regain his playing privileges for The European Tour was Sweden's Leif Westerberg, thanks, in the main, to his superb victory in the richest stand alone Challenge Tour event in history, the €330,000 Kazakhstan Open. As Westerberg collected the €52,800 top prize at the Nurtau Golf Club in Almaty, McGowan took second place to move second on the Rankings with five events of the 2007 Schedule remaining. The end of the season was in sight, and the prospect of a thrilling climax was quickly becoming a reality.

There would be no change at the top of the Rankings the following week after The Dutch Futures, where Scotland's Peter Whiteford took the title at the Golfclub Houtrack on the outskirts of Amsterdam, but McGowan's play-off defeat to Baker seven days later saw him leapfrog Aguilar at the summit with just two events until the Grand Final.

Whiteford became the eighth and final double champion of 2007 in the doc Salbe PGA

European Challenge at the Golf and Vital Park Bad Waldsee's New Course in Germany, before Lundberg's win in Italy set the scene for the final event at San Domenico Golf on Italy's Adriatic coast.

Lorenzo-Vera needed nothing less than a victory in the elite 45-man Apulia San Domenico Grand Final to overtake McGowan at the top of the Rankings, and he did so in the most dramatic fashion, closing out the year with a stunning final three holes that included two birdies and an audacious up and down from a greenside bunker for par at the 18th to win by a single stroke.

The 22 year old from Biarritz undoubtedly saved his best for last, securing his first victory of a supremely consistent year – where he racked up nine top ten finishes in total – to amass a prize money haul of €128,927, and setting a new Rankings record as he became the first French player to win the Challenge Tour.

Lorenzo-Vera, McGowan, Aguilar, Donaldson, Westerberg, Luiten, Carlsson, Dinwiddie, Lundberg, Manley, Zanotti, Baker, Whiteford, Pyman, Zapata, Molinari, Velasco, Fowler, Delamontagne and Larsen – The Challenge Tour graduates from 2007 – we salute you.

Michael Gibbons

Alvaro Velasco

The European Challenge Tour's 2007 graduates who won places on The 2008 European Tour International Schedule via the top 20 on the Rankings (from left to right) Leif Westerberg, Magnus A Carlsson, Robert Dinwiddie, Jan-Are Larsen, Mikael Lundberg, Joost Luiten, Jamie Donaldson, Felipe Aguilar, Ross McGowan, Michael Lorenzo-Vera (kneeling front), Stuart Manley, Peter Fowler, Peter Baker, Edoardo Molinari, Alvaro Velasco, Julio Zapata, Fabrizio Zanotti, Iain Pyman, François Delamontagne and Peter Whiteford

Michael Lorenzo-Vera, winner of the European Challenge Tour's season-ending Apulia San Domenico Grand Final and consequently Number One in the Challenge Tour Rankings, flanked by Alain de Soultrait (far left), Director of Challenge Tour, Sergio Melpignano, owner and President of San Domenico Golf, Franco Chimenti, President of the Italian Golf Federation, and Lello Dibari, Mayor of Fasano

François Delamontagne

i The 2007 European Challenge Tour season witnessed eight multiple winners – the most in Challenge Tour history, beating the seven attained in 1997.

European Challenge Tour Rankings 2007

Pos	Name	Country	Played	€
1	Michael LORENZO-VERA	(FRA)	(20)	128927.00
2	Ross McGOWAN	(ENG)	(20)	126645.15
3	Felipe AGUILAR	(CHI)	(23)	120409.16
4	Jamie DONALDSON	(WAL)	(24)	111747.50
5	Leif WESTERBERG	(SWE)	(25)	102322.88
6	Joost LUITEN	(NED)	(16)	99406.25
7	Magnus A CARLSSON	(SWE)	(25)	95670.31
8	Robert DINWIDDIE	(ENG)	(24)	91256.98
9	Mikael LUNDBERG	(SWE)	(23)	87916.11
10	Stuart MANLEY	(WAL)	(27)	84394.87
11	Fabrizio ZANOTTI	(PAR)	(23)	73816.44
12	Peter BAKER	(ENG)	(18)	72874.23
13	Peter WHITEFORD	(SCO)	(27)	72729.73
14	Iain PYMAN	(ENG)	(22)	70725.10
15	Julio ZAPATA	(ARG)	(23)	70158.19
16	Edoardo MOLINARI	(ITA)	(20)	65299.88
17	Alvaro VELASCO	(ESP)	(24)	59785.74
18	Peter FOWLER	(AUS)	(9)	59712.33
19	François DELAMONTAGNE	(FRA)	(12)	59232.00
20	Jan-Are LARSEN	(NOR)	(24)	56244.04
21	Nicolas VANHOOTEGEM	(BEL)	(16)	54866.63
22	Andrew MCARTHUR	(SCO)	(22)	54812.75
23	Gareth PADDISON	(NZL)	(24)	54640.79
24	Hernan REY	(ARG)	(24)	53988.49
25	Robert COLES	(ENG)	(21)	52614.71
26	Eric RAMSAY	(SCO)	(19)	51881.46
27	François CALMELS	(FRA)	(13)	51786.33
28	Anders Schmidt HANSEN	(DEN)	(24)	49090.23
29	Gary CLARK	(ENG)	(28)	46970.50
30	Richie RAMSAY	(SCO)	(9)	44425.67
31	Liam BOND	(WAL)	(20)	43728.44
32	Ben MASON	(ENG)	(21)	43265.00
33	Carlos DEL MORAL	(ESP)	(25)	41661.00
34	Colm MORIARTY	(IRL)	(16)	39388.94
35	Stephen BROWNE	(IRL)	(26)	39364.25
36	Martin WIEGELE	(AUT)	(20)	39322.75
37	Juan ABBATE	(ARG)	(21)	38546.36
38	James KAMTE	(RSA)	(14)	38116.37
39	Stuart DAVIS	(ENG)	(27)	37797.14
40	George MURRAY	(SCO)	(25)	37019.33
41	Raphaël EYRAUD	(FRA)	(16)	36125.73
42	Miguel RODRIGUEZ	(ARG)	(22)	35710.60
43	Inder VAN WEERELT	(NED)	(25)	33943.71
44	Jamie MCLEARY	(SCO)	(22)	33789.49
45	Klas ERIKSSON	(SWE)	(26)	33776.48
46	Daniel DE LEON	(MEX)	(21)	31430.39
47	Peter KAENSCHE	(NOR)	(26)	31167.44
48	Chris GANE	(ENG)	(18)	30557.45
49	Gareth MAYBIN	(NIR)	(10)	29388.00
50	Fredrik WIDMARK	(SWE)	(19)	29008.09
51	Tobias DIER	(GER)	(16)	28776.21
52	Rodolfo GONZALEZ	(ARG)	(23)	28709.65
53	Gustavo ROJAS	(ARG)	(23)	27117.07
54	Michael HOEY	(NIR)	(22)	26438.47
55	Sébastien DELAGRANGE	(FRA)	(14)	26381.27
56	Mikko KORHONEN	(FIN)	(20)	25738.03
57	Alvaro SALTO	(ESP)	(15)	25659.17
58	Adam GEE	(ENG)	(14)	25275.50
59	Tim MILFORD	(ENG)	(22)	25142.53
60	Antti AHOKAS	(FIN)	(24)	24946.86
61	Jamie LITTLE	(ENG)	(26)	24854.99
62	Sebastian FERNANDEZ	(ARG)	(18)	24255.42
63	Gustavo ACOSTA	(ARG)	(21)	24233.20
64	Richard TREIS	(GER)	(23)	24088.54
65	John E MORGAN	(ENG)	(10)	24043.62
66	Matthew KING	(ENG)	(26)	22948.66
67	Toni KARJALAINEN	(FIN)	(23)	22892.34
68	Tim DYKES	(WAL)	(21)	22152.57
69	Pablo LARRAZABAL	(ESP)	(17)	21596.25
70	Anthony SNOBECK	(FRA)	(26)	21385.61
71	Wilhelm SCHAUMAN	(SWE)	(22)	20924.38
72	Magnus PERSSON	(SWE)	(16)	20745.96
73	Pablo DEL GROSSO	(ARG)	(14)	19858.86
74	André BOSSERT	(SUI)	(13)	19621.33
75	Christophe BRAZILLIER	(FRA)	(24)	19548.28
76	Roope KAKKO	(FIN)	(18)	18608.50
77	Daniel DENISON	(ENG)	(13)	18302.03
78	Jeppe HULDAHL	(DEN)	(16)	18212.46
79	Paul WARING	(ENG)	(6)	18106.13
80	Andrew BUTTERFIELD	(ENG)	(17)	17764.96
81	Benjamin MIARKA	(GER)	(20)	17693.27
82	Carlos CARDEZA	(ARG)	(9)	17371.26
83	Paul DWYER	(ENG)	(27)	17215.60
84	Oliver WHITELEY	(ENG)	(14)	16969.78
85	Emilio DOMINGUEZ	(ARG)	(12)	16891.76
86	Scott HENDERSON	(SCO)	(25)	16550.83
87	Marco CRESPI	(ITA)	(18)	16234.81
88	Benoit TEILLERIA	(FRA)	(15)	15930.01
89	Thomas NIELSEN	(DEN)	(14)	15101.49
90	Kieran STAUNTON	(ENG)	(15)	15073.19
91	Andrew OLDCORN	(SCO)	(9)	14938.43
92	Bernd WIESBERGER	(AUT)	(19)	14859.83
93	Ally MELLOR	(ENG)	(22)	14651.89
94	Michiel BOTHMA	(RSA)	(11)	14522.00
95	Jerome THEUNIS	(BEL)	(23)	14512.14
96	Martin MARITZ	(RSA)	(8)	14475.07
97	Pontus ERICSSON	(SWE)	(22)	14415.83
98	Phil WORTHINGTON	(ENG)	(15)	14390.68
99	Mark TULLO	(CHI)	(10)	13873.11
100	Manuel MERIZALDE	(COL)	(12)	13651.42

The European Tour Golfer of the Month Awards are presented throughout the year followed by an Annual Award

Nick Dougherty (centre) is presented with The European Tour Golfer of the Month Award for October by George O'Grady (right), Chief Executive of The European Tour, at the Volvo Masters where Mel Pyatt (left), President and CEO of Volvo Event Management, was at the helm from the inaugural event in 1988 until his retirement in 2007

ANNUAL WINNERS

2006 Paul Casey

2005 Michael Campbell

2004 Vijay Singh

2003 Ernie Els

2002 Ernie Els

2001 Retief Goosen

2000 Lee Westwood

1999 Colin Montgomerie

1998 Lee Westwood

1997 Colin Montgomerie

1996 Colin Montgomerie

1995 Colin Montgomerie

1994 Ernie Els

1993 Bernhard Langer

1992 Nick Faldo

1991 Severiano Ballesteros

1990 Nick Faldo

1989 Nick Faldo

1988 Severiano Ballesteros

1987 Ian Woosnam

1986 Severiano Ballesteros

1985 Bernhard Langer

Retief Goosen - *January*

Henrik Stenson - *February*

Anton Haig - *March*

Markus Brier - *April*

Padraig Harrington - *May & July*

Angel Cabrera - *June*

Marc Warren - *August*

Lee Westwood - *September*

The European Tour Shot of the Month Awards are presented throughout the year followed by an Annual Award

Angel Cabrera - *June*

Retief Goosen - *January*

Mikko Ilonen - *February & August*

Anton Haig - *March*

Charl Schwartzel - *April*

Justin Rose - *May*

Padraig Harrington - *July*

Brett Rumford - *September*

ANNUAL WINNERS

2006 Paul Casey

2005 Paul McGinley

2004 David Howell

2003 Fredrik Jacobson

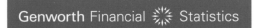
Stroke Average

Pos	Name	Stroke Average	Total Strokes	Total Rounds	Pos	Name	Stroke Average	Total Strokes	Total Rounds	Pos	Name	Stroke Average	Total Strokes	Total Rounds
1	Ernie ELS	70.10	4346	62	50	Wen-chong LIANG	71.38	3426	48	102	Carlos RODILES	71.80	5385	75
2	Justin ROSE	70.33	2813	40	50	Sergio GARCIA	71.38	2855	40	103	Simon YATES	71.81	2226	31
3	Richard GREEN	70.52	3949	56	53	Paul MCGINLEY	71.40	6140	86	103	Sam WALKER	71.81	6104	85
4	Richard STERNE	70.61	5366	76	53	Simon DYSON	71.40	6926	97	103	Matthew ZIONS	71.81	4165	58
5	Lee WESTWOOD	70.63	6569	93	55	Stephen GALLACHER	71.41	6070	85	106	Simon NASH	71.82	2442	34
6	Alan MCLEAN	70.66	2049	29	55	Charl SCHWARTZEL	71.41	4713	66	107	Birgir HAFTHORSSON	71.84	3951	55
7	Nick DOUGHERTY	70.70	7141	101	57	Pelle EDBERG	71.43	6000	84	107	Jean-Baptiste GONNET	71.84	5244	73
8	Robert-Jan DERKSEN	70.72	7567	107	57	Bradley DREDGE	71.43	5714	80	107	Terry PILKADARIS	71.84	5819	81
9	Miguel Angel JIMÉNEZ	70.76	6227	88	57	Markus BRIER	71.43	5929	83	110	Thomas BJÖRN	71.86	6108	85
10	Andrew MCLARDY	70.80	5027	71	60	Taichi TESHIMA	71.45	4001	56	111	Iain STEEL	71.88	1725	24
11	Per-Ulrik JOHANSSON	70.82	1983	28	61	Paul BROADHURST	71.46	5717	80	111	Philip GOLDING	71.88	1869	26
12	Peter HANSON	70.88	6379	90	62	James KINGSTON	71.48	5718	80	111	Marc CAYEUX	71.88	1725	24
12	Jyoti RANDHAWA	70.88	5812	82	63	Miles TUNNICLIFF	71.49	5719	80	114	Brad KENNEDY	71.89	2013	28
14	Alejandro CAÑIZARES	70.89	5317	75	63	Gonzalo FDEZ-CASTAÑO	71.49	6363	89	115	Jean VAN DE VELDE	71.91	4746	66
15	Zane SCOTLAND	70.91	2269	32	65	Ross FISHER	71.50	5577	78	115	Marcel SIEM	71.91	6112	85
16	Retief GOOSEN	70.92	4681	66	65	Damien MCGRANE	71.50	7222	101	115	Joakim HAEGGMAN	71.91	3811	53
17	Mikko ILONEN	70.94	4895	69	67	Steve ALKER	71.51	4648	65	118	Pablo MARTIN	71.92	2661	37
18	Mads VIBE-HASTRUP	70.96	5535	78	67	Anthony WALL	71.51	6507	91	119	David CARTER	71.93	5898	82
18	Padraig HARRINGTON	70.96	3548	50	69	Benn BARHAM	71.55	6583	92	120	Johan EDFORS	71.94	5108	71
20	Søren HANSEN	70.99	5963	84	70	Ian GARBUTT	71.56	6297	88	120	Carl SUNESON	71.94	6403	89
21	David LYNN	71.01	6107	86	71	Garry HOUSTON	71.57	7730	108	120	Adam BLYTH	71.94	2302	32
21	Oliver WILSON	71.01	7101	100	71	Martin ERLANDSSON	71.57	6227	87	123	Anders HANSEN	71.95	2950	41
23	Søren KJELDSEN	71.02	6747	95	71	David HIGGINS	71.57	3793	53	124	Marcus FRASER	71.96	5541	77
24	Alastair FORSYTH	71.03	6322	89	74	Oliver FISHER	71.58	6299	88	124	Prom MEESAWAT	71.96	3382	47
25	Thomas LEVET	71.05	3979	56	75	Jesus Maria ARRUTI	71.60	4081	57	127	Ricardo GONZALEZ	72.00	4680	65
26	Simon KHAN	71.06	6395	90	76	Tom WHITEHOUSE	71.61	6373	89	127	Luke DONALD	72.00	3024	42
26	Michael JONZON	71.06	2558	36	77	Henrik STENSON	71.63	3653	51	129	Alessandro TADINI	72.01	6337	88
26	Graeme MCDOWELL	71.06	6253	88	77	Peter O'MALLEY	71.63	6447	90	130	Andrew MARSHALL	72.02	6410	89
26	Martin KAYMER	71.06	6324	89	77	Paul CASEY	71.63	5372	75	130	Simon WAKEFIELD	72.02	7130	99
30	Phillip ARCHER	71.07	7462	105	80	Christian CÉVAËR	71.64	6233	87	132	Martin MARITZ	72.04	2017	28
31	Gary ORR	71.10	3626	51	80	Ariel CANETE	71.64	6376	89	133	Phillip PRICE	72.07	6126	85
32	Hennie OTTO	71.14	1992	28	82	José Manuel LARA	71.65	5087	71	133	Chapchai NIRAT	72.07	2090	29
32	Fredrik ANDERSSON HED	71.14	6474	91	83	Graeme STORM	71.66	8026	112	135	John BICKERTON	72.10	4903	68
34	Francesco MOLINARI	71.15	6546	92	83	Brett RUMFORD	71.66	6593	92	136	Scott BARR	72.11	2019	28
35	Niclas FASTH	71.16	5693	80	85	Gary MURPHY	71.68	6451	90	137	Marc WARREN	72.12	5842	81
36	Steve WEBSTER	71.18	5125	72	86	Alvaro QUIROS	71.69	2796	39	138	David BRANSDON	72.13	5482	76
37	Peter FOWLER	71.20	3204	45	87	Henrik NYSTRÖM	71.70	5234	73	139	Richard BLAND	72.14	6132	85
38	Euan LITTLE	71.23	2137	30	87	Richard MCEVOY	71.70	4302	60	139	Patrik SJÖLAND	72.14	5338	74
39	Sam LITTLE	71.24	5913	83	89	Ian POULTER	71.71	3944	55	139	Notah BEGAY III	72.14	2020	28
40	Scott STRANGE	71.25	4845	68	89	Keith HORNE	71.71	3442	48	139	Alvaro SALTO	72.14	2020	28
41	Raphaël JACQUELIN	71.26	6983	98	91	Jeev Milkha SINGH	71.72	7387	103	143	Sven STRÜVER	72.15	6349	88
42	Peter LAWRIE	71.27	7056	99	92	Peter HEDBLOM	71.73	5021	70	144	Grégory HAVRET	72.17	7073	98
43	Colin MONTGOMERIE	71.28	5774	81	92	Robert ROCK	71.73	5738	80	144	Jarmo SANDELIN	72.17	6856	95
44	Thongchai JAIDEE	71.29	6345	89	92	David GRIFFITHS	71.73	6312	88	146	Rafael CABRERA BELLO	72.19	6858	95
44	Rory MCILROY	71.29	1996	28	92	Mark FOSTER	71.73	7173	100	146	Marcus BOTH	72.19	2310	32
46	Paul LAWRIE	71.31	5990	84	96	Maarten LAFEBER	71.75	4807	67	148	Joakim BÄCKSTRÖM	72.20	6209	86
47	David FROST	71.34	4352	61	97	Gary LOCKERBIE	71.76	6028	84	148	Nicolas COLSAERTS	72.20	2527	35
47	Andres ROMERO	71.34	5279	74	97	Santiago LUNA	71.76	4449	62	148	Shiv KAPUR	72.20	5920	82
47	Grégory BOURDY	71.34	6920	97	99	Emanuele CANONICA	71.77	6675	93	151	Andrew COLTART	72.21	5632	78
50	Robert KARLSSON	71.38	5211	73	101	Alexander NOREN	71.79	5815	81	151	Chinarat PHADUNGSIL	72.21	3105	43

Driving Distance (yds)

Pos	Name	Average Yards	Stats Rounds
1	**Alvaro QUIROS**	**308.2**	**37**
2	Emanuele CANONICA	302.9	87
3	Daniel VANCSIK	302.1	71
4	Henrik STENSON	300.7	29
5	Ricardo GONZALEZ	299.8	58
6	Ernie ELS	299.4	36
7	Joakim BÄCKSTRÖM	299.2	78
8	Paul CASEY	298.7	47
9	Christian L NILSSON	297.7	72
9	Robert KARLSSON	297.7	50
11	Juan PARRON	297.6	64
12	François CALMELS	297.5	32
13	Ross FISHER	297.0	67
14	Pelle EDBERG	296.8	75
15	Johan EDFORS	296.3	56
16	Eirik Tage JOHANSEN	296.1	41
17	Anton HAIG	295.7	41
18	David BRANSDON	295.5	73
19	Martin KAYMER	295.4	81
20	James HEATH	295.2	73
21	Luis CLAVERIE	294.9	52
22	Nicolas COLSAERTS	294.6	32
23	François DELAMONTAGNE	294.4	35
24	Lee WESTWOOD	294.1	68
25	Rafael ECHENIQUE	293.9	73

Driving Accuracy (%)

Pos	Name	%	Stats Rounds
1	**Peter O'MALLEY**	**76.0**	**82**
2	Henrik NYSTRÖM	73.6	68
3	David HIGGINS	71.7	45
4	Ian POULTER	71.2	28
5	Anders HANSEN	71.1	25
6	Richard GREEN	70.8	44
7	John BICKERTON	69.8	56
8	David FROST	69.7	37
8	Peter LAWRIE	69.7	94
10	Jean-François REMESY	69.6	72
11	Gareth DAVIES	69.5	59
12	Lee WESTWOOD	69.4	68
13	Andrew BUTTERFIELD	69.3	32
14	Colin MONTGOMERIE	69.0	60
14	Robert-Jan DERKSEN	69.0	99
16	Alexandre ROCHA	68.6	65
17	Jonathan LOMAS	68.5	41
18	Thomas LEVET	68.3	52
19	Garry HOUSTON	67.4	103
20	Mads VIBE-HASTRUP	66.8	75
21	Alessandro TADINI	66.5	84
21	Matthew MILLAR	66.5	85
23	Anthony WALL	66.3	75
24	Miles TUNNICLIFF	66.2	75
25	James HEPWORTH	66.1	68

Average Putts Per Round

Pos	Name	Putts per Round	Stats Rounds
1	**Thaworn WIRATCHANT**	**27.9**	**41**
2	Marc WARREN	28.2	76
3	Kyron SULLIVAN	28.5	75
4	Richard BLAND	28.6	74
4	Marcus FRASER	28.6	65
6	Jarmo SANDELIN	28.7	88
6	David HOWELL	28.7	24
8	Shaun P WEBSTER	28.8	57
8	Robert KARLSSON	28.8	50
8	Christian CÉVAËR	28.8	81
8	Sam WALKER	28.8	76
8	Padraig HARRINGTON	28.8	24
8	Johan AXGREN	28.8	77
14	Paul BROADHURST	28.9	69
14	Richard STERNE	28.9	62
14	Damien MCGRANE	28.9	96
17	Richard GREEN	29.0	44
17	Martin ERLANDSSON	29.0	81
17	Thomas BJÖRN	29.0	66
17	Fredrik ANDERSSON HED	29.0	83
17	Patrik SJÖLAND	29.0	67
17	Graeme MCDOWELL	29.0	78
17	Jeev Milkha SINGH	29.0	75
24	Andrew MCLARDY	29.1	65
24	David DRYSDALE	29.1	58
24	Andres ROMERO	29.1	64
27	Jamie SPENCE	29.2	34
27	Mads VIBE-HASTRUP	29.2	75
27	Mikko ILONEN	29.2	62
27	Gonzalo FDEZ-CASTAÑO	29.2	85
27	Shiv KAPUR	29.2	74
27	Søren KJELDSEN	29.2	88
33	Pelle EDBERG	29.3	75
33	Andrew MARSHALL	29.3	81
33	Simon WAKEFIELD	29.3	94
33	Markus BRIER	29.3	75
33	Nick DOUGHERTY	29.3	83
33	Peter FOWLER	29.3	40
39	Darren FICHARDT	29.4	55
39	Miles TUNNICLIFF	29.4	75
39	Paul MCGINLEY	29.4	70
39	Benn BARHAM	29.4	81
39	Niclas FASTH	29.4	52
39	Alexander NOREN	29.4	76

Greens In Regulation (%)

Pos	Name	%	Stats Rounds
1	**Retief GOOSEN**	**77.0**	**44**
2	Lee WESTWOOD	76.9	68
3	Ernie ELS	76.1	36
4	Stuart LITTLE	74.9	25
5	Peter HANSON	73.8	72
6	Charl SCHWARTZEL	73.2	47
7	Steven O'HARA	73.1	80
8	Zane SCOTLAND	72.9	24
9	Jesus Maria ARRUTI	72.4	56
10	Thomas LEVET	72.3	52
10	Oliver FISHER	72.3	80
12	Ian POULTER	72.0	28
13	François DELAMONTAGNE	71.7	35
13	François CALMELS	71.7	32
15	Birgir HAFTHORSSON	71.6	51
16	Miguel Angel JIMÉNEZ	71.3	74
16	Jean-François LUCQUIN	71.3	80
18	Alastair FORSYTH	71.2	78
19	Stephen GALLACHER	71.1	80
20	Henrik STENSON	70.9	29
20	Oliver WILSON	70.9	87
22	Anthony WALL	70.8	75
22	Paul CASEY	70.8	47
24	Colin MONTGOMERIE	70.6	60
24	Niclas FASTH	70.6	52

Sand Saves (%)

Pos	Name	%	Stats Rounds
1	**Richard STERNE**	**78.7**	**62**
2	Thongchai JAIDEE	71.0	74
3	Emanuele CANONICA	70.1	87
4	David HOWELL	68.6	24
5	Thaworn WIRATCHANT	67.0	41
6	Francesco MOLINARI	65.7	83
7	Darren FICHARDT	65.6	55
8	Brett RUMFORD	63.7	82
9	David FROST	63.6	37
9	Marc WARREN	63.6	76
11	James KINGSTON	62.9	71
12	Pelle EDBERG	62.3	75
12	Paul BROADHURST	62.3	69
12	Kyron SULLIVAN	62.3	75
15	Lee S JAMES	62.1	50
16	Anthony WALL	62.0	75
17	John BICKERTON	61.5	56
18	David CARTER	61.2	74
19	Anders HANSEN	60.9	25
20	Shiv KAPUR	60.6	74
21	Christopher HANELL	60.5	66
22	Richard GREEN	60.4	44
23	Ignacio GARRIDO	60.2	77
23	Simon WAKEFIELD	60.2	94
25	Stuart LITTLE	60.0	25
25	Marcel SIEM	60.0	82

Putts Per Green In Regulation

Pos	Name	Putts per GIR	Stats Rounds
1	**Marcus FRASER**	**1.739**	**65**
2	Marc WARREN	1.741	76
3	Andres ROMERO	1.742	64
4	Richard GREEN	1.746	44
4	Ernie ELS	1.746	36
6	Fredrik ANDERSSON HED	1.747	83
7	Richard BLAND	1.749	74
7	Retief GOOSEN	1.749	44
9	Christian CÉVAËR	1.752	81
10	Sam WALKER	1.754	76
11	Thaworn WIRATCHANT	1.756	41
12	Richard STERNE	1.757	62
12	Padraig HARRINGTON	1.757	24
14	Robert KARLSSON	1.758	50
15	Henrik STENSON	1.762	29
16	Mikko ILONEN	1.764	62
16	Graeme MCDOWELL	1.764	78
18	Pelle EDBERG	1.765	75
18	Miles TUNNICLIFF	1.765	75
18	Zane SCOTLAND	1.765	24
21	Paul BROADHURST	1.767	69
22	Carlos RODILES	1.768	70
22	Peter FOWLER	1.768	40
24	Thomas BJÖRN	1.770	66
25	Martin ERLANDSSON	1.771	81
25	Kyron SULLIVAN	1.771	75
25	Alexander NOREN	1.771	76
28	Colin MONTGOMERIE	1.772	60
28	Jyoti RANDHAWA	1.772	74
28	Jeev Milkha SINGH	1.772	75
28	Johan AXGREN	1.772	77
32	David FROST	1.773	37
33	Marcel SIEM	1.774	82
33	Charl SCHWARTZEL	1.774	47
35	Miguel Angel JIMÉNEZ	1.776	74
35	Bradley DREDGE	1.776	69
35	Patrik SJÖLAND	1.776	67
38	Taichi TESHIMA	1.778	46
38	Pablo MARTIN	1.778	24
38	Shiv KAPUR	1.778	74

Scrambles

Pos	Name	%	AVE SPR	AVE Missed GPR	Total Missed GIR	Total Scrambles	Stats Rounds
1	**Padraig HARRINGTON**	**63.6**	**3.7**	**6**	**140**	**89**	**24**
2	Robert KARLSSON	62.0	3.6	6	292	181	50
3	Richard GREEN	61.3	3.5	6	248	152	44
4	Søren KJELDSEN	60.3	3.6	6	527	318	88
5	Niclas FASTH	60.0	3.2	5	275	165	52
6	Richard STERNE	59.9	3.5	6	364	218	62
7	Damien MCGRANE	59.8	4.0	7	639	382	96
8	Andrew MCLARDY	59.5	3.8	6	420	250	65
9	David LYNN	59.4	3.3	6	431	256	78
10	Raphaël JACQUELIN	59.3	3.4	6	474	281	83
11	Ian GARBUTT	59.2	3.5	6	507	300	86
11	Thaworn WIRATCHANT	59.2	4.9	8	336	199	41
13	Terry PILKADARIS	58.9	3.5	6	401	236	68
14	Gary ORR	58.8	3.3	6	240	141	43
14	Mads VIBE-HASTRUP	58.8	3.6	6	454	267	75
16	Ernie ELS	58.7	2.5	4	155	91	36
16	Jarmo SANDELIN	58.7	4.2	7	627	368	88
18	Henrik STENSON	58.6	3.1	5	152	89	29
18	Miguel Angel JIMÉNEZ	58.6	3.0	5	382	224	74
20	John BICKERTON	58.4	3.4	6	329	192	56
21	Thomas BJÖRN	58.3	3.7	6	420	245	66
22	Graeme MCDOWELL	58.2	3.6	6	476	277	78
23	Peter LAWRIE	58.1	3.6	6	580	337	94
23	Christian CÉVAËR	58.1	4.0	7	563	327	81
23	Andrew COLTART	58.1	3.9	7	472	274	71
23	Kyron SULLIVAN	58.1	4.2	7	546	317	75
23	Jeev Milkha SINGH	58.1	3.5	6	458	266	75

The European Tour Order of Merit 2007

Flags (A-K)

	Abu Dhabi
	Argentina
	Australia
	Austria
	Barbados
	Belgium
	Brazil
	Chile
	China
	Colombia
	Costa Rica
	Denmark
	Dubai
	England
	Fiji
	Finland
	France
	Germany
	Guatemala
	Hong Kong
	Iceland
	India
	Indonesia
	Ireland
	Italy
	Jamaica
	Japan
	Kazakhstan

Pos	Name	Country	Played	€	£
1	Justin ROSE	(ENG)	(12)	2944945.27	2065801.94
2	Ernie ELS	(RSA)	(18)	2496237.49	1751045.19
3	Padraig HARRINGTON	(IRL)	(15)	2463742.38	1728250.72
4	Henrik STENSON	(SWE)	(17)	2014841.29	1413358.37
5	Niclas FASTH	(SWE)	(23)	1919338.85	1346365.91
6	Angel CABRERA	(ARG)	(13)	1753023.79	1229700.26
7	Andres ROMERO	(ARG)	(23)	1741707.38	1221762.09
8	Søren HANSEN	(DEN)	(26)	1692053.60	1186931.26
9	Retief GOOSEN	(RSA)	(21)	1478244.83	1036950.01
10	Lee WESTWOOD	(ENG)	(25)	1420327.21	996322.32
11	Nick DOUGHERTY	(ENG)	(28)	1409658.29	988838.35
12	Colin MONTGOMERIE	(SCO)	(25)	1403293.38	984373.53
13	Paul CASEY	(ENG)	(22)	1389887.02	974969.33
14	Richard STERNE	(RSA)	(21)	1366544.69	958595.29
15	Sergio GARCIA	(ESP)	(13)	1228266.70	861596.90
16	Graeme STORM	(ENG)	(33)	1209672.90	848553.84
17	Søren KJELDSEN	(DEN)	(29)	1177606.32	826059.98
18	Anders HANSEN	(DEN)	(12)	1155834.00	810787.26
19	Grégory HAVRET	(FRA)	(32)	1142148.02	801186.91
20	Peter HANSON	(SWE)	(25)	1128267.60	791450.16
21	Miguel Angel JIMÉNEZ	(ESP)	(26)	1054016.44	739364.92
22	Richard GREEN	(AUS)	(17)	1050618.19	736981.13
23	Bradley DREDGE	(WAL)	(24)	1047945.94	735106.62
24	Ian POULTER	(ENG)	(16)	1046180.57	733868.26
25	Raphaël JACQUELIN	(FRA)	(28)	1045857.71	733641.78
26	Simon DYSON	(ENG)	(32)	1019828.70	715383.11
27	Robert KARLSSON	(SWE)	(22)	950506.15	666755.16
28	Yong-eun YANG	(KOR)	(21)	918386.34	644223.95
29	Phillip ARCHER	(ENG)	(33)	903377.22	633695.45
30	Oliver WILSON	(ENG)	(29)	900210.52	631474.09
31	Steve WEBSTER	(ENG)	(25)	895585.01	628229.41
32	Markus BRIER	(AUT)	(26)	881273.44	618190.23
33	Jyoti RANDHAWA	(IND)	(26)	849895.28	596179.27
34	Mikko ILONEN	(FIN)	(24)	833514.82	584688.81
35	Charl SCHWARTZEL	(RSA)	(20)	826368.27	579675.69
36	Robert-Jan DERKSEN	(NED)	(29)	809312.79	567711.71
37	Graeme MCDOWELL	(NIR)	(26)	789663.44	553928.21
38	Luke DONALD	(ENG)	(12)	775093.32	543707.66
39	Grégory BOURDY	(FRA)	(29)	763306.34	535439.39
40	Nick O'HERN	(AUS)	(12)	759817.54	532992.10
41	Martin KAYMER	(GER)	(29)	754690.79	529395.82
42	Marc WARREN	(SCO)	(30)	735956.96	516254.52
43	Ross FISHER	(ENG)	(27)	730095.93	512143.17
44	Thomas BJÖRN	(DEN)	(25)	725428.74	508869.25
45	Fredrik ANDERSSON HED	(SWE)	(26)	725254.70	508747.16
46	Jeev Milkha SINGH	(IND)	(30)	717790.32	503511.10
47	Alastair FORSYTH	(SCO)	(27)	697066.38	488973.80
48	Brett RUMFORD	(AUS)	(27)	662427.26	464675.37
49	Simon KHAN	(ENG)	(27)	660779.81	463519.72
50	Gonzalo FDEZ-CASTAÑO	(ESP)	(27)	655314.88	459686.22
51	Pelle EDBERG	(SWE)	(28)	629614.30	441657.93
52	Mark FOSTER	(ENG)	(29)	622566.43	436714.04
53	Peter O'MALLEY	(AUS)	(27)	615908.87	432043.93
54	Simon WAKEFIELD	(ENG)	(33)	604735.75	424206.28
55	Michael CAMPBELL	(NZL)	(25)	590205.41	414013.63
56	Peter HEDBLOM	(SWE)	(24)	586589.95	411477.48
57	Anthony WALL	(ENG)	(29)	586097.42	411131.98
58	Anton HAIG	(RSA)	(30)	581232.78	407719.57
59	Thongchai JAIDEE	(THA)	(27)	559997.48	392823.56
60	Francesco MOLINARI	(ITA)	(28)	552004.01	387216.35
61	Mads VIBE-HASTRUP	(DEN)	(25)	482549.46	338495.80
62	Andrew MCLARDY	(RSA)	(24)	477569.67	335002.61
63	Alexander NOREN	(SWE)	(29)	472335.66	331331.09
64	Louis OOSTHUIZEN	(RSA)	(23)	460529.36	323049.28
65	José Manuel LARA	(ESP)	(24)	454434.28	318773.74
66	Peter LAWRIE	(IRL)	(30)	450091.28	315727.24
67	Johan EDFORS	(SWE)	(24)	449714.43	315462.89
68	David LYNN	(ENG)	(25)	431600.80	302756.65
69	Alejandro CAÑIZARES	(ESP)	(25)	429014.41	300942.37
70	Ariel CANETE	(ARG)	(28)	425800.18	298687.67
71	Paul BROADHURST	(ENG)	(24)	422549.48	296407.39
72	Paul LAWRIE	(SCO)	(27)	422510.36	296379.95
73	Damien MCGRANE	(IRL)	(31)	412672.72	289479.10
74	Paul MCGINLEY	(IRL)	(25)	392852.34	275575.62
75	Daniel VANCSIK	(ARG)	(29)	390382.09	273842.81
76	Sam LITTLE	(ENG)	(27)	388452.58	272489.31
77	Martin ERLANDSSON	(SWE)	(28)	386517.96	271132.22
78	Christian CÉVAËR	(FRA)	(29)	368069.75	258191.28
79	Thomas LEVET	(FRA)	(17)	346795.71	243268.11
80	Sam WALKER	(ENG)	(31)	341292.53	239407.77
81	Jean-François LUCQUIN	(FRA)	(32)	340870.56	239111.77
82	Per-Ulrik JOHANSSON	(SWE)	(10)	335347.75	235237.66
83	James KINGSTON	(RSA)	(26)	324911.66	227917.02
84	Stephen GALLACHER	(SCO)	(26)	314240.94	220431.78
85	José-Filipe LIMA	(POR)	(30)	314185.98	220393.23
86	Carlos RODILES	(ESP)	(26)	308709.69	216551.76
87	Gary MURPHY	(IRL)	(30)	308428.17	216354.28
88	Wen-chong LIANG	(CHN)	(14)	304248.90	213422.63
89	Benn BARHAM	(ENG)	(32)	294844.16	206825.45
90	Jean-Baptiste GONNET	(FRA)	(24)	292378.99	205096.20
91	David GRIFFITHS	(ENG)	(31)	286545.62	201004.25
92	Maarten LAFEBER	(NED)	(25)	285587.99	200332.49
93	Garry HOUSTON	(WAL)	(35)	278829.84	195591.83
94	David FROST	(RSA)	(20)	277940.18	194967.75
95	Rory MCILROY	(NIR)	(4)	277255.40	194487.40
96	Zane SCOTLAND	(ENG)	(9)	277187.40	194439.70
97	Shiv KAPUR	(IND)	(28)	271050.57	190134.87
98	Marcus FRASER	(AUS)	(26)	270218.39	189551.12
99	Barry LANE	(ENG)	(28)	268764.58	188531.31
100	Tom WHITEHOUSE	(ENG)	(32)	263332.58	184720.91

Pos	Name	Country	Played	€	£
101	John BICKERTON	(ENG)	(24)	262757.97	184317.83
102	Alvaro QUIROS	(ESP)	(13)	259350.02	181927.24
103	Miles TUNNICLIFF	(ENG)	(27)	258096.12	181047.66
104	Jean-François REMESY	(FRA)	(29)	256109.75	179654.28
105	Ricardo GONZALEZ	(ARG)	(23)	255682.91	179354.86
106	Scott STRANGE	(AUS)	(21)	243796.73	171017.02
107	Jean VAN DE VELDE	(FRA)	(24)	242757.19	170287.80
108	Emanuele CANONICA	(ITA)	(30)	242093.55	169822.28
109	Oliver FISHER	(ENG)	(30)	242066.54	169803.34
110	Richard FINCH	(ENG)	(34)	235963.17	165521.98
111	Phillip PRICE	(WAL)	(28)	234918.02	164788.84
112	Henrik NYSTRÖM	(SWE)	(24)	231818.41	162614.54
113	Rafael ECHENIQUE	(ARG)	(29)	227069.28	159283.15
114	Ignacio GARRIDO	(ESP)	(27)	222757.74	156258.72
115	Michael JONZON	(SWE)	(11)	213622.96	149850.91
116	Mardan MAMAT	(SIN)	(27)	212728.22	149223.27
117	Jarmo SANDELIN	(SWE)	(33)	212657.53	149173.68
118	Lee SLATTERY	(ENG)	(29)	212580.99	149119.99
119	Ian GARBUTT	(ENG)	(29)	212469.29	149041.64
120	Alessandro TADINI	(ITA)	(30)	211090.09	148074.17
121	Alan MCLEAN	(SCO)	(8)	205938.51	144460.47
122	Stephen DODD	(WAL)	(23)	205914.68	144443.76
123	Carl SUNESON	(ESP)	(29)	202210.85	141845.61
124	Steven O'HARA	(SCO)	(31)	201033.17	141019.50
125	Sven STRÜVER	(GER)	(29)	198902.09	139524.60
126	Joost LUITEN	(NED)	(4)	198147.67	138995.40
127	Matthew MILLAR	(AUS)	(30)	193376.00	135648.20
128	Robert ROCK	(ENG)	(28)	188576.24	132281.29
129	Marcel SIEM	(GER)	(27)	182638.07	128115.82
130	Steven JEPPESEN	(SWE)	(35)	182077.31	127722.46
131	Kyron SULLIVAN	(WAL)	(31)	180642.50	126715.98
132	Gary ORR	(SCO)	(16)	179857.54	126165.35
133	Patrik SJÖLAND	(SWE)	(26)	179137.70	125660.40
134	Rafael CABRERA BELLO	(ESP)	(34)	178927.16	125512.71
135	Santiago LUNA	(ESP)	(23)	176069.05	123507.82
136	Mark PILKINGTON	(WAL)	(34)	175084.65	122817.30
137	Joakim BÄCKSTRÖM	(SWE)	(30)	173604.81	121779.22
138	Darren CLARKE	(NIR)	(20)	172110.17	120730.78
139	Mattias ELIASSON	(SWE)	(26)	171172.57	120073.07
140	Prom MEESAWAT	(THA)	(13)	166028.94	116464.95
141	Hennie OTTO	(RSA)	(8)	165242.27	115913.12
142	David HOWELL	(ENG)	(17)	164715.74	115543.78
143	Richard BLAND	(ENG)	(30)	164059.89	115083.72
144	Gary LOCKERBIE	(ENG)	(30)	162709.46	114136.42
145	Wade ORMSBY	(AUS)	(28)	162664.40	114104.81
146	Darren FICHARDT	(RSA)	(22)	162528.39	114009.41
147	Terry PILKADARIS	(AUS)	(24)	158306.59	111047.92
148	Steve ALKER	(NZL)	(21)	154316.23	108248.79
149	Christian L NILSSON	(SWE)	(30)	153646.14	107778.74
150	Andrew MARSHALL	(ENG)	(30)	152183.42	106752.68
151	Marcus HIGLEY	(ENG)	(32)	151184.87	106052.22
152	James HEATH	(ENG)	(31)	150757.93	105752.74
153	Taichi TESHIMA	(JPN)	(20)	150256.79	105401.20
154	Simon YATES	(SCO)	(10)	149052.96	104556.74
155	Sion E BEBB	(WAL)	(24)	147998.11	103816.80
156	Peter GUSTAFSSON	(SWE)	(30)	147739.25	103635.21
157	Peter FOWLER	(AUS)	(13)	142024.55	99626.50
158	Christopher HANELL	(SWE)	(28)	141923.53	99555.63
159	Alexandre ROCHA	(BRA)	(26)	141389.01	99180.68
160	Iain STEEL	(MAS)	(8)	140948.82	98871.91
161	Andrew TAMPION	(AUS)	(25)	139634.35	97949.84
162	Edward RUSH	(ENG)	(26)	136683.33	95879.78
163	David HIGGINS	(IRL)	(17)	136320.66	95625.37
164	James HEPWORTH	(ENG)	(31)	136173.35	95522.04
165	Chapchai NIRAT	(THA)	(11)	133025.61	93313.98
166	David PARK	(WAL)	(28)	130930.53	91844.34
167	Kenneth FERRIE	(ENG)	(24)	127746.29	89610.68
168	Andrew COLTART	(SCO)	(29)	127407.41	89372.96
169	David BRANSDON	(AUS)	(25)	123285.71	86481.69
170	Johan AXGREN	(SWE)	(30)	118696.23	83262.29
171	Jesus Maria ARRUTI	(ESP)	(19)	116043.66	81401.59
172	David CARTER	(ENG)	(31)	110234.05	77326.29
173	Richard MCEVOY	(ENG)	(23)	106657.11	74817.17
174	Chris GANE	(ENG)	(10)	105973.24	74337.45
175	Matthew ZIONS	(AUS)	(22)	99044.83	69477.35
176	Thaworn WIRATCHANT	(THA)	(14)	96967.59	68020.23
177	Chinarat PHADUNGSIL	(THA)	(16)	93222.48	65393.12
178	Pablo MARTIN	(ESP)	(12)	92269.40	64724.56
179	Joakim HAEGGMAN	(SWE)	(20)	90085.04	63192.30
180	Kevin STADLER	(USA)	(6)	88089.06	61792.17
181	Gareth DAVIES	(ENG)	(26)	86886.59	60948.66
182	Euan LITTLE	(SCO)	(10)	84780.98	59471.63
183	Juan PARRON	(ESP)	(27)	81554.49	57208.34
184	Birgir HAFTHORSSON	(ISL)	(18)	77955.28	54683.59
185	Simon NASH	(AUS)	(12)	75917.14	53253.88
186	Keith HORNE	(RSA)	(16)	75500.80	52961.83
187	Adam GEE	(ENG)	(3)	73276.00	51401.19
188	Cesar MONASTERIO	(ARG)	(28)	73055.01	51246.18
189	Kane WEBBER	(AUS)	(11)	69856.69	49002.64
190	Terry PRICE	(AUS)	(28)	69618.65	48835.66
191	Simon HURD	(ENG)	(14)	66920.17	46942.75
192	Jarrod MOSELEY	(AUS)	(5)	65632.91	46039.77
193	Luis CLAVERIE	(ESP)	(18)	63328.49	44423.28
194	Andrew OLDCORN	(SCO)	(10)	62711.43	43990.42
195	David DRYSDALE	(SCO)	(25)	62166.43	43608.12
196	Manuel QUIROS	(ESP)	(18)	61879.90	43407.13
197	Chris RODGERS	(ENG)	(13)	60730.53	42600.88
198	Sandy LYLE	(SCO)	(15)	60511.17	42447.00
199	Stuart LITTLE	(ENG)	(13)	59465.00	41713.14
200	François DELAMONTAGNE	(FRA)	(13)	58086.04	40745.83

Flags (M-Z)

Kenya
Korea
Malaysia
Mexico
Netherlands
New Zealand
Northern Ireland
Norway
Paraguay
Phillipines
Portugal
Puerto Rico
Qatar
Russia
Scotland
Singapore
South Africa
Spain
Sweden
Switzerland
Taiwan
Thailand
Trinidad & Tobago
Turkey
United Arab Emirates
USA
Wales
Zimbabwe

The European Tour International Schedule 2007

Date	Tournament	Venue
2006		
Nov 9-12	HSBC Champions	*Sheshan International GC, Shanghai, China*
16-19	UBS Hong Kong Open	*Hong Kong GC, Fanling, Hong Kong*
23-26	MasterCard Masters	*Huntingdale GC, Melbourne, Australia*
Nov 30- **Dec** 3	Blue Chip New Zealand Open	*Gulf Harbour CC, Auckland, New Zealand*
7-10	Alfred Dunhill Championship	*Leopard Creek, Mpumalanga, South Africa*
14-17	South African Airways Open	*Humewood GC, Port Elizabeth, South Africa*
2007		
Jan 11-14	Joburg Open	*Royal Johannesburg and Kensington Golf Club, South Africa*
18-21	Abu Dhabi Golf Championship	*Abu Dhabi Golf Club, Abu Dhabi*
25-28	The Commercialbank Qatar Masters	*Doha GC, Qatar*
Feb 1-4	Dubai Desert Classic	*Emirates GC, Dubai*
8-11	Maybank Malaysian Open	*Saujana G&CC, Kuala Lumpur, Malaysia*
15-18	Enjoy Jakarta Astro Indonesia Open	*Damai Indah G&CC, Jakarta, Indonesia*
21-25	**WGC - Accenture Match Play**	***Gallery GC, Tucson, Arizona, USA***
Mar 1-4	Johnnie Walker Classic	*Blue Canyon Country Club, Phuket, Thailand*
8-11	Clariden Leu Singapore Masters	*Laguna National GC, Singapore*
15-18	TCL Classic	*Yalong Bay GC, Sanya, Hainan Island, China*
22-25	Madeira Islands Open BPI	*Santo da Serra, Madeira, Portugal*
22-25	**WGC – CA Championship**	***Doral Golf Resort & Spa, Florida, USA***
Mar 29- **Apr** 1	Estoril Open de Portugal	*Quinta da Marinha Oitavos Golfe, Estoril, Portugal*
5-8	**MASTERS TOURNAMENT**	***Augusta National, Georgia, USA***
12-15	Volvo China Open	*Shanghai Silport GC, China*
19-22	BMW Asian Open	*Tomson Shanghai Pudong GC, Shanghai, China*
26-29	Open de España	*Centro Nacional de Golf, Madrid, Spain*
May 3-6	Telecom Italia Open	*Castello di Tolcinasco G&CC, Milan, Italy*
10-13	Valle Romano Open de Andalucia	*Aloha Golf Club, Spain*
17-20	The Irish Open	*Adare Manor Hotel & Golf Resort, Co.Limerick, Ireland*
24-27	**BMW PGA CHAMPIONSHIP**	***Wentworth Club, Surrey, England***
May 31- **June** 3	The Celtic Manor Wales Open	*The Celtic Manor Resort, Newport, South Wales*
7-10	BA-CA Golf Open, presented by Telekom Austria	*Fontana GC, Vienna, Austria*
14-17	OPEN DE SAINT-OMER presented by NEUFLIZE OBC	*Aa Saint Omer GC, Lumbres, France*
14-17	**US OPEN CHAMPIONSHIP**	***Oakmont CC, Oakmont, Pennsylvania, USA***
21-24	BMW International Open	*Golfclub München Eichenried, Germany*
June 28- **July** 1	Open de France ALSTOM	*Le Golf National, Paris, France*
5-8	Smurfit Kappa European Open	*The K Club, Straffan, Co. Kildare, Ireland*
12-15	The Barclays Scottish Open	*Loch Lomond, Glasgow, Scotland*
19-22	**THE 136TH OPEN CHAMPIONSHIP**	***Championship Course, Carnoustie, Scotland***
26-29	The Deutsche Bank Players' Championship of Europe	*Gut Kaden, Hamburg, Germany*
Aug 2-5	The Russian Open Golf Championship	*Le Meridien Moscow CC, Moscow, Russia*
2-5	**WGC – Bridgestone Invitational**	***Firestone CC, Akron, Ohio, USA***
9-12	**US PGA CHAMPIONSHIP**	***Southern Hills CC, Tulsa, Oklahoma, USA***
16-19	Scandinavian Masters	*Arlandastad Golf, Stockholm, Sweden*
23-26	The KLM Open	*Kennemer G&CC, Zandvoort, The Netherlands*
Aug 30- **Sept** 2	Johnnie Walker Championship at Gleneagles	*The Gleneagles Hotel, Perthshire, Scotland*
6- 9	Omega European Masters	*Crans-sur-Sierre, Crans Montana, Switzerland*
13-16	Mercedes-Benz Championship	*Golf Club Gut Lärchenhof, Cologne, Germany*
20-23	The Quinn Direct British Masters	*The Belfry, Sutton Coldfield, West Midlands*
27-30	*Seve Trophy	*The Heritage Golf & Spa Resort, Killenard, Co. Laois, Ireland*
Oct 4-7	Alfred Dunhill Links Championship	*Old Course, St Andrews, Carnoustie and Kingsbarns, Scotland*
11-14	HSBC World Match Play Championship	*Wentworth Club, Surrey, England*
11-14	Open de Madrid Valle Romano	*Real Sociedad Hípica Española Club de Campo, Madrid, Spain*
18-21	Portugal Masters	*Oceânico Victoria Golf Club, Vilamoura, Portugal*
25-28	Mallorca Classic	*Pula GC, Majorca, Spain*
Nov 1-4	**Volvo Masters**	***Club de Golf Valderrama, Sotogrande, Spain***

* Approved Special Events   **Play-Off victory   ^ Reduced to 54 holes due to inclement weather

Winner	Score	First Prize €	Total Prize Fund €
Y E Yang, KOR	66-72-67-69=274 (-14)	655,883	3,935,460
José Manuel Lara, ESP	64-66-66-69=265 (-15)	259,178	1,549,290
Justin Rose, ENG	69-66-68-73=276 (-12)	170,353	892,400
Nathan Green, AUS	71-67-76-65=279 (-5)	145,831	766,300
Alvaro Quiros, ESP	74-66-68-67=275 (-13)	158,500	995,000
Ernie Els, RSA	67-66-66-65=264 (-24)	158,500	1,016,070
Ariel Canete, ARG	66-68-65-67=266 (-19)	158,500	1,010,590
Paul Casey, ENG	71-68-67-65=271 (-17)	257,876	1,556,540
Retief Goosen, RSA	65-68-71-69=273 (-15)	282,743	1,706,650
Henrik Stenson, SWE	68-64-69-68=269 (-19)	309,862	1,840,540
Peter Hedblom, SWE	73-71-68-68=280 (-8)	165,895	991,660
Mikko Ilonen, FIN	66-68-71-70=275 (-9)	134,563	804,370
Henrik Stenson, SWE	def Geoff Ogilvy, 2 and 1	1,027,631	6,089,670
Anton Haig, RSA**	71-64-70-70=275 (-13)	310,801	1,887,130
Liang Wen-chong, CHN**	64-72-68-73=277 (-11)	139,075	835,720
Chapchai Nirat, THA	61-66-68-71=266 (-22)	127,046	756,340
Daniel Vancsik, ARG	68-66-68-68=270 (-18)	116,660	695,980
Tiger Woods, USA	71-66-68-73=278 (-10)	1,014,505	5,959,090
Pablo Martin (AM), ESP	73-70-66-68=277 (-7)	N/A	1,253,750
Zach Johnson, USA	71-73-76-69=289 (+1)	975,770	5,423,540
Markus Brier, AUT	72-68-67-67=274 (-10)	249,125	1,501,480
Raphaël Jacquelin, FRA	66-69-70-73=278 (-10)	283,570	1,698,330
Charl Schwartzel, RSA	69-68-68-67=272 (-16)	333,330	1,984,350
Gonzalo F'dez-Castaño, ESP**	67-68-65=200 (-16) ^	283,330	1,700,000
Lee Westwood, ENG	72-64-65-67=268 (-20)	166,660	1,005,980
Padraig Harrington, IRE**	73-68-71-71=283 (-5)	416,660	2,511,240
Anders Hansen, DEN **	74-70-67-69=280 (-8)	725,000	4,382,595
Richard Sterne, RSA	67-67-64-65=263 (-13)	368,812	2,216,195
Richard Green, AUS**	66-65-67-70=268 (-16)	216,660	1,295,150
Carl Suneson, ESP	67-70-70-69=276 (-8)	83,330	508,085
Angel Cabrera, ARG	69-71-76-69=285 (+5)	943,182	5,241,400
Niclas Fasth, SWE	67-65-73-70=275 (-13)	333,330	1,979,950
Graeme Storm, ENG	66-74-71-66=277 (-7)	666,660	3,968,700
Colin Montgomerie, SCO	69-64-71-65=269 (-11)	593,580	3,548,215
Grégory Havret, FRA**	68-64-70-68=270 (-14)	738,255	4,394,880
Padraig Harrington, IRL**	69-73-68-67=277 (-7)	1,106,620	6,162,530
Andres Romero, ARG	68-68-63-70=269 (-19)	600,000	3,648,490
Per-Ulrik Johansson, SWE	69-62-67-67=265 (-23)	244,250	1,469,915
Tiger Woods, USA	68-70-69-65=272 (-8)	989,225	5,795,580
Tiger Woods, USA	71-63-69-69=272 (-8)	914,039	5,007,920
Mikko Ilonen, FIN	67-72-67-68=274 (-6)	266,660	1,594,030
Ross Fisher, ENG	66-67-68-67=268 (-12)	266,660	1,604,800
Marc Warren, SCO**	65-73-73-69=280 (-12)	343,692	2,058,415
Brett Rumford, AUS**	68-66-66-68=268 (-16)	333,330	2,003,000
Søren Hansen, DEN	65-68-71-67=271 (-17)	320,000	2,000,000
Lee Westwood, ENG	68-70-70-65=273 (-15)	434,727	2,598,650
Great Britain & Ireland	16 ½ - 11 ½	125,000	2,000,000
Nick Dougherty, ENG	67-66-66-71=270 (-18)	562,624	3,376,090
Ernie Els, RSA	def Angel Cabrera 6 and 4	1,443,830	2,328,577
Mads Vibe-Hastrup, DEN	69-69-67-67=272 (-16)	150,000	901,350
Steve Webster, ENG	66-66-67-64=263 (-25)	500,000	3,013,490
Grégory Bourdy, FRA	69-68-64-67=268 (-12)	333,330	2,003,000
Justin Rose, ENG**	70-68-71-74=283 (-1)	666,660	3,928,500

DIRECTORS

N. C. Coles, MBE, *Chairman*

A. Gallardo, *Vice Chairman*

M. Bembridge

R. Chapman

P. Eales

D. Jones

R. Lee

J. E. O'Leary

D. J. Russell

O. Sellberg

J. Spence

J. Van de Velde

Sir M. F. Bonallack, OBE
(*Non Executive Tour Group Director*)

P. A. T. Davidson
(*Non Executive Tour Group Director, Finance*)

B. Nordberg
(*Non Executive Tour Group Director*)

K. S. Owen
(*Non Executive Tour Group Director, Broadcasting*)

CHIEF EXECUTIVE	G. C. O'Grady
DIRECTOR OF INTERNATIONAL POLICY	K. Waters
RYDER CUP DIRECTOR AND HEAD OF PLAYER RELATIONS	R. G. Hills
FINANCIAL DIRECTOR & COMPANY SECRETARY	J. Orr
GROUP MARKETING DIRECTOR	S. F. Kelly
DIRECTOR OF CORPORATE AFFAIRS AND PUBLIC RELATIONS	M. S. Platts
DIRECTOR OF TOUR OPERATIONS	D. W. Garland
DIRECTOR OF BROADCASTING & NEW MEDIA	M. Lichtenhein
MANAGING DIRECTOR, EUROPEAN SENIORS TOUR	K. A. Stubbs
DIRECTOR OF CHALLENGE TOUR	A. de Soultrait
CHIEF REFEREE	J. N. Paramor
ASSISTANT DIRECTOR OF TOUR OPERATIONS	D. A. Probyn
SENIOR REFEREE	A. N. McFee
SENIOR TOURNAMENT DIRECTOR AND QUALIFYING SCHOOL DIRECTOR	M. R. Stewart
CHAMPIONSHIP DIRECTOR	P. Adams
DIRECTOR OF CHAMPIONSHIP MANAGEMENT	J. Birkmyre
DIRECTOR OF TOURNAMENT SERVICES	E. Kitson
DIRECTOR, SPECIAL PROJECTS	M. MacDiarmid
SALES DIRECTOR	T. Shaw
DIRECTOR OF COMMUNICATIONS	G. Simpson

TOURNAMENT COMMITTEE

T. Björn, *Chairman* (DEN)

R. Chapman (ENG)

D. Clarke (NIR)

J. Haeggman (SWE)

C. Hanell (SWE)

R. Jacquelin (FRA)

M. A. Jiménez (ESP)

B. Lane (ENG)

B. Langer (GER)

P. McGinley (IRL)

C. Montgomerie, OBE (SCO)

M. Roe (ENG)

J. Spence (ENG)

H. Stenson (SWE)

Photographers

gettyimages®

David Cannon
Cancan Chu
Stuart Franklin
Sam Greenwood
Scott Halleran
Richard Heathcote
Harry How
Ross Kinnaird
Warren Little
Andy Lyons
Andrew Redington
Jamie Squire
Ian Walton

Additional Contributors
Phil Inglis
Stefan von Stengel
Annie Rose
Sean Dillow

Søren Hansen